Theories of Communication Networks

146 - Structural holes

Theories
of Communication
Networks

Peter R. Monge

Noshir S. Contractor

2003

OXFORD
UNIVERSITY PRESS

Oxford   New York
Auckland   Bangkok   Buenos Aires   Cape Town   Chennai
Dar es Salaam   Delhi   Hong Kong   Istanbul   Karachi   Kolkata
Kuala Lumpur   Madrid   Melbourne   Mexico City   Mumbai   Nairobi
São Paulo   Shanghai   Taipei   Tokyo   Toronto

Copyright © 2003 by Oxford University Press, Inc.

Published by Oxford University Press, Inc.
198 Madison Avenue, New York, New York, 10016

www.oup.com

Oxford is a registered trademark of Oxford University Press

Library of Congress Cataloging-in-Publication Data
Monge, Peter R.
Theories of communication networks / Peter R. Monge, Noshir S.
Contractor.
    p. cm.
Includes bibliographical references and index.
ISBN-13 978-0-19-516036-9; 978-0-19-516037-6 (pbk.)

ISBN 0-19-516036-3; 0-19-516037-1 (pbk.)

1. Social interaction.   2 Interpersonal communication.   3. Communication—Social aspects.
4. Social perception.   I. Contractor, Noshir S., 1959–   II. Title.
HM1111 .M664 2002
302—dc21   2002011753

9 8 7 6 5 4 3

Printed in the United States of America
on acid-free paper

To . . . the ties that bind, reciprocated with our love, connected forever:

Janet, Todd, Ryan, and Amber

Thrity and Maria

Stanley Wasserman

Foreword: Multitheoretical, Multilevel—and Multianalytical

Social network analysis has been used for the past seventy years to advance research in the social and behavioral sciences. In fact, it was almost exactly seventy years ago from the publication date of this book that Jacob Moreno presented his research on children and isolation to the Medical Society of the State of New York. His use of sociograms, highlighted in his April 1933 presentation, was the first widely recognized application of social network analysis.

Social network analysis progressed slowly, almost linearly, with the developments of sociometry (sociograms, sociomatrices), graph theory, dyads, triads, subgroups, and blockmodels, all of which served to enlighten substantive concerns such as reciprocity, structural balance, transitivity, clusterability, and structural equivalence. By 1980, all of these methods had been adopted by the small band of network analysts.

In the early 1980s, Sunbelt Conferences (now the official Annual Meeting of the International Network for Social Network Analysis) were attended by a core set of about seventy scholars. Total head counts were small; there were very few people on the periphery. It was not hard to trace the evolution of network theories and ideas from professors to students, from one generation to the next. The field of network analysis was even analyzed as a network! Users eventually became analysts, and some even methodologists. But it was easy to know the players and to keep score. It's not hard to follow a field that was the size of about three professional baseball teams!

I had a conversation about ten years ago with the then editor of a respected methodology journal. He told me, basically and with some condescension, that network analysis was just a bunch of indices applied, one at a time, to small data sets. He wanted to know where the "models" were! Network analysis to him was just a bunch of simple, disconnected data analyses, with very little statistics. At that time, this may well have been a valid observation.

But something happened in about 1990. Maybe it was the realization that the social context of actions matter; maybe it was the acknowledgment that epidemics do not progress uniformly through populations (which are almost never homogeneous); maybe it was the slightly controversial view that sex research had to consider sexual networks, even if such networks are just dyads; maybe it was the revelation that organizational network studies are at the heart of management research (roughly one-third of presentations at the Academy of Management annual meetings now have a network perspective). It could also have been that physicists, looking for alternatives to the technical problems of the universe, turned their attention to the Web, small worlds, and metabolic systems, all of which are applications of the paradigm that a few social and behavioral scientists have been working on for many, many years, unbeknownst to many of the physicists now doing network analysis.

The first course in network analysis at the Summer Quantitative Methods Program at the University of Michigan's ICPSR (July 1987) had just three students. This past year, more than forty total (the maximum allowed) were taught in two courses, with another ten on the waiting list. The journal editor I mentioned earlier, along with some colleagues, just recently wrote a clever methodological piece on networks, building on the work of others, particularly statisticians. Clearly, he now thinks network analysis is important! We have seen tremendous growth of interest in our "little field" over the past decade; major breakthroughs over the past ten years, both substantive and methodological, have allowed this paradigm to greatly expand its usefulness, especially in Internet research, organizational science, policy studies, and epidemiology. The first two of these research areas are contained within the study of communication, the focus of Professors Monge and Contractor's volume.

The new era of network analysis is marked by exponential rather than linear growth. The textbooks of the last fifteen years, whether elementary and expository (such as Dave Knoke and Jim Kuklinski's little green book published by Sage, and John Scott's small and limited but with a very readable introduction, also published by Sage) or advanced and focused (for example, the very nice volumes by Pip Pattison and by John Boyd), now appear rather narrow. Wasserman and Faust (1994), a decade old, needs about four additional chapters and two hundred pages to bring it into the present (but see the forthcoming Carrington, Scott, and Wasserman volume [2003] for overviews of new methods).

Enter Monge and Contractor (2003). Timely, broad, and detailed, the text you are holding is a welcome addition to the social network analysis canon. It is as clever as Friedkin (1998) and Watts (1999) but broader in coverage, and I expect this text to be used as recommended reading in network analysis courses, to demonstrate to researchers everywhere that network analysis must be multitheoretical. Such substantive theorizing will lead us to multilevel views of networks; but the crucial, and unique, aspect of network research of the new century is that it must be multianalytical. Monge and Contractor present a wide range of both substantive, theoretical concerns (collective action, cognition and contagion, exchange, proximity, and homophily theories, for example) and analytical approaches (particularly standard network models, and p^*).

As the authors state in their acknowledgments, I am certainly not a bystander in their research endeavors. I have worked with both, particularly Professor Contractor, for many years; we have grants together, and several of the ideas in their earlier chapters stem from work that I did with Nosh and Katie Faust several years ago. But I have tried to keep my closeness to this volume from distorting my historical perspective on it, and from influencing my critical evaluation of it.

I have some reservations about some of the analytical approaches described here: Are computational models really ready for "prime time"? *Blanche*, highlighted in this volume, appears better than most. Computational models are still in their infancy; there is very little consistency across modeling platforms, each researcher having his or her own set of idiosyncratic assumptions. No doubt, many important assumptions have been built into the code of these models, but many (most?) researchers fail to completely reveal their assumptions; it is a daunting task to understand how theory gets translated into code which then gets translated into "pseudo" data. Simulations offer a rather imperfect, and incomplete, substitute to analytical solutions, particularly those that are based on realistic, stochastic models. Data generated by computational models are not data in the conventional sense; thus, standard statistical analyses are not possible. My hope, which indeed could be facilitated by the versions of multianalyses presented by Professors Monge and Contractor, is that computational models will soon be blended with proper, statistical models, as a first step in improved network data analyses.

The start of this new century has demanded new analytic tools for networks; there is certainly a great need for wise people imparting their views on what these tools are and how to use them. This volume is the first such compilation meeting this demand. I recommend it very highly. Read it and learn how to be a better network analyst.

Work on the foreword was funded by support from the U.S. Office of Naval Research.

Preface

Though scholarly interest in the concept of networks has existed for more than two centuries (Mattelart, 2000), study of this phenomenon has certainly come of age in recent years, particularly in the areas of communication and organizations. Research has increased dramatically, scholarly and popular books abound on network topics, and the management literature is filled with articles offering advice on network issues. Books cover such topics as structural holes (Burt, 1992), strategic alliances (Yoshino & Rangan, 1995), and the network society (Castells, 1996, 2001). Academic journals contain extensive research on interlocking board directorates, corporate alliances, value chains, network organizations, and much more. Popular magazines offer countless articles on the Internet and World Wide Web, corporate intranets and extranets, e-commerce, business-to-business networks, personal and corporate networks, and virtual organizations, to name but a few of many network topics.

The ideas for this book have grown out of our collaboration over the past decade on a variety of network research and writing projects. One of these was a chapter for the *New Handbook of Organizational Communication* (Monge & Contractor, 2001), which we entitled "Emergence of Communication Networks." In organizing that chapter we were taken by the fact that very little published research on communication and organizational networks was motivated by network theories. At the same time, much network research employed some components of social science theories, or utilized the theoretical mechanisms from those theories, to develop and test network hypotheses, though often more implicitly than explicitly. Consequently, we organized that chapter around the social science theories that scholars have used to account for various network processes in organizations. Like many handbook chapters and review articles written for publication in academic journals, available space severely limits what can be said. Further, we were struck by the fractured nature of the work in this area. The field does not have a coherent, overarching framework for integrating conceptual, theoretical, and empirical work. Consequently, we set out to develop that framework, and the results of those efforts constitute this book.

But we should be more specific. Our review of the vast network research literature led us to see several problems in current network research. First, though relatively few network studies utilize theories as the basis for formulating research hypotheses, those that do use only single theories. As such, they tend to account for relatively small amounts of network variance. This, of course, contributes to our knowledge of communication networks, but not nearly to the extent that most would like. This observation led us to develop a multitheoretical perspective as a way to help compare and integrate diverse theories and to increase the explanatory power of research efforts.

A second observation regarding the existing literature is the fact that most research is conducted at a single level of analysis, typically the individual or dyad, though sometimes at the entire network level. Rarely are studies conducted that tap multiple network levels. Networks, however, are complex systems composed of components and properties that exist and can be explained at all levels. A full explanation of the particular configuration observed in any specific network is likely to require informative contributions from all levels. Thus, the framework we develop is multilevel as well as multitheoretical. By multilevel we mean all the typical levels within a specific network at both a given point in time and at earlier points in time. Further, we also include in the framework the other networks to which the focal network may be related, as well as the attributes of people who comprise these networks. This provides a much broader, comprehensive analytic context in which to situate network research than has been available to date.

Third, many contemporary scholars are exploring challenging frontiers in science that are associated with emergent system properties such as complexity (Axelrod, 1997), chaos and catastrophe (Simon, 1996), and coevolution (Kaufmann, 1993; McKelvey, 1997). This view of contemporary science has not percolated very far into the domain of network research. As a consequence, we introduce in this book the complex adaptive systems perspective. We do this via an agent-based modeling framework. We start with a population of people, organizations, or other entities that constitute a network, generically called agents. The agents follow probabilistic rules that may be independent or interconnected. They observe the behavior of other agents to whom they are connected in their local environment and respond to them. As they follow the rules, network structures emerge. Change the rules and/or the interconnections, and the structures change. This is straightforward agent-based modeling.

What is unique in our approach is that the rules assigned to agents are derived from the social theories examined in the book. For example, a generative mechanism in theories of collective action applied to network formation is mutuality. A generative mechanism in cognitive balance theories is transitivity. If we create rules for agents based on mutuality, we can create computational models to examine collective action theories of network formation. If we create rules based on transitivity, we can develop computational models to explore balance theories of networks. And, by developing computational models that provide agents both sets of rules, we could explore both theories together from a multitheoretical perspective.

Fourth, most network analysis is static and cross-sectional. Of course, this observation is not unique to the area of networks as the same observation can be made about most social science research. Nonetheless, those who are interested in finding ways to study network evolution and dynamics must find tools that facilitate that goal. One set of tools to explore coevolutionary dynamics is computational modeling, an emerging field in organizational analysis and the social sciences more broadly (Carley, 1995). In this book we introduce ideas pertaining to the computational modeling of communication networks. By using the Blanche computer program we create dynamic simulations of network evolution. We also explain how to use these results to generate interesting hypotheses and to analyze research data.

Finally, we think that it is extremely important to empirically test the ideas and framework presented in this book. Recent developments in network analysis provide highly useful tools to accomplish this. Thus, we describe the p^* statistical framework (Crouch & Wasserman, 1998; Wasserman & Pattison, 1996) and PSPAR computer programs (Richards & Seary, 2001; Seary, 1999) that provide opportunities to examine the various components of multitheoretical, multilevel network data. These techniques can be applied to network data gathered in the empirical world or generated by computer simulation to show the extent to which theoretically derived generative mechanisms function as rules to guide individual behavior that, in turn, creates emergent network structures. If we were to employ multiple theories and multiple rule-generating mechanisms, the p^* analysis techniques and PSPAR computer programs would enable us to test the multitheoretical, multilevel framework proposed in this book. Of course, that is a huge task, the subject of considerable future research. Consequently, we present in the book illustrative examples rather than definitive results, which should provide the basis for considerable future work.

The book has ten chapters organized into two major parts and a concluding chapter. The first four chapters provide the theoretical framework for studying communication networks. The next five chapters explore a wide range of social science theories that contain network-relevant generative mechanisms. Chapter 10 integrates the two parts.

Chapter 1 provides a general introduction to networks and a preview of the major theories covered in greater detail in the second half of the book. Chapter 2 provides an overview of network concepts and measures and presents the multitheoretical, multilevel framework. Here, we show how different theories imply different network theoretical mechanisms. As a consequence, different theories should generate different network configurations or realizations. We present this framework for individual, dyadic, triadic, group, and global network properties. We also include influence from the same network at earlier points in time and from networks of other relations at the same or earlier points in time. Finally, the framework permits exploration of a wide variety of network participant attributes or traits. Chapter 3 presents our views of networks as complex systems. We employ agent-based models in which agents follow rules. These rules are derived from the social science theories covered in the remainder of the book and hence provide a way to compare and contrast how they operate, individually and together, to generate emergent structures. Chapter 4 discusses the emerging field of computational organizational modeling. We provide our perspective on how computer simulations can best be used to study network and related phenomena. And, we introduce and describe Blanche, an object-oriented, multi-agent network-based simulation modeling environment that can be used to study dynamic network formulations of social science theories.

Chapters 5 through 9 focus on specific families of theories and show how our multitheoretical, multilevel approach can be used to examine their theoretical mechanisms. Chapter 5 explores theories of self-interest and mutual interest (collective action). These include transaction cost economics, public goods theories, as well as Burt's (1992) theory of structural holes.

Chapter 6 examines theories of cognition and contagion. Here, we explore balance mechanisms, inoculation theory, semantic networks, and transactive memory theory. Chapter 7 presents exchange and dependency theories. Chapter 8 explores theories of proximity and homophily. Chapter 9 focuses on coevolutionary theory.

Chapter 10 provides an integration of the first nine chapters. We begin by summarizing the essential arguments of the MTML framework. We review how p^* analytic approaches and computational modeling enable us to specify and test MTML models. Next we recount the key theoretical statements and empirical findings for each of the network mechanisms. We preview some of the more exciting recent theoretical advances in social network analysis, focusing special attention on *small world* and *scale-free* networks. We offer some thoughts about how these efforts, in conjunction with the MTML framework proposed in the book, are well poised to help us investigate some of the novel, twenty-first-century network forms of organizing enabled by peer-to-peer infrastructures. We note that many of the most innovative examples appear in nontraditional organizational settings such as nongovernmental organizations and terrorist networks.

Acknowledgments

Though as yet you may only have scanned the table of contents, read the preface, or skimmed the chapters, it should come as no surprise that we viewed the process of writing this book as a complex, self-organizing co-evolutionary organizational system created out of multilevel heterarchical communication networks. Yet it wasn't until we completed the book and began to think about writing the acknowledgments that we came to fully appreciate how extensive the network of support has been during the years we have worked on this project. A large number of colleagues, family, friends, and institutions have shared in almost every aspect of its preparation from early conceptual discussions to the final nuances of production. Some of these contributions greatly influenced the volume you now hold in your hands, leading us in directions we could not have anticipated at the outset.

The preparation of this book was supported in part by several grants from the U.S. National Science Foundation. We are deeply grateful for the funding that NSF has provided to our research projects over the years, which has enabled us to develop and explore many of the ideas and techniques described in this book. We want to extend special thanks to our research partners: Francois Bar, Kathleen Carley, Janet Fulk, Andrea Hollingshead, John Kunz, Ray Levitt, and Stanley Wasserman on IIS-9980109, "Co-Evolution of Knowledge Networks and 21st Century Organizational Forms," Janet Fulk on SBR-9602055, "Collective Action in Communication and Information-Based Public Goods: Interorganizational Computer-Supported Collaborative Work II," and Michael Case, Patricia Jones, Stephen Lu, and Barbara O'Keefe on ECS-94-27730, "The Sustainable Management of Civil Infrastructure: A Methodology and Testbed to Bridge Information Technology and Application." Our work with these colleagues has challenged us to make the arguments presented in this book more sophisticated yet, at the same time, more accessible to a larger interdisciplinary community of scholars.

Our personal networks of scholars provided us with extensive feedback and commentary on various chapters in this book (as well as the *Handbook* chapter that served as the springboard for this endeavor). The nodes in this network include George Barnett, Lucio Biggiero, Ann Bishop, Pablo Boczkowski, Phil Bonacich, Steve Borgatti, Moses Boudourides, Dan Brass, Ron Burt, Steve Chaffee, Steve Corman, Jerry Davis, Marya Doerfel, Eric Eisenberg, Andrew Flanagin, Les Gasser, Fred Jablin, David Johnson, Renee Houston, Toru Ishida, David Krackhardt, Anna Langhorne, Leah Lievrouw, Bill McKelvey, Kathy Miller, Scott Poole, Linda Putnam, Ron Rice, Bill Richards, Everett Rogers, Ramon Sangüesa, Craig Scott, Andrew Seary, David Seibold, David Stark, Cynthia Stohl, Emanuela Todeva, Duncan Watts, and Barry Wellman. To you all we want to express our gratitude for your time, effort, and creative contributions to this work.

For stimulating discussions of networks nothing could have been better than the ideas generated at the weekly Illinois "Net-Coffee" group meetings over the past five years, many of which informed and refined ideas presented in this book. The Net-Coffee group has included Ruth Aguilera, Shin-Kap Han, Caroline Haythornthwaite, Ravi Madhavan, and Stanley Wasserman.

We extend special gratitude to Stan Wasserman and his collaborators Katie Faust, Laura Koehly, Pip Pattison, and Garry Robins for their extensive efforts at helping us improve our understanding of p^* methodologies. The framework we propose here has benefited greatly from their advice and assistance.

Our respective universities have been exceptionally supportive of our work. We particularly wish to mention Patti Riley, director of the School of Communication, and Geoffrey Cowan, dean of the Annenberg School, University of Southern California, as well as Jesse Delia, dean of the School of Liberal Arts and Sciences, and David Swanson, head of the Department of Speech Communication, University of Illinois, who provided release time and other support to facilitate the completion of this book. In addition, we thank the Committee on Institutional Cooperation (the academic counterpart to the "Big Ten") and the Office of the Chief Information Officer at the University of Illinois as well as Dean Geoffrey Cowan of the Annenberg School for their generous technical and financial support that enabled us to coteach our graduate seminars on communication network analysis via Internet2 videoconferencing. These courses were an important forum that helped us to develop and advance the ideas presented in this book. Additionally, we would like to thank the Annenberg School for Communication at the University of Pennsylvania, and in particular Elihu Katz, for inviting Noshir Contractor to serve as a resident Annenberg Scholar in the fall of 1997. The community of Annenberg Scholars, and other faculty at the school, and in particular Joseph Cappella, served as an excellent testing ground for some of the early development of the ideas presented in this book.

Class discussions with the students who participated in the graduate seminars we cotaught on communication network analysis between USC and Illinois were always lively, stimulating, and challenging. Others who joined us remotely from the University of Wisconsin-Madison, Purdue University, and Pennsylvania State University also contributed. The students in these seminars were patient, diligent, and tough early critics of most of the ideas advanced in this book. Many have continued over the years to bring new ideas, articles, and chapters to our attention, and some have joined us in various research collaborations. In particular, at the University of Illinois's Team Engineering Collaboratory (TEClab) we would like to recognize the contributions of Anne Cummings, Nora Danner, Fabio Fonti, Susan Grant, Maureen Heald, Annika Hylmo, Laurie Lewis, James Miller, Edward Palazzolo, Tim Pollock, Kasey Walker, Dana Serb, Christine She, Chunke Su, Rob Whitbred, and Pascal Yammine. We are especially grateful to Edward Palazzolo for assistance with the computational models. At the Annenberg School, USC, we acknowledge the contributions of Alison Bryant, Elisia Cohen, Francesca Gardini, Laura Hawkins, Hao Huang, K. J. Kim, Jack Qiu, Michelle Shumate, Luminita Voinescu, Jenny Xu, and Connie Yuan. To our delight, many of these former students have now become faculty colleagues.

We wish to recognize the truly creative and impressive skills of several communication, computer science, and engineering graduate and undergraduate students in the University of Illinois TEClab. They were the lead software programmers of Blanche, the computational modeling environment presented in this book, and IKNOW, a network capture and visualization tool to support knowledge networks, also referenced in this book. Especially noteworthy are the tireless efforts of Mike Armstrong, Mike Chan,

Tom Ferrone, Feihong Hsu, Andrew Hyatt, Ryan Kanno, Shailesh Kocchar, Shyam Kurup, Peter Taylor, Emily Wang, and Dan Zink.

Most books are a creative blend of new ideas and revisions to former thinking. This volume is no exception, and we wish to acknowledge former work that we have incorporated herein, both directly and by adaptation. Most important, we thank Sage Publications for permission to adapt and reproduce material from our chapter, "Emergence of Communication Networks," in *The New Handbook of Organizational Communication*, which appears in several chapters throughout the book. Chapter 1 is based in part on writings on globalization and organizational networks found in Monge (1998) and Monge and Eisenberg (1987). The discussion of the CRADA project in chapter 2 is based partially on the final project report by Fulk et al., (1998), and a paper presented by Contractor, Wasserman, and Faust at the International Communication Association annual convention in 2000. Chapter 3 includes material adapted from Monge's (1977) article on alternative systems perspectives, Contractor's (1994) chapter on self-organizing systems, Contractor and Seibold's (1993) article in *Human Communication Research*, and the Contractor et al. (1998) NSF proposal. For table 3.1, Knowledge Framework, and other materials on knowledge networks, we acknowledge Contractor's and Carley's chapters in *The Handbook of New Media* (2002), as well as contributions by our graduate student, Connie Yuan. Chapter 4 provides an extensive discussion of the Blanche network computer simulation environment. Much of the introductory material in this chapter is based on the Hyatt, Contractor, and Jones (1997) article published in *Computational and Mathematical Organizational Theory*. The discussion of public goods and communication dilemmas in chapter 5 is based on ideas and text found in Fulk et al. (1996), Monge et al. (1998), Kalman et al. (2002), and a paper by Contractor, Danner, Palazzolo, Serb, and She (2001) presented at the annual convention of the International Communication Association. The discussion of network organizations in chapter 7 is based in part on Monge and Fulk (1999). Chapter 9 includes ideas and written contributions on community ecology by Alison Bryant and on the NK(C) model by Connie Yuan, both graduate students at the Annenberg School. The discussion of small worlds in chapter 10 was adapted from a review published by Nosh Contractor in *Chance*, the material on peer-to-peer networks from Contractor (in press), and the work on transnational criminal organizations from Bryant, Shumate, and Monge (2002).

Many thanks go to our fine editor at Oxford University Press, Martha Cooley, and her excellent assistant, Frank Fusco. It was a delight to work with them, making the entire production process much more enjoyable than it might otherwise have been.

Finally, and to us most important, we would like to express our deepest affection to the members of our families for their encouragement, support, patience, and love throughout this lengthy process, especially Janet Fulk, Sarosh and Thrity Contractor, and Maria Mastronardi. And, to you, our colleagues, our delight in having you read whatever part of our book you choose, and for engaging with us, wherever possible, in this fascinating quest to understand the theoretical basis for the multilevel, complex, co-evolving web of networks that comprise all our lives.

Contents

1 Networks and Flows in Organizational Communication   *3*

Part I
The Multitheoretical, Multilevel Framework

2 Network Concepts, Measures, and the Multitheoretical, Multilevel Analytic Framework   *29*

3 Communication and Knowledge Networks as Complex Systems   *79*

4 Computational Modeling of Networks   *99*

Part II
Social Theories for Studying Communication Networks

5 Theories of Self-Interest and Collective Action   *141*

6 Contagion, Semantic, and Cognitive Theories   *173*

7 Exchange and Dependency Theories   *209*

8 Homophily, Proximity, and Social Support Theories   *223*

9 Evolutionary and Coevolutionary Theories   *241*

Part III
Integration

10 Multitheoretical, Multilevel Models of Communication and Other Organizational Networks   *293*

Appendix: Data Sets Used in Chapter 2   *329*

References   *331*

Author Index   *377*

Subject Index   *387*

Theories of Communication Networks

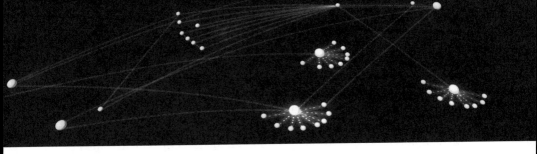

1

Networks and Flows in Organizational Communication

Communication networks are the patterns of contact that are created by the flow of messages among communicators through time and space. The concept of message should be understood here in its broadest sense to refer to data, information, knowledge, images, symbols, and any other symbolic forms that can move from one point in a network to another or can be cocreated by network members. These networks take many forms in contemporary organizations, including personal contact networks, flows of information within and between groups, strategic alliances among firms, and global network organizations, to name but a few. This book offers a new multitheoretical, multilevel perspective that integrates the theoretical mechanisms that theorists and researchers have proposed to explain the creation, maintenance, dissolution, and re-creation of these diverse and complex intra- and interorganizational networks (Monge & Contractor, 2001). This focus provides an important new alternative to earlier reviews of empirical literature, organized on the basis of antecedents and outcomes (Monge & Eisenberg, 1987) or research themes within organizational behavior (Krackhardt & Brass, 1994).

Although examining the emergence of communication networks is in itself an intellectually intriguing enterprise, the inexorable dynamics of globalization provide an even more compelling impetus for communication researchers and practitioners (Held, McGrew, Goldblatt, & Perraton,

1999). This chapter begins by underscoring the rationale for studying the emergence of communication networks and flows in a global world. The chapter also situates the contributions of this book in previous communication perspectives on formal and emergent communication networks in organizations as well as current philosophical perspectives on the study of emergence in structures.

Communication Networks and Flows in a Global World

Communication networks and the organizational forms of the twenty-first century are undergoing rapid and dramatic changes (Fulk & DeSanctis, 1999). What is unfolding before our collective gaze is being driven by spectacular advances and convergences in computer and communication technology and by the collective economic, political, societal, cultural, and communicative processes collectively known as globalization (Grossberg, Wartella, & Whitney, 1998; Monge, 1998; Robertson, 1992; Stohl, 2001; Waters, 1995). While many of the changes brought about by globalization are beneficial to humankind, others are clearly detrimental (Scholte, 2000). Key to the changing organizational landscape is the emergence of network forms of organization (Monge, 1995) as an integral part of the coevolution of the new "network society" (Castells, 1996). These organizational and social forms, which are neither classical markets nor traditional hierarchies (Powell, 1990), nor both (Piore & Sabel, 1984), are built around material and symbolic flows that link people and objects both locally and globally without regard for traditional national, institutional, or organizational boundaries.

The emphasis here is on the flow as well as the form. In fact, Appadurai (1990) theorizes globalization as a series of five flows that he calls "scapes": ethnoscape, technoscape, financescape, mediascape, and ideoscape. These represent the movements of peoples, technologies, finance capital, entertainment, and ideology/politics through global networks. Thus, capital, material, labor, messages, and symbols circulate through suppliers, producers, customers, strategic partners, governing agencies, and affiliates to form what Hall (1990) calls the "global postmodern culture" (p. 29), one that is simultaneously global and local. Built on the basis of flexible, dynamic, ephemeral relations, these network flows constitute the bulk of organizational activity (Monge & Fulk, 1999). Thus, global organizations are processes, not places.

Globalization processes are fundamentally altering our perceptions of time and space. Harvey (1989) points to *space-time compression* where both time and space collapse on each other as instantaneous communication obliterates the time it takes for messages to traverse space. Scholte (2000) discusses a fundamental change in the social geography caused when people inhabit supraterritorial spaces that transcend specific locales. Giddens (1984) articulates *space-time distanciation*, a process by which social relations, or in our case, organizational communication relations, are stretched across space and time, making them more abstract and remote.

Historically, organizations were organized by place, that is, by locale, and "when" was associated with "where." Organizations were established at specific locations, and events tended to occur in the particular locations where organizations existed. As early communication technology enabled people to communicate at a distance, organizations came to be organized by time (Beniger, 1986). Today, at the dawn of the new millennium, communication technology makes it possible for people to experience the same event at the same time anywhere in the world (O'Hara-Devereaux & Johansen, 1994). Distance no long matters, and time shrinks space. Communication and computer technologies have merged to generate "virtual organizations" so that people at a distance can work as if they were in the same space at the same time (DeSanctis & Monge, 1999). As virtual organizational forms proliferate, the virtual will become "real," in that it will be seen as the natural and accepted way to organize (DeSanctis & Monge, 1999).

Castells (1996) points to the emergence of "timeless time," a phenomenon that is created by hypertext and other new multimedia features, like hyperlinks, message permutations, and image manipulations, that destroy what was historically perceived as the natural sequence and time ordering of events (p. 462). These communication forms alter the way organizations, people, and the rest of the world are experienced. As Castells says, "All messages of all kinds become enclosed in the medium, because the medium has become so comprehensive, so diversified, so malleable, that it absorbs in the same multimedia text the whole of human experience, past, present, and future" (p. 373). These dramatic changes in time, space, and virtual experiences are likely to intensify in the coming decades as communication technologies continue to converge. These are processes we need to understand.

Granovetter (1985, 1992) chastised organizational scholars for failing to see organizations as *embedded* in the network of larger social processes, which they influence and which also influence them, particularly those that generate trust and discourage malfeasance. But as important as Granovetter's arguments have been, they tell only one side of the story. In contrast, Giddens

(1984, 1991, 2000) applies the concept of embeddedness to the processes of globalization. He and a number of other scholars have argued that people and organizations around the globe have traditionally been focused on their local networks rather than global contexts. People tend to be more embedded in home, neighborhood, community, and organizational networks in their hometowns, states, and countries than they are in distant connections around the globe. But, Giddens argues, the processes of globalization are changing this. Specifically, they are leading to *disembedding*, the process by which traditional network ties are broken. Equally important, globalization leads people to establish new ties at a distance through a process of *reembedding*, thus restructuring the world and shifting the focus from the local to the global. In some cases, others argue, these new ties at a distance can restructure and strengthen local diasporas (Tsgarousianou, Tambini, & Bryan, 1998). For organizations, too, disembedding is important because it generates restructuring processes, new networks and connections with distant organizational communities around the world. Communication plays a central role in these embedding and disembedding processes as it provides the information, knowledge, and motivation that enable people to envision alternative relations. How these processes work will be central to our understanding of twenty-first-century organizations.

Another aspect of globalization is *reflexivity*, a "deepening of the self" that provides opportunities for new forms of personal relations and participation in new kinds of communication networks (Lash & Urry, 1994, p. 31). As communication technology conveys news, information, and entertainment about organizational and societal processes around the globe, people become more informed about the world, themselves, and their place in the larger scheme of things. These identity-altering experiences include processes of *individuation*, whereby people come to rely less on traditional norms, values, and institutions and more on their own knowledge of things (Giddens, 1991; Lash & Urry, 1994). This leads to individualized patterns of consumption and mass customization of products, both important challenges for future organizations. It also changes the nature of work expectations and experiences, as well as affiliations within a wide range of social, political, religious, and recreational organizations. Thus, over the next decades we are likely to see substantial global transformations in the ways in which people view themselves, in how they relate to organizations, and in what they are willing to tolerate (Held, McGrew, Goldblatt, & Perraton, 1999).

One early manifestation of these changes is the development of "e-lancers," that is, electronically connected freelancers, people who work together on a temporary basis to produce goods and services (Malone &

Laubacher, 1998). This new breed of worker brokers their services on the open market, see themselves as transients, and have little if any loyalty or commitment to the organizations for which they work. Instead, their loyalty is invested in their craft. Indeed, Internet Web sites like guru.com thrive by connecting e-lancers with each other and with contract projects.

Another manifestation of these global transformations is the emergence of the disposable workforce, "people who have several years of skills development and tenure with a firm who lose their jobs through no fault of their own and cannot find comparable employment elsewhere" (Conrad & Poole, 1997, p. 582). From a network perspective, these are people who have had their organizational ties severed, who are floating unconnected in the workforce, and who must establish new connections in order to survive economically. These are people who have been disembedded by their work-day world and who seek reembedding. Both of these examples are a long way from the world of long-term tenured university professors or the Japanese corporate model of lifelong employment.

If the phenomenon we take as our stock in trade, organizational communication, is itself undergoing radical transformation, then we too must change our ways of studying it. And to be effective, the ways in which we change must reflect the transformations that we seek to understand. Since the nature of organizations is radically changing in the twenty-first century we will need to abandon former notions of what constitutes organizations and explore new possibilities—among them, networks of flows and connections, perhaps even rhizomes (Eisenberg, Monge, Poole, et al., 2000)—irrespective of traditional names, charters, boundaries, or walls. We must transcend our disciplinary parochialism in favor of incorporating insights from other perspectives not normally included in our analytic frameworks, including economics, philosophy, political science, new forms of systems thinking like coevolutionary, complexity, and self-organizing systems theories, and many others.

Finally, we must recognize that globalization is producing as many if not more negative outcomes than positive ones. We must incorporate in our work explicit attention to problems generated by globalization, including the displacement of labor, the exploitation of child workers, the migration of workforces, the degradation of the environment, and many other important problems. With all this and much more ahead of us, the twenty-first century should be a most interesting and challenging time to study communication networks and flows within and among organizations. The following section situates the arguments of this book within the context of previous communication research on formal and emergent networks.

Formal Versus Emergent Networks

Historically, organizational communication scholars have made important theoretical and empirical distinctions between formal and emergent networks. Theoretically, the notion of "emergent network" was a designation that originally differentiated informal, naturally occurring networks from formal, imposed, or "mandated" networks (Aldrich, 1976), the latter of which represented the legitimate authority of the organization and were typically reflected by the organizational chart. The formal networks were presumed to also represent the channels of communication through which orders were transmitted downward and information was transmitted upward (Weber, 1947). Early organizational theorists were aware that the formal organizational structure failed to capture many of the important aspects of communication in organizations and discussed the importance of informal communication and the grapevine (Barnard, 1938; Follett, 1924). Several scholars developed ways to study the grapevine and informal networks such as Davis's (1953) Episodic Communication in Channels of Organizations (ECCO) analysis, a technique for tracing the person-to-person diffusion of rumors and the flow of other information in an organization.

Fukuyama (1999) argues that social and organizational structure spans a continuum that ranges from formal to informal. He says, "No one would deny that social order is often created hierarchically. But it is useful to see that order can emerge from a spectrum of sources that extends from hierarchical and centralized types of authority, to the completely decentralized and spontaneous interactions of individuals" (p. 146). Researchers have provided considerable evidence over the years for the coexistence of the two networks. For example, using a variant of ECCO analysis, Stevenson and Gilly (1991) found that managers tended to forward problems to personal contacts rather than to formally designated problem solvers, thus bypassing the formal network. Similarly, Albrecht and Ropp (1984) discovered that "workers were more likely to report talking about new ideas with those colleagues with whom they also discussed work and personal matters, rather than necessarily following prescribed channels based upon hierarchical role relationships" (p. 3). Stevenson (1990) argued that the influence of formal organizational structure on the emergent structure could be best understood on the basis of a status differential model. In a study of a public transit agency, he found evidence that the social distance across the hierarchy reduced the level of communication between higher- and lower-level employees, with middle-level employees serving as a buffer.

An important rationale for studying emergent communication networks has evolved out of the inconclusive findings relating formal organizational structure to organizational behavior (Johnson, 1992, 1993; also see McPhee & Poole, 2001). Jablin's (1987) review of the empirical research on formal organizational structures pointed to the inconclusive nature of studies involving structural variables such as hierarchy, size, differentiation, and formalization. More recently, a series of meta-analytic studies have concluded that the relationships between formal structure, organizational effectiveness (Doty, Glick, & Huber, 1993; Huber, Miller, & Glick, 1990), and technology (Miller, Glick, Wang, & Huber, 1991) are largely an artifact of methodological designs. The fact that formal structural variables have failed to provide much explanatory power has led several scholars to question the utility of further research on formal structures. Rather, they have argued that it is preferable to study emergent structures because they better contribute to our understanding of organizational behavior (Bacharach & Lawler, 1980; Krackhardt & Hanson, 1993; Krikorian, Seibold, & Goode, 1997; Roberts & O'Reilly, 1978; Roethlisberger & Dickson, 1939).

A creative alternative to abandoning formal networks in favor of studying emergent ones is to find new ways to examine both. The problems with formal structures have prompted some scholars to develop network measures that capture in emergent networks the key concepts used to describe formal organizational structure. For example, Krackhardt (1994) has developed four measures of informal structure—connectedness, hierarchy, efficiency, and least-upper-boundedness (unity-of-command)—that map onto theories of an organization's formal organizational structure.

Further, the increased use of new computer-mediated communication systems has spawned research that uses formal organizational structure as a benchmark against which to compare emergent communication networks, for example, those that emerge in an electronic medium. Several interesting, though somewhat conflicting, findings have been generated. In a two-year study of more than eight hundred members of an R&D organization, Eveland and Bikson (1987) found that electronic mail served to augment, and in some cases complement, formal structures. Similarly, Bizot, Smith, and Hill (1991) found that electronic communication patterns corresponded closely to the formal organizational structures in a traditionally hierarchical R&D organization. However, Rice (1994a) found that the electronic communication structures initially mirrored formal organizational structures, but these similarities diminished over time. Hinds and Kiesler (1995) explored the relationship between formal and informal networks in a telecommunications company. They found that communication technologies were increasingly used as a tool for lateral communication across formal organizational boundaries; this finding was most pronounced for technical workers. Lievrouw and Carley (1991) argued that new communication technologies might usher in a new era of "telescience" by offering alternatives to the traditional organizational structures in universities and industry.

The literature comparing face-to-face or mediated emergent communication structures to formal structures generally demonstrates a *pro-emergent bias*, that is, the theory and empirical evidence focus on the advantages of informal communication to individuals and organizations. However, Kadushin and Brimm (1990) challenged the assumption that three types of emergent networks, (1) the shadow networks (the "real" way things get done), (2) the social interaction networks, and (3) the career networks (the venue for so-called networking) always serve to augment the limitations of the organization's formal network. Instead, they argued that these three informal networks frequently work at cross-purposes, thereby restricting rather than promoting the organization's interests. In a study of senior executives in a large international high technology company, they found that by saying, "Please network, but don't you dare bypass authority," organizations create what Bateson (1972) called a *double bind*, a choice situation where each alternative conflicts with the others. They argued that "an important first step is to recognize the incompatibilities between emergent network structures and corporate authority structures and to move this inconsistency from the realm of double bind to the domain of paradox" (Kadushin & Brimm, 1990, p. 15).

Clearly, scholars continue to be interested in the study of the differences between formal and emergent networks in organizations. Ironically, however, the distinction between formal and informal structures in organizations has diminished significantly in recent years and may become increasingly irrelevant in coming decades. The reasons for this convergence center on shifts in organizational structure and management philosophy. Prominent among these are changes to more team-based forms of organizing, the adoption of matrix forms of organizational structure (Burns & Wholey, 1993), and shifts to network forms of organizing (Miles & Snow, 1986, 1992, 1995; Monge, 1995). At the core of these changes has been the explosion of lateral forms of communication (Galbraith, 1977, 1995) made possible by new information technologies that facilitate considerable point-to-point and broadcast communication without regard for traditional hierarchy (Fulk & DeSanctis, 1999).

These developments have eroded the distinction between prior structural categories used to characterize organizations, specifically, between formal and informal and/or between formal and emergent. Contrary to traditional views, contemporary organizations are increasingly constructed out of emergent communication linkages, linkages that are ephemeral in that they are formed, maintained, broken, and reformed with considerable ease (Palmer, Friedland, & Singh, 1986). As Krackhardt (1994) says, "An inherent principle of the interactive form is that networks of relations span across the entire organization, unimpeded by preordained formal structures and fluid enough to adapt to immediate technological demands. These relations can be multiple and complex. But one characteristic they share is that they *emerge* in the organization, they are not preplanned" (p. 218, italics in the original). The networks that emerge by these processes and the organizations they create are called network organizational forms.

The Emergence of Structure from Chaos

The concept of emergence represents a complex and intricate set of beliefs about how order appears out of randomness in nature and society. As such, it has attracted considerable interest in the physical and social sciences as well as philosophy (Dyson, 1997; Gell-Mann, 1994; Holland, 1995, 1998). In the context of organizations, McKelvey (1997) defines emergence as "any order, structure, or pattern appearing in complex random events that cannot be attributed to some specific prepensive purposeful activity or decision by some identifiable official or unofficial component entity" (p. 359).

Emergence typically refers to a set of arguments that higher-level phenomena appear to exhibit properties that are not revealed at lower levels. Clearly, notions of level and by implication, the notion of multilevel systems, are an integral part of the concept of emergence. Kontopoulos (1994) argues that differences in interlevel orderings reflect the nature of different types of emergent structures. As shown in figure 1.1, levels may be nested or nonnested. Nesting implies that lower levels are at least partially included in higher levels. Nested structures may be fully nested as in the case of hierarchies, or partially nested, as in the case of heterarchies, also called "tangled composite structures" (p. 55, see also Hofstadter, 1979; McCulloch, 1945, 1965).

Tangledness refers to the fact that relations between levels lead to overlapping structures. Tangledness typically produces considerably more autonomy and complexity at each level than the nonoverlapping relations found in hierarchies. For example, based on the well-worn notion of a "unitary chain of command," people in organizational hierarchies report to one

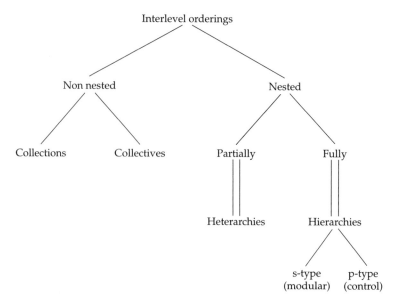

Figure 1.1
Interlevel ordering. Redrawn from K. M. Kontopoulos, *The Logics of Social Structure*.
Copyright 1993 by Cambridge University Press. Used by permission of Cambridge
University Press.

and only one boss, each of whom also reports to one and only one boss
throughout the organization, which makes for clear-cut and unambiguous
lines of authority. People in heterarchies, such as the "matrix" form of
organization, typically report to multiple bosses, who also report to several
bosses. This tangled composite form of structure is considerably more complex and autonomous than the simple, fully nested hierarchy. Finally, two
types of hierarchies are differentiated. The first is the p-type hierarchy
(named after Howard Pattee who formulated early principles of hierarchy)
that operates on the basis of strong control principles from the top down.
The second is the s-type (named after Herbert Simon, who pioneered the
logics of emergent structures), which operates on the basis of a weaker principle of modularity from the bottom up (Kontopoulos, 1994, p. 54–55).

The notion of emergence also raises questions regarding which levels
determine other levels. Microdetermination occurs when the lower level
parts influence the behavior of the higher levels. Macrodetermination occurs
when the higher levels determine the behavior of the lower level parts. Of
course, other possibilities exist. Each level could determine the other in equal

or differential amounts. Or, neither level could determine the other, in which case, each might be determined by externalities, which are other processes outside of the structure and its parts, which impact one or more levels of the structure. And, finally, we must permit the possibility of each level causing itself via feedback loops over time and via self-organizing processes. As shown in figure 1.2 heterarchies permit all of these forms of influence. In fact, adequate accounts of the emergence of networks are likely to require some degree of all of them.

Holland (1997) argues that one major theme runs through the various notions of emergence: "In each case there is a procedure for freely generating possibilities, coupled to a set of constraints that limit those possibilities" (p. 122). One example is neural networks. In this case, Holland says, "We have the possible ranges of behavior of individual neurons (firing rates) constrained by their connections to other neurons" (pp. 122–123, see also Cilliers, 1998). Holland extends this view by arguing that all emergent so-

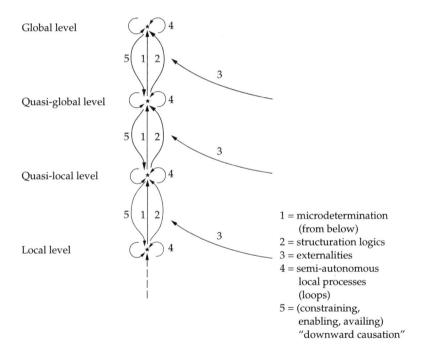

Figure 1.2
The general form of heterarchical level structure. Redrawn from K. M. Kontopoulos, *The Logics of Social Structure*. Copyright 1993 by Cambridge University Press. Used by permission of Cambridge University Press.

cial behavior can be accounted for by a general algorithm in which the interactions between agents is determined by the inputs to each and the set of rules that constrain possible reactions. He calls this algorithm "constrained generating procedures." We will have more to say about this strategy in chapter 3.

Emergence implies the idea of incorporation. As Kontopoulos (1994) says,

> A dominant, higher, emergent structure appears, subsuming fully or partially various previous modes of organization. This new structure re-organizes the possibility space, the resources and the processes, sets a new boundary for the emergent structure on the basis of which new laws and properties may appear, and ecologically asserts its new-found unity. This amounts to what Pattee and Polayni have called a new closure property that operates as a new law of organization, the logic of the emergent structure. (p. 39)

Kontopolous (1993) identifies five different epistemic positions on emergence. These views comprise alternative ways of conceiving of structural emergence. The five consist of three forms of emergence that can be arrayed on a continuum that is anchored on one end by "reductionism" or upward determinism and at the other by "holism" or downward determinism. Philosophers have debated these two polar positions since the early Greeks. It is the three intermediary positions that have emerged during the last half of the twentieth century as alternatives to the two traditional positions.

The first position is *reductionism,* in which all of the elemental parts of a system are aggregated into higher-level structures. An aphorism that captures the essence of reductionism states that "the whole is equal to the sum of its parts." Emergence refers to the fact that the collection shows properties not shown by the individual elements. The collective phenomena show "'synchronized aggregation,' that is, formation of higher collective quasi-entities exhibiting novel properties and new stabilities" (Kontopolous, 1994, p. 26). Reductionism also implies that higher levels of structure are completely determined by the lower levels. (Reductionism also refers to the epistemic belief that all observable phenomena, and therefore all knowledge, ultimately can be explained by the laws of physics, that is, reduced to the behavior of elementary particles. Thus, society can be reduced to psychology; psychology can be reduced to biology, biology to chemistry and chemistry to physics. This view has been thoroughly discredited. See Holland, 1998.)

The second view is *construction or compositional emergence.* This epistemic strategy contains a partial microdeterminism but also includes a focus on "relational-interactional and contextual-ecological variables" (p. 12). This is a form of microdeterminism in which the parts and their interactions comprise the structure of the larger system. Holland (1995, 1998) argues that the interaction of a large number of agents following a small number of rules can generate highly complex macrostructures. Hofstadter's (1979) description of the behavior of ant colonies provides one classic example. The behavior of individual ants follows about a dozen rules, yet the structure and behavior of the entire colony is highly complex (Wilson, 1971). Thus, the emergent structure depends in important ways on the relationships that exist among the parts as well as the context of external variables.

Heterarchy is the third conception of emergence. Heterarchies are "tangled composite structures" that have multiple overlapping, relations across levels. To use McKelvey's (1997) terms, heterarchies represent "multiple orders" (p. 355) that are determined by multiple other levels. Rather than being determined solely from the bottom up as in compositional models, or from the top down, as in hierarchies, heterarchical levels codetermine each other. Heterarchies operate on the basis of "partial determination from below, partial determination from above, partial focal-level determination, (and) residual global indeterminacy.... This is possible by virtue of the fact that heterarchies involve multiple access, multiple linkages, and multiple determinations" (Kontopoulos, 1994, p. 55). McKelvey (1997) points out that this multiple determination makes heterarchies more complex than hierarchies, and therefore, these multiple orders may be difficult to trace. To illustrate this problem, he provides the example of a division manager who wishes to introduce structural "reengineering" processes into a firm. Resistance to the change can stem from subordinates or superiors, thus crossing three levels, and making identification of emergence more difficult than in a simple top down hierarchy or bottom up reductionism.

The fourth view of emergence is hierarchy. As shown in figure 1.1, hierarchies are largely (fully) nested structures, which means that higher levels include lower levels. In hierarchies, the microparts are partially overdetermined by the higher levels. Everyone is familiar with traditional organizational authority hierarchies, where each person reports to one and only one boss. All bosses have authority over all bosses below them in the hierarchy, thus subsuming their authority. The top boss has authority over all. Hierarchy is the dominant form of civil, religious, and other forms of bureaucracy. In organizational networks, hierarchies frequently represent the formal organizational structure.

The anchor on the continuum is holism, sometimes also called transcendence, which constitutes a strong downward determination of the microparts by the macrosystem. Holism is sometimes summarized by the aphorism that "the whole is greater than the sum of its parts." This view emphasizes the totality of the structure, the autonomy of higher levels of structure from lower levels, and the macrodetermination of the parts of the structure by the total structure. In network analysis, holism would emphasize that the overall organizational structure is independent of the particular people who comprise the network. It would also focus on the ways in which the network structure imposes constraints on the behaviors of individuals in the network.

Emergence and Time

Emergence can be viewed from two perspectives with regard to time. *Synchronous* emergence refers to the fact that at any given point in time it is possible to examine both the parts of the network and the entire cross-level structure and see properties such as stability and modularity at one level that do not exist at other levels. Synchronous emergence could show both the parts and their associated network configurations as well as the entire network restraining the behavior of the parts. *Diachronic* emergence refers to the fact that the behavior of the system over time generates properties at one or more levels that did not exist at prior points in time. Diachronic emergence provides much more interesting views of the dynamics of network emergence because it reveals a much greater portion of the emergent process than the synchronic perspective (see Monge & Kalman, 1996, for a further discussion of sequentiality, simultaneity, and synchronicity).

This section has introduced, in the abstract, key concepts and epistemic perspectives associated with the notion of emergence. In order to relate these abstractions to the emergence of organizational networks, the next two sections review the genesis of network forms in organizational contexts as well as the perspectives that have been used historically to study the emergence of structure in organizations. Following that review, we will examine several families of multilevel theories and theoretical mechanisms that can be used to understand the implications of emergent structure.

Network and Organizational Forms

Communication network patterns that recur in multiple settings are called *network forms*. An early theoretical paper by Bavelas (1948), based on Lewin's (1936) psychological field theory, identified a number of small group communication network forms in organizations, including the chain, circle, wheel, and "comcon" (*completely con*nected), and theorized about how the different forms processed information. These network forms varied in the degree to which they were centralized, with the wheel being the most centralized, since all links centered on one individual, and the comcon the least centralized, since everyone was connected to everyone else and thus had the same number of links.

This theoretical article and an imaginative experimental design created by Leavitt (1951) generated hundreds of published articles over some twenty-five years. The primary focus of these efforts was the impact of information processing via the different network forms on productivity and satisfaction (see Shaw, 1964, for a review of this literature). Two prominent findings emerged from this research. First, centralized organizations were more efficient for routine tasks while decentralized networks were more efficient for tasks that required creativity and collaborative problem solving. Second, people in decentralized organizations were more satisfied with the work processes than people in centralized organizations, with the exception in the latter case that the central person in centralized networks was extremely satisfied. Unfortunately, little further theoretical development accompanied this plethora of empirical research. As a result, this line of inquiry has essentially died; almost no articles have been published on small group network forms in organizations during the past twenty years.

Organizational structures, including communication networks that share common features or patterns across a large number of organizations, are called *organizational forms* (McKelvey, 1982). Weber (1947) argued that bureaucracy was the universal organizational form. Three principle theoretical mechanisms that created bureaucracy were rationalization, differentiation, and integration. Rationalization occurred by specifying legitimating instructions that produced standard operating procedures, thus leaving little opportunity for individual autonomy. Rationalizing the network meant specifying who could say what to whom, often summarized by the injunction that commands should flow downward and information upward in the bureaucracy. Differentiation was the process of breaking work up into its various components. This often led to job specialization particularly as production processes proliferated and increased in size and complexity. As work became differentiated, the various parts needed to be coordinated, and thus processes of integration came into operation. Weber argued that bureaucracy differentiated along vertical organizational lines and primarily integrated that way as well. Bureaucracy allowed little room for lateral, cross-level, or cross-boundary communication networks, that is, informal or emergent networks, a feature for which it has been frequently criticized (Galbraith, 1977; Heckscher, 1994).

Miles and Snow (1986, 1992) identified four major organizational forms that have developed over the past century. These are: (1) the traditional functional form, which emerged during the early part of the century, (2) the divisional (or multidivisional) form, which was begun by Alfred P. Sloan at General Motors in the 1940s (see Chandler, 1977), (3) the matrix form, which evolved during the 1960s and 1970s, and (4) the network form, which has emerged over the past decade. Miles and Snow (1992) argue that each of these forms contains its own operating logic, or in terms of this book, its own theoretical mechanism.

The functional form uses a logic of "centrally coordinated specialization" (p. 58), which enables it to efficiently produce a limited set of standardized goods or services for a stable, relatively unchanging market. The divisional form operates by a logic of "divisional autonomy with centrally controlled performance evaluation and resource allocation" (p. 60). Divisions produce separate products or focus on separate markets but are collectively accountable to centralized authority through their communication networks. The ability to develop new divisions enables the multidivisional form to pursue new opportunities in changing markets. The matrix form combines the operating logic of functional and multidivisional forms, using the functional form to produce standardized goods and services and the shared resources of the multidivisional form to explore new opportunities via project groups or teams. The network form uses flexible, dynamic communication linkages to connect and reconnect multiple organizations into new entities that can create products or services.

Three Historical Perspectives on Emergence of Structure in Organizations

Communication network analysis falls within the intellectual lineage of structural analysis, which has had a long and distinguished history. In sociology, Herbert Spencer (1982) and Emile Durkheim (1989/1964) are often credited with introducing structural concepts into sociological thinking. In anthropology, Radcliff-Brown (1959) incorporated structural-functionalist ideas into his watershed analysis of cultures. And in linguistics, structural thinking can be traced to the pioneering work of de Saussure (1916/1966). Most structural analyses of organizations and communication can be located in one of three traditions: (1) positional, (2) relational, and (3) cultural.

The *positional* tradition is rooted in the classical work of Max Weber (1947), Talcott Parsons (1951), and George Homans (1958). Organizational structure is viewed as a pattern of relations among positions. Sets of organizational roles are associated with positions and specify designated behaviors and obligatory relations incumbent on the people who assume the positions. The positions and attached roles constitute the relatively stable and enduring structure of the organization independent of the people who fulfill the roles. This tradition leads to the view that positions and roles determine who communicates with whom, and consequently, the communication structure of the organization. White, Boorman, and Breiger (1976) and Burt (1982) have developed the most significant recent positional theories applicable to organizational communication under the rubric of structural equivalence. This theory argues that people maintain attitudes, values, and beliefs consistent with their organizational positions irrespective of the amount of communication that they have with others in their organizational networks. The positional tradition has been criticized for its inability to take into account the active part individuals play in creating and shaping organizational structure (Coleman, 1973; Nadel, 1957; White, Boorman, & Breiger, 1976).

The *relational* tradition focuses primarily on the direct communication that establishes and maintains communication linkages. Taken collectively, these linkages create an emergent communication structure that connects different people and groups in the organization irrespective of their formal positions or roles. Rooted in systems theory (Bateson, 1972; Buckley, 1967; and Watzlavick, Beavin, & Jackson, 1966), the relational tradition emphasizes the dynamic, constantly changing, enacted nature of structure created by repetitive patterns of person-to-person message flow. Rogers and Kincaid (1981) claim that it is the dominant tradition for studying communication in organizations.

The *cultural* tradition examines symbols, meanings, and interpretations of messages transmitted though communication networks. As part of the resurgence of interest in organizational culture (Frost, Moore, Louis, Lundberg, & Martin, 1985), much of the work has been based on Giddens's (1976, 1984) writings on structuration, which attempt to account for both the creative and constraining aspects of social structure. These studies are characterized by an explicit concern for the continual production and reproduction of meaning through communication, examining simultaneously how meanings emerge from interaction and how they act to constrain subsequent interaction. The cultural tradition has spawned recent work on semantic networks (Monge & Eisenberg, 1987) described later in this book. These three traditions are discussed in greater detail in Monge and Eisenberg (1987).

Although interesting and useful, these network traditions focus attention at a metatheoretical level and fail to specify the *theoretical mechanisms*, such as self-interest, contagion, and exchange, which describe how people, groups, and organizations forge, maintain, and dissolve linkages. As such, the three network traditions demonstrate an unfortunate bias toward the consequences of network structures on attitudes and behavior rather than generating a better understanding of how and why people create, maintain, dissolve, and reconstitute network linkages. Further, while a number of scholars over the past decade have called for greater explication of network theory (e.g., Rogers, 1987; Salancik, 1995; Wellman, 1988), almost none have provided it. Finally, while several reviewers have identified theories that are applicable to network research within and between organizations (Galaskiewicz, 1985; Grandori & Soda, 1995; Mizruchi & Galaskiewicz, 1994; Smith, Carroll, & Ashford, 1995), few have systematically explored the theories and their theoretical mechanisms (Monge & Contractor, 2001).

This book addresses these issues in four ways. First, it provides a new theoretical framework that incorporates multiple theoretical mechanisms to generate network configurations. Second, it offers agent-based models of rule following behavior that incorporate theoretical mechanisms for generating complex adaptive networks. Third, it shows how computational modeling, and in particular the *Blanche* computer simulation environment, can be useful for exploring the evolutionary dynamics of networks. Finally, it reviews new developments in network analysis that permit direct estimation of network parameters of multitheoretical, multilevel models. This facilitates empirical exploration of multitheoretical explanations of the dynamics of communication networks.

In the next section we present a brief overview of the theoretical framework. In the following section we offer a synopsis of the different families of theories that provides the basis for the multitheoretical, multilevel model.

Overview of the Theoretical Framework

Chapter 2 describes the new framework, which we call the multitheoretical, multilevel model (MTML). We argue that alternative social science theories make differential predictions about communication networks. Some of the theoretical mechanisms are unique, even complementary. Others are duplicative, at least in part. Still others compete, offering contradictory explanations. None of the theories, on their own, provide definitive, exhaustive explanations of network phenomena. The MTML framework identifies network properties such as mutuality and density and shows how these properties correspond to theoretical mechanisms in social theories. We argue that utilizing multiple theories should improve our explanations of network evolution as well as significantly increase the amount of variance accounted for by these theoretical mechanisms.

Since networks are inherently multilevel, the MTML framework identifies network properties that exist at individual, dyad, clique, and network levels. Further, it expands this perspective to include the same network at earlier points in time as well as other networks to which it might be related, both contemporaneously and historically. Finally, the framework permits incorporation of attributes of the nodes at all relevant levels. This provides a much more general framework for examining the evolution of communication networks than existing alternatives.

Chapter 3 presents an agent-based, rule-guided model of complex networks. When agents follow rules complex structures emerge. This process need not be planned in advance; it can be self-organizing. The key that ties agent-based models to the MTML framework is to make the rules correspond to the generative mechanisms of social theories. We argue and show that models built on the different theoretical mechanisms inherent in different theories lead to different emergent structures. Since some of these are complementary and others are overlapping in their explanatory value, we argue that a multitheoretical perspective will improve our explanations and our explained variance.

Chapter 4 focuses on the role of computational modeling in network research. We introduce *Blanche*, a program specifically designed to model the emergence of communication networks. We also discuss the role that computer simulations can play in exploring the dynamics and evolution of communication networks. Computational models enable us to incorporate theoretical mechanisms from social theories as the rules that agents follow. As agents follow different rules, different structures evolve over time.

Overview of the Families of Theories

The second part of the book focuses on the role of theory and theoretical mechanisms in explaining the emergence and evolution of communication networks. This review demonstrates that a wide array of theories can be used to develop network formulations. In some cases different theories, some using similar theoretical mechanisms, offer similar explanations but at different levels of analysis. The five epistemic perspectives on the emergence of structure from chaos, reviewed earlier, provide a useful context in which to integrate the heterarchical ordering of multitheoretical explanations. The review also underscores the considerable variation in the depth of conceptual development and empirical research across the different theories and theoretical mechanisms. Since the book focuses on theoretical mechanisms, many other interesting network articles that have little or no bearing on these issues have not been included. The theories and their theoretical mechanisms are summarized in table 1.1. These families are briefly summarized in the following paragraphs.

Chapter 5 presents theories of self-interest and theories of collective action. *Theories of self-interest* focus on how people make choices that favor their personal preferences and desires. Two primary theories in this area are the theory of social capital and transaction cost economics. Distinct from human capital, which describes individual personal characteristics, social capital focuses on the properties of the communication networks in which people are embedded. Structural holes in the network provide people opportunities to invest their information, communication, and other social resources in the expectation of reaping profits. Transaction cost economics examines the information and communication costs involved in market and organizational transactions as well as ways in which to minimize these costs. Network forms of organization provide an alternative to markets and hierarchy, focusing instead on embeddedness in complex networks. Information flows are essential in determining to whom a firm should link and joint value maximization offers an alternative principle to minimizing transaction costs.

Theories of mutual interest and collective action examine how coordinated activity produces outcomes unattainable by individual action. One theory that exemplifies this perspective is public goods theory, which examines the communication strategies that enable organizers to induce members of a collective to contribute their resources to the realization of a public good. Mutual self-interest often conflicts with the individual self-interests of the members of a collective and sometimes leads to free riding and other social and communication dilemmas. Network relations are often essential to the provision and maintenance of the good.

Chapter 6 discusses contagion and cognition theories. *Contagion theories* address questions pertaining to the spread of ideas, messages, attitudes, and beliefs through some form of direct contact. Contagion theories are based on a disease metaphor, where exposure to communication messages

Table 1.1
Selected Social Theories and Their Theoretical Mechanisms

Theory	Theoretical Mechanism
Theories of Self-Interest	Individual value maximization
Social Capital	Investments in opportunities
Structural Holes	Control of information flow
Transaction Costs	Cost minimization
Mutual Self-Interest & Collective Action	Joint value maximization
Public Good Theory	Inducements to contribute
Critical Mass Theory	Number of people with resources & interests
Cognitive Theories	Cognitive mechanisms leading to
Semantic/knowledge Networks	Shared interpretations
Cognitive Social Structures	Similarity in perceptual structures
Cognitive Consistency	Avoid imbalance & restore
Balance Theory	balance
	Reduce dissonance
Cognitive Dissonance	
Contagion Theories	Exposure to contact leading to
Social Information Processing	Social influence
Social Learning Theory	Imitation, modeling
Institutional Theory	Mimetic behavior
Structural Theory of Action	Similar positions in structure and roles
Exchange and Dependency	Exchange of valued resources
Social Exchange Theory	Equality of exchange
Resource Dependency	Inequality of exchange
Network Exchange	Complex calculi for balance
Homophily & Proximity	Choices based on similarity
Social Comparison Theory	Choose comparable others
Social Identity	Choose based on own group identity
Physical Proximity	Influence of distance
Electronic Proximity	Influence of accessibility
Theories of Network Evolution	Variation, Selection, Retention
Organizational Ecology	Competition for scarce resources
NK(C)	Network density and complexity

leads to "contamination." Inoculation theory provides strategies that can be used to prevent contamination. Two competing contagion mechanisms have received considerable attention in the research literature. Contagion by cohesion implies that people are influenced by direct contact with others in their communication networks. Contagion by structural equivalence suggests that those who have similar structural patterns of relationships within the network are more likely to influence one another. Social information processing (social influence) theory suggests that the attitudes and beliefs of people become similar to those of the others in their communication networks. Social learning theory and institutional theory posit that mimetic processes lead to contagion, whereby people and institutions imitate the practices of those in their relevant networks.

Cognitive theories explore the role that meaning, knowledge, and perceptions play in communication networks. *Semantic networks* are created on the basis of shared message content and similarity in interpretation and understanding. A complementary perspective views interorganizational networks as *structures of knowledge*. Creating interorganizational alliances requires building extensive knowledge networks among prospective partners and maintaining them among current partners. These knowledge networks are the mechanisms though which organizations share both explicit and tacit knowledge. *Cognitive communication structures* represent the perceptions that people have about their communication networks, that is, about who in their networks talk to whom. These individual cognitive communication networks can be aggregated to provide a collective or consensual view of the entire network. Cognitive consistency theory examines the extent to which the attitudes, beliefs, opinions, and values of network members are governed by a drive toward consistency. The theory suggests that network members tend toward cognitive similarity as a function of the cognitive balance in their networks rather than alternative mechanisms such as contagion.

Transactive memory systems consist of knowledge networks in which people assume responsibility for mastery among various aspects of a larger knowledge domain. In this way the collective is more knowledgeable than any component. Knowledge repositories linked to the larger knowledge network facilitate knowledge storage and processing. While knowledge flow is essential to an effective knowledge network, communication dilemmas sometimes lead people to withhold potentially useful information.

Chapter 7 focuses on *exchange and dependency theories*. These theories seek to explain the emergence of communication networks on the basis of the distribution of information and material resources across the members of a network. People seek what they need from others while giving what others also seek. The exchange form of this family of theories is based largely on equality, assuming that giving and getting generally balances out across the network. The dependency form emphasizes inequality and focuses on how those who are resource rich in the network tend to dominate those who are resource poor. Consequently, power, control, trust, and ethical behavior are central issues to both theories. Exchange and dependency theories have both been used to examine the flow of information and the power dependencies that develop under interlocking corporate boards of directors. Exchange theory also partially accounts for the emergence of network forms of organization.

Chapter 8 discusses *homophily and proximity theories*. These account for network emergence on the basis of the similarity of network members' traits as well as their similarity of place. Traits represent a variety of personal and demographic characteristics such as age, gender, race, and professional interests. Social comparison theory suggests that people feel discomfort when they compare themselves to others who are different because they have a natural desire to affiliate with those who are like themselves. Of course, this ignores the old adage that opposites attract, which would argue for a heterophily mechanism. Proximity theories argue that people communicate most frequently with those to whom they are physically closest. The theory of electronic propinquity extends this to the realm of e-mail, telephones, and other forms of electronic communication.

Chapter 9 explores *coevolutionary theory*. Traditional evolutionary theory is based on mechanisms of variation, selection, retention, and struggle or competition. Random and planned variations in organizational traits occur, which are selected and retained on the basis of their contribution to organizational fitness and survival. Coevolutionary theory articulates how communities of organizational populations linked by intra- and interpopulation networks compete and cooperate with each other for scarce resources. In order to survive, firms must adapt to the constantly changing environmental niches in which they find themselves while also attempting to influence the ways in which their environments change.

The tenth and final chapter of the book integrates the four major contributions of the book. We begin with a review of the essential arguments advanced in this book in terms of the MTML framework and the theories discussed in chapters 5 through 9. We then discuss recent developments in "small world" research. This is an interesting and surprisingly common property where networks display considerable local connectedness while also having a low degree of separation with the other nodes in the network. Next, we discuss an agenda for future research on the emergence and evolution of organizational communication networks. We offer a number of suggestions for areas that need exploration and for the confluence of analytic strategies that could significantly advance our knowledge of network processes and novel forms of organizing in the twenty-first century. Finally, we conclude by exploring the implications of networks and flows for the globalizing world of the twenty-first century.

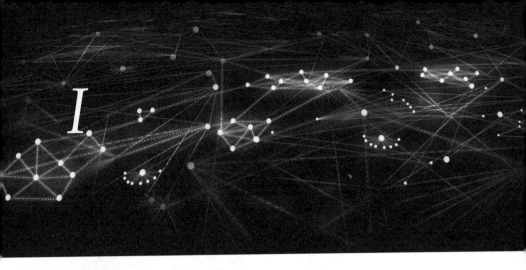

The Multitheoretical, Multilevel Framework

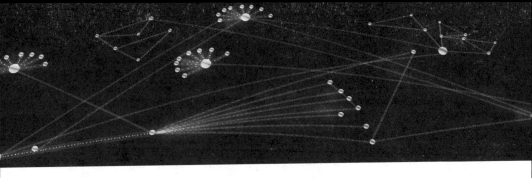

2

Network Concepts, Measures, and the Multitheoretical, Multilevel Analytic Framework

This chapter begins with an overview of network analysis concepts and measures. Those readers who are new to the area, or who are familiar with the social theories described in this book but not with network analysis itself, should find a careful reading of the first section of this chapter to be essential in understanding the remainder of the chapter and book. Network analysis has become a fairly technical topic, and there are a number of concepts, measures, and analytic strategies that require careful explication.

This section of the chapter should provide sufficient background in network analysis to enable an informed reading of the network literature. We hasten to emphasize, however, that it is only a brief introduction. Hence, like all other introductory materials, an attempt is made to trade-off conceptual rigor with simplicity. An extensive literature exists on network analysis, including several fine texts and a number of excellent review chapters. Those who wish to explore further the network analysis material presented in the first third of this chapter should consult the sources in the references that we have identified under "Relations in a World of Attributes." Those who are more familiar with network analysis will find the first section of this chapter less important. A quick skim should provide ample insight into our selection and use of concepts and definitions.

The second section introduces the MTML framework. It shows how various network properties at different levels of analysis can represent the generative mechanisms from different social theories. It also shows how combining theories can provide broader explanations of emergent networks than each theory can alone. As a part of that framework we introduce the statistical ideas pertaining to realizations of a graph and discuss p^* analytic strategies and the PSPAR computer program that can be used to analyze relevant data. This section concludes with an extended presentation of the MTML model, which broadly classifies variables into endogenous and exogenous factors, each with multiple levels. Examples are provided for each of the ten classes of hypotheses generated by this framework.

Network Analysis

The concept of network is extremely general and broad, one that can be applied to many phenomena in the world. At its core, network analysis consists of applying a set of relations to an identified set of entities. Road networks tie together various locales by the relationship, "can travel to," while electrical networks link different power sources and outlets with the relationship, "provides power to." In the context of organizational communication, network analysts often identify the entities as people who belong to one or more organizations and to which are applied one or more communication relations, such as "provides information to," "gets information from," "knows about," and "communicates with." It is also common to use work groups, divisions, and entire organizations as the set of entities and to explore a variety of relations such as "collaborates with," "subcontracts with," and "joint ventures with." As we will discuss later in the book, the entities could also be nonhuman agents such as knowledge repositories, avatars, and so on.

Relations in a World of Attributes

Relations are central to network analysis because they define the nature of the communication connections between people, groups, and organizations. This focus stands in sharp contrast to other areas of the social sciences, which have tended to study "attributes," the characteristics of people, groups, and organizations rather than the relations between them. Relations possess a number of important properties, including strength, symmetry, transitivity, reciprocity, and multiplexity. A large literature exists that describes these properties and other fundamentals of network analysis, including network concepts, measures, methods, and applications (see, for example, Haythornthwaite, 1996; Marsden, 1990; Monge, 1987; Monge & Contractor, 1988; Scott, 1988, 2000; Stohl, 1995; Wasserman & Faust, 1994; Wigand, 1988). Tables 2.1, 2.2, and 2.3 from Brass (1995a) summarize major network concepts. These tables describe measures of network ties, measures assigned to individuals, and measures used to describe entire networks. The measures described in this chapter and several additional metrics can be computed using network analysis software programs such as UCINET 6 (Borgatti, Everett, & Freeman, 2002), MultiNet (Richards & Seary, 2000), and Pajek (Batagelj & Mrvar, 2002). Since the focus of this book is on theory and research, we provide only a brief overview of some of the more widely used network measures and analytic techniques rather than extensive coverage.

Network Linkages

Network linkages are created when one or more communication relations are applied to a set of people, groups, or organizations. For example, in

Table 2.1
Typical Social Network Measures of Ties (Brass, 1995a)

Measure	Definition	Example
Indirect Links	Path between two actors is mediated by one or more others	A is linked to B, B is linked to C; thus A is indirectly linked to C through B
Frequency	How many times, or how often the link occurs	A talks to B 10 times per week
Stability	Existence of link over time	A has been friends with B for 5 years
Multiplexity	Extent to which two actors are linked together by more than one relationship	A and B are friends, they seek out each other for advice, and work together
Strength	Amount of time, emotional intensity, intimacy, or reciprocal services (frequency or multiplexity often used as measure of strength of tie)	A and B are close friends, or spend much time together
Direction	Extent to which link is from one actor to another	Work flows from A to B, but not from B to A
Symmetry (reciprocity)	Extent to which relationship is bidirectional	A asks B for advice, and B asks A for advice

Table 2.2

Typical Social Network Measures Assigned to Individual Actors (Brass, 1995a)

Measure	Definition
Degree	Number of direct links with other actors
In-degree	Number of directional links to the actor from other actors (in-coming links)
Out-degree	Number of directional links from the actor to other actors (out-going links)
Range (Diversity)	Number of links to different others (others are defined as different to the extent that they are not themselves linked to each other, or represent different groups or statuses)
Closeness	Extent to which an actor is close to, or can easily reach all the other actors in the network. Usually measured by averaging the path distances (direct and indirect links) to all others. A direct link is counted as 1, indirect links receive proportionately less weight.
Betweenness	Extent to which an actor mediates, or falls between any other two actors on the shortest path between those actors. Usually averaged across all possible pairs in the network.
Centrality	Extent to which an actor is central to a network. Various measures (including degree, closeness, and betweenness) have been used as indicators of centrality. Some measures of centrality weight an actor's links to others by centrality of those others.
Prestige	Based on asymmetric relationships, prestigious actors are the object rather than the source of relations. Measures similar to centrality are calculated by accounting for the direction of the relationship (i.e., in-degree).
Roles	
Star	An actor who is highly central to the network
Liaison	An actor who has links to two or more groups that would otherwise not be linked, but is not a member of either group
Bridge	An actor who is a member of two or more groups
Gatekeeper	An actor who mediates or controls the flow (is the single link) between one part of the network and another
Isolate	An actor who has no links, or relatively few links to others

organizational contexts Farace, Monge, and Russell (1977) identified three distinct important communication networks in terms of production, maintenance, and innovation relations. Other kinds of communication linkages are possible. For example, Badaracco (1991) distinguished two types of knowledge, which he called migratory and embedded, each associated with

Table 2.3
Typical Social Network Measures Used to Describe Networks (Brass, 1995a)

Measure	Definition
Size	Number of actors in the network
Inclusiveness	Total number of actors in a network minus the number of isolated actors (not connected to any other actors). Also measured as the ratio of connected actors to the total number of actors.
Component	Largest connected subset of network nodes and links. All nodes in the component are connected (either direct or indirect links) and no nodes have links to nodes outside the component.
Connectivity (Reachability)	Extent to which actors in the network are linked to one another by direct or indirect ties. Sometimes measured by the maximum, or average, path distance between any two actors in the network.
Connectedness	Ratio of pairs of nodes that are mutually reachable to total number of pairs of nodes
Density	Ratio of the number of actual links to the number of possible links in the network
Centralization	Difference between the centrality scores of the most central actor and those of all other actors in a network is calculated, and used to form ratio of the actual sum of the differences to the maximum sum of the differences
Symmetry	Ratio of number of symmetric to asymmetric links (or to total number of links) in a network
Transitivity	Three actors (A, B, C) are transitive if whenever A is linked to B and B is linked to C, then C is linked to A. Transitivity is the number of transitive triples divided by the number of potential transitive triples (number of paths of length 2).

a different type of linkage. Migratory knowledge is information that exists in forms that are easily moved from one location, person, group, or firm to another. Migratory knowledge tends to be contained in books, designs, machines, blueprints, computer programs, and individual minds, all of which encapsulate the knowledge that went into its creation. Embedded knowledge is more difficult to transfer. It "resides primarily in specialized relationships among individuals and groups and in the particular norms, attitudes, information flows, and ways of making decisions that shape their dealings with each other" (p. 79). Craftsmanship, unique talents and skills, accumulated know-how, and group expertise and synergy are all difficult to transfer from one place to another and particularly difficult to transfer across organizational or even divisional boundaries.

The two types of network linkages Badaracco (1991) identified were the product link, associated with migratory knowledge, and the knowledge link, associated with embedded knowledge. In the interfirm context, a product link is an arrangement whereby a company relies on "an outside ally to manufacture part of its product line or to build complex components that the company had previously made for itself" (p. 11). Knowledge links are alliances whereby companies seek "to learn or jointly create new knowledge and capabilities" (p. 12). These "alliances are organizational arrangements and operating policies through which separate organizations share administrative authority, form social links, and accept joint ownership, and in which looser, more open-ended contractual arrangements replace highly specific, arm's length contracts" (Badaracco, 1991, p. 4).

Research on interorganizational linkages began more than forty years ago with the work of Levine and White (1961) and Litwak and Hylton (1962), which spawned a quarter century of interest on the exchange of goods and material resources (see, e.g., Mitchell, 1973; Warren, 1967). More recent work has focused on communication, information, and knowledge linkages (Gulati, 1995; Powell, Koput, & Smith-Doerr, 1996; Tsai, 2001). Eisenberg et al. (1985) developed a two-dimensional typology of interorganizational linkages based on linkage content and linkage level. The content dimension separated (1) material content from (2) symbolic or informational content. The level dimension distinguished three forms of exchange. Eisenberg et al. (1985) state that

> an *institutional* linkage occurs when information or materials
> are exchanged between organizations without the involvement
> of specific organizational roles or personalities (e.g., routine data
> transfers between banks). A *representative* linkage occurs when a
> role occupant who officially represents an organization within
> the system has contact with a representative of another organiza-
> tion (e.g., an interagency committee to formulate joint policies).
> The emphasis here is on the official nature of the transaction
> and the representative capacities of the individuals. Finally, a
> *personal* linkage occurs when an individual from one organiza-
> tion exchanges information or material with an individual in
> another organization, but in a nonrepresentative or private capac-
> ity (i.e., via friendship or "old school" ties). (p. 237, italics in the
> original)

Network Concepts and Measures

Network analysis is an analytic technique that enables researchers to represent relational data and explore the nature and properties of those relations. The entities mentioned earlier in this chapter—for instance, people, work groups, and organizations—are typically represented as nodes or points in a network analysis, with one node assigned to each entity.

The *relations*, such as "communicates with" or "provides data to," are represented as lines connecting the various nodes. These lines are typically called links, ties, or arcs. Links are typically assigned properties that are believed to be inherent to the relations. Two important properties are *directionality* and *strength*. Relations can be either directional or nondirectional. Directional links are those that go from one point to another. That is, they have an origin and a destination. Nondirectional links are those that do not have a direction, representing instead a shared partnership. The relation "supplies parts to" is a directional tie since the parts go from one organization, the supplier, to another organization, the receiver. The relation "is strategically allied with" is a nondirectional relation, since it ties together two firms without a direction between the two.

The second property is *strength*, which indicates the quantity of the relation. The strength of a tie could be "dichotomous" or "valued." A dichotomous tie simply indicates whether the relation is present or absent. Thus, the dichotomous relation "communicates with" simply indicates whether two people, work groups, or organizations communicate with each other without any indication of how much communication occurs. A valued link represents the intensity or frequency of the link. Thus, the strength of the same relation, "communicates with" represented as a valued link could indicate the amount of time people spend communicating with each other, for instance, less than five minutes per week, an hour a week, several hours a week, and so on. Alternatively, it could represent the frequency with which they communicate, for example, once a month, once a week, daily, or their satisfaction with that communication on a numerical scale.

Researchers can examine one or more relations on the same set of nodes. When relations are studied one at a time, they are called *uniplex* relations. Two or more relations studied together are considered *multiplex*. Historically, most network research, including much of the work reviewed in this book, has examined uniplex relations, but there is no theoretical or analytic reason why researchers must limit themselves to single relations.

Indeed, Wasserman and Faust (1994) have argued that network research could be significantly improved if it moved from uniplex to multiplex analysis.

Representing Networks

It is customary in network analysis to organize network data in square data matrices (the same number of rows and columns) that are sometimes called *sociomatrices*. The columns and rows of the matrices are typically assigned the names or numbers of the nodes in the analysis, that is, the people, work groups, or organizations. The cells of the matrices contain entries that represent the relations between all possible pairs of nodes. If the relations are dichotomous, the entries are 1 and 0, with the one representing the presence of the relation and the zero representing its absence. A sociomatrix of 1s and 0s representing binary relations is called an *adjacency* matrix. If the relation is valued, then numbers are entered into the matrix to represent the strength (the frequency, duration, or amount) of the relation between each pair of nodes in the network. It is common to think of these matrices as "who to whom" matrices with the rows representing the "who" and the columns representing the "whom." Thus, it is possible to "read" a matrix from left to right by selecting a row representing "who," moving to a particular cell to find the nature of the relationship that exists, and then moving to the top of the column to read "with whom" it occurs. In a nondirectional network, the value associated with the tie from node A to node B is the same as the value associated with the tie from node B to node A. Hence, these matrices are symmetric, with values above the diagonal being a mirror reflection of values below the diagonal. Directional networks, however, are almost always asymmetric.

Another way to represent network data is via *graphs*. Each participant in the network is assigned a numbered or labeled point. Lines between points represent relations. If relations are directional, arrowheads are placed at the front of the line indicating the direction of the relation. Graphs with directional relations are called *digraphs*. If the relations are dichotomous, a line represents the relation while the absence of a line represents the absence of the relation. If the relations are valued, numbers can be placed on each line to represent the frequency, duration, or other quantity of the relation. These are called *valued graphs*.

In some cases the rows and columns used to represent a network may not be the same entities. For instance, the rows may represent individuals and the columns may represent different knowledge repositories. These would then be represented in rectangular (rather than square) matrices. Such networks are sometimes referred to as *bimodal* or *affiliation* networks.

In summary, networks represent relational ties among a set of nodes. The nodes may be individuals, groups, organizations, or any other well-defined set of entities. The relations can be communication, affect, shared interpretations, or transfer of tangible or symbolic resources. Relations can be directional or nondirectional, binary or valued, and uniplex or multiplex. These networks can be represented as matrices or graphs.

Measuring Network Properties

In addition to representing the network as graphs and matrices, analysts have also developed a suite of metrics to calculate various properties of the network. These properties can be computed at various levels of analysis. Wasserman and Faust (1994) suggest that there are five distinct levels. The *individual actor* level is the level of the participants represented by the nodes or points in the network, whether individuals, groups, or organizations. At this level analysis would focus on such things as the number of contacts each participant has or the number of others who indicate contact with them. The *dyad* level examines pairs of network members together with their relations. At this level researchers might ask the extent to which ties are reciprocated between each pair in the network. The *triad* level examines three nodes at a time, focusing perhaps on the level of balance among all triads in the network. The fourth level is the *subgroup*. At this level analysts frequently want to identify who belongs to subgroups and who does not. The final *global* level is the network as a whole. Here the focus might be on the proportion of possible ties that actually exist in the network.

Individual Level of Analysis

DEGREE, INDEGREE, AND OUTDEGREE

For any given node, the number of directional ties emanating from it is called the node's *outdegree*. Similarly, the number of ties directed to that node, in other words, terminating there, is called the node's *indegree*. The number of nondirectional ties associated with a node is simply called *degree*. The interpretation of the degree metrics depends on the nature of the networks being examined. In a directional communication network, a node's out-degree could be interpreted as "expansiveness," while the node's indegree would signal its "popularity." Some researchers have used degree as one indicator of the node's social capital or centrality. It might seem reasonable to interpret a high degree of centrality as a positive and desirable feature of the network, but it could also be justifiably interpreted as signaling a strain such as communication overload or a constraint on the node's ability to function effectively. Nodes that have a degree of zero are referred to as *isolates*; that is, they have no ties to others in the network.

BETWEENNESS

While degree metrics gauge the extent to which a node is directly connected to all other nodes in the network, *betweenness* measures the extent to which a node is directly connected only to those other nodes that are not directly connected to each other. That is, it measures the extent to which a node serves as an intermediary "between" other nodes in the network. Between-ness measures can be computed either by accounting for the direction of ties or simply the presence of these ties. In a communication network, a node with a high betweenness score is often interpreted as deriving power by controlling or brokering the flow of information as well as managing the interpretation of that information. Clearly, the removal or departure of a node with a high betweenness measure would eliminate the indirect connections among many other nodes in the network. As such it offers an alternative conceptualization of centrality in the network. Nodes that serve as an intermediary between *groups* of people that are not directly connected to other groups (rather than unconnected individuals) are sometimes referred to as *liaisons* or *bridges*.

CLOSENESS

While degree metrics gauge the extent to which nodes are directly connected to all other nodes in the network, and betweenness measures indirect connections, *closeness* measures the extent to which nodes are directly or indirectly connected to all other nodes in the network. Hence a node can have a high closeness score even if the node has a low degree score, but is connected to nodes that either have high degree scores or are, in turn, connected to other nodes that have high degree scores. Closeness is therefore interpreted as a useful measure to assess a node's ability to efficiently access information directly or indirectly "through the grapevine." In that sense, it offers a third conceptualization of an individual's centrality in the network. It also serves to measure the reach of a node's indirect network.

Padgett and Ansell's (1993) analysis of the marital and business ties among sixteen families in fifteenth-century Florence, Italy, offers an interesting illustration of the differences in degree, closeness, and betweenness measures of centrality. Padgett's data reveal that in the marital network, the Lambersteschi and the Peruzzi families were approximately equally likely to forge marital ties with other families. Hence their degree centrality in the marital network was about the same. However, the Peruzzi family had a substantially higher betweenness centrality measure than the Lambersteschi family. This suggests that members of the Peruzzi family married into other families who in turn did not marry members of one another. Another sharp contrast, involving the Medici and Ridolfi families, can be found in the business network. While the Medicis had only a marginally higher degree of closeness than the Ridolfis, their betweenness centrality was five times as large. That is, while the Medicis and the Ridolfis were equally connected via direct and indirect business ties to the remaining Florentine families, the Medicis were much more likely to engage in direct business ties with families that were not themselves involved in direct business relationships. These contrasts offer some useful explanations and understandings of the role these families played in fifteenth-century Florence.

STRUCTURAL HOLES

Burt (1992) developed a series of measures that describe the extent to which an individual fills *structural holes* in the network. These measures examine various properties of the "ego-centered" network, that is, the subset of the overall network that exists among the partners in an individual's network. Using the egocentric network, Burt computes a measure of the individual's *effective network size*. It is based on the premise that ties among a person's network partners attenuate the effective size of that individual's network. The maximum effective size of a network occurs when an individual's communication partners are not connected to one another. However, it is reduced by the average number of ties that each of the partners have with other partners in an individual's network. Burt (1992) argues that *efficiency* is an index of the extent to which individuals have maximized the effective size of their egocentric networks. An individual's *structural constraint* is the extent to which an individual has strong ties with partners who in turn have strong ties with other partners of the individual. Finally, an individual's *hierarchical constraint* measures the extent that a single partner in the network is the source of that individual's structural constraint.

This section has provided conceptual definitions and some illustrations of network properties that can be measured for each individual or node in the network. That is, we can obtain measures for each individual's degree, betweenness, closeness, effective size, efficiency, structural constraint, and hierarchical constraint in the network. Next we describe measures that can be computed between pairs of individuals.

Dyadic (or Link or Tie) Level of Analysis

Wasserman and Faust (1994) note that the directional ties between any two individuals in a network can be characterized as symmetric, asymmetric, or null. Ties are symmetric if individuals have ties to each other. They are asymmetric if only one individual has a link to the other. They are null if neither has ties to each another. *Mutuality* or *reciprocity* is defined as the extent to which ties between two individuals are symmetric. For binary relations, mutuality can be present or absent, depending on whether symmetric links exist between two individuals. For valued relations, mutuality measures the similarity between the values of the links between two individuals. While mutuality measures the extent to which two individuals are directly connected to one another, it is possible to also measure the extent to which two individuals are either indirectly connected through the network (distance and geodesics) or share similar patterns of interactions with others in the network (structural equivalence). These two metrics are discussed next.

DISTANCE AND GEODESICS

For any pair of nodes, two types of links can exist: direct and indirect. *Direct links* are connections between any pair of nodes that involve only those two nodes. *Indirect links* occur between any two nodes by virtue of their connections with other nodes. A direct link between two nodes is said to be a one-step connection. The smallest indirect connection is two-step, which ties together three nodes with two direct links. Here, the first node is directly connected with the second node, the second is directly connected with the third, which leads the first and third nodes to be indirectly connected to each other with a two-step linkage or two *degrees of separation*. Two nodes can have both direct and indirect connections. To complete the example just given, the first and third nodes could also have a direct link, in which case these two nodes would have a direct link to each other as well as an indirect link through the second node.

Higher levels of indirect links exist within many networks such as three-step connections, which tie together four nodes, four-step links, which tie together five nodes, and so on. It is this measure that is referenced in the "small world" hypothesis that any two individuals on the planet are separated on the average by six degrees of separation (Milgram, 1967). The notion of multiple-step linkages, called *n-step links* where *n* represents the number of links, naturally leads to the idea of *chains* or *paths* within the network. There are many applications of these in organizational contexts. Wasserman and Faust (1994) provide the example of dissemination of information among employees in organizations. "An important consideration is whether information originating with one employee could eventually reach all other employees, and if so, how many lines it must traverse in order to get there. One might also consider whether there are multiple routes that a message might take to go from one employee to another, and whether some of these paths are more or less efficient" (p. 105).

There are a number of network concepts that describe how to get from one point to another in a network. One of the most important of these is the *distance* between two points. The distance, typically represented by the symbol *d*, is the number of links between two nodes. The shortest distance between two points is called a *geodesic*. The largest distance is called the *diameter*.

In summary, the indirect links between two individuals provide at least two useful measures at the dyadic level. First, *reachability* is the shortest path (or the geodesic) that connects two individuals in a network. Reachability has a minimum value of one if two individuals are directly connected, a value of two if they are one-step removed, and so on. Reachability has an infinite (or undetermined) value if it is not possible for one individual to directly, or indirectly, reach the other individual.

Second, *redundancy* measures the number of alternative shortest paths (or geodesics) that connect two individuals indirectly. A high redundancy score would indicate a greater likelihood that information will flow from one individual to another via one of the multiple indirect paths.

STRUCTURAL EQUIVALENCE

While mutuality is a measure based on the direct links between two individuals, and reachability and redundancy are based on the indirect links between two individuals, there are additional measures of *structural equivalence* that are based on the similarity of interaction patterns between two individuals. In its strictest form, two individuals have a high degree of structural equivalence if they are tied to—and not tied to—the same other individuals in the network. A more general measure of structural equivalence, sometimes called regular equivalence, measures the extent to which two individuals have ties to similar other individuals in the network though not necessarily the same others. Similar other individuals can be defined a priori based on attributes such as profession. So, for instance, two doctors may have a high degree of regular equivalence if they both have ties to nurses, even if they are not the same nurses. However, more commonly, "similar other individuals" is defined based on their patterns of interaction in the network.

Triadic Level of Analysis

Properties of the network can also be measured for individuals in the network taken three at a time. *Transitivity* and *cyclicality* measure the extent to which every set of three actors, say, A, B, and C, in the network demonstrates certain structural patterns. If A directs a link to B and B directs a link to C, the network triad is *transitive* if A also directs a tie to C. For instance, if a group of three organizations is in a transitive relation, then if A makes a donation to B, B will make a donation to C, *and* A will also donate to C.

A network triad is *cyclical* when A directs a tie to B, B ties to C, and C in turn links to A, thereby completing the cycle. Transitivity and cyclicality are identical if the network involves nondirectional links. In essence they both assess the extent to which, for instance, we are friends with friends of our friends.

Subgroup Level of Analysis

COMPONENTS AND CLIQUES

A graph or network is *connected* if it is possible to get from one point to all other points in the graph, that is, if every point is reachable from every other point. This typically happens only in relatively small networks. More likely, the graph is unconnected or *disconnected*, meaning that it is not possible to get to all points in the graph from the other points. This implies that there are subsets of points in the network that are connected to one other, called *subgraphs*; it also implies that the subgraphs are not connected to each other. These connected subgraphs of the network are called *components* of the network. A *strong component* is composed of all individuals who have direct or indirect ties to all other individuals in the component. A *weak component* is composed of individuals who are connected to all other individuals in the subgraph irrespective of the directionality of the link.

The criteria to define these components are somewhat flexible. Substantively, components index the extent to which clearly identifiable and distinct cliques exist within the network. Although the term *clique* has a very specific definition in network methodology, it was used here in the preceding sentence in its more colloquial sense. In network theory, a *clique* is defined as a maximally complete subgraph, that is, the maximum number of individuals in the network who are all directly connected to one another, but are not all directly connected to any additional individuals in the network. One or more individuals can be member(s) of more than one clique. Again, more relaxed criteria are also used to identify cliques. An *n-clique* includes the maximum number of individuals in the network who are all directly or indirectly connected to one another via no more than n links. Further, they are not directly (or indirectly) connected via n or fewer links to any other additional individual in the network. Clearly, a 1-clique (that is, where $n=1$) is equivalent to the strict definition of cliques. A 2-clique or a 3-clique is a less conservative definition thereby allowing more members to be included in the clique.

While *n*-cliques relax the requirement of a *direct* link to all members in the clique, *k-plex* relaxes the requirement of a direct link to *all* members in the network. A *k*-plex therefore includes the maximum number of individuals in the network who are directly connected with, at least, all but k of the individuals in the group. Further, they are not all directly connected to any other additional individual in the network. Clearly, a 1-plex group is identical to a clique, comprising individuals who are directly connected to all but one of the members in the group (that is, themselves), while a 2-plex comprises a group of individuals who are each connected directly to all but two in the group (that is, themselves and one other member).

POSITIONS

While components and cliques help measure the extent to which subgroups of individuals in a network are cohesively connected, there are other measures which index the extent to which individuals in the network engage in similar structural interactions (or are structurally equivalent), and thereby enact similar roles or positions. While components and cliques help identify subgroups of individuals who are relationally tied to one another, role analyses identify groups of individuals who occupy similar positions. The distinction between the two sets of measures reflects the traditional intellectual distinctions between the relational and positional approaches described in chapter 1.

Global Network Level of Analysis

Density is a concept that refers to the extensiveness or completeness of the relations in the network. Another frequently used term for density is *connectedness*. Density is measured as the ratio of total links to possible links, that is, the percentage of possible relations that actually exist. Networks with few linkages are called *sparse* or sparsely connected networks; networks with many links are said to be *dense* or highly connected.

Network centralization is an umbrella concept that examines the variation in individuals' centralities within a network. Individuals' centrality scores were defined in a previous section discussing network measures at the individual level of analysis. In general, a network is centralized if a few individuals (perhaps, just one) have considerably higher centrality scores than others in the network. A network is decentralized if the members in the network have roughly the same centrality scores. This implies that people are not more (or less) central than others. Consequently, network centralization indexes the variability among the individuals' centrality. Degree network centralization measures the extent to which some individuals have a much higher degree centrality score than others.

Betweenness and closeness network centralization provide corresponding indices based on individuals' betweenness and closeness centrality scores.

The Multitheoretical, Multilevel (MTML) Analytic Framework

Representing networks as matrices or graphs and measuring properties of the network serve useful descriptive purposes. However, *explaining* the emergence of networks requires an analytic framework that enables inferences to be made on the basis of theories and statistical tests. Consequently, this section introduces the MTML framework and p^* statistical network techniques, an integrated theoretical and analytic framework that provides an appropriate basis for studying multiple substantive theories across several analytic levels on the basis of valid statistical inference techniques (Contractor, Wasserman, & Faust, 2001).

The problem of explaining network emergence explored in this book challenges network analysts to make four key moves: (1) from single theoretical to multitheoretical analyses, (2) from single level to multilevel analyses, (3) from purely network explanations to hybrid models that also account for attributes of the individual nodes, and (4) from descriptive or exploratory techniques to inferential or confirmatory ones. These four issues are discussed in greater detail in the following subsections.

Multitheoretical Analyses

First, our review of the vast network research literature (Monge & Contractor, 2001) led us to realize that relatively few network studies utilize theories as the basis for formulating research hypotheses, and those that do use only single theories. As such, they tend to account for relatively small amounts of network variance. This, of course, contributes to our knowledge of communication networks, but not nearly to the extent that most would like. This observation led us to develop the MTML perspective as a way to help compare and integrate diverse theories and to increase the explanatory power of research efforts.

Alternative social theories make differential predictions about communication networks. Some of the theoretical mechanisms are unique, even complementary. Others are duplicative, at least in part. Still others compete, offering contradictory explanations. None of the theories, on their own, provide definitive, exhaustive explanations of network phenomena. The MTML framework identifies theoretical mechanisms in social theories and shows how they correspond to network properties such as mutuality and density. We argue that utilizing multiple theories should improve our explanations of network evolution as well as significantly increase the amount of variance accounted for by these theoretical mechanisms.

Multilevel Analyses

Second, one of the key advantages of a network perspective is the ability to collect and collate data at various levels of analysis (person, dyad, triad, group, organizational, and interorganizational). However, for the purposes of analyses most network data are either transformed to a single level of analysis (e.g., the individual or the dyadic level) that necessarily loses some of the richness in the data, or are analyzed separately at different levels of analysis thus precluding direct comparisons of theoretical influences at different levels. For instance, social exchange theory suggests that the likelihood of a communication tie from person A to person B is predicated on the presence of a communication tie from person B to person A. However, balance theory suggests that the likelihood of a communication tie from person A to person B is predicated on the configuration of ties the two people have with third individuals, C through, say, person Z. While social exchange theory makes a prediction at the dyadic level, balance theory makes a prediction at the triadic level.

Jones, Hesterly, and Borgatti (1997, p. 912) extend this dilemma even beyond the triadic level, noting that although many organizational studies adopt a network perspective, "these studies most often focus on exchange dyads, rather than on the network's overall structure or architecture." Yet, by limiting attention to dyads and ignoring the larger structural context, "these studies cannot show adequately how the network structure influences exchanges" (Jones et al. 1997, p. 912). This is the problem of *dyadic atomization* noted by Granovetter (1992). While network analysis offers independent statistical tests for theoretical predictions at each of these levels of analysis, combining and comparing effects simultaneously necessitates an analytic framework that offers multilevel hypotheses testing. The MTML framework combined with the p^* analytic techniques provides these capabilities.

Incorporating Attributes

Third, a long-standing debate among structural scholars has centered on the merits and feasibility of incorporating information about attributes of nodes into network studies. Typical examples are gender or an individual's organizational affiliation in interorganizational networks. While formalists tend to dismiss the utility of looking at attributes, the majority of network scholars embrace the idea (Wellman, 1988). Unfortunately, even those who would like to create hybrid models that incorporate attribute information to explain network patterns are sometimes deterred by the difficulty of doing it in a statistically defensible manner.

Further, while some empirical network research exists that incorporates data on individual attributes, these studies are often limited to one level of analysis, as described previously. For instance, theories of homophily would suggest that in an interorganizational network, people with similar organizational affiliations are more likely to have communication ties with one another than with people who have different organizational affiliations. In a potentially conflicting prediction, theories of collective action would argue that individuals with similar organizational affiliations are more likely to be structured in centralized networks among themselves rather than with individuals from different organizations. Simultaneously combining and contrasting these two predictions involving individuals' attributes goes beyond the capabilities of most contemporary network analytic methods.

Valid Statistical Inference

In the past two decades scholars have made considerable progress in the development of descriptive network metrics. Since network data are relational, they constitute, by definition, nonindependent observations. Consequently, "standard" statistical methods that assume independent units such as regression analysis and ANOVA are not appropriate. The efforts to develop statistical estimation of network properties have been relatively sparse, unconnected, and esoteric, thereby making them relatively inaccessible to the larger research community and inapplicable for integration across multiple levels of analysis. For instance, there are measures that can be used to describe the level of reciprocity in a network, that is, the extent to which communication links from person A to person B also exist from person B to person A. However, network analysts have been less successful in formulating statistically defensible and computationally accessible tests that can determine if the degree of reciprocity in a network is statistically significant.

In summary, there is a pressing need for a multitheoretical, multilevel approach to organizational network analysis. Further, this framework needs to include the capability to incorporate theoretical explanations that are based on information about attributes and other external characteristics outside the bounds of the properties of the focal network. Finally, valid statistical inferential techniques need to simultaneously incorporate multiple theoretical explanations at the individual, dyad, triad, and global levels of analyses.

The following section describes the p^* statistical analytical techniques for network analysis. This framework has three potential benefits. First, it serves as a template to stimulate a conscious attempt to specify hypotheses grounded in multiple theories and at multiple levels. Second, it provides an omnibus assessment of the complementary and contradictory influences of these multiple theories. Finally, it focuses attention on areas where opportunities remain to develop new theoretical explanations. This discussion provides the context in which it is possible to develop the genres of multitheoretical, multilevel hypotheses that influence the structural tendencies of a network. We turn to that task after describing the logic of p^* analysis.

Realizations of Graphs and Networks in p* Analysis

Statistically, every observed network, that is, every network data set, can be viewed as one "realization" of a network or graph. A *realization* is one particular configuration of ties in a network out of the set of possible configurations. These possible configurations are anchored at one end by a completely connected network where everyone is tied to everyone else. It is anchored at the other end by a completely empty network, one in which no one is tied to anyone else in the network. Obviously, many different realizations exist between these two poles. For example, in one realization of a three-person network, person A might be connected to persons B and C, but B and C might not be connected to each other. In an alternative realization, A might not be connected to B or C, who are themselves connected to each other.

Consider an interorganizational consortium of 17 members representing various industry and government organizations that we will examine in detail later in this chapter. The observed communication relations in the data constitute only one realization of a graph consisting of 17 people and the possible ties among them. Theoretically, there are many other graph realizations that could have arisen based on the communication ties among the 17 members. Further, it should be apparent that as the number of nodes in a network gets larger, the number of possible network realizations increases dramatically. The statistical question of interest is why the observed realization occurred out of the rather large set of other possible graph realizations.

The answer to this question resides in whether the observed graph realization exhibits certain hypothesized structural features, such as reciprocation, balance, and density. If these features exist, they increase the likelihood of some realizations and decrease the likelihood of others. The presence of these structural features are captured by estimating parameters that quantify the effects of the hypothesized structural property on the probability of ties being present or absent in the network. These estimates indicate whether graph realizations that contain the theoretically hypothesized property have significantly higher probabilities of being observed. If so, then the hypothesized property is statistically important for understanding the structural configuration of the observed network. This logic is central to random graph models, including Markov random graph models (Frank & Strauss, 1986; Strauss & Ikeda, 1990) and the p^* family of models (Anderson, Wasserman, & Crouch, 1999; Pattison & Wasserman, 1999; Robins, Pattison, & Wasserman, 1999; Wasserman & Pattison, 1996).

Recall our discussion in the preceding paragraphs that a network of 17 individuals can have a very large, but finite, number of realizations or configurations. At one end of the continuum is a network of 17 individuals with no directed communication links between them. At the other end of the continuum is a network of 17 individuals, all of whom have direct communicative links to one another, a completely connected network. Along this continuum there is a very large number of possible configurations. In a network of 17 individuals, each individual can have links to 16 other individuals. Hence the network of 17 individuals can have a total of 272 (17 times 16) links. If the network is a binary network (that is, links to individuals are either present or absent), each of the 272 links can be in one of two states, either present or absent. Hence there are 2^{272} possible configurations of the network or approximately 7.5885×10^{81}, that is, the number of configurations is over 7 followed by 81 zeros! The number of possible configurations of the network is referred to as the *sample space* (Wasserman & Faust, 1997).

Our general goal is to see if certain structural characteristics of the observed network are more, less, or just as likely to occur by chance among the various possible configurations within the sample space. These structural characteristics could be, for instance, the number of links in the observed network, the number of reciprocated links in the observed network, the number of transitive triads in the observed network, or the overall network centralization of the observed network. In order to assess tendencies for these structural characteristics in the observed network, we must begin by making some assumptions regarding the probability of finding each of the 2^{272} possible realizations within the sample space. To do so we make a simple—and as we shall argue later, somewhat simplistic—assumption, that each of the links in the network has a 50-50 chance of being observed. In our 17-person example with 272 links that are equally likely to be present or absent, each of the possible 2^{272} configurations is also equally likely to be observed. That is, each realization of the 2^{272} possible network configurations has a $\frac{1}{2}^{272}$ probability of being observed. Our assumption here implies that the various realizations follow a "uniform probability distribution," where each alternative is equally likely to occur.

Since we assumed that each link has a 50-50 chance of occurring, it also follows that in a large proportion of the 2^{272} configurations of the network the individuals will chose about half (or 8) of the 16 other individuals in the network. These would be distinct configurations because the individuals could choose different sets of 8 other individuals in each of these network realizations. We could then conclude, based on our assumption of a uniform probability distribution, that if the observed network were equally likely to occur as any of the 2^{272} possible configurations of the network, the "expected" number of links for each actor in the observed network would be 8, which is half of 16. That is, the expected number of links present in the observed network would be 136 (17 times 8). Further, if the observed network had considerably more or less than 136 links present, we would be able to assess the likelihood (or the probability) that such a configuration is likely to occur within the sample space of all possible configurations. By doing so, we will be able to statistically determine the probability that the observed network has a structural tendency for a larger or smaller number of links than one would expect purely on the basis of chance.

An important consideration in determining if the theoretically hypothesized property has a significantly higher probability of being observed is to ensure that this probability is not an artifact of other properties of the network itself. For instance, consider 2 networks of 17 individuals each. Assume that the first network has many more communication links present than in the second network. Further, suppose we observe that the first network exhibits a much higher degree of reciprocity (a larger number of mutual links) than in the second network. This observation alone does not warrant a claim that the first network has a greater structural tendency toward reciprocity. The higher reciprocity in the first network may well be an artifact of the greater number of links in that network. That is, if there were more links in a network, one would expect higher reciprocity purely on the basis of chance. Hence, in order to determine if the first network exhibits a greater tendency toward reciprocity, statistical techniques need to be applied that *condition* on the number of links in the network (see Wasserman & Faust, 1997).

More generally, these techniques facilitate testing for higher-level structural characteristics, such as reciprocity, after conditioning for lower level structural characteristics, such as the number of links chosen by each individual. For instance, one can statistically test for a structural tendency toward transitivity in the network, after conditioning for lower level structural effects such as the number of links chosen by individuals in the network, as well as the number of reciprocated links in the networks. By doing so, it is possible to ensure that the structural tendency for transitivity observed in the network is not simply an artifact of the number of ties or the number of reciprocated ties in the network.

The statistical "conditioning" just described works on the basis of a fairly simple logic. Suppose that in our example of 17 individuals, we were interested in assessing whether the observed network exhibited a structural tendency toward reciprocity (or mutuality). In statistical terms, we want to assess the probability that reciprocity in the observed network is more, less, or just as likely to be found from the sample space of all possible network configurations of 17 individuals. Since, as noted previously, the reciprocity in the observed network may to some extent be an artifact of the number of links in the observed network, we would need to condition for this artifact.

This conditioning is done quite simply by reducing the sample space to include only those realizations of the graph that have exactly the same number of links as was found in the observed network. If, in the observed network, each individual had on average ties to only 3 other individuals, the total number of links present in the network would be 51 (17 times 3). In order to determine if there were a structural tendency toward reciprocity in this observed network, one would compare it to a subset of the 2^{272} network realizations that also had only 51 links. That is, the sample space used to test the structural tendency toward reciprocity would include only those network realizations where the number of links is the same as the number of links present in the observed network (51, in this example). By doing so, one is in effect comparing the degree of reciprocity in the observed network to the family of networks that have exactly the same number of links. For this reduced sample space, estimates of the reciprocity that is most likely to occur can be made. This "expected" reciprocity can then be compared to the observed reciprocity. If the observed reciprocity is much larger or smaller than the expected reciprocity one can justifiably claim that the observed network exhibits a statistical tendency toward reciprocity. Hence the process of "conditioning" is tantamount to reducing the number of possible configurations (or the sample space) to which the observed network is compared. In statistical terms, it implies that the observed network is being compared to the expected value based on a conditional probability distribution. This procedure follows the general logic of statistical inference in which systematic or expected variation is compared to a known distribution. The extent to which the observed component exceeds the expected indicates whether the observed is statistically significant at a selected probability level. As mentioned earlier, the logic of conditioning can be used to assess higher order structural tendencies such as network centralization after conditioning for lower level structural tendencies such as the number of choices made by an individual, the degree of reciprocity, the tendency toward transitivity. As such it lays the framework for multilevel statistical tests for structural tendencies in the network.

The discussion so far has been based on an overly simple premise that must now be revisited. We have assumed that, in the sample space of all possible network realizations, a link between two individuals has a 50–50 chance of being either present or absent. We then described how the structural tendency in the observed network could be compared to what would be expected from this uniform distribution of all possible network realizations. Wasserman and Faust (1997) note that this assumption can be usefully described in terms of coin tosses. In order to determine one possible network realization, suppose we used the toss of a coin to determine if a link were present between the first and the second individual in the network. Let us suppose heads counts as the presence of a link and tails counts as the absence of a link. We could toss this coin 272 times and use each result to assign the presence (or absence) of a link between each pair of individuals in the network. The 272 coin tosses will generate one possible realization of the network of 17 individuals. If we repeated this exercise of 272 coin tosses and recorded the outcome each time, we would generate a large number of possible network realizations. Assuming the coin is not "biased" toward heads or tails, each coin toss has an equal, 50-50, chance of coming up heads or tails. Further the likelihood of each coin toss is totally independent of any of the preceding coin tosses. That is, each link from one individual to another is assumed to have a 50-50 chance of occurring and each link is independent of every other link between any pair of individuals. This is equivalent to the assumption of a *uniform probability distribution* for the realization of various network configurations.

Suppose we replace the coin with a "biased" coin—one that comes up heads 60 percent of the time, and tails 40 percent. If we repeat the above exercise we can generate a very large number of network realizations but in this case there is an unequal 60-40 chance of a link from one individual to another. Further, as in the previous case, the link from one individual to another is independent of the links from any individual to any other individual. This assumption is equivalent to what is described in statistical terms as a family of *Bernoulli distributions* that is defined by the parameters n and p. Parameter n is the number of trials, or in this case the number of possible links among the individuals, 272. The p parameter is the probability of a "success" for each trial, in this case, 60 percent for the presence rather than the absence of a link between each pair of individuals.

Extending this exercise further, suppose we were to consider a scenario where each coin toss was not independent of preceding coin tosses. This is a scenario hard to conceive in practice but one that is entirely plausible when considering networks of individuals. That is, the presence of a tie from individual A to individual B is not independent of a tie from individual B to A, individual B to C and/or individual C to A, or even in some circumstances individuals D and E. Indeed, these may be exactly the sorts of structural tendencies that we are interested in examining.

The "conditioning" process outlined is in fact one way of assessing these structural tendencies. It does so by assessing the propensity toward these structural effects based on a uniform probability distribution—after conditioning by shrinking the sample space for the plausible lower order effects, such as number of choices, degree of reciprocity, and so on. An alternative interpretation is that we assess the degree of reciprocity in an observed network using a *conditional uniform distribution* that includes all possible network realizations that have the same number of links as the observed networks. Likewise, we assess the degree of transitivity in the observed network using a conditional uniform distribution that includes all possible network realizations that have the same number of links as well as the same number of mutual and asymmetric links as the observed network.

If one assumes a uniform probability distribution, the probability of a specific realization of the network can be considered as a product of the independent probabilities of ties being present between every pair of individuals in the network. Hence, the probability of a particular network realization is analogous to a traditional contingency table such as one classifying people on the basis of gender and managerial position. In this case, the rows of the contingency table might be divided into males and females and the columns into managers and nonmanagers, where the expected value for a particular cell such as female managers can be computed as the product of the probability of being in the female row times the probability of being in the manager column. Typically, a researcher would assess a tendency for the observed number of female managers to be higher, lower, or equal to what would be expected, based on the proportion of females and managers in the sample.

In similar fashion it is possible to assess the likelihood for links or higher order structural characteristics in the network to be higher, lower, or equal to what would be expected based on the proportion of links sent and received by individuals in the network. For categorical or ordinal data, which is typical of network linkages studied by most social scientists, these effects can usually be estimated using *log linear analysis*. In a simple form of this analysis, the likelihood or expected probability of ties in the network is the product of the independent probabilities of the number of ties sent by individual A and the number of ties sent by individual B. However, a straightforward mathematical transformation, the logarithm of this likelihood, called simply the *log likelihood*, can be computed as the sum of the logarithms of the independent probabilities. This logarithmic transformation of a product of probabilities to a linear sum of probabilities is what gives this technique the name log-linear analysis. Converting the probability, which ranges from 0 to 1, to its logarithmic value widens its range from $-\infty$ to $+\infty$ enabling it to better capture the variations among the explanatory structural characteristics of the network that can theoretically occur over that range. To keep the statistical estimation analytically tractable, rather than computing the probability of a tie, techniques are used to estimate the odds of a tie. The odds are defined as the ratio of the probability of a tie being present to the tie being absent. The logarithm transformation of the odds is called a *logit*. Wasserman and his colleagues (e.g., Anderson, Wasserman, & Crouch, 1999; Wasserman & Pattison, 1996) have shown that a specific family of p^* logit network models can be appropriately estimated using *logistic regression*. Details on how to compute p^* network analyses with the PSPAR computer program are illustrated using an example at the end of this chapter.

The Multitheoretical, Multilevel Model

The brief statistical overview of the challenges and opportunities for the analysis of networks demonstrates the increasing plausibility to empirically assess the structural tendencies of networks informed by multiple theories at multiple levels. Table 2.4 provides a summary of a multitheoretical, multilevel (MTML) framework to test hypotheses about organizational networks. The table describes ten classes of network hypotheses. Each represents a different set of relational properties that can influence the probabilities of graph realizations. In each case, the hypothesis is that graph realizations with the hypothesized property have larger probabilities of being observed than those that do not have the hypothesized property.

The table is organized by endogenous and exogenous variables that influence the probability of ties being present or absent in the focal network. *Endogenous variables* (rows 1 through 4) are relational properties inherent in the focal network that influence the realization of that network. *Exogenous variables* (rows 5 through 10) refer to various properties outside the focal network that influence the probability of ties being present or absent in the focal network, that is, its realization.

It should be noted that the exogenous-endogenous distinction being made here is not equivalent to similar terminology used in the development of causal models in general and structural equation models in particular. Unlike its use in causal modeling, endogenous variables here are not predicted by exogenous variables. Here, both explain structural tendencies of the network. *Endogenous variables* are characteristics of the relations within the network that are themselves used to explain the structural tendencies of that relation. *Exogenous variables* are characteristics of the network, other than the relation itself, that are used to explain the structural tendencies. Exogenous variables include the attributes of the people or other nodes in the network, other relations within the network, as well as the same relation in the network in the previous points in time. The following two sections review the influence of endogenous and exogenous predictors in structuring network realizations at each of the individual, dyadic, triadic, and global levels. Each of the ten classes of hypotheses is illustrated with one of the theoretical mechanisms for emergence of communication networks discussed more fully in the remaining chapters of the book.

Endogenous Network Variables

Table 2.4 contains three columns. The first identifies endogenous (rows 1–4) and exogenous (rows 5–8) predictor variables at the four levels of analysis and in relation to other networks (rows 9 and 10). The second column provides examples of specific network measures for each of the ten classes

Table 2.4

Summary of the Multitheoretical, Multilevel Framework to Test Hypotheses About Organizational Networks (Variable of Interest: Probability of the Realization of a Graph)

Independent Variable	Examples of Specific Measures	Hypotheses
1. Endogenous (same network): *Actor level*	Individual network metrics such as choice actor centrality, structural autonomy	Graph realizations that have higher values of actor level measures (e.g., centrality, structural autonomy) have larger probabilities of occurring (e.g., *theory of social capital, structural holes*)
2. Endogenous (same network): *Dyad level*	Mutuality, reciprocation	Graph realizations that have more mutuality or reciprocation (i.e., a tie from i to j and a tie from j to i) have larger probabilities of occurring (e.g., *exchange theory*)
3. Endogenous (same network): *Triad level*	Transitivity, cyclicality	Graph realizations that have more cyclicality (i.e., a tie from j to k, k to i, and i to j) or more transitivity (i.e., a tie from i to k, k to j, and i to j) have larger probabilities of occurring (e.g., *balance theory*)
4. Endogenous (same network): *Global level*	Network density, centralization	Graph realizations that have more network centralization have larger probabilities of occurring (e.g., *collective action theory*)
5. Exogenous: Actor attributes (*actor level*)	Age, gender, organization type, education	Graph realizations where there are ties between actors with similar attributes (age, gender, org type, education) have larger probabilities of occurring (e.g., *theories of homophily*)
6. Exogenous: Actor attributes (*dyad level*)	Differential mutuality and reciprocation	Graph realizations where there is a greater likelihood of mutual (or reciprocated) ties between actors with similar attributes have larger probabilities of occurring (e.g., *exchange theory*)
7. Exogenous: Actor attributes (*triad level*)	Differential transitivity and cyclicality	Graph realizations where there is a greater likelihood of transitive (or cyclical) ties between actors with similar attributes have larger probabilities of occurring (e.g., *balance theory*)
8. Exogenous: Actor attributes (*global level*)	Differential network density, centralization	Graph realizations where there is a greater likelihood of network centralization among subgroups with similar attributes have larger probabilities of occurring (e.g., *collective action theory*)
9. Exogenous: Network (*other relations*)	Advice, friendship network	Graph realizations where, say, communication ties between actors co-occur with their ties on a second relation (e.g., advice or friendship) have larger probabilities of occurring (e.g. *cognitive theories*).
10. Exogenous: Network (*same network at previous point in time*)	Communication network	Graph realizations where the ties between actors at one point in time co-occur with ties at preceding points in time have larger probabilities of occurring (e.g., *evolutionary theories*)

of hypotheses. The final column provides typical network hypotheses. Rows 1 through 4 present the four levels of endogenous relational properties of the focal network that influence the realization of the network.

Figures 2.1 through 2.10 accompany the discussions of each of the ten rows in table 2.4. Each of these figures shows a simple hypothetical network of people, departments, organizations, and so on, represented by circles that are linked to one another by lines. The solid lines represent links that are observed in the network. The dotted lines represent the likelihood for an additional link to exist in the network based on predictions made by a specific theoretical mechanism. The positive or negative sign used to label these dotted lines indicates whether the theory would predict a higher or lower likelihood for this additional link to be present. While the theory might predict several additional ties in the hypothetical network, for simplicity the figures illustrate the likelihood of only one additional tie that is more likely to be present and one additional tie that is less likely to be present.

THE INDIVIDUAL LEVEL

The *endogenous* individual level (sometimes also called the nodal or actor level) refers to network properties of the entities that comprise the network. The individual level can be people, groups or even entire organizations in the case of an interorganizational network. Column 2 of row 1 shows endogenous, nodal level properties, measured at the individual level as discussed earlier in the chapter. These include degree, betweenness, and closeness centrality, as well as measures such as effective size, efficiency, structural autonomy, and hierarchical constraint. These endogenous network properties are different from the exogenous attributes of individual nodes such as age, gender, and affiliation in that the former are viewed as inherent in the network , that is, defined by the node's relations, and the latter are viewed as attributes that are external to, and independent of, the network. (The external measures will be discussed shortly.) For instance, the theory of structural holes (Burt, 1992) suggests that individuals seek to enhance their structural autonomy by forging ties with two or more unconnected others, thus creating indirect ties between the people with whom they link. Hence, as illustrated in figure 2.1, the theory of structural holes would suggest a lower probability for a tie between the actor at the top-center and the actor at the lower left corner because the former is already indirectly connected with the latter via an indirect link. However, the theory would suggest a

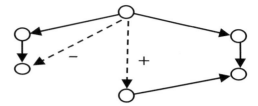

Figure 2.1
Endogenous actor level: Theory
of structural holes

higher probability of a tie from the actor at the top and center to the actor at the bottom and center because the former is not otherwise indirectly connected to the latter. As indicated in row 1, column 3 and illustrated in figure 2.1, this hypothesis claims that there are greater probabilities for the realization of a particular network configuration in those situations in which individuals or organizations have a high degree of structural autonomy.

THE DYADIC LEVEL

The endogenous *dyad* level (also called the link or tie level) refers to various network measures that characterize the ties between nodes in the network (row 2). These dyadic level properties include mutuality and reciprocation. For instance, theories of social exchange (Blau, 1964; Homans; 1958, 1974), network exchange (Willer & Skvoretz, 1997), and resource dependency (Emerson, 1962, 1972a, 1972b; Pfeffer & Salancik, 1978) suggest that individuals and organizations forge ties by exchanging material or information resources. In its most elemental form, this hypothesis claims that the probabilities for the realization of a graph are higher in networks that have a high degree of reciprocated or mutual ties (see figure 2.2). As illus-

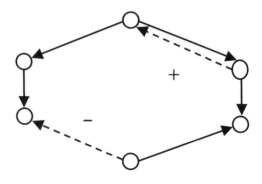

Figure 2.2
Endogenous dyad level: Theory
of social exchange

trated in figure 2.2, the theory of social exchange would suggest a higher probability of a tie from the actor at the top right corner of the network to the actor at the top-center because a tie already exists between these two leading from the actor at the top-center to the actor at the top right corner, thus reciprocating the contact. In contrast, there is a lower likelihood of a tie from the actor at the bottom-center of the network to the actor toward the bottom left of the network because the left-center node does not have any ties with the bottom center node.

The endogenous triadic level refers to measures defined on the set of possible three-node combinations in the network. In the case of endogenous variables (row 3), these triadic level network properties include transitivity and cyclicality. As defined previously, a triad is transitive if person A has a tie to person B, B has a tie to a third person C, and A also has a tie to C. Transitivity can be interpreted in a number of ways, depending on the substance of the relation under study. If the relation is one of sentiment, such as liking or friendship, then theories of cognitive balance (Heider, 1958; Holland & Leinhardt, 1975) suggest a tendency toward consistency in relations. Colloquially, friends of friends should be one's own friends, that is, people typically like their friends' friends. In contrast, transitivity in formal relations, such as exercise of authority, reflects a hierarchical tendency in the network—one's boss's boss is also one's boss. Hypotheses about transitive behavior should be supported in network realizations that contain triads that exhibit a high degree of transitivity (see figure 2.3).

Cyclicality in triads occurs when there is a link from persons A to B, a link from B to C, and a link from C to A, completing the cycle. Interpreta-

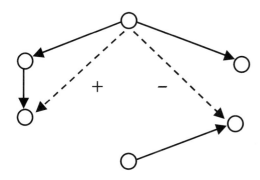

Figure 2.3
Endogenous triad level: Balance theory

tion of cyclicality depends on the substance of the relation. When the tie is one of flow of resources, such as doing favors or providing information, then cyclicality is a network property that can be thought of as illustrating the theory of generalized exchange (Bearman, 1997). Node A does a favor for B, and B, rather than returning the favor directly to A does a favor for node C, who in turn does a favor for A, thereby returning A's favor to B indirectly.

As shown in figure 2.3, balance theory suggests the likelihood of a tie from the actor at the top-center of the network to the actor at the lower left of the network. This is expected because this tie would complete a transitive triad involving the actor at the top-center of the network and the two actors on the left side of the network. However, there is a lower likelihood of a tie from the actor at the top-center of the network to the actor at the bottom right of the network because this tie would not facilitate the completion of a transitive triad. It is also worth noting that while balance theory, as indicated in figure 2.3, suggests a positive likelihood of a tie from the actor at the top-center of the network to the lower left part of the network, the theory of structural holes, as indicated in figure 2.1, suggested a lower likelihood of a tie from the actor at the top-center of the network to the actor at the lower left of the network. Taken together, these observations underscore how the MTML framework can be used to examine simultaneously two different theoretical mechanisms that may provide contradictory explanations for the likelihood of network ties.

THE GLOBAL LEVEL

The global level (row 4) refers to properties of the entire network that influence the probability of the realization of a specific observed network. As column 2 of row 4 shows, endogenous global properties include the network's density and its degree of centralization. The degree of centralization of the entire network depends on the extent to which a subset of people in the network has a much higher degree of centrality than the rest of the other people. This type of configuration concentrates message flow or other network activities on those nodes rather than distributing it more evenly to all the nodes. For instance, theories of collective action (Coleman, 1973, 1986; Marwell & Oliver, 1993) and public goods (Fulk, Flanagin, Kalman, Monge, & Ryan, 1996; Samuelson, 1954) suggest that people or organizations in a network are more likely to obtain a collective good if the network is centralized (Marwell, Oliver, & Prahl, 1988). This hypothesis would be supported if there were greater probabilities for the realization of networks that have a high degree of centralization (see figure 2.4).

The theory of collective action illustrated in figure 2.4 predicts a higher probability of a tie from the actor at the top-center to the actor at the lower right of the network. This occurs because the actor at the lower right of the network is a central actor and adding a link from the actor at the top-center to the actor at the lower right would enhance the network centralization of the network. However, the theory of collective action would also suggest a lower probability of a tie from the actor at the top-center of the network to the actor at the bottom-center because this tie would not increase the overall network centralization.

Exogenous Variables

Exogenous variables are elements outside the focal relation within the network that influence the probability of ties being present or absent in the focal network. As mentioned earlier, these exogenous variables derive from attributes of the nodes (rows 5 through 8), as well as properties of other relations among the network of nodes (row 9), and the same network of relations at previous points in time (row 10). These cases are discussed in the following paragraphs.

THE INDIVIDUAL LEVEL

The individual level of exogenous variables (row 5) refers to individual or organizational attributes that influence the probability of ties being present or absent in the observed network. These individual level attributes include

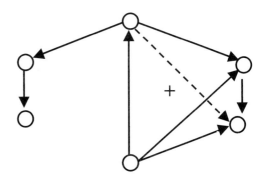

Figure 2.4
Endogenous global level:
Theories of collective action

such things as age, gender, and membership in an organization, or the type of organization. Exogenous nodal properties are different from endogenous nodal properties (row 1) in that the former are externally specified attributes of the entities that comprise the network, such as age, education, organizational affiliation, while the latter are derived from properties of the network itself, such as an individual's popularity or an organization's centrality. For instance, theories of homophily suggest that individuals seek to forge links to others with whom they share similar attributes. Homophily has been studied on the basis of similarity in age, gender, education, prestige, social class, tenure, and occupation (e.g., Carley, 1991; Coleman, 1957; Ibarra, 1992, 1993a, 1993b, 1995). As column 3 of row 5 shows, hypotheses based on homophily would be supported if the probabilities of ties being present or absent in the network reflected the propensity of nodes to link to others with similar attributes. In the case of the 17-member interorganizational consortium discussed earlier, the attribute of interest may be the type of organization—government or industry—in which an individual is employed (see figure 2.5).

Homophily theory suggests the greater likelihood of a tie from the actor of the top-center of the network in figure 2.5 to the lower left of the network because the two actors share a similar attribute—both represent government organizations. In contrast, the theory of homophily predicts the lower likelihood of a tie from the actor of the top-center to the actor toward the lower right of the network because the former represents a government organization while the latter represents the industry.

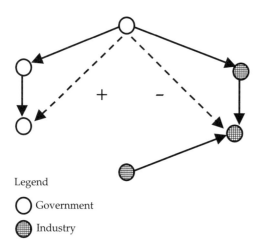

Legend

◯ Government

⊕ Industry

Figure 2.5
Exogenous attribute actor level:
Theories of homophily

The influence of exogenous variables at the dyadic level (row 6) refers to the influence of shared exogenous attributes on dyadic properties of the network. Typical dyadic level properties include mutuality and reciprocation. As discussed previously, the endogenous influence of the focal network at the dyadic level (row 2) leads to a greater likelihood that the link from one individual to another in a network will be reciprocated. The exogenous influence described here is the "differential" (positive or negative) influence of individual's exogenous attributes on the likelihood that these links will be reciprocated. For instance, social exchange theory suggests that any two individuals are more likely to engage in interactions where they are exchanging or reciprocating resources. However, in some cases it makes sense to argue that there is an even greater (in this case, positive differential) likelihood for this reciprocation to occur between individuals who share common attributes such as gender or organizational affiliation. Thus, an extension of social exchange and resource dependence theories suggests that exchange ties, that is, mutual or reciprocated ties, are more likely to occur among people who share similar attributes. This additional likelihood is referred to as a *differential* effect. Hypotheses based on this *differential mutuality or reciprocation* would be supported if there were greater probabilities for the realization of graphs in which attributes are shared by pairs of nodes. In other words, these hypotheses would be supported if the probabilities of ties being present or absent in the network would reflect nodes' tendencies to reciprocate ties with others who share similar attributes (see figure 2.6).

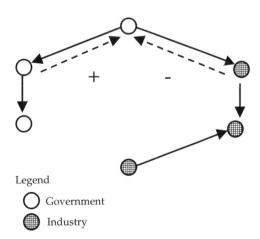

Figure 2.6
Exogenous attribute dyad level:
Resource dependency theory

Legend

◯ Government

⊕ Industry

Social exchange theory extended in conjunction with homophily theory specifies that there should be a greater likelihood of a tie from the actor at the upper left to the actor at the top-center of the network. This tie would reciprocate a tie from the actor at the top-center to the actor on the left of the network, and in addition both actors share the same attribute, namely representing a government organization. However, the same logic would suggest a lower probability for a tie from the actor at the upper right to the actor at the top-center of the network because even though this would reciprocate a tie from the actor at the top-center to the actor at the top-right, the two actors do not share a similar attribute. The actor at the top-center of the network represents a government organization while the actor at the upper right represents industry.

THE TRIADIC LEVEL

The triadic level for exogenous variables (row 7) refers to the influence of shared exogenous attributes on triadic properties of the network. The triadic level properties of the network include transitivity and cyclicality (defined previously in the discussion of row 3). As with the prior level, the shared exogenous attributes of the individuals in the network, differentially (positively or negatively) influence the propensity for the network to be transitive or cyclical. Theories of cognitive balance and generalized exchange can be extended to cover situations in which transitive and cyclical ties are even more likely to exist among actors who share similar attributes. Hypotheses based on this *differential transitivity and cyclicality* would be supported if there were greater probabilities for the realization of graphs in which actors with shared attributes are more likely to have transitive and cyclical ties with one another (see figure 2.7).

Balance theory can be examined in conjunction with homophily, as shown in figure 2.7. This combination suggests that there is a greater likelihood of a tie from the actor at the top-center to an actor at the lower left of the network because this tie would complete a transitive triad among three actors who share the same attribute, all representing government organizations. On the other hand, the same logic would suggest a lower probability of a tie from the actor at the top-center of the network to the actor at the lower right-hand because this tie would complete a transitive triad between three actors who do not share a similar attribute. The actor at the top-center of the network represents a government organization, while the other two actors in the triad represent private industry.

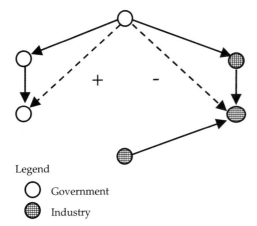

Legend

○ Government

⊕ Industry

Figure 2.7
Exogenous attribute triad level:
Balance theory

Note that the probabilities for additional ties indicated in figure 2.7 are identical to those reported in figure 2.5 and later in this section in figure 2.8. This illustrates how multilevel models might offer complementary explanations for the structural tendency of the network. In this case, theories of homophily at the exogenous attribute actor level (illustrated in figure 2.5), theories of balance at the exogenous triad level (figure 2.7), and theories of collective action at the exogenous global level (figure 2.8) complement one another's explanation for a higher probability of a network that includes a tie from the actor at the top and center to the actor at the lower left-hand corner; further, they complement one another in indicating a lower probability of a network that includes a tie from the actor at the top and center to the actor at the lower right-hand corner of the network.

THE GLOBAL LEVEL

The global level for exogenous variables (row 8) refers to the influence of shared exogenous attributes of the individuals on the global properties of the network. These global properties include network density and centralization (where some nodes in the network are much more central than others). The discussion of endogenous influences on the global properties of the network (row 4) noted that the configuration of links in the network may exhibit structural tendencies toward greater network centralization. That is, individuals may have a propensity to selectively forge ties with others in the network, thereby making some individuals more central than others. While these explanations seek to explain the global structural tendency toward centralization of the network based on the endogenous network itself, one can also examine the global properties of the network based on the influence of shared exogenous attributes of the individuals in the network. In an extension of the theories of collection action and public goods, the argument proposed here is that there is a greater likelihood for network centralization to occur among actors who share similar attributes such as organizational affiliation than among individuals who do not share these attributes. Hypotheses based on this *differential* network centralization would be supported if there were greater probabilities for the realization of graphs in which actors with shared attributes are more likely to have higher levels of subgroup network centralization. In other words, these hypotheses would be supported if the probabilities of ties being present or absent in the network would reflect actors' tendencies to forge more centralized subgroup networks with other actors who share similar attributes (see figure 2.8). In this figure, theories of collective action in conjunction with homophily predict that the government organization at the top-center of the network is more likely to forge a tie with the government organization at the lower left side because this link would further the centralized position of the latter within the network of government agencies. However, the government entity at the top-center of the network is not more likely to link with the industry representative at the lower right because this tie would not enhance the centralized position of the latter within the network of industry representatives.

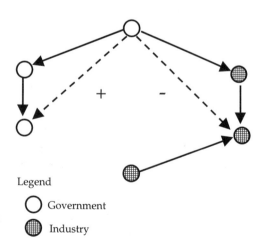

Legend

Figure 2.8
Exogenous attribute global level:
Theories of collective action

◯ Government

⊕ Industry

In addition to the exogenous influences of attributes of the network nodes, additional *relations* among nodes represent a second set of exogenous variables that may influence the probability of ties being present or absent in the focal network (see row 9). For instance, the convergence theory of communication (Richards & Seary, 1997; Rogers & Kincaid, 1981; Woelfel & Fink, 1980), cognitive theories (Carley, 1986, 1991; Carley & Krackhardt, 1996; Krackhardt, 1987a), and the theory of transactive memory systems (Hollingshead, 1998a, b, c; 2000) offer arguments that can be used to predict the influence of cognitive or semantic networks (Monge & Eisenberg, 1987) on their communication networks. These theories argue that the presence or absence of a cognitive or semantic tie between people is associated with the presence or absence of a communication tie between them. Hypotheses based on the influence of exogenous networks would be supported if there were greater probabilities for the realization of graphs in which the individuals' ties in the focal network corresponded to their ties in the exogenous networks. In other words, these hypotheses would be supported if the presence or absence of ties in the exogenous networks increased the probabilities of ties being present or absent in the focal network (see figure 2.9). This figure indicates that a person or organization at the top-center of the network is more likely to have a friendship relation with a person or organization at the top left side of the network because they already have a communication tie. However, the entity at the lower left of

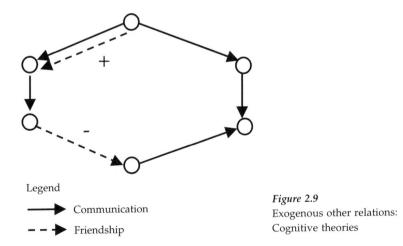

Legend

⟶ Communication

- - ➤ Friendship

Figure 2.9
Exogenous other relations:
Cognitive theories

the network is less likely to have a friendship tie with the entity at the bottom-center because they do not communicate.

It may appear that the objective sought here could be far more easily obtained by computing a simple correlation between the two relations in the network. In fact, Krackhardt (1987b) used techniques introduced by Hubert and Schultz (1976) to develop the Quadratic Assignment Procedure (QAP), which tests the significance of association between two networks. Several organizational communication researchers (e.g., Stohl, 1993) have used QAP, but in its present form the technique does not generalize to the multilevel framework proposed here.

EXOGENOUS PRIOR RELATIONS

Finally, the probability of ties being present or absent in the focal network can also be influenced by the presence or absence of ties in that same network at previous points in time (row 10). At its most primitive form, theories of evolution (McKelvey, 1997) would argue that inertia alone would predict that a tie between people at a previous point in time would increase the likelihood of the tie being maintained at subsequent points in time. For instance, Gulati (1995) hypothesized that "the higher the number of past alliances between two firms, the more likely they are to form new alliances with each other" (p. 626). Hypotheses based on the influence of the same network at previous points in time would be supported if there were greater probabilities for the realization of graphs in which links in the focal network

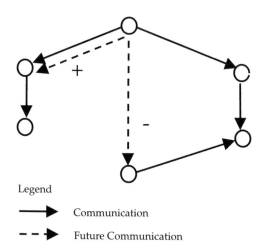

Legend

Figure 2.10
Exogenous prior relations:
Evolutionary theories

⟶ Communication

-- ▶ Future Communication

corresponded to links in the preceding networks (see figure 2.10). This graph shows that there is a greater likelihood of future communication between the actor at the top-center of the network and one at the upper left of the network because they currently communicate. However, there is a lower likelihood of future communication between the actor at the top-center of the network and the actor at the bottom-center because they have not had a prior communication tie.

The treatment of exogenous variables described in this book does not address the interactions among the exogenous variables just described. The reason for this is that current statistical techniques cannot as yet address these issues. Two scenarios are worth considering. First, the influence of exogenous networks (either of different relations on the same network of actors or the same network at previous points in time) on the focal network can be moderated based on a third set of exogenous variables, the attributes of the actors. In other words, the tendency to build on preexisting ties may be different for actors with different shared attributes. An illustration of this situation is represented in Stevenson and Gilly's (1993) study of organizational problem solving networks where they note that "managers are more likely than non-managers to use preexisting ties when forwarding organizational problems" (p. 103). A second instance would be the influence on the focal network by an exogenous network (which is a different relation on the same network of people) *and* at a previous point in time. This is the case when new kinds of ties might be established against the backdrop of existing relationships of a different type. For example, as Granovetter (1985, 1992) has argued, economic transactions are often "embedded" in social relations. This would suggest that economic relationships between people or organizations might be more likely when they have a prior social relationship. While the statistical models, including Markov random graph models and the p^* family of models, have developed techniques to test hypotheses in the ten cells described in this section, additional efforts are being made to address more complicated interaction scenarios, such as the two illustrated earlier.

Summary

This section has introduced the MTML integrative analytic framework that seeks to examine the extent to which the structural tendencies of organizational networks are influenced by multitheoretical hypotheses operating at multiple levels of analysis. The exigencies of nonindependence in relational data preclude the use of standard statistical testing procedures. Hence, this section introduced the notion of graph realizations and described how the hypothesized properties of networks influence the probabilities of realizing a specific network configuration. These properties were broadly classified as endogenous, which means they belong to the focal relation in the network itself, and exogenous, including attributes of the actors and relations distinct from the focal relation in the network. The properties in each of these two categories were further classified on the basis of their level: actor, dyad, triad, and global. For each subcategory, theoretically motivated hypotheses were used to illustrate the influence of that property on the structural tendency of the network. Figure 2.11 presents a schematic of the overall MTML model.

A Multitheoretical, Multilevel p* *Network Analysis Example*

This final section of the chapter introduces an example to illustrate the concepts in the preceding sections of this chapter. Specifically, it tests eight hypotheses deduced from three theories at two levels. It tests these hypotheses by statistically estimating the extent to which structural tendencies implied by these hypotheses influence the probabilities of observing certain realizations of the network.

The data used in this example was collected from 17 individuals representing 7 organizations who were preparing to sign a cooperative research and development agreement (CRADA). The CRADA was estab-

The MTML Network
Structuring Processes

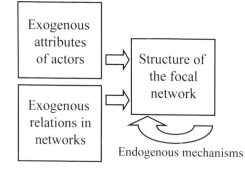

Figure 2.11
The MTML network structuring process

lished to commercialize production of software for improving the building design process for large institutional facilities. The 17 individuals were representatives from four agencies of the U.S. Army and four private corporations. The U.S. Army partners included a research laboratory, a district office, a unit of the army reserves, and members from the headquarters. The four private companies were a CAD operating systems developer, a construction software firm, a software development company, and an architectural firm.

The organizations they represented were blocked into two types: Block 1 comprised 9 individuals representing private sector companies, and Block 2 comprised 8 individuals representing government agencies. The individuals provided these data while they were in the process of negotiating the CRADA. The data represent the amount of communication reported by each of the individuals in the time period immediately prior to the signing of their strategic alliance agreement. The data were dichotomized for use in this analysis.

Theoretical Rationale for the Hypotheses

The goal of this example is to test hypotheses about the extent to which the CRADA network demonstrates a structural tendency toward mutuality, transitivity, and cyclicality. According to *exchange and dependency theories* (discussed in greater detail in chapter 7) individuals are more likely to forge network ties with others if there are resources (material or informational) they need from others and if there are resources that they can offer those others. That is, the impetus for a network tie is the possibility of exchanging resources that make the two individuals dependent on one another. Earlier in this chapter, this structural tendency was defined as *mutuality*. In the present example, according to theories of exchange and dependency, two individuals who are involved in this collaboration to develop software are more likely to have mutual communication ties, which will enable them to exchange resources.

While theories of exchange and dependency posit structural tendencies at the dyadic level, theories of cognitive consistency (discussed in greater detail in chapter 6) examine structural tendencies at the triadic level. According to consistency theories, individuals are more likely to be friends with friends of their friends. That is, the impetus for a network tie from A to C is positively influenced by the presence of a tie from A to another individual, say B, and the tie from B to C. Earlier in this chapter we defined this structural property between A, B, and C as *transitivity*. Consistency theories can also be used to support a related claim: that a network tie from A to B and a network tie from B to C will increase the likelihood of a tie from C to A. This "closing the loop" impetus reveals a structural property that we described earlier as *cyclicality*.

Of course, hypotheses regarding structural tendencies at the dyadic level and the triadic level can only be assessed if individuals choose others in the network—a structural tendency toward *choice* at the individual level. On the basis of these relatively simple previews of theoretical arguments to be expanded in later chapters of the books, the following five hypotheses were tested.

H1: The network demonstrates a structural tendency toward choice (that is, to choose other actors).

H2: The network demonstrates a structural tendency toward choice and mutuality.

H3: The network demonstrates a structural tendency toward choice, mutuality, and cyclicality.

H4: The network demonstrates a structural tendency toward choice, mutuality, and transitivity.

H5: The network demonstrates a structural tendency toward choice, mutuality, transitivity, and cyclicality.

In addition, we test three hypotheses about the extent to which these structural tendencies are differentially higher among actors that have been subgrouped into blocks based on one of their exogenous attributes (that is, whether they represent an organization in the private sector or the government sector). Theories of homophily (discussed in greater detail in chapter 8) suggest that individuals are more likely to forge ties with other individuals with whom they share similar attributes—in this case their organizational affiliation in the government or private sector.

H6: The network demonstrates a structural tendency toward choice, mutuality, transitivity, and in addition a differential tendency toward choice with other actors in the same block (either private sector or government).

H7: The network demonstrates a structural tendency toward choice, mutuality, transitivity, and in addition differential tendencies toward choice with other actors in the same block and mutuality with other actors in the same block (either private sector or government).

H8: The network demonstrates a structural tendency toward choice, mutuality, transitivity, and in addition differential tendencies toward choice with other actors in the same block and transitivity with other actors in the same block (either private sector or government).

Downloading and Installing PSPAR

PSPAR, developed by Andrew Seary, a graduate student of Bill Richards at Simon Fraser University, is a DOS-based program that conducts p^* analysis on computers running the Windows operating system. The software can be downloaded from the PSPAR web site at: http://www.sfu.ca/~richards/Pages/pspar.html by clicking on the link: http://www.sfu.ca/~richards/Pdf-ZipFiles/psparw32.zip

The network data used in this example, and included at the end of this chapter, is a text file named *crada.neg*. PSPAR requires the network data to be in a linked list format. The linked list format specifies the ID of the source of a network link, followed by the target of the network link, followed by the strength of the network link. So for instance, a line that reads 3 4 1 means that actor ID 3 has a link to actor ID 4 of strength 1. The linked list format is a particularly compact form for describing relations in a large sparsely connected network. It was also the format used by Bill Richards's Negopy program. Bill Richards provides a utility program, ADJ2NEG.exe, which automates this conversion of data in adjacency matrix format (which is what UCINET, a popular network analysis software program, uses) to the linked list format. The conversion utility program can be downloaded from http://www.sfu.ca/~richards/Pages/utility.htm. The network data set used in this example has already been converted to linked list format.

The attribute data used in this example, and included at the end of this chapter, is a text file named crada.atr. PSPAR requires the attribute data to be stored in a file that has the first column for actor IDs and additional columns for actor attributes. Since in this example there is only one attribute (representing a private or government organization), the first column is the ID of the actors and the second column is a number that indicates the attribute of that actor. So, for instance, a row that reads 4 1 indicates that actor ID 4 has attribute 1 (a private sector representative). Likewise, a row that reads 11 2 indicates that actor ID 11 has attribute 2 (a government sector representative).

P* Analysis using PSPAR

1. To launch the PSPAR program, double click on the file named Psparw32.exe.

2. You will see a DOS window with the command prompt line reading *Enter name of network file:*
   Type *crada.neg* and hit *Enter*.

3. You will be prompted *Include diagonal (y or n):*
   Since diagonals are irrelevant in this context, type *n* and hit *Enter*.

4. You will be prompted *Fit to block parameters (y or n):*
   To test the first five hypotheses, you are not interested in the differential effects of the blocks. Type *n* and hit *Enter*.

5. You will be prompted *Enter name of output file:*
   To save the output for the first hypotheses type: *crada1.out* and hit *Enter*.

6. You will be prompted to select *How many global parameters?* to use in the model. You will be provided with a selection of various parameters that are numbered from 1 through 16.
   To test hypothesis 1, you will need one parameter: the Choice parameter.
   Type *1* and hit *Enter*.

7. You will be prompted to enter parameter numbers:
   The Choice parameter (i>j) called edges in PSPAR is Parameter Number 1.
   Type *1* and hit *Enter*.

8. The program returns the results of the analysis. These results are also saved in the crada1.out file.
   You will be prompted to *Continue? (y or n):*
   To continue testing additional hypotheses type *y* and hit *Enter*.

9. You will be prompted if you want to use *Same files? (y or n):*
   To test Hypotheses 2 through 5 type *y* and hit *Enter*.

10. You will be prompted to select *How many global parameters?* to use in the model. Repeat steps 6 through 9 for Hypotheses 2 through 5.
    For Hypothesis 2, the number of parameters will be 2: Choice or Edges (Parameter Number 1), Mutuality or R(eciprocated) Edges (Parameter Number 2).
    For Hypothesis 3, the number of parameters will be 3: Choice, Mutuality, and Cyclicality (Parameter Number 7).
    For Hypothesis 4, the number of parameters will also be 3: Choice, Mutuality, and Transitivity (Parameter Number 6).

For Hypothesis 5, the number of parameters will be 4: Choice, Mutuality, Cyclicality, and Transitivity.

After completing the test for Hypothesis 5, you will be prompted *Continue? (y or n)*

Type *n* and hit *Enter*.

11. To continue with tests for the differential Hypotheses 6 through 8, repeat steps 1 through 3.

    You will be prompted *Fit to block parameters (y or n)*:
    Since we want to test hypotheses about differential effects within blocks, type *y* and hit *Enter*.

12. You will be prompted *Enter name of attribute file*:
    Type *crada.atr* and hit *Enter*.

13. You will be prompted *How many attributes (not including id)?*
    Since the only attribute is type of organization represented type *1* and hit *Enter*.

14. To save the output for Hypothesis 6 type: *crada6.out* and hit *Enter*.

15. You will be prompted to *Enter attribute number for blocking*:
    Since there is only one attribute, type *1* and hit *Enter*.

16. You will be prompted to *Accept this block structure? (y or n)*:
    The block structure shows how there are two blocks of actors who belong to private and government sector. Type *y* and hit *Enter*.

17. You will be prompted to select *How many parameters?*
    For Hypothesis 6 you will need to estimate four parameters: choice, mutuality, transitivity, and choice within blocks. Type *4* and hit *Enter*.

18. You will be prompted to *Enter Parameter Numbers*: it will also prompt you to *Add 100 for corresponding block parameter*.
    For Hypothesis 6 you will need to estimate Parameter 1 (for Choice), Parameter 101 (for Choice within blocks), Parameter 2 (for Mutuality), and Parameter 6 (for Transitivity). Type *1 101 2 6* and hit *Enter*.

19. You will be prompted to *Continue (y or n)*:
    To continue testing Hypotheses 7 and 8, type *y* and hit *Enter*.

20. If you typed y, you will be prompted *Same files? (y or n)*:
    Type *y* and hit *Enter*.

21. You will be prompted *Same blocking?*
    Type *y* and hit *Enter*.

22. Repeat steps 18 through 20. For Hypothesis 7 you will need to estimate Parameter 1 (for choice), Parameter 101 (for choice within blocks), Parameter 2 (for mutuality), Parameter 102 (for mutuality within blocks), and Parameter 6 (for transitivity). For Hypothesis 8,

Table 2.5

Summary of the p* Analysis Testing the Eight Multilevel, Multitheoretical Hypotheses

Hypothesis	Model	Number of Parameters	−2L ("Badness" of fit)
1	Choice	1	354.387
2	Choice + Mutuality	2	254.251
3	Choice + Mutuality + Cyclicality	3	241.973
4	Choice + Mutuality + Transitivity	3	228.836
5	Choice + Mutuality + Cyclicality+ Transitivity	4	228.068
6	Choice + Choice within blocks + Mutuality + Transitivity	4	222.754
7	Choice + Choice within blocks + Mutuality + Mutuality within blocks + Transitivity	5	221.723
8	Choice + Choice within blocks + Mutuality + Transitivity + Transitivity within blocks	5	218.925

you will need to estimate Parameter 1 (for Choice), Parameter 101 (for choice within blocks), Parameter 2 (for mutuality), Parameter 6 (for transitivity), and Parameter 106 (for transitivity within blocks). You are now ready to review the results of the analyses.

Table 2.5 summarizes the results obtained from the tests of all eight hypotheses. The last column in the table, the log likelihood measure, is a measure of *badness of fit*. It indicates how unlikely it is to find the observed realization of the graph if the structural tendencies are governed by the specific hypothesis posited. Hence, lower log likelihood values indicate a model that has a better fit. A quick inspection of the results reported in Table 2.5 would suggest greatest support for Hypothesis 8 since it has the lowest log likelihood value (218.925). However, since the number of parameters estimated (that is the number of explanatory variables, five) in Hypothesis 8 was the largest, it may not be the most parsimonious model. That is, the fact that it had the best fit may simply be an artifact of there being more explanatory variables in Hypothesis 8 than in the preceding hypotheses. To assess if this was the case, one can compare the fit of Hypothesis 8 with other hypotheses that had fewer explanatory variables. The best fitting model with four explanatory variables (Hypothesis 6) had a log likelihood value of 222.754. This is considerably larger than the log likelihood value (218.925) of Hypothesis 8. Further, Hypothesis 6, the best fitting model with four explanatory variables, was considerably superior to Hypothesis 4 (a log likelihood value of 228.836), the best fitting model with three explanatory variables. Likewise, Hypothesis 4 is significantly superior to Hypothesis 2 (a log likelihood value of 254.251) with two explanatory variables, which in turn was overwhelmingly superior to Hypothesis 1 (a log likelihood value of 354.387) with one explanatory variable. Hence, one can conclude that Hypothesis 8 is the best supported of the eight hypotheses. It offers the best explanation of the structural tendencies observed in the network after accounting for the fact that it had more explanatory variables than the remaining hypotheses.

Substantively, Hypothesis 8 suggests that the structure of ties among the individuals in the network was influenced by desire to engage in mutual ties, as proposed by theories of exchange and dependency at the dyadic level, and transitive ties, as proposed by theories of consistency at the triadic level. Further, consistent with theories of homophily, individuals demonstrated a structural tendency to enhance their direct and transitive triadic ties with other individuals who shared similar attributes, in this case membership in governmental or private sector organizations.

This example has attempted to illustrate how one can use p^* analytic techniques to provide one omnibus test of the structural tendencies of a network based on multiple theories (theories of exchange and dependency, theories of consistency, and theories of homophily) at multiple levels of analysis (individual, dyadic, and triadic). The first five hypotheses illustrate how to test endogenous hypotheses about the network, structural tendencies at the individual, dyadic, and triadic levels. The three additional hypotheses illustrate how to incorporate into the MTML framework the influence of the individuals' exogenous attributes on the structural tendencies of the network. The results of the analyses provide a straightforward test to assess how probable is the observed realization of the network among all possible realizations of the network that exhibit the hypothesized structural tendencies.

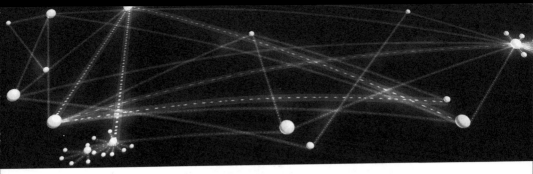

3

Communication and Knowledge Networks as Complex Systems

The concept of a system has a long and distinguished history in the social sciences. In fact, Mattelart and Mattelart (1998) claim that "the idea of society as an organism, that is, a whole composed of organs performing predetermined functions, inspired the earliest conceptions of a 'science of communication'" (p. 6). We begin this chapter with a brief historical overview of the major systems perspectives that have been utilized in social theory and research: structural-functionalism, cybernetics, and general systems theory. We then apply recent developments in complex systems theories to organizational networks. In doing so, we look at communication and knowledge networks from the perspective of agent-based modeling and self-organizing systems.

A Brief History of Systems Models

Mattelart and Mattelart (1998) trace the early growth of systems thinking in the social sciences. Adam Smith's (1776) classic work, *The Wealth of Nations*, postulated that a laissez-faire system, the division of labor, and channels of communication and transportation were crucial aspects of economic prosperity. The key to economic and therefore social success was the unrestricted circulation of messages, materials, and money through secure networks. According to Mattelart and Mattelart (1998), Francois Quesnay, a French physician and economist, published an economic chart (*tableau economique*) in 1758. "The chart offers a macroscopic vision of an economy of 'flows' in the form of a geometrical zigzag figure in which the lines expressing exchange between human beings and the land, as well as among the three classes making up society, cut across each other and become intertwined" (pp. 6–7). The Mattelarts note that Claude Henri de Saint Simon's eighteenth-century work also applied systems theory to the concept of networks. Saint-Simons's theory conceived of society as "an organic system, a bundle or fabric of networks. . . . He attributed strategic importance to the development of a system of communication routes" (p. 7). Out of this background Herbert Spencer (1820–1903) developed the first integrated theory of society built on a direct analogy with biological systems.

> The physiological division of labor and the progress of the organism went together. From the homogeneous to the heterogeneous, from the simple to the complex, from concentration to differentiation, industrial society is the embodiment of "organic society": an increasingly coherent, integrated society-as-organism in which functions are increasingly well defined and parts increasingly interdependent. In this systematic whole, communication is a basic component of organic systems of distribution and regulation. Like the vascular system, the former (made up of roads, canals, and railways) ensures the distribution of nutritive substance. The latter functions as the equivalent to the nervous system, making it possible to manage the complex relations between a dominant centre and its periphery. This is the role of information (the press, petitions, surveys) and of all the means of communication by which the centre can "propagate its influence," such as the postal service, the telegraph and news agencies. Dispatches are compared to nervous discharges that communicate movement from an inhabitant of one city to that of another. (Quoted in Mattelart & Mattelart, 1998, pp. 8–9)

Several variations of systems theory have been developed during the twentieth century (Simon, 1996). Three that have made important contributions to the study of organizational communication are structural-functionalism, cybernetics, and general systems theory. These variants are briefly reviewed in this section to provide a context in which to develop a model of communication networks as complex adaptive self-organizing systems.

Functionalism

Functionalism (also called structural-functionalism) is perhaps best represented in Talcott Parsons's (1937) attempt to create a unified social systems theory, and in the functionalist theorizing of Lasswell (1948), Lazarsfeld (1941), and Merton (1949). The logic of functionalist systems theory contains five steps (Monge, 1977). First the relevant components of the system must be identified, including the boundary so that it is possible to distinguish the system from its environment. Second, the relevant parts of the environment—those that affect and influence the operation of the system—are identified. Third, a trait, attribute, or some other property of the system must be identified that is essential to the continued operation of the system, that is, for it to continue functioning. Fourth, the different values that the trait can assume must be specified along with the range in which the traits must be kept in order for the system to survive. It is assumed that if the values of the trait do not stay within the acceptable range, the system will cease to function. Finally, the relations among the parts must be described to show how their collective operation keeps the traits within the range required to sustain the system.

The overall idea of functional analysis is to identify how systems maintain themselves despite constantly changing environmental conditions. Cannon (1932) described functional systems such as these as *homeostatic* (open) systems and identified many that exist in the human body, including the temperature control, breathing, and the endocrine system.

A number of scholars have identified social and communication functions. Lasswell (1948) argued that communication fulfils three functions in society: (1) surveillance of the environment to identify threats and opportunities, (2) coordination of response to threat, and (3) transmission of social and cultural heritages between generations. Lazarsfeld (1941) and Merton (1949) suggested that entertainment was a fourth important communication function.

Functional systems have been severely criticized over the years for emphasizing stability and the status quo rather than growth and changes. In a sense, they are structure-preserving systems, ones that are designed to keep the network of relations, the system, intact despite constant change in the environment. Maruyama (1982) called these *morphostatic* systems, emphasizing their fixed structure. Of course, there are times at which it is extremely important to maintain the structural and operational integrity of the systems we have created, such as when an economy is working well, an airplane is flying across country, or a physician is performing an operation. On the other hand, there are times when the structures of systems need to be changed to make them better. Maruyama (1982) called systems that were capable of changing their structures *morphogenetic* systems. More important, some system change is inevitable; consequently, our theories and models need to account for morphogenetic properties.

Cybernetics

Weiner (1948, 1956) developed the second form of systems theory, *cybernetics*. This type of system operates by a somewhat different logic than functional systems (Monge, 1977). First, the system and its environment must be distinguished, implying the creation of boundaries between the two. As a part of this process, an attribute of the system is identified or selected, which becomes the target of the control effort. Second, after the system is identified, a control center must be created for this attribute of the system. This control center contains goal parameters (sometimes called the reference signal) that can be set to alternative values. Third, influence must be taken by the control center to achieve the established goal. Typically this is a signal that the control center sends to turn on or off a device like a heater or air conditioner that is capable of influencing the temperature. Fourth, there must be a monitor in the system that reads the current state of the system and provides this information back to the control center regarding the influence of the control center's output on the part of the system being controlled. A thermometer could provide this form of feedback to a control center for temperature. Fifth, the control center then makes a "comparator" test between the reference signal (the goal) and the feedback signal (the current state of the system being controlled). In the case of the thermostat, the comparator test would examine the difference between the temperature goal and the current temperature. Finally, the control center would decide what action to take next. If the current temperature matches the goal, no further action is taken. If the feedback suggests that the temperature is too cold, the control center would send a signal to turn on the furnace. If the comparator test indicated that the temperature was hotter than the goal parameter, the control center would send a signal to turn on the air conditioner. One of the most interesting things about cybernetic systems is that they are extremely broad, general devices that can work in open systems and irrespective of the source of object they are attempting to control. Literally thousands of different kinds of cybernetic devices (such as autopilots on airplanes) have been developed since Weiner first articulated their general logic, and he himself applied the general cybernetic concepts to an analysis of society (Weiner, 1956), as did a number of other scholars (see, for example, Deutsch's 1963 classical work on governments). However, like functionalism, cybernetics is very control oriented, focusing on preserving the status quo, at least insofar as this is reflected in the goals and values of the control center.

General Systems Theory

Ludwig von Bertalanffy (1968) formulated a project he called *general systems theory*. His basic goal was to organize and codify all scientific knowledge into a single unified whole. Rather than employ reductionism, which reduces all knowledge to the level of physics, Bertalanffy used *perspectivism*, by which he meant the isomorphism of scientific laws across various fields. He observed that a number of concepts seemed to occur in almost all scientific explanations. Thus, knowledge structures could be built at least in part around the following concepts: "*information*, the symbolic patterning of matter and energy; *networks*, the channels through which information flows and the limitations imposed upon message processing by channel characteristics; *memory*, the storage, manipulation, and retrieval of information; *boundary processes*, the interface between communication systems at the same or different levels and the seeking, avoiding, and filtering of information; *control*, feedback processes and the use of information to manipulate and influence other systems or subsystems or components within the communication system" (Monge, 1977, p. 29). J. G. Miller's (1978) tome, *Living Systems*, attempts this task for the life sciences, containing hundreds of cross-level hypotheses about many aspects of living systems. Of course, totalizing projects such as this are now somewhat out of favor. While a noble enterprise, few now think that a grand integrative scheme is possible, and others argue that even if it were possible, it would be undesirable.

Critique

Contractor (1994) provided a critique of earlier work with systems theory as a basis for advocating complex systems theory. Specifically, he claimed that theorizing and research in organizational communication failed to adequately account for five problems. First, he argued that while much of systems theory is based on process thinking and dynamics, most empirical research is cross-sectional in nature and therefore fails to capture the dynamics inherent in systems theories. Of course, this is not a criticism of systems theory per se but of the research efforts that have been mounted to test it. Further, this criticism can be leveled at most of the published research in the social sciences, not just systems-based research. Second, he argued that system formulations in organizational communication were based too much on linear contingencies that did not adequately capture the circularity implicit in mutual causal loops, especially those in morphogenetic systems. Monge (1982) made a similar point, arguing that systems theories could only be properly tested with analytical techniques that captured the feedback and causal loop properties of systems. An analogy formulated in that article captures the essence of the argument: systems research is to systems theory as traditional research is to traditional theory.

The next two problems Contractor (1994) identified were *historicity* and *time irreversibility*. These refer to the fact that in nonlinear systems the magnitude of the relationship between two or more variables depends on the history of the system and the direction of time, that is, whether it is currently near the front, the middle, or the end of its processes. In linear systems, the relations between variables will be the same, no matter where the system is in its history. In nonlinear systems, the relations vary across time. Monge, Contractor, and Cozzens (1990) provide an example of nonlinear systems modeling that accounts for historicity. The final problem that Contractor identified was discontinuity often represented by sizeable qualitative system changes or by systems that operate far from equilibrium. Systems that import large amounts of energy from their environments, that use that information to renew themselves, and that export the accumulated disorder back to the environment are called *dissipative structures*.

Addressing these issues with recent developments in systems theory provides the possibility of examining and explaining important nonlinear dynamic changes in complex social systems. The first of these is the transition from a state of organization or order to chaos, which is the domain of what is popularly referred to as chaos theory. The second important change is from a state of disorder to a state of self-organization, the domain of self-organizing systems theory. Finally, there is the move from one state of self-organization to a new discontinuous state of self-organization or chaos, typically treated under the rubric of catastrophe theory.

Complexity Theory and Complex Systems

Complexity has played an important role in organization science ever since the open-system view of organizations was developed in the 1960s (Anderson, 1999). Scholars such as Emery and Trist (1965) and Thompson (1967) theorized about how the interdependent parts of organizations interacted with each other and with the larger environment to exchange resources. These interdependencies and complex "double interacts" were viewed as the very essence of organizing (Weick, 1979) often incorporated with notions of loose coupling (Weick & Bougon, 1986). But, with the exception of Simon's (1996) classic work in 1969 (first edition) on the architecture of complexity in the sciences of the artificial, little of this work actually used the concept of complexity or complexity theory until the 1990s.

A sizeable literature on complex systems has developed over the past three decades, though much of it exists outside of organizational contexts (e.g., Eve et al., 1997). Though Markovsky (1997) claims that knowledge about complexity has yet to be integrated into a coherent theory and remains a loose set of concepts, orientations, heuristics, and analytic tools, Simon (1996) argues that considerable progress has been made. Merry (1995) observes that different scholars tend to emphasize different aspects of the construct. Simon (1996) defines *complexity* as a system that is "made up of many parts that have many interactions" (pp. 182–184). Axelrod and Cohen (1999) add the constraint that the interactions must be strong rather than weak so that current events will strongly influence future ones. Holland (1998) explores complexity from the perspective of agent-based modeling, which examines how complex patterns of behavior emerge from the interactions between lower-level agents following relatively simple rules. Gell-Mann (1996) defines complexity as the length of *algorithmic information content* that is required to describe and predict the properties of incoming data streams. This approach seeks the smallest subset of data that can predict the complex regularities in the larger set at a selected level of accuracy. Finally, Kauffman (1993) believes that self-organization is an inherent part of complex evolutionary systems that can offer important insights.

The essential idea of complex systems is that *rule-governed interaction* among a set of interconnected individuals can generate emergent structures (Holland, 1995, 1998). Complex systems are often studied using computer simulations in order to explore the "large scale effects of locally interacting agents" (Axelrod, 1997). In the following subsections we describe the main elements of complex systems: the networks of agents, their attribute or traits, their rules of interaction, and the structures that emerge from these rules of interaction.

Network of Agents

Complex systems analysis explores the behavior of a network of people, groups, organizations, or other entities generically called *agents* or actors. The network is important because it provides the context or the environment for the individual agents. The network includes the relations among the agents from which, for instance, other agents learn and to which agents can transfer new information and improvements (Axelrod & Cohen, 1999).

Attributes or Traits

Agents typically possess *attributes* or *traits*. Those individuals that have the same traits would typically be considered as being of the same type. Traits may be any of the elements described in chapter 2, such as gender, education, occupation, attitudes, skills, expertise, experience, and behavior. In their discussion of complex systems, Axelrod and Cohen (1999) identify three important classes of traits: location, capabilities, and memory. Location represents where the agents exist and operate. These could be considered their spatial coordinates vis-à-vis other agents. Capabilities refer to the behaviors in which agents can engage. These could be skills required by an agent to accomplish a certain task or the activities carried out by an agent. Memory is information or knowledge about past behaviors. This could include previous experience with a certain task or an agent's recollection of "who knows whom" or "who knows what" in the network.

Rules of Interaction

Agents follow *interaction rules* (Holland, 1995). Rules prescribe, or in some cases describe, how agents behave in specific situations. The agents consciously pursue rules that are prescribed. Rules that are described may not require a conscious effort on the part of agents. The rules are not necessarily deterministic. Instead, they could be stochastic, suggesting a greater likelihood for how agents behave in specific situations. The rules may describe how an agent's traits or attributes are likely to change as a conse-quence of the network's characteristics. Additionally, the rules may describe how an agent's relations to others are likely to change as a consequence of the network's characteristics. Further, the rules may themselves be "meta-rules," describing which specific rules are more likely to be followed in a particular context. For instance, a metarule may specify that the rules of interaction may depend on agent's attributes, thus allowing for the possi-bility that different agents in the network follow different rules, potentially at different times.

It is important to note that different authors use a variety of related concepts to refer to rules. For example, Anderson (1999) uses the concept of schemata, which emphasizes the cognitive aspects of rules (Rumelhart, 1984). Axelrod and Cohen (1999) use the concept of strategies, which privi-leges a more conscious, societal level game-theoretic approach. Complex systems where agents follow rules that explicitly and sometimes consciously seek to improve their fitness in terms of performance, adaptability, or sur-vival are called *complex adaptive systems*. The theoretical mechanisms that generate the specification of such fitness-motivated rules are discussed in greater detail in chapter 9. Despite these differences, the concepts gener-ally refer to the set of behaviors available to agents.

A good example of a game-theoretic rule is "tit for tat," which was developed in the context of the prisoner's dilemma, a game that facilitates exploration of the problem of mutual cooperation (Axelrod, 1984; Rapoport & Chammah, 1965). The basic idea is that two individuals are placed in a situation where they must independently choose whether to cooperate with each other. The rewards they receive are based on the combination of their joint choices. The game is designed so that the best choice for each player individually is noncooperation. However, if both choose noncooperation, the payoff is worse than if both choose to cooperate. Hence, while non-cooperation is the best individual choice, cooperation is the best mutual choice. Mixed outcomes, where one person chooses to cooperate and the other chooses to defect via noncooperation, lies between the two alterna-tives where both cooperate or defect.

People are often asked to play repeated rounds of the prisoner's dilemma game. The outcome of the first round provides both players with information about the others' choices. On subsequent rounds people can make the same or different choices as the ones they made on the preceding rounds. The tit-for-tat rule is "simply one of cooperating on the first move and then doing whatever the other player did on the preceding move" (Axelrod, 1997, p. 16).

The tit-for-tat strategy clearly is based on the principle of reciprocity. As we saw in chapter 2, reciprocity is an important characteristic of many types of network relations. As we shall see in the second section of the book, reciprocity is also an important generative mechanism in some social theories of exchange (chapter 7) and collective action (chapter 5). Thus, rules can reflect or represent the generative mechanisms contained in social theories. This is important because it enables us to capture the essence of the theories in our models and apply them as the rules governing complex adaptive behavior. Some representative communication rules discussed later in the book are:

1. I try to keep the costs of my communication to a minimum (chapter 5, theories of self-interest).
2. I try to maximize the collective value of my communication to all others (chapter 5, theories of collective action).
3. I try to keep my interactions balanced among the people I communicate with (chapter 6, balance theory).
4. I am more likely to communicate with this person if the person has resources I need or if the person needs resources I have (chapter 7, resource dependency theory).
5. I am more likely to communicate with this person in order to reciprocate the way they have communicated with me in the past (chapter 7, exchange theory).
6. I am more likely to communicate with people who are like me and less likely to communicate with people who are different (chapter 8, theories of homophily).
7. I am more likely to communicate with people who are physically proximate or electronically accessible (chapter 8, theories of proximity).
8. I am more likely to communicate with people in order to improve my fitness (chapter 9, evolutionary theory) or the network's overall fitness (chapter 9, coevolutionary theory).

Emergence of Structure

When agents follow these rules, structures emerge. In agent-based models, emergent structures reflect the underlying theoretical mechanisms that generated them. If all agents follow the same rule, a unique structure will emerge that reflects the theoretical mechanisms that generated the corresponding rule of interaction. In most cases, in the real world, (i) different agents follow different rules, (ii) the same agents follow different rules at different times, and (iii) the different rules may operate simultaneously at different levels:

actor, dyadic, triadic, and global. Thus, a multitheoretical, multilevel (MTML) framework is necessary in order to capture this complexity in modeling a network of agents. The probability distribution of network realizations should reflect this multiplicity of theoretical generative mechanisms.

Summary

Complex systems can be studied as agent-based models. Populations of agents, a generic term that can be applied to a wide variety of entities, have attributes and traits such as capabilities, memory, and levels of intelligence. Agents follow rules of engagement, which describe or prescribe how they act and interact in particular circumstances. Interaction creates networks of connections among the agents. Rules can represent the theoretical mechanisms articulated in social theories. When, as in this book, we use theoretical mechanisms as stochastic rules in agent-based models, the rules influence the probabilities of emergent structures implied by the relevant social theories. This strategy enables us to create multitheoretical and multilevel models that reflect diverse social theories at multiple levels of analysis.

Self-Organizing Complex Systems

Not all complex systems are *self-organizing systems*. And self-organizing systems are not always poised to self-organize. In this section we briefly review the essential ideas of self-organization, particularly as it applies to complex systems (Contractor & Seibold, 1993). Ilya Prigogine and his colleagues proposed the theory of self-organization. Glansdorff and Prigogine (1971) proved that systems that exhibit emergence of spontaneous order must have at least the following four features:

1. At least one of the components in the system must exhibit auto-catalysis, that is, self-referencing.
2. At least two of the components in the system must be mutually causal.
3. The system must be open to the environment with respect to the exchange of energy and matter.
4. The system must operate in a far-from-equilibrium condition.

Fukuyama (1999) describes an interesting example of a self-organizing system called slugs. Slugs began in the Washington, D.C., area in 1973 when the U.S. government designated one lane of Interstate Highway 95 connecting the suburbs in Virginia and downtown Washington as a three-person carpool lane. Soon after the change occurred, lines of people and cars began to form spontaneously each morning in Virginia next to entrances to the I-95 highway. Drivers of cars with fewer than three people began offering rides to one or two people who were usually complete strangers, thus meeting the three-person carpool requirement. Each evening, the same thing happened in Washington, D.C. By meeting the carpool requirement commuters were able to save forty minutes in their daily round trip.

Interestingly, this pattern continues to today. "Slugging" as it has come to be called, has developed a set of rules that people are expected to observe. For example, smoking is forbidden and people are expected to avoid controversial topics of conversation. Fukuyama points out that the slug culture wasn't purposively created by anyone. "No government bureaucracy, historical tradition, or charismatic leader initially laid down the rules of where to meet or how to behave; it simply emerged out of the desire of commuters to get to work faster. . . . The practice of slugging emerged spontaneously in the ecological niche created by the government mandate, a bit of social order created from the bottom up by people pursuing their own private interests in getting to work" (p. 144).

Fukuyama (1999) also observed that "complex activities need to be self-organizing and self-managing. The capabilities for doing so, if not given in the underlying culture, will be supplied by private firms because their productivity depends on it. We can see this in the new forms of organization that have spread in American factories and offices over the past twenty years, and particularly in the concept of the network" (p. 255).

While this is an excellent illustration of the self-organizing processes described in this chapter, it also underscores an important qualifying statement about the self-organizing nature of complex systems. Not all complex systems are self-organizing. Many of these systems are termed chaotic— often driven by simple nonlinear mechanisms and sometimes vulnerable to relatively miniscule perturbations (or fluctuations). In general, the traffic on interstate highways tends to be chaotic. Fukuyama describes certain specific conditions that made it possible for this complex system to transcend its chaotic state. Indeed, what makes Fukuyama's illustration so compelling is its relative uniqueness.

Knowledge Networks as Complex Systems

The agent-based approach to the study of complex systems is especially suited to understanding knowledge networks among agents where some of the agents may be humans or aggregates of humans, such as groups and organizations, while others may be nonhuman, such as computer software, computing hardware, and mobile communication devices. The emergence of human communication networks is inextricably linked to and embedded in these larger knowledge networks. The number of agents as well as the quantitative and qualitative complexity of the relations among them makes agent-based modeling a particularly useful framework to study the emergence of communication and knowledge networks. The remainder of this chapter describes how agent-based models can be used to conceptualize multiagent knowledge networks as complex systems and to theoretically specify the conditions under which communication and knowledge networks are more likely to self-organize. We begin by introducing the concepts of knowledge networks and cognitive knowledge networks.

Knowledge has been defined in a number of ways, each definition reflecting the goals of its respective discipline. A common hierarchy offered in computer science is that data (bits, bytes, pixels, voxels), when combined with content (e.g., metadata, often implicit), lead to information. The integration, analysis, and synthesis of information lead to knowledge (Carley & Newell, 1994). In artificial intelligence, the knowledge level is one in a hierarchy of many representational schemes (Newell, 1981). At this level, knowledge is represented symbolically (Johnson-Laird, 1983; Minsky, 1975; Schank & Abelson, 1977). Researchers in many other fields have adopted similar representations (see, e.g., Blumer, 1969; Knorr-Cetina, 1981). At the knowledge level, the symbols or concepts acquire meaning through their relation to other concepts (Carley, 1986a, 1986b; Gollob, 1968; Heise, 1969, 1970; Minsky, 1975). These formalisms imply that knowledge can only be understood within a network of other knowledge concepts (Carley & Newell, 1994; Lesperance, 1991).

From the standpoint of studying organizations, it is useful to conceptualize knowledge networks as they map on to a population of agents. The location of knowledge within this network of agents varies along a continuum. This continuum spans from a centralized sector, where knowledge resides with one agent, to a distributed one, where knowledge exists among many (Farace, Monge, & Russell, 1977). Further, distributed knowledge may refer to the flow or diffusion of knowledge, which increases the level of knowledge among all actors. Alternatively, distributed knowledge may refer to the parts of a larger knowledge base, each possessed by separate agents within the network. In this form of distributed knowledge, people bring relatively unique, nonredundant knowledge, which enable a collective to accomplish complex tasks (Gore, 1996). Distributed knowledge occurs at many levels in the empirical world, including work groups, large scale project teams, and interorganizational strategic alliances, to name but a few.

In addition to these characteristics of the observable knowledge networks, people have their own "cognitive" perceptions of the knowledge network, that is, each person embodies her or his own idea of how knowledge is distributed among others in the network. For example, a common, if idealized, analogy depicts a set of networked computers in which knowledge about a given domain is available on one of the hard disks (i.e., with one of the agents), while the *directory* of information on all of the other hard disks (i.e., the entire knowledge network) is available to all agents (Wegner, 1995). In reality, the directory of information possessed by each of the agents (i.e., each agent's perception of "who knows what") may be incomplete and/or inaccurate. Hence, all agents within an observable knowledge network have their own *cognitive knowledge networks*, which refers to their perceptions of the overall observable knowledge network (Contractor, Zink, & Chan, 1998).

A final important characteristic of knowledge networks is their fluidity, in terms of both agents and linkages. People join or leave a knowledge network on the basis of tasks to be accomplished, and their levels of interests, resources, and commitments. The links within the knowledge network are also likely to change on the basis of evolving tasks, the distribution of knowledge within the network, or changes in the agents' cognitive knowledge networks (Hollingshead, Fulk, & Monge, 2002).

In chapter 2 we cited Badaracco's (1991) useful distinction between migratory and embedded knowledge. Migratory knowledge such as that contained in books, designs, blueprints, and computer programs exists in forms that are easily encoded and therefore moveable from one location, person, group, or firm to another. This form of knowledge can be easily distributed both within and across organizations. Embedded knowledge—like craftsmanship, unique talents, and skills, accumulated know-how, and group expertise and synergy—is more difficult to transfer and thus more difficult to develop in term of knowledge networks.

Multiagent Knowledge Networks: Avatars, Webbots, and Repositories

The MTML communication network framework presented in chapter 2 and the complex systems perspective developed earlier in this chapter can be usefully applied to characterize knowledge relations. Focusing on knowledge networks also enables us to explore an interesting extension to our framework. So far we have treated network entities or agents as if they were humans, either as individuals or as collectives such as groups or organizations. Let us now consider a network where the agents could include nonhuman agents. These nonhuman agents could be knowledge repositories that range from simple file cabinets to sophisticated electronic databases. Nonhuman agents could also include avatars and webbots. *Avatars* are software products that provide electronic representations of human agents. They are designed by human agents to act as semiautonomous agents capable of interacting with other agents, be they human, knowledge repositories, or others' avatars. *Webbots* are web-based robots that are programmed to repeat structured tasks, such as continually searching the web for topics of interest to the webbot's owner. They may then "push" certain knowledge to their owners.

In the work context, both human and nonhuman agents seek to accomplish certain tasks or activities while utilizing certain skills and expertise. Table 3.1 (adapted from Carley, 2002, and Contractor, 2002) provides a framework for relating human agents, nonhuman agents, tasks, and expertise. All four categories are arrayed as the rows and columns of the matrix so that the cells provide all possible combinations of relations between the categories. The range of interactions between human agents, nonhuman agents, tasks, and skills also can be represented as a multimodal network. *Multimodal* networks, unlike the networks we have discussed so far, do not necessarily have the same set of actors who can all potentially interact with one another. Sometimes these are also referred to as s-partite graphs (Wasserman & Faust, 1994, p. 121).

The first cell in the first row of the matrix in table 3.1 represents the typical communication network among human agents. However, the cell to the right describes links between human agents as the rows and knowledge repositories as the columns. A link here indicates an individual's attempt to access, retrieve, or publish data and knowledge to the repository. Moving in table 3.1 to the next section to the right, the rows remain the human agents, but the columns indicate skills or expertise possessed by individuals. A link here indicates a human agent's expertise in a certain area. Finally, the top right section of table 3.1 refers to the relations between human agents and tasks or activities. The presence of a link here could signify that a particular human agent has been assigned to a task. The second row represents the possible relations among nonhuman agents such as avatars, webbots, and repositories, and human agents, tasks, and skills.

Table 3.1
A Network Framework for Relating Human Agents, Nonhuman Agents, Tasks, and Expertise

	Human Agents	*Nonhuman Agents (Webbots, Avatars, etc.)*	*Expertise/Skills*	*Tasks/Activities*
Human agents	Traditional communication networks	Publish, retrieve/access	Expertise/skills offered by human agent	Tasks/activities accomplished by human agent
Nonhuman agents (Webbots, Avatars, etc.)	Push technology applications (e.g., Infogate)	P2P technology applications (e.g., Gnutella)	Expertise/skills offered by non-human agent	Tasks/activities accomplished by nonhuman agent
Skills/expertise	Skills/expertise needed	Skills/expertise needed	Constraints among expertise/skills	Skills needed for tasks/activities
Tasks/activities	Tasks assigned to human agent	Tasks assigned to nonhuman agent	Expertise/skills developed from tasks/activities	Constraints among tasks/activities

Taken together the multimodal network provides a network characterization of the interactions among human agents, nonhuman agents, skills, and tasks. From a network standpoint, the MTML approach outlined previously can be usefully employed to study the structural tendencies of this larger network rather than simply focusing on the communication interactions among humans.

Two examples of theoretical mechanisms discussed in greater detail in later chapters illustrate the utility of this approach. First, the MTML approach provides a network framework to examine and explain the structural tendencies for actors to publish, retrieve, or access information. By doing so, it provides an opportunity to examine and extend theories of collective action that have been proposed for the study of new information technologies as connective and communal public goods (Fulk et al., 1996; Monge et al., 1998).

Second, the multimodal network can be used to situate simultaneously the structural tendencies for actors to communicate with one another in terms of three related knowledge network functions described by theories of transactive memory (Hollingshead, Fulk, & Monge, 2002; Moreland, 1999; Palazzolo, Serb, She, Su, & Contractor, 2002; Wegner, 1995). First, communication provides agents the opportunity to learn what others know, a process that is known as *directory updating*. Next, these communication links are used to seek information from knowledgeable others on issues relevant to agents' tasks. Finally, the communication also gives actors an opportunity to "allocate" information they might receive to others in the network who are considered knowledgeable in that area and hence intellectual custodians of that knowledge.

The framework proposed here, summarized in table 3.1 and illustrated in the preceding examples, extends our traditional notions of communication network analysis to include nonhuman agents, which are increasingly pervasive in the workplace. While the preponderance of research on new media has focused on considering them as channels for communication among a network of human agents, the framework formulated here additionally considers the role of new media as nodes within a larger knowledge network. Further, by considering task and expertise as part of the network the framework enables examination of the increasingly dynamic relations that twenty-first-century workers have with tasks and the skills required to accomplish those tasks.

Knowledge Networks as Complex Self-Organizing Systems

As a complement to the multilevel, multimodal framework just presented, the theory of complex systems provides a rich vocabulary to describe the self-organization of knowledge networks. The first condition for self-organizing systems as discussed above emphasizes that the components of a system are self-generative. The concept of *autocatalysis* is used to capture the capabilities of the parts of a system to self-create and self-renew independent of the forces from the outside environment (Luhmann, 1990; Luhmann, 1992; Maturana & Varela, 1980). Although self-referential closure is emphasized in both Maturana and Varela (1980), and Luhmann's discussion of autopoiesis, it does not mean that no resource exchange with the external environment is needed. The key point here is on how the parts enact their environment for their self-renewal and self-production (Morgan, 1997). As such, in *autopoietic systems*, one seeks to explain the apparent stability of a network by processes of active self-generation or renewal. This distinguishes it from other approaches that seek to explain change rather than stability in a network. In knowledge networks that are formed on the basis of social networks for generating and sharing knowledge, there are two types of components in the system that exhibit autocatalysis, the knowledge per se and the people. As discussed before, human cognizance plays a key role in the creation of new knowledge. Through complicated cognitive processes, new knowledge can be generated by the accumulation of new information and integration with preexisting knowledge. The social network is self-generative in that the charisma or reputation of a person can by itself serve as a strong magnet to attract more participants to the network.

Mutual causality is another key feature of the self-organizing system. The proposal that current levels of X can be partially predicted by prior levels of Y and current levels of Y can be partially predicted by prior levels of X captures a significant portion of the dynamism of evolutionary process (Contractor, 1994). In the context of knowledge networks this type of mutual causality is reified again in the relationship between knowledge (X) and people (Y). On one hand, once people decide to share their knowledge with others, the knowledge becomes independent of the provider, and becomes information circulated in the network that can be used as raw material to generate more knowledge. Although we cannot say for sure what type of new knowledge will be created, accumulation and distribution of information and knowledge are necessary for the creation of new knowledge. On the other hand, as people are the actual inventors of new ideas, pooling together the intelligence of better informed and motivated people can spin off much more new knowledge

The third condition states that maintaining a self-organized state requires importing energy into the system (Anderson, 1999; Prigogine and Stengers, 1984). Following the *law of requisite variety* as first proposed by Ashby (1964; Coleman, 1990; Morgan, 1997), the level of internal complexity of a system has to match the level of complexity of the external environment if it is to deal with the challenges posed by that environment. In the context of knowledge networks, it can be argued that only when the span of knowledge people have within the network matches the external complexity of the environment, could a knowledge network be considered valuable and attract more contributors. Each time a new person is recruited into the network, the network gains new resources for self-organizing. New members are important new resources because they are possible carriers of knowledge, experience, skills, and expertise that may be previously unknown to the system. The acquisition of new skills or new knowledge by any member of the network can also bring in new energies. In line with this argument we would propose that the probability for the network to generate more new ideas and attract more members is an accumulative function of the size of the contributor pool. This is consistent with the hypothesis proposed by Monge et al. (1998) for the study of information sharing in interorganizational communication systems.

The last condition for self-organizing behavior is that the system has to operate in a *far-from-equilibrium* state. *Critical value* is an important concept in self-organizing systems (McKelvey, 1999b). Certain threshold values are critical for self-organizing activities because at these critical points the growth trajectory of complex systems may change dramatically. Below the first critical value of adaptive tension, the system's activities can be explained using traditional science. Above the second critical value, the system will behave chaotically. The transition region, on the edge of order and chaos, is the far-from-equilibrium state, or the *complex regime*, in which self-organizing adaptive activities are most likely to happen (Cramer, 1993; Kauffman, 1993).

So far we have argued that knowledge networks can be studied from the perspective of complex systems that have the capability to self-organize. The ultimate goal of this position is not to assert another analogy for the theory of complexity in order to demonstrate that it works for social science as well as for physics and biology. In face of an ever-growing body of publications on complex systems, Contractor (1999) proposed that system thinkers should move beyond a metaphorical fascination for definitions, conceptualizations, and collecting analogies. In addition, scholars need to think about what new insights would be gained if the theoretical mechanisms of self-organization were to be used to study organizations. To what extent can the theory of complexity as a general framework of thinking that applies to multiple disciplines be employed in organizations? In chapter 9 we will return to the issues of studying knowledge networks as complex adaptive systems in the context of coevolutionary theory.

Summary

Systems theory evolved in the last half of the twentieth century from its earlier focus on stable, homeostatic phenomena to a deep concern over complex dynamic adaptive systems. Some of these systems are chaotic and very difficult to analyze. Others are frozen in their current locations with little possibility for change. Others are more orderly, existing at the edge of chaos, capable of adapting more quickly to changes they encounter (Kauffman, 1993, 1995).

This chapter has provided a brief overview of the historical roots of systems theory as well as an introduction to contemporary thought on complex systems. Organizational communication networks can now be viewed as self-organizing complex systems, ones that often emerge from the interconnected rule-governed behavior of a population of interacting agents. In terms of the models of networks described in chapter 2, network realizations can be seen as depending on internal network properties, specifically, changes in the attributes of the network members and the dynamic interactions with other network members in the environments in which they coexist.

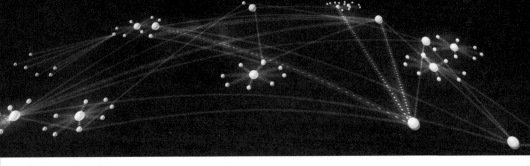

4

Computational Modeling of Networks

Computer simulations have long been used as an effective tool in engineering, economics, psychology, and a number of other social sciences. Engineers typically use simulations to predict performance of a system that has known dynamic characteristics. These characteristics are typically obtained from theory and are then articulated in the simulation as difference or differential equations. The goal of engineering simulation is then to assess the dynamic performance of a system based on a priori knowledge of the dynamic relationships among the various elements of the system.

Forrester (1961, 1973) was one of the earliest and most influential advocates of simulation modeling of dynamic social systems. Forrester advocated this approach as a way to model and assess the dynamics of industrial and world phenomena. Sterman (2000) provides a recent review of research on dynamics simulation from this tradition. While this approach has produced a considerable number of studies, it too is based on the assumption that the researcher has a priori knowledge of the dynamic relationships among elements of the system. Indeed, many of the results of these models have been criticized for specifying relationships that were at best untested and at worst flawed. In response to these criticisms, more recent interest has focused on redefining the utility of simulations in the social sciences. Rather than using simulations to test the long-term dynamics of systems with known interrelationships, theorists (Carley &

Prietula, 1994; Contractor, 1994; Hanneman, 1988) have suggested that social scientists should use simulations to help construct theory, to identify the heretofore-unknown interrelationships. This section describes the traditional use of computer simulations as well as the adaptation of this approach toward theory construction and testing in the social sciences. Later sections will apply these general approaches to the computational modeling of networks in particular.

Carley and Prietula (1994) suggest that the emergence of the new field of computational organizational theory (COT) signals the growing interest in the construction of computational models to augment and assist theory building. Most social science theories are richly evocative but highly abbreviated (Poole, 1997), that is, they offer explanations that suggest complex interrelationships but do not provide precise, falsifiable mathematical formalizations of the theory. Of course, not all theories are designed to be, or lend themselves easily to, unambiguous and specific descriptions of these relationships. Computer simulations, which require completely unambiguous specifications of the interrelationships, require theorists to articulate their models with greater precision and rigor. Often this implies that the same theory may generate several alternate models depending on the interpretation of the theoretical statements. In fact, Hanneman (1988) advocates the use of computer simulations to gain insights into the long-term implications of dynamic social models, even those ambiguous theories that may have alternative interpretations. It is important to emphasize that the results of a computer simulation are not a surrogate for empirical data. Rather, they help to identify the emergent processes implied by the theory. As such, simulations provide researchers with opportunities to deduce hypotheses about differences in the emergent process implied by theories. Often, the differences in these emergent processes are implicit but not immediately obvious or intuitive.

Traditional theoretical approaches rely on synthetic verbal statements and deductive reasoning strategies to generate hypotheses from the theory (Blalock, 1964, 1969). COT moves theorists to the next level of theory building by requiring them to formalize and make explicit the deduction of hypotheses from the theoretical statements.

The distinctions between traditional and COT research processes are summarized in figure 4.1. Researchers in the traditional approach to theory construction deduce hypotheses by examining the logical interrelationships among the verbal statements offered by the theory. Some researchers convert the verbal statements to mathematical equations and explore the logic of the theory via structural equation models (Blalock, 1989; Bollen, 1989;

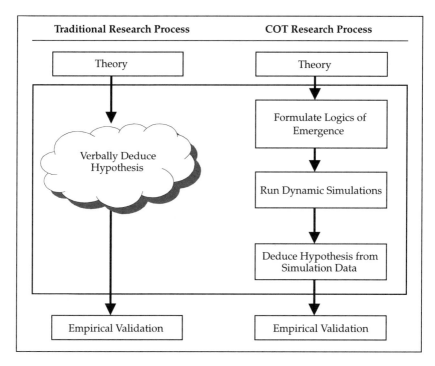

| Traditional Research Process | COT Research Process |

Theory

Theory

Verbally Deduce Hypothesis

Formulate Logics of Emergence

Run Dynamic Simulations

Deduce Hypothesis from Simulation Data

Empirical Validation

Empirical Validation

Figure 4.1
Traditional vs. computational organizational theory research processes

Land, 1969). These verbally or mathematically deduced hypotheses are then empirically validated. Empirical rejection of the hypotheses leads to refinements in the theory.

Researchers who use the COT approach first identify the logics of emergence or other generative mechanisms in the theory, and then articulate these logics in a computational model. Given the frequent verbal ambiguities in theoretical statements, the process of identifying the logics is nontrivial. However, the exercise is an important and useful step in adding precision and rigor to the articulation of the theory. Since these logics are typically nonlinear, it is extremely difficult to mentally construe their implications over time for a large number of entities (e.g., individuals, groups, organizations) or at multiple levels of analyses. Hence, simulations of computational models are used to explore the nonlinear, transient and long-term dynamics implied by the logics of emergence for the system. Of course, as with traditional approaches, the results of the simulation must be fitted to empirical data. A good fit would imply validation of the theory or, more accurately, an inability to reject validation of the theory. A poor fit would suggest refinements, modifications, further disambiguation, or rejection of the theory.

Computational Organizational Network Models

An explicit focus on the generative mechanisms whereby networks enable and constrain organizational behavior has led to an interest in creating formal mathematical and computational network models of organizational activities. It has, in effect, led scholars to combine two streams of research: (1) computing organizational simulations based on theoretically derived generative mechanisms, and (2) testing or validating properties of these simulated networks in organizational contexts (Carley, 1995).

There are a few promising examples of this integration. Zeggelink (1993) modeled the evolution of friendship networks based on a set of generative mechanisms derived from social exchange theory (Blau, 1964), classical conditioning theory (Lott & Lott, 1960), social comparison theory (Festinger, 1954), and balance theory (Heider, 1958). Levitt et al. (1994) developed the virtual design team (VDT), a computational model of an engineering design organization based on information processing theory (Galbraith, 1977), contingency theory (Thompson, 1967), media richness, and social influence theories (Fulk & Steinfield, 1990). Lin and Carley (1995) present a computational model for examining organizational performance that draws on various factors articulated by contingency theories (Scott, 1987; Thompson, 1967), including task environment, organizational design, and stressors such as crises and time pressures. Corman (1996) offered a cellular automata model, POWERPLAY, to demonstrate the emergence of a dominance hierarchy based on principles inspired by structuration theory (Giddens, 1984). Contractor and Grant (1996) described a computational model to examine the emergence of shared interpretations in organizations based on Burt's (1982) structural theory of action and Heider's (1958) balance theory. Hyatt et al. (1997) used Fulk et al.'s (1990) social information processing theory and Burt's structural theory of action to model the adoption of new communication technologies.

All of these studies represent a genre of scholarship that attempts to model explicitly and dynamically the attributes and relationships among a network of agents based on generative mechanisms suggested by one or more social theories. Further, they employ computer simulations to help envision the dynamic, often nonintuitive, implications of their models. The following section describes the concepts used in the computational modeling of networks.

Concepts in the Computational Modeling of Networks

Core issues in modeling networks include (1) the articulation of the attributes or characteristics of the nodes in the network (i.e., the human agents, such as individuals, groups, or organizations, or nonhuman agents such as databases, avatars, and webbots), (2) the relationships among the nodes, and (3) the coevolution of the attributes and relationships over time. *Blanche* is a computational environment designed to assist in the modeling of simulation of networks. Along with other agent-based computational environments, *Blanche* has some significant differences from many of the better-known simulation environments used to model systems dynamics (Hanneman, 1988; Sterman, 2000).

Systems dynamics simulation programs such as *Dynamo* (Hanneman, 1988), *STELLA/iThink* (Richmond & Peterson, 1993), *Vensim*, and *Powersim* are especially appropriate to study the often nonlinear interrelationships among variables or concepts such as net labor, schedule pressure, fatigue, and productivity. Hence the building blocks in these environments are typically *concepts* that measure flows, rates, and levels based on an aggregate of entities (Sterman, 2000).

Agent-based modeling environments, like *Blanche*, are a more recent entry to the field of simulation. As Sterman (2000, p. 896) notes, "In an agent-based model, the individual members of a population such as firms in an economy or people in a social group are represented explicitly rather than as a single aggregate entity. Important heterogeneities in agent attributes and decision rules can then be represented." The building blocks in these environments are *agents*. There has been considerable recent interest in the development of agent-based computational models and multiagent simulation environments (Bond & Gasser, 1988; Drogoul & Ferber, 1994; Epstein & Axtell, 1996; Langton, Burkhart, Lee, Daniels, & Lancaster, 1998; Latane, 2000; Page, 1997; Prietula, Carley, & Gasser, 1998; for a recent review see Gilbert & Troitzch, 1999). While all computational network models can be considered as agent-based models, the reverse is not always true. An agent-based computational model may describe dynamics among a set of agents based solely on the attributes of the agents. In order to qualify as an agent-based computational *network* model, the dynamics must also consider the relations among the agents. As we will describe later, *Blanche* is especially well suited to model changes in both attributes of, and relations between, agents.

In *Blanche* these agents are defined as computational "objects." Each agent has a set of attributes and each agent can have one or more relations to other agents. Further each agent (or "object") has associated with it a set of rules (or, in the language of object-oriented programming, "methods") that specify how the values of the agents' attributes, as well as the values of their relations with other agents, can change over time. Hence an agent-based computational environment, such as *Blanche*, provides a flexible platform for the specification of models and the visual and statistical analysis of the often nonlinear interrelationships between the attributes and relations among a network of agents (Contractor, Whitbred, Fonti, Hyatt, Jones, & O'Keefe, 2000).

In addition to the "objects" (the attributes and relations; see Rock-Evans, 1989), a set of generative mechanisms, which comprise the logics of emergence, is needed to examine the evolution of networks. A discrete set of generative mechanisms provides flexibility and expressiveness such that dependencies among attributes and relations over time are modeled as a function of values at contemporaneous and/or prior points in time. For example, we can think of an agent's attribute, A, at a point in time, t, as a function of the value of A at prior points in time, $t - 1$, as well as a function of the value of some of the agent's relations (Rs) to other agents in the network contemporaneously at time, t, or at preceding points in time, such as $t - 1$. Under the assumption that attributes and relations take on real values, *Blanche* employs nonlinear difference equations to represent the evolution of an agent's attributes and relations over time. These distinctions are described more fully below.

Attributes

As described in chapter 2, an attribute is simply a measure of a property of a node. Nodes can have many attributes. Attributes can be binary, categorical, or continuous. *Binary* attributes are represented by dichotomous phenomena such as whether the agent is human or nonhuman, male or female. "State" information, such as whether an agent is engaged in a certain activity, can also be modeled as a binary attribute. An example of *categorical* attributes is whether a human agent is in sales, marketing, or R&D. Similarly, categorical attributes of nonhuman agents could be whether they are webbots, avatars, or databases. Examples of *continuous* attributes are an agent's level of expertise, attitudes, or workload. Some agent attributes may not change over time, such as gender or whether an agent is human or nonhuman, while others may change to varying degrees. For instance, an agent's expertise may change relatively slowly, while an agent's workload may fluctuate rapidly. Change is indexed in terms of discrete time intervals, called *iterations*, which can be thought of as seconds, days, weeks, or any other consistent unit of time. With each new iteration of the simulation, time is incremented, and the agent's attributes may change values. As we will illustrate later, the values of an agent's attributes are specified at each iteration by nonlinear difference equations.

The values of an agent's attributes at any point in time can depend in four ways on the same or other *attributes* of the agent or other agents in the network. First, an agent's attributes are often influenced by their own previous states, thereby reflecting the forces of inertia. For instance, an influential predictor of an agent's contemporaneous expertise is the agent's prior expertise. Second, an agent's attributes may be influenced by other attributes of the same agent. For example, an agent's workload, an attribute, could depend on the efficiency of the same agent, another attribute. Third, an agent's attributes may be influenced by the same attribute of other agents in the network. In the previous example, an agent's workload could depend on the workload of other agents in the network. Fourth, an agent's attributes may be influenced by other attributes of other agents in the network. Continuing this example, an agent's workload could depend on the efficiency of other agents in the network. While the examples here illustrate simple additive influences on the changes in an agent's attributes, specific social theories may posit more complex multiplicative or other nonlinear influences.

An agent's attributes can also be influenced by one or more relations it has with other agents in the network. For instance, an agent's workload may be higher if it receives communication ties from several other agents in the network, that is, the agent has a high in-degree in their communication network.

Relations

A relation specifies a link of variable strength between two nodes. Relations may represent communication, influence, workflow, activation, or any other relationship of interest between two nodes in the network. In terms of the knowledge networks discussed in chapter 3, it may also represent what one agent, A, thinks another agent, B, knows about a particular topic. Strength can be interpreted in a variety of ways. For example, in a communication network, a relation from node A to B can represent the volume of communication such as the number of messages that A receives from B. The relation strength is either dichotomous (0 or 1), signifying presence or absence, or continuous. Typically, a higher strength value indicates a stronger relation. The value of a relation may change depending on the attributes of the source agent, the destination agent, both agents, and other agents in the network, as well as relations between the agents. For every relation specified, there will be a maximum of $n^2 - n$ possible relations in the simulation, where n is the number of nodes in the simulated network.

Changes in Agents' Attributes and Relations

As discussed earlier, some of the agents' attributes (such as gender) and relations (such as reporting relationships) may not change over time. However, the primary goal of a computational model is to use theoretically motivated mechanisms to generate a set of rules about how agents' attributes and relations influence one another over time. In general, these rules can be specified as a nonlinear difference equation for each of the agents' attributes and relations. That is, at any point in time, t, an agent i's attribute, $X_{i,t}$, may be influenced by its own previous value at time $t - 1$, $X_{i,t-1}$, as well as the contemporaneous or prior values of *other* attributes of the *same* agent i (e.g., $Y_{i,t}$, $Z_{i,t-1}$, etc.), the values of the same or other attributes of *other* agents j (e.g., $X_{j,t}$, $Y_{j,t}$, $Z_{j,t}$, etc.), the relations between agent i and other agents, j (e.g., $C_{ij,t-1}$), as well as the relations among other agents j and k (e.g., $R_{jk,t-1}$). The latter can be at the dyadic, triadic, group, or global levels.

Schematically, a nonlinear difference equation for one attribute can be specified as:

$$X_{i,t} = \text{function } (X_{i,t-1}, Y_{i,t-1}, Z_{j,t-1}, \ldots C_{ij,t-1}, \ldots R_{jk,t-1})$$

This equation indicates that the value of attribute X for an agent i at time t is influenced by its own value for that same attribute at time $t - 1$, its own value for another attribute Y at time $t - 1$, the value of another attribute Z for all other agents j at time $t - 1$, the value of its relation C with all other agents j at time $t - 1$, and the value of the relation R among other agents j and k at time $t - 1$. The exact function, which could be additive, multiplicative, logarithmic, exponential, or other combinations of these variables is based on the theoretical mechanism(s) used to posit the dynamics. In some cases, the nonlinear difference equation could also be a series of if-then logic statements.

Similar nonlinear difference equations must be specified for each of the remaining attributes as well as for each of the relations. Hence if the computational model identified, say, three attributes for each agent and two relations among the agents, there will be a total of five nonlinear difference equations that will be used to specify how each of the attributes and relations change over time.

Initial Conditions

A computational network model is fully specified once we have identified the attributes, relations, and the nonlinear difference equations that represent how these attributes and relations change over time. However, in order to use the model for simulations, one must additionally specify the *initial conditions* or state of the network. That is, one must specify *starting values* for the agents' attributes and relations. The computational model uses these starting or initial values at $t = 0$ to assess the agents' attributes and relations at subsequent iterations or points in time. Indeed, one of the potential benefits of computational modeling is to determine how initial conditions may influence the transient and long-term dynamics of a network. Many nonlinear systems are very sensitive to initial conditions; and it is virtually impossible for the human mind to intuit the dynamics of a theoretically derived computational model based on different initial conditions. For instance, consider a network where initially the agents share a great deal of interest on a particular topic, X, but do not communicate much with one another. That is, they all have high initial values for a particular attribute, X, and low initial values for a communication relation, C, between the agents. As an alternative, consider another network where initially the agents do not share a great deal of interest on a particular topic but communicate extensively with one another. In this case, the agents have low initial values for attribute X and high initial values for the communication relation, C, between agents. The same set of theoretical mechanisms (and as a result nonlinear difference equations) about the extent to which shared interest and communication mutually influence one another will potentially lead to very different dynamics in these two networks. To understand these differences, one must execute the same computational model using different initial values for the attributes and relations among the network of agents. In the section titled "Designing Virtual Experiments," later in this chapter, we discuss the manipulation of initial conditions in greater detail.

To summarize, a network in this computational modeling framework consists of (1) a list of agents or nodes, each characterized by a set of attributes; (2) a list of relations relating agents to each other; (3) nonlinear difference equations that represent how each of the attributes and relations change over time; and (4) initial conditions for the values of each of the attributes and relations at time $t = 0$.

Overview of Blanche

Once a network computational model is defined, there are many ways to implement it. Using a general-purpose computer language to hard-code a particular model may be efficient in the short term but does not promote reusability or extensibility. Hence simulation software, such as STELLA (Richmond, 2001), can be used to implement these agent-based computational network models. But since such simulation environments are designed for modeling a system of variables rather than a network of agents, they can be unwieldy, especially for networks of different sizes and for batch processing of many randomly generated data sets. Since the computational network models described above have a common framework, an attractive solution is to create a generic, reusable architecture to support the framework and provide the end user with easy-to-use tools to define models in terms of attributes, relations, and equations specifying the interrelationships among them. *Blanche* is such a system; it is designed so that researchers can use it as a tool for building and evaluating quantitative simulations of organizational networks. It is implemented in Microsoft Visual C++ and runs on Windows operating systems. *Blanche* embodies an object-oriented framework in which a network is defined as a collection of node objects that each have internal attributes and relations to other nodes. Both attributes and relations are objects themselves. *Blanche* is publicly available on the Internet at http://www.spcomm.uiuc.edu/Projects/TECLAB/BLANCHE/ as of the date of publication of this book. The use of computer simulations to study the evolution of networks could require considerable programming knowledge by researchers. However, *Blanche* strives to provide an easy user-interface to support the specification of mathematical models, execution of network simulations, and the dynamic analysis of network evolution.

As underscored earlier, the goal of computational network modeling is to discern emergent characteristics implied by generative mechanisms derived from one or more theories at one or more levels of analysis. Importantly, the results of these computational experiments do not, by themselves, confirm or validate knowledge claims about how networks emerge in organizations. Hence a principled use of theoretically guided computational modeling is inextricably linked to two other scientific enterprises: (1) a research design to collect the empirical data of the phenomena being examined, and (2) the use of appropriate statistical techniques to specify and test the likelihood of obtaining the observed realization of the network from among the set of possible configurations. The nexus between computational modeling and the latter of these two enterprises will be discussed next.

Deterministic Versus Stochastic Models

Computational models can be either deterministic or stochastic. That is, a computational model could comprise a system of generative mechanisms that specify unequivocally, and hence deterministically, the logics codetermining changes in the attributes of the nodes and the relations among them. The underlying assumption is that the generative mechanisms specified in the computational model provide a comprehensive explanation for the emergence of the network. No additional theoretical mechanisms need be considered. Replicating such models will always lead to exactly the same emergent outcomes. Clearly, such totalizing assumptions, while attractive in the ideal, are unrealistic on at least two counts. First, the logics embodied in the verbal descriptions of most social theories suggest the likelihood of an increase or decrease in certain changes, rather than their inevitability. Second, social theories typically offer explanations that contribute to rather than singularly explain changes associated with attributes or relations within networks. Hence, deterministic mechanisms are likely to have very limited relevance to the computational modeling of social systems. A relatively simple, though often simplistic, response to this problem is to introduce a random error term as an additive component to the model.

Nondeterministic or stochastic computational modeling is therefore a more realistic, albeit more complex, enterprise. The most elementary manner in which to add a stochastic component to a computational model is to introduce a random component that will influence the outcomes of the generative mechanisms. Thus, while a deterministic computational model would unequivocally specify the computed value associated with an outcome (either an attribute or a relation), a stochastic computational model will specify an *expected value*, where an underlying probability distribution contributes to the selection of the computed value. This value would occur within the range specified by the distribution. For example, if a normal distribution were used, values near the center of the distribution would be more likely and those in the tails increasingly unlikely. The simulation is more likely to compute a value that is closer to the expected value than it is to select a value that is substantially farther away from the expected value.

In summary, stochastic computational models seek to determine the probability rather than the actual value of an agent's attribute or the relation between two agents. The key theoretical decision is to select the appropriate underlying probability distribution that would be used in assigning the computed value. Several possible distributions are available for this purpose, but two are used most frequently, depending on the nature of the data. If the variables were binary, the distributions of choice are binomial. Examples of binary variables include attributes of a node like the decision to adopt or not adopt a new technology or their relations such as whether they communicate or not with one another. If the phenomena being modeled were continuous variables, the preferred option would be to use a Gaussian random distribution. Examples of continuous variables would include attributes of the node such as expertise of an individual or their relations as in the amount of time spent communicating with one another.

As one would expect, repeatedly executing stochastic computational models will not necessarily yield the same emergent outcomes. Instead, the outcomes will vary and can be summarily viewed as a distribution with some emergent outcomes more likely to occur than others. Normally, modelers would take a measure of central tendency, such as the mean, median, or mode of the distributions as the most likely expected values for the model. Likewise, they would use measures of dispersion, such as the variance of the distribution, as a measure of confidence in the predictions. Of course, valid simulations that have narrower distributions and smaller variances around the midpoints of the variables make more accurate predictions of emergent phenomena. In a subsequent section we will describe how varying certain characteristics of the model, such as the values of the parameters or the initial values of the data, can be used to conduct *virtual experiments*. Analyzing the results of these virtual experiments could be useful in streamlining the research design for an empirical study as well as deducing hypotheses for empirical validation in field studies.

Examples of Deterministic and Stochastic Models

Consider a computational model where the value of the contemporaneous communication relations between two agents is influenced by their prior communication relation, their desire to reciprocate communication, and their propensity to communicate with "friends of friends." This would suggest that the communication relation, $C_{ij, t}$, from agent i to agent j at time t is influenced by (1) the communication relation, $C_{ij, t-1}$, at the previous point in time, $t-1$, (2) the communication relation, $C_{ji, t-1}$, from agent j to agent i, at the previous point in time, $t-1$, and (3) the presence of prior relations, $C_{ik, t-1}$, from agent i to all agents, k, in the network who in turn have similar prior relations, $C_{kj, t-1}$, with agent j.

A *deterministic* model of this process can be represented as:

$$C_{ij, t} = p_1 C_{ij, t-1} + p_2 C_{ji, t-1} + p_3 \Sigma(C_{ik, t-1})(C_{kj, t-1}) \tag{1}$$

In equation 1, the computational model is entirely deterministic with the contributions of the three components weighted by p_1, p_2, and p_3 respectively. p_1, p_2, and p_3 are parameters and are specified by the modeler, ideally on the basis of theory. The Σ (the capital Greek letter sigma) indicates a summation of the communication from source agent i to every other agent k multiplied by the communication of each of these agents k to the target agent, j.

A simple, though somewhat simplistic, stochastic version of this model, which includes a *random error term*, can be represented as:

$$C_{ij, t} = p_1 C_{ij, t-1} + p_2 C_{ji, t-1} + p_3 \Sigma(C_{ik, t-1})(C_{kj, t-1}) + \tag{2}$$
$$\text{Random (Mean, Variance} = \sigma)$$

In equation 2, the computational model is essentially deterministic but includes, as an "error" term, some random fluctuations. The Mean and the Variance are parameters that are specified by the modeler. Typically, the random "error" term will have a mean of 0, but this does not necessarily have to be the case. The value of the Variance parameter will determine the likely range of random error.

A more sophisticated *stochastic* version of this model can be represented as:

$$C_{ij,\,t} = \text{Normal}[\text{Mean} = p_1 C_{ij,\,t-1} + p_2 C_{ji,\,t-1} + \tag{3}$$
$$p_3 \Sigma (C_{ik,\,t-1})(C_{kj,\,t-1}), \text{Variance} = \sigma]$$

In equation 3, the computational model includes a stochastic component that makes the expected value of the relation the mean of a probability distribution. The "realized" value for the communication relation would therefore be selected from a probability distribution. The realized value could be more or less than the expected value. However, if the same computational model were run repeatedly, say a 1,000 times, the average of the realized values will increasingly approximate the "expected" value. Unlike equation 2, the modeler does not need to specify a parameter value for Mean. Instead one need only specify a value for the Variance parameter. This indicates the variability due to the stochastic component around the mean value that is deterministically computed.

Including a stochastic component in the above two equations is further complicated if some of the explanatory mechanisms include noncontinuous variables. Specifically, if some of the relational or attribute variables are binary or categorical, then including a stochastic error term that is normally distributed is not appropriate.

Special Issues in Computational Modeling of Networks

While the approaches outlined above would be appropriate for computationally modeling a wide variety of social phenomena, alternative or additional constraints must be considered in modeling *network* phenomena. These constraints arise from the recognition that relations within a network are not independent from one another. As discussed in chapter 2, the likelihood of a relation between any two agents, A and B, is not conceptually independent of the likelihood of relations between A and some other agent C, agent B and some other agent D, or between agents C and D. This is in contrast to nonnetwork data where it is normally appropriate to assume that the values of two individuals' attributes (such as age) are independent of one another. The Gaussian and binomial distributions described above assume that the observations are independent and are therefore generally inappropriate for specifying the dependency structures that may exist among the relational ties in a network. It is, therefore, important to specify statistical distributions that take into account specific theoretically derived dependencies among the relational ties in a network. The p^* approach outlined in chapter 2 provides a framework to specify such dependencies in empirical data. It can also be used as the basis for computer simulations of networks, as we now describe.

Let us begin with the premise that we seek to model the probabilities of ties among a network of agents. As discussed in chapter 2, a set of g nodes can have as many as $(g)(g - 1)$ directed ties on each relation. Since each of these ties can be either present or absent, there can be as many as $2^{(g)(g - 1)}$ possible configurations or realizations of the network. So, modeling the probabilities of ties being present among the members of a network can be aggregated to modeling the probabilities of specific configurations of all the $(g)(g - 1)$ ties in the network. If the probabilities of these ties are all independent of one another, then the probability of a specific configuration of the network will simply be the product of the probability of each tie in the network.

Suppose the probability, p_{AB}, of the tie from A to B is independent of the probability of all other ties in the network including, for instance, the probability of a tie from A to C, (p_{AC}), the probability of a tie from A to D, (p_{AD}), the probability of a tie from C to D, (p_{CD}), and so on. Then the probability of a specific configuration of a network of ties among A, B, C, and D is given by the product of the probabilities of the individual ties in the network. However, when the probability of a tie from A to B is not independent of the other probabilities in the network, a more complex situation occurs. Then, the probability of a tie from A to B may be *conditionally dependent* on other ties in the network.

Wasserman and Faust (1994), building on earlier work, develop an approach that provides for modeling the probability of ties in a network as a function of several explanatory variables. These explanatory variables are often characteristics of the network and are computed as network "statistics." Examples would include the network's density, centralization, mutuality, and transitivity. Each of these explanatory variables can potentially influence the probability of a particular realization (or configuration) of the network. The magnitude of the influence is estimated by parameters associated with each explanatory variable.

The probability of a *specific network* realization, x, of a random network X, is given by $Pr\,(X = x)$. Note that x is a network with a specific configuration and X represents a family or distribution of networks. The probability refers to the likelihood that the specific configuration, x, be found among all the possible configurations that can be found in X.

The probability of a *specific tie* being present is given by the expression $Pr\,(X_{ij} = 1)$. This refers to the probability that the random variable X_{ij}, the relation from agent i to agent j, is 1. This probability may be conditional on the probability of other ties being present. If it is, then the conditional probability is written as $Pr\,(X_{ij} = 1)\,|\,X_{ij}{}^C$ where $X_{ij}{}^C$ refers to the *complement* of the network—that is, all ties in the network except the one from i to j.

Probabilities can vary only between 0 and 1. Explanatory variables, however, are often continuous and can range from $-\infty$ to $+\infty$. Consequently, we need to employ a transformation that allows us to map the variation of explanatory variables that have a large range to the variation of a response variable, the probability of x in this case, that has a range attenuated to be between 0 and 1. Logarithmic transformations are appropriate for this purpose.

To summarize, $Pr\,(X = x)$ is a function of several characteristics of the network and its actors, such as network density, mutuality, and transitivity. These are given by a family of terms $z_1(x)$, $z_2(x)$, $z_3(x)$, and so on. The magnitude of influence exerted by each of these characteristics on the probability of a tie being present is denoted by parameters. These are given by a family of terms θ_1, θ_2, θ_3, and so on. Since the probabilities range from 0 to 1 and the explanatory variables can range from $-\infty$ to $+\infty$, we model the logarithm of the probabilities thus:

$\log_e Pr\,(X = x)$ is explained by $\theta_1\,z_1(x) + \theta_2\,z_2(x) + \theta_3\,z_3(x)$ and so on.

Taking the inverse of logarithms, $Pr\,(X = x)$ is explained by the exponential function:

$e^{\theta_1\,z_1(x) + \theta_2\,z_2(x) + \theta_3\,z_3(x) + \ldots + \theta_r\,z_r(x)}$.

So far we have discussed, at the network level, the probability, Pr $(X = x)$, of a configuration of ties, and at a dyad level, the probability, $Pr\,(X_{ij} = 1)$, of a tie being present in the network. For computational simplicity, Wasserman and his colleagues focus on the odds ratio of a tie being present to a tie being absent. This odds ratio takes the form:

$Pr\,(X_{ij} = 1)\,/\,Pr\,(X_{ij} = 0)$

If the probabilities of a tie from i to j are conditional on other ties in the network, then the odds ratio takes the form:

$Pr\,(X_{ij} = 1)\,|\,X_{ij}{}^C\,/\,Pr\,(X_{ij} = 0)\,|\,X_{ij}{}^C$

Wasserman and his colleagues have derived a model that expresses the conditional log odds of a tie being present to a tie being absent to be equal to $e^{\theta' d}{}_{ij}(z)$. Applying the logarithmic transformation, the logarithm of the odds of a tie being present is given by:

$\theta' d_{ij}(z)$, where $d_{ij}(z) = [z(x^+_{ij}) - z(x^-_{ij})]$.

x^+_{ij} is the observed network with the tie from agent i to j forced to be present, and x^-_{ij} is the observed network with tie from agent i to j forced to be absent. Recall that $z(x_{ij})$ is a set of network statistics that influence the probability (and, by extension, the odds ratio) of a tie being present. These network statistics could include the network density, transitivity, centralization, and so on. Therefore, $z(x^+_{ij})$ represents these network statistics computed on a network that is very similar to the actual network but that forcibly includes the presence of a tie from agent i to agent j. Likewise $z(x^-_{ij})$ represents these network statistics computed on a network that is very similar to the actual network but that forcibly includes the absence of a tie from agent i to agent j.

In the following example, we will see how we can use *Blanche* to model the probabilities of a tie from i to j and at the aggregate level the probability of a particular network configuration. These probabilities are computed as a function of several characteristics of the network weighted by preassigned parameters. We will see that this approach is distinct from the deterministic and stochastic approaches reviewed earlier in this chapter.

Example of Specifying a p* Computational Network Model

The probability distribution to be associated with the "expected" value is selected on the basis of the structural dependencies that are hypothesized among the relations. For instance, a well-known hypothesis based on theories of consistency (see chapter 6 for a detailed description) is that "friends tend to be friends of friends." This would suggest a transitive triadic structural dependency, such that if A has a tie to B and B has a tie to C, the likelihood of A having a tie to C is above and beyond what may have been predicted based on (1) the prior relation between A and C, (2) the similarity in their attributes, and (3) their mutual desire to exchange resources. Thus, if there are N agents in a network, the probability distribution that is used to select a "realized" value for the communication relation between A and C must take into account all the N-2 triads in which A and C are embedded. We will refer to this approach as the *p* stochastic computational modeling approach*.

A useful way to conceptualize and visualize the theoretically hypothesized dependencies among relational ties is to use dependence graphs (Frank & Strauss, 1986). A *dependence graph* looks very similar to a social network. However, the nodes and relations in a dependence graph differ from social networks where the nodes represent agents and the relations represent relational ties. In a dependence graph, the nodes represent relational ties among the actors and the relations represent the theoretically specified structural dependencies among these network ties. For example, in a social network that involves 4 people, the number of nodes is 4 and the number of ties could range from 0, if there were no relational ties among everyone, to 6 if the ties were nondirected, or 12 if the ties were directional. The dependence graph for this social network has 12 nodes representing the 12 possible relational ties that can occur among the 4 people in the social networks. The number of ties among these 12 nodes could range from 0, if there were no structural dependencies specified among the relational ties, to 66, if each relational tie were theoretically deemed to depend on every other relational tie.

In most cases, the number of theoretically specified structural dependencies, that is, the number of ties in the dependence graph, will not be at either extreme of this range. As discussed previously, having no ties in the dependence graph assumes that each relational tie in the social network is structurally independent of every other relational tie. The presence of a tie from person A to person B is not influenced by the presence of a tie from B to A or person A to any other person C, or the presence of a tie between any two other people, D and E. This special case, where all relational ties are theoretically specified to be independent of all other relational ties, is called the Bernoulli graph distribution. Note that the tie from person A to person B can be in one of two states, 0 or 1, that is, present or absent. Assuming that there are no differences among the attributes of the people, the probability of a tie from person A to person B is simply the total number of relational ties initiated by all people divided by the number of relational ties that can be initiated by all people. Since the probability of a tie from person A to person B is specified to be structurally independent of all other ties in the network, the probability of realizing a particular network configuration of ties among the people is simply the product of the independent probabilities of each tie. This is analogous to the statement that if a coin is tossed twice and the probability of getting heads on the first toss is 0.5 and the probability of getting heads on the second toss is 0.5, the probability of getting a configuration of two successive heads is 0.25 (the product of the two independent 0.5 probabilities). Likewise the probability of getting a configuration of two successive tails, or one with one head followed by one tail, or a configuration of one tail followed by one head are each 0.25. Since these are the only possible configurations, it is not surprising that the probabilities of these four configurations total to 1, that is, if we flip a coin twice, one of these four configurations is bound to be realized.

In the case of networks, we are interested in computationally modeling the probabilities of various configurations of the network, each with its unique representation of ties present or absent. In the case described above, we are interested in the probability of finding configurations of relational ties based on the assumption of structural independence among all ties. To specify this theoretical mechanism in a computational model, in this case, structural independence among all relational ties, we specify the likelihood of network configurations that meet this criterion of structural independence. In this case the probability that the network X has a specific realization x can therefore be represented as

$$Pr(X = x) = (1/c)e^{\{kL\}}$$

where L is the sum of all ties present in the network and k is a weighting coefficient; c is a normalizing constant to ensure that the sum of the probabilities for all the possible configurations totals to 1.

The approach introduced in this section is particularly important because the assumption of structural *independence* among the relational ties as largely implausible. However, the theoretically more useful applications arise when applying this approach to modeling structural *dependencies* among relations. The simplest extension to the independence model described above is to relax the assumption of independence between pairs of agents. This extension specifies that the presence or absence of a relation from agent A to agent B is conditionally dependent on the presence or absence of a relation from B to A. The remaining assumptions of independence specified earlier are still preserved in that the ties between a dyad are independent of ties between any other dyad. Hence, these models are sometimes referred to as *dyadic independence models* (Wasserman & Faust, 1994).

In this case, each dyad can assume one of three distinguishable states: (1) no ties between the two agents, called the *null state*, (2) a tie from one agent to the other but not vice versa, or the *asymmetric state*, and (3) ties between both agents, known as the *mutual state*. Unlike the coin toss analogy stated earlier where each toss of the coin can take on two states, here the dyad can take on three states. Like that analogy, where sequential tosses resulted in "configurations of heads and tails" that were independent of one another, the configuration of a network here also assumes independence. Thus, the state of a dyad being null, asymmetric, or mutual is viewed as independent of every other dyad being null, mutual, or asymmetric. Thus, the probability distribution used to select a value for the communication relation from agent i to j takes into account the mutual structural dependencies at the dyadic level as well as the transitive structural dependencies at the triadic level. Similar extensions, though not discussed here, can be developed at the global level of the network as well.

Although this section has outlined the promise of using p^* approaches to computationally model networks, much statistical work remains to be done to in order to fully realize its potential. Until those advances have been accomplished, considerable insights can be gleaned by using the more traditional, though somewhat flawed, approaches to deterministic and stochastic modeling outlined in the preceding section. Indeed the example provided at the end of this chapter relies on a more traditional approach to computational modeling.

Strategies for Empirical Validation of Computational Models

Once a theoretically defined computational network model is specified, we must explore strategies by which the model can engage with phenomena observed in empirical contexts. From a conceptual standpoint, the most direct strategy to empirically validate a computational model is to compare the results generated from a simulation with empirically collected longitudinal network data. For instance, Contractor, Whitbred, Fonti, Hyatt, O'Keefe, and Jones (2002) developed a computational model to explain the evolution of a communication network based on multiple theories (including theories of self-interest, contagion, balance, proximity, and homophily) at multiple levels (individual, dyadic, triadic, and group levels). They also collected communication network data from a public works department at thirteen points in time over a twenty-six-month period. They used the computational model to simulate the evolution of the network, using the empirical data collected at the first point in time as the initial values for the computational model. They then compared the computationally generated network with the observed network at each of the subsequent twelve points in time. In general, they found significant correlations between the observed communication networks and the networks generated from the computational model. As would be expected of most autoregressive processes, these correlations were weaker for later points (such as time points 10, 11, and 12) than for earlier points (such as 2, 3, and 4). Further, they were able to identify specific theoretical mechanisms in the computational model (such as proximity and balance) that were more influential in predicting the evolution of the networks than other mechanisms (such as theories of self interest). Given the resource-intensive nature of collecting most social science data, the strategy of empirically validating computational data as described here is compelling but also very challenging.

Consequently, researchers have explored several alternative strategies for engaging computational network data with empirical data in ways that are less resource-intensive. Broadly, these strategies seek to discern patterns in the data generated from computational models and "validate" them by testing for similar patterns in empirical data. As such, these strategies rely on investing greater efforts in generating large volumes of computational data from "virtual experiments." Given the dramatic reduction in computational costs, this approach is far less resource-intensive than collecting equivalent empirical data. It is possible to analyze the data generated from these virtual experiments to discern patterns and hypotheses that can be validated using relatively modest amounts of empirical data.

Virtual experiments are carried out using a large number of artificial "virtual" agents as a sample. These virtual agents selectively constitute a "virtual" network. A virtual experiment provides researchers with an opportunity to create a large number of such artificial or "virtual" networks that have characteristics relevant to the researchers' theoretical questions. The term *virtual* is used here to underscore that these are not real groups identified in the field, but "virtual" groups created in the computer. It should not be confused with the use of the term *virtual* to reference teams (Lipnack & Stamps, 1997) and organizations (DeSanctis & Monge, 1999) that are geographically distributed. This distinction is important to bear in mind because it is possible, and we argue desirable, to use virtual experiments to study various characteristics and dynamics of geographically distributed virtual teams and organizations.

Virtual experiments are used to examine the transient and long-term emergent characteristics of a set of theoretical propositions. Theoretical propositions serve to explain the change in one variable (attribute or relational) based on some or all of the remaining variables in the model. The theoretical propositions are represented as a system of generative mechanisms or rules in a computational model. Each element of the generative mechanism has associated with it a weighting coefficient called a parameter. It represents the influence of a specific variable on the change of another variable. The virtual experiments are used to collectively explore and examine the changes in the levels of variables being examined in the social system.

Virtual experiments can be used to determine how the initial conditions influence the emergent characteristics of virtual agents and networks. The initial conditions of the system may be randomly varied or may be obtained from empirical field or experimental data. For instance, we may want to better understand how differences in the initial conditions may influence the dynamics posited by the theory. These initial conditions may be specified in terms of the attributes of the agents or in terms of the relations among them (see Hyatt, Contractor, & Jones, 1997; and Palazzolo et al., 2000, for examples).

Consider a computational model that seeks to describe the evolution of a network based on a theory of collective action (Coleman, 1986; Marwell & Oliver, 1993; Monge et al., 1998). In general terms, such a model seeks to predict the likelihood of collective action based on the interests and resources of the agents as well as the relations that exist among them. Clearly the likelihood of collective action will depend in part on the initial conditions of the group. For instance, a group that has agents who have a high degree of interest is more likely to accomplish collective action than a group whose agents have a lower average degree of interest. Likewise, the potential to mobilize in a group that begins as a well-connected network may differ from a group that is not so well connected. Further, a group that has agents who have a high degree of interest and are well connected will demonstrate different characteristics from groups that may have a low degree of interest and are not well connected.

It is easy to see that even with a well-specified theory, predicting the complex interactions that influence the likelihood of collective action in different scenarios over a period of time is an extremely difficult task. Without the aid of computer models it is nearly impossible to deduce hypotheses comparing the likelihood of collective action in groups that vary in terms of their levels of interest and communication. It is in such instances that conducting virtual experiments helps guide the deduction of hypotheses based on different initial conditions.

The above example illustrates how virtual experiments can be used to determine the ways in which emergent characteristics are influenced by different initial conditions. There are at least two other ways in which virtual experiments can be useful. First, they can also be used to determine how emergent characteristics are altered by *parameter changes*, that is, the relative influence of the variables on one another. The parameters that are used for modeling virtual experiments may be based on prior field and experimental empirical studies. Second, they can also be used to study the transient and long-term influence of *interventions* (such as the introduction of a new technology) on an ongoing social system. Finally, virtual experiments are an excellent approach to explore the conditions under which a system will transition from a state of chaos to a state of self-organization or move from a stable equilibrium state or a self-organized far-from-equilibrium state into a state of chaos.

Executing Virtual Experiments

For the example on collective action in the previous section, it is possible to create a large number of artificial networks each made up of artificial agents. The agents in these networks each have several attributes such as age, expertise, affiliation, and individual interest in accomplishing a certain collective action, and may be connected to other agents via several relations like communication and workflow. Different artificial networks of agents can be created, such that in different networks the agents can be assigned high or low interest in accomplishing a particular collective goal as well as high or low communication ties with other artificial agents.

To execute the virtual experiment, the network of artificial agents evolves by each agent following certain rules or generative mechanisms specified by the theory and implemented in the computational model. The changes in the attributes of, and relations among, these agents provide data, which enable the researcher to discern differences in the likelihood of collective action based on the initial conditions of the networks of artificial agents. At the end of a virtual experiment, it should be possible for the researcher to examine if, when, at what level, and for how long the various artificial networks of agents would be able to sustain collective action. Further, by aggregating and analyzing across the various artificial networks, the researcher can identify trends and patterns about how characteristics of the artificial networks such as connectedness of the communication relations or characteristics of its agents such as high or low interest influence the likelihood of collective action.

It is important that any inferences made by the researcher derive entirely from the rules or generative mechanisms in a computational model. These rules reflect the tenets of the specific theory. To the extent that the rules implemented in the model fail to reflect the specific theory, the inferences drawn by the researcher are suspect.

In many instances the verbal description of theories may lead to more than one plausible interpretation of the generative mechanisms. Hence it is often necessary to implement each of these plausible sets of generative mechanisms. One focus of virtual experiments is to examine the extent to which the underlying dynamics are robust to small changes or differences in the models. It may be the case that multiple interpretations of a model may not yield substantially different patterns of emergence. In such cases, the differences in interpretation can be considered trivial. However, in other instances, differences in interpreting a theory may lead to very different emergent patterns. In such cases, the differences will help to refine, extend, and clarify the theory.

Interpreting the Results of Virtual Experiments

In the preceding section we observed that field studies can help with the formulation and execution of virtual experiments. Results from field studies can be used to specify effect sizes that are used as parameters or weighting coefficients in the computational model. Further, field studies can provide the initial data that can then be used in the computational model to consider various possible outcomes.

In turn, virtual experiments can inform the design of field studies. They can specify under what conditions the theory is most likely to predict differences. These can help with the judicious use of resources for the collection of appropriate data at appropriate points in time. For instance, computational models may help the researcher identify the key differences in initial conditions that would theoretically lead to substantially different outcomes. This finding can assist the researcher in designing an empirical study that will focus resources on finding samples that would most clearly highlight those differences in initial conditions. As such the theoretical predictions made by the computational model would help the researcher avoid investing extensively in samples that may vary on other less critical variables. The economies that can be obtained by using computational models to pursue a more selective data collection strategy are particularly salient for social scientists interested in collecting resource-intensive longitudinal data.

Example of Specifying and Implementing a Computational Model in Blanche

We conclude this chapter by offering a ten-step example to illustrate how computational network modeling can advance our understanding of the emergence of networks from a multitheoretical, multilevel perspective. For this example, we will specify and implement a simple, theoretically motivated, computational model to examine the relationship between communication relations and attitudes among a network of actors.

Step 1: Downloading and Installing Blanche

Before specifying the computational model, you will need to download the *Blanche* software on your computer. *Blanche* works with computers running on Windows platforms. The Web site for *Blanche*, as of publication of this book, is: http://www.spcomm.uiuc.edu/Projects/TECLAB/BLANCHE/. The example described below is based on the current version of *Blanche*. The Web site contains updated descriptions as well as interactive tutorials for use with this and subsequent versions of *Blanche*.

To download the software, click on the link marked "Downloads." After downloading the file into a temporary directory, double click the file name to start the install process. By default, the program will install in a folder called *Blanche* in the Program Files folder. It is highly recommended to use this default folder to store the program, models, and data. To launch *Blanche*, go to Programs under the Start menu and click *Blanche. Blanche* integrates three major functionalities: *model building* or design, *data generation*, and *model analysis*. First, *Blanche* allows users to build a computational model based on one or more of the specific theoretical mechanisms described in this book. Second, *Blanche* can generate initial data sets based on specific probability distributions when empirical data is not available or appropriate for the model. Third, the model analysis function of *Blanche* executes the simulations specified in the model building process. In addition to the *Blanche* program, the downloaded files also include a Tutorial model named Tutorial.mdl. This tutorial is the computational model we will implement in the following example.

Step 2: Identifying Theoretical Mechanisms for the Computational Model

Before we specify and examine the implementation of the Tutorial model, let us consider briefly a couple of theories that seek to explain the relationship between communication and attitudes among a network of actors. *Contagion theories*, described in greater detail in chapter 6, suggest that individuals are influenced by the attitudes of others in their network with whom they communicate. *Theories of homophily*, described in greater detail in chapter 8, suggest that individuals seek to communicate with others who have similar attitudes to them. Each of these theories offers generative mechanisms. Contagion theories provide generative mechanisms for changes in individuals' attitudes based on communication. Homophily theories provide generative mechanisms for changes in individuals' communication networks based on their attitudes.

Step 3: Specifying the Computational Model

The computational model, Tutorial.mdl, specifies these theoretical generative mechanisms. We will begin by *reviewing* and modifying the Tutorial model using the model building functionality of *Blanche*. After launching the *Blanche* program, click on *File* → *Open* and select the Tutorial.mdl file. Make sure the Program Files\Blanche\Tutorial folder is selected before selecting the Tutorial.mdl file.

We begin by identifying the attributes and relational variables to be used in the computational model. The tutorial model contains two attributes and two relational variables. Each actor in the network has two attributes, AttX and AttY, which represent the actor's attitudes about topics X and Y, respectively. Once the Tutorial.mdl file is opened, a small window will appear that contains the two attributes and the initial data for these two attributes. Click on *View* → *Attributes (Ctrl+A)* to view the two attributes' variables. The relational variable, PComm, indicates the actor's probability of communication with each other actor in the network. The second relational variable, Comm, describes the actual presence or absence of a communication tie in particular instances between pairs of actors. To view these two relational variables, click on *View* → *Relations (Ctrl+R)*. Double click on the relational variable PComm to see details about that variable (you can also highlight it and then click the *Modify* button). You should see the following:

- The field for the *Variable Name*: PComm is the name of the variable.
- The field for the *Level* of the variable. The PComm variable is level 0. This means that it is the first variable to be calculated at each iteration. Variables that are at higher levels (1, 2, . . .) are computed after those at level 0 in consecutive order.
- The radio buttons specify whether the variable is an *attribute* variable, a *relation* variable, a *cognitive attribute* variable, or a *cognitive relation* variable. An attribute variable is a single value

for each actor. A relation is a variable specified for each pair of actors. A cognitive attribute variable is each actor's perception of some attribute for each other actor in the network. A cognitive relation is each actor's perception of some relation between each pair of actors.

- The section titled *Equation* includes a window to specify the equation (e.g., PComm = . . .) that serves as a mathematical specification of the generative mechanism for that variable and how it should change (or not) over time. Above the equation window are two smaller windows: the window on the left lists the names of all other variables that could be included in the equation; the window on the right is a list of mathematical and logical functions that can be used to specify the generative mechanism.
- The *Data File* includes a window to specify the initial data set that contains the actor's probability of initial communication with the other actors in the network.
- The *Browse* button is used to select an initial data set that may have been previously generated or collected as part of a study.
- The *Generate* button is used to generate a new initial data set.
- The *Save* button at the top right of the window saves any changes made to the model and closes the *Edit Variable* window, returning you to the main *Blanche* screen.
- The *Cancel* button does not save any changes you made and returns you to the main screen.
- The *Description* text box is a place to enter notes about the equations and variables that have been created. Any information stored in this field is for informational purposes only and has no effect on the model. Annotating and documenting the model is extremely helpful to capture and communicate the modeler's intent.
- Additionally, there are fields for advanced features (e.g., Pass Data). A pass variable indicates a variable to be "passed" to another computational model. This feature enables *Blanche* to be "docked" or connected with other computation models. *Docking* is a innovative strategy to leverage the capabilities of other computational models rather than replicate their functionality in *Blanche*. Additional information about advanced features is available in the documentation provided with the software.

Next, let us familiarize ourselves with the computational model specified by clicking on each of the two attributes and relations and reviewing the equations and descriptions associated with each of the four variables: AttX, AttY, Comm, and PComm.

The changes in AttX, an actor's attitude about topic X, is specified as follows:

$$= \text{IF SIGMA(Comm\_ij\_t)} != 0 \text{ THEN CNRAND(SIGMA(Comm\_ij\_t*AttX\_j)} / (\text{SIGMA(Comm\_ij\_t))}, 0.05, 0, 1) \text{ ELSE AttX.}$$

Conceptually, this equation indicates that AttX, the ego actor's attitude about X, is based on the sum of the attitudes about X among the alter actors with whom the ego communicates weighted by the amount the ego communicates with each of these other actors. If the ego actor does not communicate with any other actor, the ego's actor remains unchanged. SIGMA (Comm_ij_t) is the sum of ego actor i's communication with all other actors, j. The != notation is used to represent the "not equal to" function. The CNRAND function specifies that the actual attitude of the ego actor is generated from a random normal distribution with the value computed above as the mean and with a standard deviation of 0.05. That is, the actual attitude of an actor about X will be a number that will typically be between the mean value computed above and plus or minus twice the standard deviation of 0.05. Further, the value of the actor's attitude is constrained to be between 0 and 1. That is, if the value is computed to be larger than 1, it will be set at 1. Likewise, if the value is computed to be lower than 0, it is constrained to be 0. If the ego actor does not communicate with any other actor, the actor's attitude about X remains unchanged.

The changes in AttY, an actor's attitude about topic Y, are identical in form to AttX. The only difference is that AttY is substituted for AttX in the previous equation.

Finally, the changes in PComm, actor i's probability of communicating with actor j, is specified as follows:

$$= 0.9 * \text{PComm\_ij} + 0.1 * (1-\text{ABS(AttX\_i–AttX\_j))} * (1-\text{ABS(AttY\_i–AttY\_j))}.$$

This equation indicates that PComm is based on: (1) the probability of communication at the previous point in time, and (2) the similarity in their attitudes about X and Y. The more similar their attitudes, the more likely they are to communicate. If two actors are in complete agreement about their attitudes toward X and Y, then their probability of communication will be the same as it was in the previous time period. If the actors disagree somewhat in their attitudes toward X and Y, their probability of communication will be above 90% but below 100% of what it was in the preceding time period. If the two actors totally disagree on their attitudes about X and Y, the probability of communication will be 90% of what it was in the preceding time period.

The changes in Comm, the presence of a communication tie from actor i to actor j, is specified as follows:

$$= \text{If URAND(0,1)} <= \text{PComm\_ij\_t THEN 1 ELSE 0.}$$

This equation indicates that the presence of a communication tie from actor i to actor j is based on the probability of communication, PComm, from actor i to actor j at the current time t. If the probability of communication is, say, 0.70, it means that a link from actor i to actor j will occur 7 out of 10 times or 70% of the time. In order to decide whether a communication tie is present in a particular instance, we pick a random number from 0 to 1. We want any number from 0 to 1 to be equally likely to be picked at random. Hence, we use a uniform random distribution, the function URAND, to pick the number. If this random number is less than or equal to (denoted as <= in the equation above) the probability of communication, PComm, there is a communication tie, Comm, from actor i to actor j as indicated by the value 1 (0 would indicate that there is no tie between actors i and j). Note that if the probability of communication is high, it is more likely that the random number picked from a uniform distribution is less than the PComm. Hence, it is more likely that there will be a communication tie from actor i to actor j when PComm takes on higher rather than lower values. For example, say, the probability of communication from one actor to another is 0.15. Further, say, the number picked from a uniform random distribution ranging from 0 to 1 was 0.30. Since this random number is larger than 0.15, there will be no communication from that actor to the other actor. Instead, say, the number picked from a uniform random distribution ranging from 0 to 1 was 0.10. Since this value is less than 0.15, there will be a communication tie from that actor to the other actor. Since the number is picked from a uniform distribution, it is equally (or uniformly) likely that any number from 0 to 1 would be picked at random. So, in general, a low probability of communication would mean that there would be a few instances where communication would occur, while in most instances communication would not occur. On the other hand, a high probability of communication would mean that there would be many instances where communication would occur, while in a few instances it would not. This probabilistic approach to modeling the likelihood of a communication tie is distinct from a deterministic modeling approach that would specify with absolute certainty the presence or absence of a communication tie and, thus, can account for some of the random fluctuations found in among real actors.

Step 4: Selecting Research Questions to Computationally Deduce Hypotheses

After developing a computational model, it is possible to computationally deduce hypotheses about the association between two variables, taking into account the multiple theories specified—in this case, Theories of Contagion and Homophily. Analyzing the results from a computational model provides a method to deduce hypotheses based on your research questions. In this example, let us examine how initial attitudes and communication co-evolve among a network of six actors based on the mechanisms specified by theories of contagion and homophily. Here are four plausible research questions:

RQ1: Based on the generative mechanisms of contagion and homophily theories, how do the initial attitudes among a network of actors influence their subsequent attitudes?

RQ2: Based on the generative mechanisms of contagion and homophily theories, how do the initial attitudes among a network of actors influence their subsequent communication relations?

RQ3: Based on the generative mechanisms of contagion and homophily theories, how does the initial communication relations among a network of actors influence their subsequent attitudes?

RQ4: Based on the generative mechanisms of contagion and homophily theories, how does the initial communication relations among a network of actors influence their subsequent communication relations?

Step 5: Designing a "Virtual Experiment"

In order to answer these research questions, we need to "design" a virtual experiment. Like other experimental or survey research designs, we want to make sure we have data that provide us enough variability in the concepts we want to study. In this case, let us design three scenarios. That is, we want to examine what the two theories imply about the co-evolution of attitudes and communication networks when the actors in the network have the following three scenarios for initial conditions:

Scenario I:

Attitude toward topic X (on a scale of 0 to 1): Normal Distribution Mean = 0.5, Std. Dev. = 0.1.

Attitude toward topic Y (on a scale of 0 to 1): Normal Distribution Mean = 0.5, Std. Dev. = 0.1.

Probability of communication between two actors: Normal Distribution Mean= 0.5, Std. Dev. = 0.1.

In this scenario, agents in the network have moderate interest (0.5 on a scale of 0 to 1) in the two topics X and Y and moderate likelihood of communicating among themselves (0.5 on a scale of 0 to 1).

Scenario II:

Attitude toward topic X (on a scale of 0 to 1): Normal Distribution Mean = 0.5, Std. Dev. = 0.1.

Attitude toward topic Y (on a scale of 0 to 1): Normal Distribution Mean = 0.5, Std. Dev. = 0.1.

Probability of communication between two actors: Uniform Distribution ranging from 0 to 1.

In this scenario, agents in the network have moderate interest (0.5 on a scale of 0 to 1) in the two topics X and Y and a random likelihood of communicating among themselves (ranging uniformly from 0 to 1).

Scenario III:

Attitude toward topic X (on a scale of 0 to 1): Uniform Distribution ranging from 0 to 1.

Attitude toward topic Y (on a scale of 0 to 1): Uniform Distribution ranging from 0 to 1.

Probability of communication between two actors: Uniform Distribution ranging from 0 to 1.

In this scenario, agents in the network have random level of interest (ranging uniformly from 0 to 1) in the two topics X and Y and a random likelihood of communicating among themselves (ranging uniformly from 0 to 1).

Step 6: Generating Initial Data for the Computational Model

Prior to generating data for a model, you need to decide on the number of actors (nodes) that you would like to include in the virtual experiment. By default, the Tutorial model is set to six actors. However, no one is restricted to that by any means. To change the number of actors in the model, click *Simulation → Model Parameters* from the main *Blanche* window. Where it requests that you specify the number of nodes in the network, type in any number you choose. Once the number of actors has been set, you can generate the initial data for these scenarios using the *Generate* button in the *Edit Variable* window for each variable. For instance, for Scenario I you need to generate actors who have an attitude toward topic X with a mean of 0.5 and a standard deviation of 0.1.

From the *Attributes* window (click *View → Attributes* if they are not already showing), double click on the AttX variable or click on *Modify* button after you highlight the AttX variable. In the AttX *Edit Variable* window, click on the *Generate* button at the lower right part of the window. This launches the Data Generator Wizard and will create datasets for the number of actors specified above based on the parameter that you will set next.

Now it is a matter of filling out the form. First, select the number of sets of data to generate. In this example we want to examine how the attitudes and communication co-evolve for a single set of actors; so select 1 (in an actual experiment you would want to increase this number in order to run multiple simulations for analysis purposes, which is discussed further later).

Next, decide on the type of distribution you would like your dataset to possess. In this case, the distribution should be normal, but it should also be confined to between zero and one. So, select *Constrained Normal Distribution*.

Now, specify the parameters for the Constrained Normal Distribution. Select 0.5 for Mean, 0.1 for Std. Dev., 0 for Min., and 1 for Max. When you are satisfied with the settings, click the *Next* button.

On the next screen, summary statistics will appear for the data just generated. In particular, it computes the minimum, maximum, mean, and standard deviation of the data generated. The values for the mean and standard deviation will typically be close, but not exactly identical, to the parameters specified (Mean = 0.5, Std. Dev. = 0.1 in this case). Click on the *Regenerate* button, if the values are not satisfactorily close, and *Blanche* will calculate a new distribution of numbers based on the same parameters previously specified.

When you are satisfied with the summary statistics for the generated data, click on the *Save* button. Save the data for this variable using the name of the variable with the Scenario number as a suffix. The file will be saved as an ASCII text file with the extension .dat. In this case, the data should be saved as AttX1.dat. If you wish to view the actual values in the dataset, open the file in Notepad (or a similar text reader). It is easiest if you save the datasets in the same folder as your model. After saving the data, click on *Finish*. Doing so will automatically add the name of the file to the Data File field. If you choose to save your datasets in a separate folder, specify the full path and file name so that the model knows where to find the data.

Repeat the above data generation instructions for the AttY variable and the PComm variable. Note that AttY is an attribute variable, while PComm is a relational variable. Go to the main *Relational Variables* screen *(View →️ Relations* from the main screen) and double click on each relational variable to generate initial data for them. Save the data in files labeled AttY1.dat and PComm1.dat, respectively. It is not necessary to enter initial data for Comm because it is computed from the PComm variable.

Repeat the above procedure to generate data for Scenarios II and III. Save the data for AttX in files labeled AttX2.dat and AttX3.dat; AttY in files AttY2.dat and AttY3.dat, and PComm in files PComm2.dat and PComm3.dat according to the parameters explained in the Scenarios section.

Step 7: Selecting Initial Data for Specific Scenarios

After the data has been generated, it is important to go back to the *Attributes (View →️ Attributes)* and *Relations (View →️ Relations)* screens to specify the location of the initial data sets just generated. For example, to seed initial data for Scenario I:

In the *Attributes* screen, double click on AttX, or click on the *Modify* button after you highlight the AttX attribute. When you are in the AttX *Edit Variable* screen, click on the *Browse* button to the right of the Data File window. Select the AttX1.dat file from the dialog box. Alternatively, simply type in the name of the data file with the .dat extension in the *Data File* field.

Click *Save* to save changes and return to the main screen. Repeat this step for the AttY1 and PComm1 variables.

After making these changes, it is important to save the model. On the main screen of the *Blanche* program, click on *File →️ Save Model As* and enter the file name Tutorial1.

Repeat the steps outlined in this section to save models, which have initial data for Scenarios II and III in files labeled Tutorial2 and Tutorial3.

Step 8: Executing the Computational Model

You are now ready to use the model analysis capability of *Blanche* to run the simulation based on the computational model specified using the initial data created by the data generation function of *Blanche*. First, close any models that may be open on the *Blanche* screen. Next, click *File→ Open Model* and select the first model, Tutorial1, from the dialog box. To run the model, simply click on the green play button. This will allow the model to run for 99 iterations (the default setting).

If you are interested in seeing how the dynamic properties of a model play out over a longer period of time, use the *Simulation → Model Parameters* command to adjust the number of iterations to suit your interests. The multiple runs tab of the *Model Parameters* window is used for conducting a series of simulations based on the same model, but with different initial data sets. This is an advanced feature that we will not be using here; the documentation provides a detailed description on how to use these features. For now, since we only want to run the model based on a single dataset for the specified scenario, ignore this tab and click the *OK* button to return to the main screen. After you have clicked the Play button, a pop-up window will appear labeled *Simulation Progress*. For a small model such as this, it will only take a few seconds to run the simulation; thus you will only see this pop-up window for a brief moment (if you set the model to run for more than 99 iterations, then it will take longer to run the simulation). When the *Simulation Progress* window disappears, the simulation is completed.

Step 9: Viewing the Results

THE DATA

The *Attributes* window contains the attribute data, in this case AttX and AttY, for the six actors for the last (99th) iteration. The iteration number is listed at the bottom right-hand corner of the window. The blue left and right double-arrow buttons on the tool bar can be used to scroll back through the simulations iterations one step at a time. To "jump" to an earlier iteration, click *Simulation → Jump* and enter the iteration number. The data in the *Attributes* window will reflect the values for each actor for the iteration represented in the lower right. (In the *Jump* case, you will "jump" to the iteration specified and the data will reflect the number you entered.)

To view the relation data, click on *View → Relation Data* and then select the relation you want to view. (You may want to resize this window to show all the actors simultaneously.) Again, the iteration number is listed at the bottom right-hand corner of the window. The blue left and right double-arrow buttons on the tool bar can be used to scroll back through iterations, and the *Jump* feature can be used here as well.

GRAPHING THE DATA

To view time series plots of the attribute or relational data, click on *View* → *Graph*. The Graph dialog box allows you to select specific variables to be plotted. For any variable, you can plot *Values* or *Statistics*. Values refer to the actual values for that variable for each actor for either attributes or relations. Statistics refer to aggregate values of attributes (such as the attribute's mean or standard deviation) or relations (such as network density or centralization). Clicking on the + sign before each variable provides the opportunity to select specific options. After you highlight a specific variable, click on the *Add* button to include it in the plot.

So, for instance, to add the mean value of actors' attitude toward X, select *AttX* → *Statistics* → *Mean*. Click on the *Add* button to transfer this to the right-hand window in the dialog box. Repeat this procedure for *AttY* → *Statistics* → *Mean* and for *Comm* → *Statistics* → *Density*. After selecting these three variables, click the *OK* button.

You should see, in a new window, a two-dimensional plot of the values for the variables you selected (on the Y-axis) and the iterations or change in time (on the X-axis). In most cases, the scale that appears on the X-axis and the Y-axis will be appropriate for the data you are viewing. However, if you would like to focus in on a specific time period or value set, adjust this by editing the section titled *Zoom Area* at the bottom of the window:
- Set the *X-Axis* view from *a* to *b* (where *a* reflects the number of the first iteration to plot and *b* reflects the last iteration to plot).
- Set the *Y-Axis* view from 0 to 1 to reflect the range of the AttX, AttY, and the Comm variables. Alternatively, change these values if you wish to "zoom in" on a particular range.
- Click on the *Apply* button.

You should now be able to view plots of the actors' mean attitudes toward X and Y over the 99 iterations. You should also be able to view the plot of the actors' communication network density over the 99 iterations. In order to review and compare later, click on the *Copy* icon. The phrase *Copy to Clipboard* will appear if you hover your mouse over the icon. Select the *As a Bitmap* option. Click the *Close* button on the plot.

To preserve this plot for later review, paste the plot into any word processing or graphics program.

Next, click *File → Close* menu item from the main *Blanche* screen to close this model and run another model.

Repeat the procedure outlined in this section for the remaining two scenarios, using the Tutorial2.mdl and Tutorial3.mdl files. In each case *Copy to Clipboard* and paste into a word processing file the plots for the AttX, AttY, and PComm variables.

Click the *File → Exit* menu item from the main *Blanche* screen to close this model and quit the *Blanche* program entirely when you have finished.

Figures 4.2 through 4.4 illustrate the results from one execution of the computational model. Figure 4.2 presents the results of one "artificial" network that represents Scenario I as described in Step 5. The actors in this network of actors started with similar and moderately positive attitudes toward X and Y and a similar and moderate amount of communication with one another. The time series plot suggests that over time the amount of

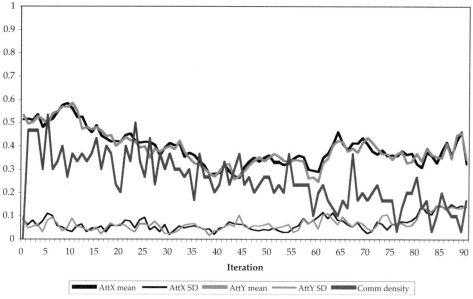

Figure 4.2

Mean communication (Comm) and attitudes (AttX and AttY) among a network of actors over time. Scenario I: Similar initial attitudes on X and Y (mean = 0.5, SD = 0.1) and a moderate initial probability of communication (PComm: mean = 0.5, SD = 0.1).

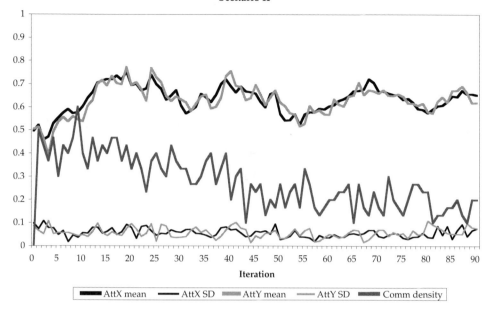

Scenario II

Legend: AttX mean · AttX SD · AttY mean · AttY SD · Comm density

Figure 4.3
Mean communication (Comm) and attitudes (AttX and AttY) among a network of
actors over time. Scenario II: Similar initial attitudes on X and Y (mean = 0.5,
SD = 0.1) and a uniform distribution in the initial probability of communication
(ranging from 0 to 1).

communication in the group decreased. Further, their positive attitudes
toward X and Y also tended to trend downward.

Figure 4.3 presents the results of one "artificial" network that represents
Scenario II. The actors in this network started with similar and moderately
positive attitudes toward X and Y. But in this scenario, their probability of
communicating with one another ranged uniformly from 0 to 1. The time
series plot suggests that the actors' attitudes toward X and Y grew more
positive, although their communication with one another declined. This
chart also includes the standard deviation for the actors' attitudes. The low
and consistent values for standard deviation suggest that while on average
the actors' attitudes toward X and Y grew more positive, their attitudes
continued to be similar to one another.

Figure 4.4 depicts the evolution of network of actors described in Scenario III. The actors in this network started with attitudes toward X and Y
that ranged uniformly from 0 to 1. In addition, their probability of commu-

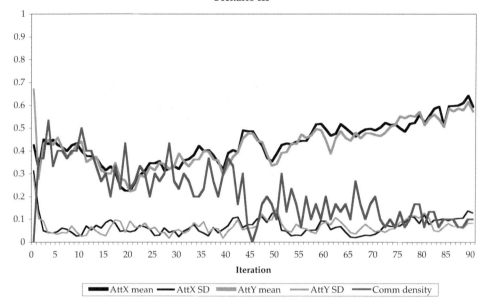

Figure 4.4
Mean communication (Comm) and attitudes (AttX and AttY) among a network of
actors over time. Scenario III: Uniform distribution in the initial attitudes on X and Y
(ranging from 0 to 1) and a uniform distribution in the initial probability of
communication (ranging from 0 to 1).

nicating with one another also ranged uniformly from 0 to 1. Here again,
the actors' attitudes trended in a positive direction, while the communication appeared to decline.

Clearly, the interpretation of these results might appear counterintuitive. Since the computational model used in this example is stochastic, one
should not expect to replicate these results exactly in future runs (but the
overall trends are likely to be similar). Further, the qualitative observations
about trends in these figures may not be statistically significant. More important, since these plots represent single instantiations of the model, it is
equivalent to examining the responses of a single "participant" in an empirical study. Hence, it is not appropriate to deduce hypotheses about the
relations between communication and attitudes based on inspecting single
instances within each of the three scenarios. The following, and final, step
describes how one can prepare to statistically analyze the results of the simulation to computationally deduce hypotheses.

Step 10: Computationally Deducing Hypotheses

In order to respond systematically to the RQs listed in this example, we would need to run these models for each of the scenarios with hundreds of data sets, which would simulate hundreds of "virtual" groups of actors. This process can be automated by:

- Generating hundreds of initial data set using the Data Generator Wizard in *Blanche*.
- Running all of these sets by specifying the number of sets using the Multiple Runs tab from the *Model Parameters* window.
- Saving the data by clicking *File → Save Data* and specifying the name of a folder in which to save the data.
- Statistically analyzing the saved data using programs such as SPSS, UCINET, or PSPAR.

The results of our statistical analysis would provide us with answers to the research questions. Since these answers are based on simulation data, they can be considered as hypotheses deduced from the theory through the process of computational modeling. The hypotheses thus deduced would need to be empirically validated. Instead of research questions, we could have begun with hypotheses that we verbally deduced from the theory. Computational modeling would allow us to "logically" validate such hypotheses. The statistical analysis of the results would allow us to assess whether computational modeling logically validates the verbally deduced hypotheses (see Palazzolo et al, 2002).

Summary

This chapter has introduced a framework for the computational modeling of networks. In it we have argued that it is difficult for people to discern the evolution of networks at multiple levels based on multiple relations. However, the generative mechanisms derived from one or more theories at multiple levels can be used to develop computational models of the network. The computational models can be deterministic or stochastic. Simple models can assume that the likelihood of ties is independent of other ties in the network. However, p^* approaches offer new opportunities to develop computational models that specify dependencies among the ties (at the dyad, triad, or global levels). Running simulations based on computational models provides the researcher an opportunity to examine the evolution of the network specified by the underlying generative mechanisms. A resource-intensive approach to validating results from these computational models is to assess how well the simulated network data compares with the empirical longitudinal network data. Alternatively, virtual experiments can be conducted by running simulations for a large number of artificial groups where the agents vary in terms of the level of their attributes, the relations among them, or even the size of the network. These experiments provide researchers an opportunity to (1) systematically observe how changes in initial conditions can influence the evolution of a network; (2) detect if changes in the values of the parameters used in the computational model influence the evolution; (3) identify if the size of the network influences the evolution of the network; and (4) assess if an intervention such as change in membership of the network or introducing a technology has a short- or long-term influence on the evolution of the network. Hypotheses deduced from these analyses can then be validated using empirical data.

Throughout this chapter we underscore the importance of relating the results of a theoretically derived computational model to empirical data. The empirical data can inform the selection of specific values for the parameters, especially in cases where the theory is not articulated at that level of precision. Further, the results of computational models can help identify key variables that serve as important "levers" in the evolution of the network. This would help direct resources to guide the judicious selection of empirical samples that maximize variances on these key variables.

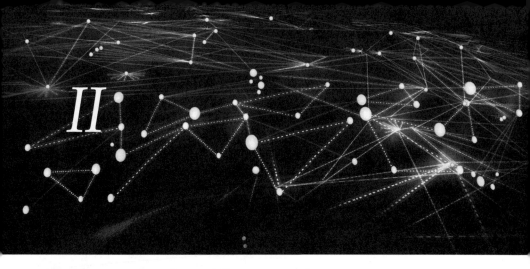

II

Social Theories for Studying Communication Networks

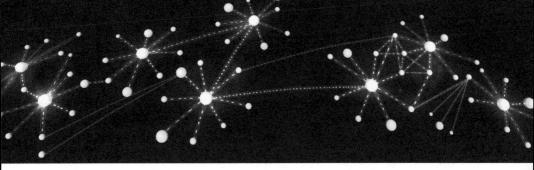

5

Theories of Self-Interest and Collective Action

Many social theories are based on generative mechanisms that are directly relevant to the emergence and coevolution of human networks. Ironically, as Monge and Contractor (2001) demonstrate, many published network studies fail to acknowledge or explicitly identify the social theories and generative mechanisms that motivate their research. In much of the rest of this book we examine a number of social theories in order to identify their generative mechanisms. These mechanisms can be used in conjunction with others to populate the multitheoretical, multilevel framework for the realization of communication and other networks described in chapter 2. For example, the theory of social capital suggests that people who try to exploit social holes will do so by seeking to improve their structural autonomy. On the other hand, theories of social exchange suggest that individuals and organizations forge ties by exchanging material or information resources. Of course, it is quite possible that people do both at the same time, thus requiring a multitheoretical framework. If this were the case, we would develop multitheoretical hypotheses. These would predict that statistical p^* analysis of observed networks would reveal significant components for structural autonomy, mutuality, and reciprocation. Further, we would expect that other possible network components, such as transitivity and cyclicality, which are generative mechanisms in other theories, would not be statistically significant in the realization of this particular observed network.

In this chapter we examine theories of self-interest and theories of mutual interest, the latter sometimes called theories of collective action, in order to identify their theoretical mechanisms. The self-interest theories are the theory of social capital, specifically Burt's theory of structural holes, and transaction cost economics. The theory of collective interest that we examine is public goods theory.

Theories of Self-Interest

Social theorists have long been fascinated by self-interest as a motivation for economic and other forms of social action (Coleman, 1986). *Theories of self-interest* postulate that people make what they believe to be rational choices in order to acquire personal benefits. The strong form of this theoretical mechanism, originally postulated by Adam Smith, is "rationality." It stipulates that people attempt to maximize their gains, or equivalently, minimize their losses. Early rational choice theorists (e.g., Homans, 1950) assumed that people who face problems, especially allocation of scarce resources, routinely examined all possible solutions. After carefully weighing the alternatives, in essence conducting a personal cost-benefit analysis, they chose the one they believed was best for them. Thus, they attempted to "maximize" their decision processes and desired outcomes.

Simon (1976) formulated a weaker form of this theoretical mechanism, which he termed "bounded rationality." *Bounded rationality* asserts that people rarely have the time, energy, or resources at their disposal to evaluate all possible alternatives. The principle of bounded rationality asserts that people *satisfice* (satisfy and suffice) rather than *maximize*, which means that people choose the first satisfactory or acceptable alternative that they find rather than exploring all alternatives and selecting the best. This chapter examines how theories of self-interest would explain the emergence of network links within and between organizations. Two theories of self-interest, the theory of social capital and transaction cost economics, that have been used to explore communication network issues are examined in this chapter.

Theory of Social Capital

The deployment of social capital (Coleman, 1988, 1990; Lin, 2001) in networks is best represented in Burt's (1992, 1997, 1998, 2001) *theory of struc-*

tural holes. This theory argues that people accumulate social resources, or *social capital*, which they invest in social opportunities from which they expect to profit. These investments are largely motivated by self-interest, defined as the return people expect to get on the social capital they invest, in short, the profits or benefits they expect to reap from their investments. As Bourdieu and Wacquant (1992) put it, "Social capital is the sum of the resources, actual or virtual, that accrue to an individual or group by virtue of possessing a durable network of more or less institutionalized relationships of mutual acquaintance and recognition" (p. 119).

Social capital is different from human capital, which represents the individual attributes and characteristics that people possess, such as intelligence, attractiveness, and prestige. Theories of human capital usually assume that people with higher amounts of valued human attributes will invest them in various settings, reaping higher personal benefits than people with smaller amounts of human capital or people with socially undesirable human capital (see Becker, 1976; Blau & Duncan, 1967). Thus, while human capital represents characteristics (or attributes) of people, social capital accrues from relationships such as those embedded in communication networks. As we have seen in our introduction to the multitheoretical multilevel p^* framework and *Blanche* modeling, network analysis focuses primarily on the network properties of the focal network. In terms of the theory described in the first part of this chapter, the focal property is social capital. However, we have also seen that attributes of people, that is, their human capital, can be an important part of generating network realizations. Thus, the multitheoretical, multilevel p^* network framework contains the potential to combine human capital and social capital explanations into a single framework.

Network holes are those places where people are unconnected in a network. Consequently, holes provide opportunities where people can invest their social capital. People invest in, fill, or exploit these holes by linking directly to two or more unconnected others, thus creating indirect ties between the people to whom they link. Filling structural holes enables investors to "broker" the relationships among the others. Naturally, this maneuver enables investors to control or, at least, influence the flow of information and knowledge among these others.

The social role of *brokers*, people who exploit holes between others, was first introduced into sociology by Georg Simmel (1955) with the concept of the *tertius gaudens*, which translates literally as "the third who benefits." Burt (1992) traces the concept to an early Italian proverb, "Between two fighters, the third benefits," and to a Dutch variation, "Between two fighters, the third laughs" (pp. 30–32). Of course, three is simply the minimal context in which a third between two others can occur. Both Simmel and Burt extend the concept to situations in which there are multiple unconnected people brokered by another. "Divide and conquer" is a well-known application of this same general principle.

Two different *tertius* situations and message strategies exist. The first occurs when two individuals are competing for the same thing. In this case, the third can communicate with the other two to play one bid off the other for the object of their desire, with one winning and the other losing, and a higher price paid to the *tertius* than if only one person wanted the object. The second *tertius* situation occurs when people want conflicting rather than the same thing. In this case, the "third" communicates as a mediator attempting to control the flow of information among the others so as to arrive at a resolution or compromise.

Investing social capital provides people the opportunity to exploit structural holes. If they are successful, they attain a competitive advantage. However, before they can attempt this they must first learn who talks with whom, in other words, the communication linkages, as well as who does not talk with whom, the communication holes or voids. To be able to invest in social holes, people must cognitively perceive both their communication networks and their "nonnetworks." Later in the book we will review work on cognitive social networks that provides individual and aggregated cognitive representations of communication networks. For now let us define the communication void network (also called the structural hole network) as represented by a set of linkages among people who do not communicate with one another. Figure 5.1 represents two such networks: the first, a communication network, and the second, a communication holes network. In each there are holes where lines exist in the other. Thus, they are the *complement* of each other.

There are multiple benefits that can accrue to those who bridge communication holes. Burt (1992, 1998) identifies three forms of information benefits: access, timing, and referrals. *Access* takes two forms: getting information that others might not get, and filtering unwanted information to avoid overload (see Dutton, 1999). *Timing* means simply being connected to the right people in the network so as to receive crucial information early enough to provide a competitive advantage. And *referrals* pertain to the fact that others who know the structural entrepreneur are likely to seek that person out for mutual benefit. Similarly, entrepreneurs are able to strategically contact selected others and bring them into important projects, thus reaping the benefits of brokering.

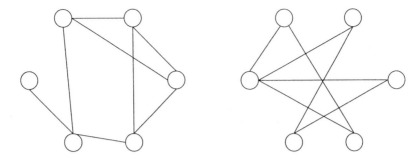

Figure 5.1
Comparing two communication networks. The structural holes in one network correspond to links in the other.

While it is important to recognize that structural holes provide social entrepreneurs with investment opportunities, like economic investments, social investments contain risks (Kahneman, Slovic, & Tversky, 1982; Kahneman & Tversky, 1979). There are no guarantees that making investments will turn a profit or produce a reward. People may lose some or all of their investments if things don't go as planned. For example, the others to which a *tertius* links may discover that they are being exploited by the *tertius* and may establish their own direct contacts with each other, thereby eliminating the "person in the middle." When this happens, entrepreneurs may fail to earn a profit, or may lose some or all of their investments, thereby incurring losses. Of course, entrepreneurs rarely put all their investments in one basket of opportunities. They are likely to invest in multiple alternatives. As yet, no research exists that provides a "balance sheet" of gains and losses accrued by multiple investments in multiple structural hole opportunities.

People who link others by filling structural holes also enhance their own structural autonomy because they can control the information that flows between others. Access, timing, and referrals also provide control in that they determine who the players will be in a network, how early they will acquire crucial information, and how they will relate to others in the network. Consequently, Burt (1992) argues that the diversity of individuals' networks is a better predictor of their social capital than network size. Researchers have examined the relationships between social capital and organizational effectiveness, efficiency, and innovation. Each area is reviewed below.

SOCIAL CAPITAL AND EFFECTIVENESS

Researchers (Burt, 1992; Benassi & Gargiulo, 1993) have argued that net-work linkages enable and constrain the flexibility, autonomy, and therefore the effectiveness, of organizational members. Consistent with Burt's (1992) argument, Papa (1990) found that organization members with diverse net-works across departments and hierarchical levels were significantly more likely to increase productivity and hasten the speed with which this change occurred. Similarly, Burt (1992) found that the occurrence of structural holes in managers' networks was positively correlated with managerial effective-ness. However, he notes that this finding was not supported among female managers and recent recruits, where effectiveness was correlated with strong ties to others. Ibarra and Andrews's (1993) research showed that individuals who were central in the advice and friendship networks were more likely to perceive autonomy in their work. Benassi and Gargiulo (1994) found that the flexibility of managers in an Italian subsidiary of a multina-tional computer manufacturer significantly impacted their likelihood of success in coordinating critical interdependencies. Managers were rated as having high flexibility if (1) their communication networks were constrained by a low level of aggregate interdependencies and consultations with others in their network, and (2) their communication network had "structural holes" among the people imposing these constraints. More recently, Burt (1997) reported that social capital is especially valuable for managers with few peers because such "managers do not have the guiding frame of refer-ence provided by numerous competitors, nor the legitimacy provided by numerous people doing the same kind of work" (p. 356). Burt (1991) devel-oped computational measures of "structural autonomy" to assess the level and distribution of constraints impacting individuals in a network. These measures are described in chapter 2.

Walker, Kogut, and Shan (1997) tested Burt's theory of structural holes at the interorganizational level. Their research showed that developing and nurturing social capital in the biotechnology industry was a significant factor in "network formation and industry growth" (p. 109). In the development of enduring relationships, firms choose to increase social capital rather than exploit structural holes. However, they argue that "structural hole theory may apply more to networks of market transactions than to networks of cooperative relations" (p. 109). In the case of market transactions, firms are not bound by structural constraints to cooperate over time and may there-fore be more inclined to exploit structural holes.

In related research, Baker (1987) found that organizations with low levels of debt improved their autonomy in managing transactions by establishing communication relationships with many, rather than one or a few, investment banks. Kosnik (1987) found that companies who had more outside directors from firms that had transactions with the focal firm had less autonomy in engaging in "greenmail," the private repurchase of company stock. Further, the CEOs of firms that had more outside directors had greater autonomy in negotiating "golden parachute" policies for the firms' top executives (Cochran, Wood, & Jones, 1985; Singh & Harianto, 1989; Wade, O'Reilly, & Chandratat, 1990).

SOCIAL CAPITAL AND EFFICIENCY

Granovetter (1973, 1974, 1982) developed a theory of the *strength of weak ties* that is related to the notion of structural holes. Conventional wisdom at the time he developed his theory held that people received most of their crucial information from others with whom they communicated on a regular basis. The communication linkages with these others were viewed as "strong ties" and these contacts typically made up their primary affiliation groups.

Granovetter studied the way people searched for jobs, expecting that they would use their strong ties to acquire information for the job search. His empirical research showed that this was not the case. Rather than using their strong ties, people employed "weak ties," their connections to others with whom they had only occasional contact. Granovetter theorized that strong ties lead to information and attitudinal similarity because everyone within the primary group communicated with everyone else, thus distributing the same information to everyone. The information that people needed to acquire jobs was unique information, which was not readily available from their strong-tie contacts. This forced them to go outside their primary groups to people with whom they communicated less frequently but who were more likely to possess scarce job-related information. From a structural holes perspective this implied that the people with whom a person has weak ties are less likely to be connected to one another, that is, these people are embedded in structural holes. Consequently, the information obtained from these weak ties is less likely to be redundant and more likely to be unique, thereby making weak ties "information rich."

The concept of *embeddedness* has also been explored by a number of scholars in related economic and communication contexts. Schumpeter (1950) first introduced the concept to describe the structure of modern markets (see Uzzi, 1997). Polanyi (1957) and later Granovetter (1985) raised this notion in the general context of "economic action and social structure," which he took to include both individuals and organizations. He observed that many theorists treated social institutions as if they were independent entities that were unconnected to other social institutions. He called this the "undersocialized" (or unembedded) view of economic action and argued that it represented one pole of a continuum on which various social theories could be placed. The other end of the continuum was anchored by the notion of "oversocialized" (or overembedded), which focused on the fact that many human and organizational economic actions were theorized to be extensively if not completely constrained by the social structures in which they are located (Piore, 1975). This view did not grant individuals or organizations much autonomy.

Granovetter argued that most organizational theory was undersocialized, a view that Biggart and Hamilton (1992) later described as the "Western bias" in organizational theory. This bias led theorists to see organizations as independent entities that operated at "arms length" under legal norms of contracts. In contrast, they argued that many Asian organizations operated in the context of important, long-standing personal networks of social and business relations that were rarely formalized via contracts. Further, they said, most Western organizations also operated this way, even if Western theorists didn't view it this way. Granovetter (1985) argued that economic theories needed to be revised to include embeddedness, and should avoid the overembedded and underembedded extremes of the continuum.

Burt (1992) argued that being embedded in a structural hole allows people to be more efficient in obtaining information. Using data from the 1985 and 1987 General Social Survey, Carroll and Teo (1996) found that the members of managers' core discussion networks were less likely to be connected to one another than members of nonmanagers' networks; consequently, nonmanagers core discussion networks were less efficient in obtaining information. As indicated above, Granovetter's (1982) research supported his theory that individuals were more likely to find jobs through their weak ties than through strong ties or formal listings. However, Lin, Ensel, and Vaughn's (1981) research showed that weak ties were only effective if they connected individuals to diverse others who could provide nonredundant information.

SOCIAL CAPITAL AND INNOVATION

The diversity of information obtained from ties has also been used to explain the introduction of innovations in organizations. Rogers (1971) identified two types of people that represented different orientations to the world: *localites* and *cosmopolites*. Localites are people whose primary orientation is to their immediate surroundings such as home, neighborhood, and community. Cosmopolites are people whose primary orientation is to the larger world, the nation, and the large city. Rogers (1971) noted that innovations were more likely to be introduced to an organization by cosmopolites, that is, people with diverse networks, including several external to the organization. In a study of the inventory and control systems manufacturing industry, Newell and Clark (1990) reported that British firms were less innovative than their U.S. counterparts in part because they were less central in their interorganizational communication networks. More recently, Burns and Wholey (1993) found that hospitals that were centrally located in an interorganizational network were more likely to be early adopters of an innovation (the matrix form of management) than other hospitals in their network. Brass (1995b) suggested that being embedded in networks with structural holes could also enhance employees' ability to provide creative solutions to organizational problems.

EXTENSIONS TO SOCIAL CAPITAL

Since the introduction of the social capital concept in the 1980s an impressive body of theoretical and empirical evidence has demonstrated its relevance. Many of the informal means by which individuals accrue social capital rely on their knowledge of the existing communication networks. As the workforce moves from being physically colocated to working in "virtual environments," it is plausible that individuals will be able to increase the scope and range of their weak ties. However, it is unclear whether electronic forms of communication such as e-mail, which provide such things as distribution lists and records of messages, make it easier or more difficult for individuals to assess the existing social structure and, in particular, the structural holes. Hence, as scholars examine the workforce of the twenty-first century, there is a pressing need for research that examines the distinctive strategies by which individuals can identify structural holes and thereby accumulate social capital in virtual organizations.

Transaction Cost Economics Theory

The second self-interest theory we examine is transaction cost economics, most fully developed by Williamson (1975, 1985). From the viewpoint of traditional economic theory, the market was the classical organizational form, where buyers and sellers communicated their intentions to each other, and where supply and demand were presumed to determine prices for goods. This is the purest form of self-interest theory (Becker, 1976). By contrast, neoclassical economics examined the development of hierarchical and vertically integrated forms as a more efficient alternative to markets (Coase, 1937), though one that is equally self-interested. However, over the past decade important changes in theories and views of organizational structuring have been occurring. A new organizational form, the network organization, has emerged as an alternative to both markets and vertically integrated organizations (Powell, 1990). This section examines these two traditional organizational forms, the market and hierarchies; the following section explores the development of the new alternative, the network form.

Classical economics was based on the idea that people can acquire the information they need to make rational choices as to when they can exchange, buy, or sell at the best price. In this sense, a market is a particular type of human organization designed to facilitate economic exchange. From a network perspective, the interesting feature of the classical view of market as organization is that each person is assumed to be connected to every other person so they know what price each is willing to pay or accept for a given transaction. Thus, in theory, markets are completely connected networks. (Bavelas, 1948, called a *completely connected* network a COMCON.) Of course, it may have been possible to connect all interested parties in small, traditional village markets, but it is essentially impossible to achieve complete or even extensive connections in the contemporary world except under special conditions.

Williamson (1975, 1985) developed transaction cost economics to explain the organization of economic activity. Whereas classical economics had focused almost exclusively on the costs of production, Coase (1937) and Williamson (1975, 1985) focused on the costs of all transactions involved in exchanging goods and services. All organizations require information and raw materials or components to manufacture goods and provide services. The information searches that organizations must undertake to determine the least costly alternatives often are fairly expensive. One alternative to the costs for repeated information searches is to acquire the means to produce the needed components within the firm. Thus, Williamson argued, organizations face a choice between buying resources from other firms and acquiring other firms in order to obtain the suppliers' goods or services at lower cost than what they could buy them for on the open market. This is frequently called the "buy or make" decision. (It is also possible to develop internal capabilities, but this is generally seen as a more expensive option since it requires a firm to develop the requisite capabilities from the start.)

Williamson viewed the first alternative as governed by market mechanisms, where an organization hunts for the best prices among the alternative supplier firms. *Transaction costs* are the expenses associated with finding information about prices and quality from the available firms and negotiating contracts. He saw the second alternative, vertical integration, as governed by *hierarchical forces*, the administrative costs, including communication, associated with managing the internal production of acquired supplier firms. Economic organizations, Williamson argued, attempt to minimize transaction costs by making a choice between markets and hierarchies. Vertical integration, he said, is the efficient alternative when the transaction costs for markets are greater than the administrative costs of production through hierarchical ownership (Zajac & Olsen, 1993, p. 133).

Clearly, the theoretical mechanism in Williamson's theory is efficient self-interest. Organizations make self-interested choices among alternative organizational forms by attempting to minimize the communication, information search, and decision-making costs associated with finding sellers in the market or acquiring suppliers. It should be clear that this mechanism is centered very much in the decision framework of individual firms. The alternative forms generated by this mechanism differ considerably in the nature of their communication networks. For example, using a market form requires firms to develop and maintain extensive external networks in order to acquire and evaluate information from suppliers, negotiate contracts, and monitor performance. Alternatively, using a hierarchical form requires organizations to develop extensive internal networks to manage the vertical integration of the acquired firms into the company and the production of the acquired firm's components.

Helper (1993) has articulated a related perspective to the "make or buy" decision as the "exit-voice" choice. Firms that choose to buy rather than make components for their own products sometimes encounter problems with their suppliers' products. When problems arise, they have two choices. They can "exit" the relationship with the supplier, terminating the connection, or they can engage in "voice" to attempt to resolve the problem.

Both of these choices have implications for communication networks. In the *exit* strategy, firms must employ extremely flexible external networks and be capable of terminating relations with nonperforming suppliers and establishing new network linkages with alternative suppliers. Of course, this strategy works only if an acceptable set of alternative suppliers exists in the marketplace. This perspective must also be recognized as explicitly explaining the dissolution of networks, rather than only their creation or maintenance. In the *voice* case, Helper (1993) argues that firms must establish "a communications system that will allow the rich flow of information which is essential to the 'let's work things out' approach" (p. 144).

She suggests that three levels of connection and information flow are possible. In the first, only market information is made available. In the second, firms may exchange information about things such as plant equipment, production processes, and finances. However, at the highest level "the information flow is characterized by 'feedback' between the customer and supplier; suggestions for improvement can be initiated by either party" (p. 144). It should be obvious that as firms move from an exit to a voice strategy they must change their communication networks and the patterns of information flow from the lowest to the highest level. Helper's research in the U.S. and Japanese auto industries suggest that the Japanese have traditionally used a voice strategy while U.S. automakers have used an exit strategy. However, that difference has been changing in recent decades as U.S. automakers have moved toward the voice strategy and developed higher levels of communication networks and information flow with their suppliers.

Gupta and Govindarajan (1991) have extended Williamson's theory to the arena of multinational corporations. They argued that governance in multinational corporations can be viewed as a network of transaction cost exchanges. Home offices govern subsidiaries by regulating three critical transaction flows: capital, product, and knowledge. The fact that subsidiaries are located in different countries creates different strategic contexts and communication problems that determine the magnitude and direction of transaction flows.

A number of criticisms have been leveled against transaction cost economics. As described earlier, Granovetter (1985) expressed the concern that most analyses of human and organizational economic behavior are clustered at either the undersocialized or the oversocialized ends of the embeddedness continuum. By contrast, Granovetter argued for the alternative embedded view that economic behavior of both individuals and organizations occurs within existing communication structures and ongoing social relations. "The embeddedness argument," he says, "stresses instead the role of concrete personal relations and structures (or 'networks') of such relations" (p. 490).

This view was supported by Uzzi's (1997) ethnographic study of twenty-three New York dress apparel firms. Uzzi conducted extensive interviews with people to identify the characteristics of embedded ties and contrast them with the features of "arms-length" ties. Uzzi discovered that embedded ties contained (1) higher levels of trust, (2) richer, more finely grained transfers of information, (3) and higher levels of problem-solving mechanisms than arms-length ties. Interestingly, he also found that his interviewees possessed both embedded and arms-length ties, suggesting that more complex types of networks than that represented by a simple dichotomy. In support of Granovetter's position, Uzzi's research showed that "embeddedness is an exchange system with unique opportunities relative to markets and that firms organized in networks have higher survival chances than do firms which maintain arm's-length market relationships" (p. 674).

The theory and research just reviewed indicate that network embeddedness is an important theoretical mechanism to account for the emergence of communication networks. The notion of embeddedness implies that network relations are mutual and reciprocal. This theoretical idea can be explored with the MTML model presented in this book. To do so a researcher would hypothesize that generative mechanisms of mutuality and reciprocity would account for a statistically significant portion of the realization of an observed network. Consistent with the MTML framework, other theoretical mechanisms would need to be specified to account for larger portions of the network realization.

Of course, there are drawbacks to embeddedness. Just as theory about the behavior of individual people or organizations can be over- or under-socialized, so can organizations be overembedded or underembedded. As Grabher (1993) says, "Too little embeddedness may expose networks to an erosion of their supportive tissue of social practices and institutions. Too much embeddedness, however, may promote a petrifaction of this supportive tissue and, hence, may pervert networks into cohesive coalitions against more radical innovations" (pp. 25–26). Similarly, Uzzi (1997), recognizing the paradox of embeddedness in the New York apparel economy, identified three conditions that turn embeddedness into a liability: "(1) there is an unforeseeable exit of a core network player, (2) institutional forces rationalize markets, or (3) overembeddedness characterizes the network" (p. 57).

Another criticism developed by Granovetter (1985) and Powell (1990) is that the dichotomy between markets and hierarchies does not exhaust all of the important organizational forms. Lazerson (1993) claims that "the false promises of vertical integration have stimulated interest in alternative organizational forms that are neither hierarchies nor markets" (p. 203). Williamson (1985, 1991) acknowledged this possibility in his discussion of alliances as hybrid forms. These, he said, exist between the other two and occur when the transaction costs associated with market exchange are too high but not high enough to justify vertical integration. However, a number of scholars, including Powell (1990), have argued that at least one alternative, the network organization, is neither market nor hierarchy in form. This argument, based on the theoretical mechanism of exchange, is discussed later in chapter 7.

Zajac and Olsen (1993) critiqued Williamson's perspective on two accounts. First, they pointed out that Williamson's analysis fails to fully account for communication and other processes encountered in the transaction costs analysis. Instead, they proposed an alternative three-stage process that they argue enables firms to determine whether they should enter into the relation. These three are the initializing stage, the processing stage, and the reconfiguring stage. During the first stage each potential partner to the relation determines its own objectives, reviews exchange alternatives, and begins exploratory contacts to examine the feasibility of the relationships. Here, Zajac and Olsen (1993) contend, the first rounds of exchange "often take the form of preliminary communication and negotiation concerning mutual and individual firm interests, and/or feasibility studies and general information exchange" (p. 139). During the second stage firms engage in both serial and parallel information processing, "interfirm communications . . . occurring between individuals at multiple organizational levels and multiple functional areas" (p. 140). The third stage, reconfiguration, consists of evaluation of the relationship followed by a return to either of the previous two stages to (1) seek relational changes or (2) reaffirm the status quo. In essence, this stage affirms the information and communication network linkages upon which the organizational relations can be established.

Research by Fulk and colleagues (1998) on the development of a cooperative research and development agreement (CRADA) provides an example of these three stages. CRADAs are legal mechanisms by which U.S. government agencies can partner with private firms to convert innovations created under federal contracts into commercially viable products. The CRADA studied by Fulk et al. included two federal agencies and four private firms that were involved in developing architectural design software. In the *initializing* stage, which lasted several months, both government agencies and private firms met regularly to explore whether a CRADA was feasible in this area and if so, whether the various partners thought it would be mutually beneficial. At the end of the first stage the potential partners concluded that they should develop a CRADA to produce the product. During the second stage, which Zajac and Olsen call the *processing* phase, the potential partners set up a series of working groups to negotiate the terms of the CRADA. During this time extensive contacts occurred among the partners, which created the basic interfirm communication networks that were necessary to organize the relationship. At the end of this time, which lasted nearly eight months, the partners signed a CRADA agreement amid considerable fanfare. In the *reconfiguration* phase, the partners began to rearrange their working relationships into ones that seemed to fit their individual interests, and one firm actually bought out one of the partners thus providing it with a competitive advantage in the context of related products. Needless to say, this action led to a reevaluation of the viability of the CRADA and an attempt to renegotiate the terms of the relationship.

The second problem that Zajac and Olsen (1993) identified is that Williamson's view of transaction cost minimization takes the perspective of only one organization. This is an error, they claimed, because a relationship has two sides, both of which should be included in any comprehensive account. Thus, they argued that transaction cost minimization from the perspective of one firm be replaced by a *joint value maximization principle* that focuses on the benefits to both or multiple firms. More specifically, they propose that "value estimations of interorganizational strategies require that a focal firm consider the value sought by that firm's exchange partner. By taking the partner's perspective, the focal firm can better estimate the value and duration of the interorganizational strategy, given that value and duration are determined interdependently by other firms" (p. 137).

It is enlightening to note that Zajac and Olsen's critique transforms the self-interest theoretical mechanism for creating organizational communication networks into one that is jointly rather than individually self-interested. Further, it attempts to maximize collective value rather than minimize individual costs. This theoretical mechanism to account for the emergence of communication networks, mutual self-interest, is reviewed more fully in the second half of the chapter.

Theoretical Mechanisms of Self-Interest

Self-interest mechanisms seek to explain an actor's attributes, based on the focal actor's configuration of relations with other actors and the attributes of these actors. Further, it seeks to explain a focal actor's decision to create, maintain, or dissolve relations with others based on the existing configuration of relations among the actors in the network and the attributes of these actors. The actors may be individuals or organizations. Let us say the focal actor is i and each other actor is j. Also, each actor i has attributes $A1_i$, $A2_i$, and so on. Based on the research reviewed above, these attributes could include an actor's efficiency in seeking information, effectiveness, productivity, creativity, innovativeness, and flexibility. Finally, the relations from actor i to actor j are $R1_{ij}$, $R2_{ij}$, and so on. The relations among the actors include communication relations, information flows, cooperative relations, trust relations, market transactions, and transaction costs.

Theories of social capital suggest that the attributes of actors may be influenced by the social capital they are able to marshal from the network in which they are embedded. In its most primitive form, attributes of actors, such as their ability to garner information will be influenced by the degree of their connectedness in the network. That is:

$$A1_i = \text{function } [\Sigma(R1_{ij})] \qquad (1)$$

where the value of an attribute, $A1$, for actor i is influenced by the sum (hence the Σ symbol) of actor i's relation, $R1_{ij}$, with all other actors j. The right-hand side of this equation reflects a network-based theoretical mechanism (the degree of each actor) that is computed at the individual (or nodal) level of analysis.

However, as discussed above, more sophisticated treatments argue that social capital does not accrue simply on the basis of the number of other actors to which the focal actor is connected. At least three extensions can be considered based on the discussion in the preceding section.

First, the range (or diversity) among the attributes of the actors with which the focal actor has relations can influence the focal actor's social capital. That is:

$$A1_i = \text{function } [\Sigma(R1_{ij}) \ast \text{Var}(A2_j)] \text{ if } R_{ij}/0 \qquad (2)$$

where the value of an attribute, $A1$, for actor i is influenced by the product of the sum of actor i's relation, $R1$, with each other actor j and the variance in some attribute, $A2$, such as the organizational demographics of the actors j connected to actor i. The right-hand side of this equation reflects a network-based mechanism, degree, which is computed at the individual or nodal level of analysis moderated by an attribute of the actor.

Second, the embeddedness of actors in the network can influence their social capital. As described in the previous section, one indicator of embeddedness is the extent to which actors are enmeshed in mutual or reciprocal ties with others. That is:

$$A1_i = \text{function } [\Sigma\{R1_{ij} * R1_{ji}\}] \tag{3}$$

where the value of an attribute, A1, for actor i is influenced by the sum of the product of actor i's relation, R1, with each other actor j and that actor j's relation, R1, in turn with the focal actor i. The right-hand side of this equation reflects the network-based mechanism of mutuality that is computed at the dyadic level of analysis. The functional relationship in equation 3 is not necessarily a linear positive relationship. Rather, the arguments in the preceding section regarding the paradox of embeddedness suggest a nonlinear inverse-U relationship, where embeddedness may enhance attributes up to some optimal level after which point they may serve as a debilitating influence.

Third, the theory of structural holes argues that social capital accrues to those who fill a structural hole, thereby enhancing their potential to serve as a *tertius* or broker in the network. That is:

$$A1_i = \text{function } [\Sigma\Sigma\{R1_{ij} * R1_{ik} * R1_{jk})\}] \tag{4}$$

where the value of an attribute, A1, for actor i is influenced by the sum of the triple product of actor i's relation, R1, with each other actor j, that actor j's relation, R1, with each other actor k, and actor i's relation, R1, with that actor k. The double summation ($\Sigma\Sigma$) symbol indicates that first one must sum across all actors k with which actors i and j have ties and then one must sum across all actors j with which actor i has ties. The right-hand side of this equation reflects a network-based mechanism, transitivity, which is computed at the triadic level of analysis. The functional relationship in equation 4 is a negative relationship. Smaller values on the right-hand side would indicate a greater ability to serve as a *tertius*.

In addition to offering theoretical mechanisms to explain actors' attributes, the theories of social capital also offer mechanisms to explain actors' relations with one another. As discussed in the previous section, theories of self-interest posit that actors strategically and selectively choose to forge ties in order to maximize (1) their ability to fill structural holes, (2) their structural autonomy, or (3) their nonredundant contacts (and hence their effective network size). While the specific formulations for these three concepts are defined in chapter 2, the theoretical mechanisms in these cases take forms, such as:

$$R1_{ij} = \text{function } [\Sigma_k \{R1_{ik} = 1 \text{ and } R1_{kj} = 0\}] \tag{5}$$

where the relation, R1, of actor i to an actor j is additively influenced by the simultaneous presence of a tie from actor i to each other actor k and the absence of a tie from each of these actors k to actor j.

Next we turn to the theoretical mechanisms in the second theory of self-interest discussed in the preceding section. In its most primitive form, transaction cost economics theory explains why organizations decide to either acquire a product or service from the market, that is, "buy" it, or create the product or service from within their own hierarchies and thus "make" it. From a self-interest perspective, it argues that the decision to forge a network relation with an outside vendor is based on a comparison of costs. The costs of forging a market relationship include, besides the cost of the product or service, the transaction costs involved in seeking information about alternative vendors and the costs that will be incurred in engaging with them via "voice," that is, in discussions and negotiations, or exiting these relations. The cost of making the product or service within the organization includes, besides the cost of the materials and labor, the administrative costs of production through hierarchical ownership. Hence from a network perspective, the theoretical mechanisms of self-interest articulated by transaction costs economics can be characterized as:

$$R1_{ij} = \text{function} \left[\{ \Sigma(R2_{ij}) \} + R3_{ij} + A1_j \} - (A2_i + A3_i) \right] \tag{6}$$

where $R1_{ij}$ is a market relation from a purchasing organization i to a potential vendor organization j, $R2_{ij}$ is the cost of communicating and information seeking on prices from each of the potential vendors j, $R3_{ij}$ is the cost of engaging (or exiting) a relation with vendor j; $A1_j$ is the cost of the product charged by vendor j. These costs collectively represent the potential costs of a market transaction. $A2_i$ is the administrative costs of production through hierarchical ownership, $A3_i$ is the cost of the materials and labor. Together they represent the potential costs of production through hierarchical ownership. According to the network mechanisms outlined in transaction cost economics, the likelihood of an organization initiating a market relation with another organization is greater if the total costs incurred to buy are lower than the total costs entailed in making the product or service.

Summary

The first half of this chapter has explored two theories representing how self-interest motivations influence human behavior. The theory of social capital emphasized that structural holes in communication networks and other social structures provide people with opportunities to invest their human resources by linking with people who are not themselves linked. In return for brokering this relationship, they expect to earn a profit on their investment. This suggests that control over the flow of information between people is a crucial element in the operation of communication networks, an insight that organizational entrepreneurs frequently and actively exploit. Structural autonomy is a theoretical generative mechanism inherent in social capital and specifically in structural holes theory that accounts for the occurrence of network realizations containing structural holes.

Transaction cost economics explores the information, communication, and other coordination costs involved in organizational production. Firms seek to minimize these costs when making decisions about how to organize. Frequently, they discover that the search for best market buys is more expensive than organizing hierarchically. However, the cost to administer hierarchies is also often quite high. Theoretical generative mechanisms that account for markets are exchange and reciprocity. Hierarchy is a generative mechanism that could be used in a multitheoretical, multilevel p^* analysis to account for vertical organizational structure.

An alternative form of organization, the network organization, can reduce both information search costs in markets and administrative costs of hierarchies. Network organizations seek to maximize joint value of exchanges with the organizations to which they are linked. Network organizations are themselves embedded in larger networks of organizational relations that make economic behavior neither over- nor undersocialized. Network organizations are discussed in chapter 7 under network exchange theory.

Mutual-Interest and Collective Action Theories

Collective action is a term that has been broadly applied to a wide range of phenomena in the social sciences (Coleman, 1973, 1990), including organizational communication. Its main focus is on "mutual interests and the possibility of benefits from coordinated action" (Marwell & Oliver, 1993, p. 2) rather than on individual self-interests. While a number of different views on collective action exist, we focus primarily on public goods theory. There are three reasons for this. First, public goods theory is the most fully developed collective action theory to date. Second, several communication scholars have recently employed the theory to examine communication public goods (Fulk, Flanagin, Kalman, Monge, & Ryan, 1996; Monge, Fulk, Kalman, Flanagin, Parnassa, & Rumsey, 1998). Finally, recent work has focused quite explicitly on the role of communication networks in creating and maintaining the public good. In the second half of this chapter we review the logic of public goods forms of collective action and examine its implications for communication networks.

Public Goods Theory

Samuelson (1954) first articulated public goods theory to explain the economics of collective ownership such as public bridges, parks, and libraries, entities to which everyone in a given society is entitled. It was this focus on the collective that distinguished this new branch of economics from the traditional realm, which pertains to private ownership, commonly called private goods. Samuelson sought to explain how the people in a collective could be induced to contribute to the creation and maintenance of public domain collective goods. Public goods are sometimes referred to as "commons," as in "owned in common," meaning by everyone. This notion goes back to the early English practice of building towns around a common area. Homes were owned privately, but the open land in the middle was owned collectively and called the town commons. Today, a number of features of the world are considered to be "commons" in that they are owned by the citizens of the world rather than by specific nations. These include the atmosphere, the oceans, space, and the Arctic/Antarctic regions (Bock, 1998).

Public goods are defined by two characteristics: *impossibility of exclusion* and *jointness of supply* (Hardin, 1982; Olson, 1965; Samuelson, 1954). Impossibility of exclusion simply means that everyone in the collective has an equal right to use the public good. No person or classes of persons can be excluded from using it. This condition holds even if people do not contribute to its creation and/or maintenance. Thus, everyone can use a public library, even those who do not earn enough money to pay taxes or in other ways contribute to its creation or ongoing costs of operation.

Jointness of supply means that one person's use of the good does not deplete or diminish the level of the good for other users. The idea here is that public goods are not consumable in the traditional sense, or are continuously renewed so that the good is of as high quality for subsequent users as it is for early users. In reality, most public goods display crowding or overuse, which can diminish the quality of the good for subsequent users. Books get lost, bridges get crowded, and parks get trashed, which lowers the quality of each over time. Thus, public goods tend to be thought of in terms of relative jointness of supply (Chamberlain, 1974; Head, 1972). Public "bads" also exist.

Smog is a prime example of a public bad to which almost everyone contributes by driving cars, burning leaves, and running factories. As a result, all who contribute to the smoggy air and live in smoggy areas are forced to breath the polluted air. Ironically here, "free riders" are essentially forced to breath the public bad air even if they don't contribute to it.

It is important to point out that public goods are not confined to public institutions; they frequently exist in the context of private organizations. For example, the Sematech alliance among semiconductor manufacturers was designed to improve the competitiveness of the U.S. industry infrastructure. All domestic, private semiconductor firms benefited even if they didn't contribute, because the results of the collective research was available to all (Browning, Beyer, & Shetler, 1995).

Public goods theory focuses on how to convince people to contribute to the creation and/or maintenance of public goods so that everyone in the collective will be able to use them. In the first half of the chapter we saw that individual interest theorists argue that people will contribute only to those things that are in their own self-interest. The first condition of a public good, impossibility of exclusion, guarantees everyone rights of equal access to public goods even if they do not contribute to making or preserving them. Self-interest theories claim that people attempt to get things for the lowest price possible. One implication of this view is that making no contributions to the creation or maintenance of the good while having free use of it is the best possible arrangement for people. It follows that people will be motivated to use public goods without contributing to them, a situation that is known as the "free rider" problem. Olson (1965) pointed out that since most societies have norms that encourage people to contribute to public enterprises, visibility is a crucial factor in whether people engaged in free riding. He argued that people are much less likely to free ride if their behavior is public enough to be seen by relevant others.

Marwell and Oliver (1993) described four components of the processes by which individuals in a collective could be convinced to contribute to a public good. They identified features of the good, characteristics of the individuals, characteristics of the collective, and the action process itself. We briefly review each in the following four sections.

FEATURES OF PUBLIC GOODS

Public goods theory has traditionally been used to study different material public goods such as roads, parks, and libraries. Recently, however, Fulk,

Flanagin, Kalman, Monge, and Ryan (1996) and Monge, Fulk, Kalman, Flanagin, Parnassa, and Rumsey (1998) have applied this perspective to interactive communication public goods. The two public goods they identified were connectivity and communality provided by communication and information systems. *Connectivity* as a public good refers to the ability to contact other members of the collective. If everyone can reach everyone else, the communication system is fully connective. If people can contact only some others in the collective, the communication system is only partially connective. There are two aspects to connectivity. *Physical connectivity* is the physical infrastructure that provides direct contact. If every employee in a firm has a computer and an e-mail account so that anyone can send e-mail messages to anyone else, the organization has full physical connectivity. Of course, the fact that people can connect does not mean that they necessarily will. Hence, *social connectivity* is the actual use of the physical connections made available by physical connectivity.

Communality occurs when people collectively store and share information providing a communal source for data and knowledge. Typically, this common pool of information resources is created by people and deposited in knowledge repositories such as shared databases and electronic bulletin boards. Communication public goods have other characteristics, of course. Two are *divisibility* and *concentration*. A library is composed of nearly equal divisible increments called books. Even a small library has value, though perhaps not as much as a larger one. Bridges and buildings, on the other hand, are "lumpy" in that neither has much value until they are complete. Finally, information public goods vary considerably in terms of concentration. Some are widely distributed while others are narrowly clustered.

CHARACTERISTICS OF INDIVIDUALS

Four characteristics of individuals that are critical to the creation of a public good are interests, resources, benefits, and costs. *Interests* refer to the fact that people see potential benefits in the creation of the good. For example, they would like to be able to borrow books without having to purchase them, or they would like to be able to cross the river quickly by bridge rather than having to take a slow-moving ferry. *Resources* refers to the fact that people possess various things they could contribute to the creation of the public good. Most often this refers to money, but time, energy, expertise, and similar capabilities also qualify as resources. For example, people often have books that they can contribute to libraries and some may even have land that they could contribute to the creation of a park. Others may contribute their time to work as docents to help keep the park as pristine as possible or to stack books returned to the library.

When a public good is created, people in the collective acquire the *benefits* of the good. Of course, these benefits are not distributed equally, as people value the good differentially. For example, some people may go to a library daily while others not at all. And, those who contribute to the public good incur the *costs* of their contributions. Finally, one or more people, usually with some leadership ability, must come forward to champion the good to others in the collective. Marwell and Oliver (1993) call this person the organizer, and Aldrich (1999) describes her or him as the entrepreneur.

GROUP CHARACTERISTICS

Characteristics of the group extend the focus on individual interests and resources to the collective. At the group level, both interests and resources are likely to vary considerably across the members of the group, from little or none to a large amount. Of course, if no one has any interest in or resources to contribute to the formation of the public good, it is highly unlikely that it will be created. On the other hand, if the collective has high interest and extensive resources, creation of a public good should be relatively easy. Neither of these cases occurs very often in everyday life. Olson (1965) argued that *interest* and *resource heterogeneity* were important collective features because they increased the likelihood that at least some individuals in the group had sufficient interests and resources to generate the good. At the extreme, one benefactor can provide the public good for all, as when an individual donates all the land for a public park or endows a university building or program.

THE ACTION PROCESS

The action processes focus on things that produce the contributions that make the good possible. Obviously, having a well-regarded champion or entrepreneur can make a big difference. But Oliver (1993) and Markus (1990) also pointed to the concept of *critical mass* as a determining factor in generating public goods. Critical mass refers to the fact that in most collective processes people decide to contribute at various times. Typically, a few people with high interest and at least some resources make the initial contributions. As interest spreads among the members of the collective interest grows and more people make contributions. Critical mass is the point in this process where enough interest is generated that the majority of people contribute to the realization of the good. When this happens, the process becomes self-sustaining and the good is usually achieved.

Original formulations of public goods theory treated individuals as if they were isolated and independent of others making similar decisions. Oliver (1993), Markus (1990), and Marwell and Oliver (1993) have criticized this view and emphasized the importance of the network of relations in which people are embedded. They argued that communication networks provide several mechanisms that influence the realization of the good. First, networks contain cliques, which are likely to be organized around some set of interests or resources that are relevant to the good. It is easier to reach others with similar interests within cliques than it is to reach people in other cliques. So, if someone with even modest resources decides that they want to organize the collective to produce a particular good, they can begin by contacting those to whom they are tightly connected. Since these people are also likely to have resources, they know they have a good chance to generate sufficient initial resources to get things going. Further, cliques can facilitate organizing in other ways. Since information flows quickly in groups with strong ties, an organizer can exploit this fact by using weak ties to contact leaders within other cliques, thus enlisting their assistance in promoting the good within their cliques. Results of computer simulations by Marwell and Oliver (1993) demonstrated that network cliques facilitated realization of the good.

Marwell and Oliver (1993) observed that organizers often do not have the resources to reach everyone in the network. Reach is here defined as the number of people who organizers can contact. Consequently, they must be selective in whom they contact. *Selectivity* is the ability to communicate with those members of a network "who are most likely to contribute or who are likely to contribute the most" (p. 130). Obviously, selectivity requires information about how interested each person is in seeing the collective good established, as well as their personal level of resources as an indicator of how much each is able or likely to give. This also suggests that the organizers need to know how to craft messages that focus on maximizing benefits for contributors while minimizing their costs.

The optimal strategy for organizers is one of "high reach and high selectivity" where everyone in the network is contacted, particularly those with the highest interests and resources. Unfortunately, the costs of this option are often prohibitive. Of course, "low reach and low selectivity" is the worst strategy as few would be contacted and they are unlikely to be the ones who would be able to contribute sufficiently to provide the good. This leaves "high reach and low selectivity" and "low reach and high selectively" as the two viable strategies available to organizers. The high reach, low selectivity option implies an impersonal, mass-mediated approach to getting messages to network members. The low reach, high selectivity option implies a personalized, communication networks approach. Interestingly, computer simulations showed that *both* strategies were effective in mobilizing resources. Marwell and Oliver's (1993) work also showed that the extent to which people are interconnected in communication networks increases their willingness to support the collective good. Marwell, Oliver, and Prahl (1988) showed that centralization and resource heterogeneity in the network influenced aggregate contributions to a collective good.

The Tragedy of the Commons and Communication Dilemmas

Hardin (1968) described the *tragedy of the commons* as a conflict between individual and collective interests, the two theoretical orientations described in this chapter. The English (and colonial New England) village commons were collectively owned by all landowners in the town and available for a variety of uses including grazing of cattle. Like all natural resources, the commons has a natural carrying capacity, in this case, the level of grazing that can occur while preserving the commons. Exceeding this capacity begins to degrade the commons, and if carried to extreme, will eventually destroy it. Hardin observed that town farmers were individually motivated to add an additional animal to the grazing field even if the carrying capacity had been reached because they stood to individually gain from the extra cow and the negative impact seemed minimal. However, if all the farmers were similarly motivated and if each did in fact add an extra animal, the collective outcome was the destruction of the common (Schelling, 1978). Hardin saw this collective negative outcome, which happened as a by-product of individually self-interested motives, as a tragedy because no one intended it to occur yet all contributed to it.

Situations that contrapose the interests of the collective such as groups or organizations against the self-centered interests of its members are known as *social dilemmas* (Dawes, 1980; Kalman, Monge, Fulk, & Heino, 2002; Messick & Brewer, 1983; Rutte & Wilke, 1992; Van Lange, Liebrand, Messick, & Wilke, 1992). Social dilemmas account for a host of societal problems involving publicly shared goods and resources, in terms of both undersupply (e.g., public television; roads and bridges; national defense) and overconsumption (e.g., overfishing; overpopulation; environmental pollution). The tragedy of the commons is a particular case of an over-consumption social dilemma.

Bonacich and Schneider (1992) employed the term *communication dilemma* to specify a social dilemma that impedes communication (Kalman, Monge, Fulk, & Heino, 2002). In organizational settings, communication dilemmas exist whenever the organization's interests demand that people share discretionary information but their individual interests and desires for individual-level gain motivate them to withhold it instead. The particular characteristics of a work setting, communication system, and the activities where people use shared information all influence where and how communication dilemmas impinge on an organization's interests (Fulk, Flanagin, Kalman, Monge, & Ryan, 1996; Monge et al., 1998). But the overall structure of incentives to individuals may ultimately inhibit discretionary information sharing.

Bonacich and Schneider (1992) recounted an especially striking case where a communication dilemma led in 1986 to the destruction of the U.S. space shuttle *Challenger*, killing all the astronauts aboard. Behind the mechanical failure and explosion lay a failure by senior managers at NASA in the months preceding the accident to share enough safety-related information. This could be traced back to their conflicting responsibilities toward the whole NASA organization and the more parochial interests of their separate divisions. Thus, the organizational structure, including formal and informal networks, failed to provide the necessary information to the right people at the right time to prevent the tragedy.

Kalman, Fulk, and Monge (2001) indicate that there are two principal ways to resolve communication dilemmas (Kerr, 1992). On the one hand, management can mandate that people use it. For example, consider the shared databases that companies seek to achieve in knowledge management systems, such as the "lessons learned" repositories to which all persons are expected to contribute their experience. Organizations could reward people who contribute information and/or penalize people who do not. Rewards and penalties that depend only on a person's individual cooperation (e.g., to contribute information) create selective incentives. They guarantee benefits to contributors independent of collective success in making good use of the shared information. Effective selective incentive schemes perform a *cooperation-contingent transformation* on the situation (Kerr, 1992), such that participants no longer perceive a social dilemma because the collective's demands on their behavior coincide with their individual interests. However, the use of selective incentives places a burden on organizations, rather than individuals, to ensure that the rewarded behaviors closely match the organization's needs.

One problem with using selective incentives to create information products is the difficulty of adequately specifying desirable performance (Kalman et al., 2001). The organization could require people to consult a specific set of information sources or follow a predetermined set of procedures to ensure that information is accurate and timely. Automated information systems might even help to centralize control over the assumptions people use in formulating information contributions (Simon & Marion, 1996). Yet, the content of information products is intrinsically uncertain prior to delivery, and all the more so when people must exercise on-the-scene judgment to generate this content. Especially difficult to program are information products whose purpose is to innovate, to challenge assumptions, or to revise how work is done. For such nonroutine information sharing, users need discretion to obtain, process, and share information based on what they judge will advance organizational, group, and private interests (Daft & Weick, 1984).

An alternative way to resolve social dilemmas is to create a *public-good transformation* (Kerr, 1992). This transformation occurs when participants place increasing value directly on collective gain. Once the collective gain available is valued sufficiently in comparison to other individual gains, conflicts of interest disappear. An example of such a transformation is found in the classic work of Sherif (1958), who demonstrated that creation of a common enemy united conflicting individuals into a collective-oriented group with a common goal.

An advantage of the public-good transformation is that contributors use their own best judgment to maximize collective gains. A public-good transformation should support participative, self-managed uses of shared databases. It avoids difficulties that attend selective incentives because it shifts responsibility for evaluating and regulating individual performance from management to each information producer. One mechanism that supports a public-good transformation is identification with the collective by individual participants.

Empirical studies using collective action as an explanatory mechanism fall into two categories: the group's mobilization as indexed by its level of involvement, and the adoption of innovations. Research using a collective action mechanism has focused on the effect of the network on mobilization, as well as more specifically the adoption of innovations. Each of these two areas is discussed below.

Collective Action and Mobilization

In a retrospective study of the insurgency in the Paris Commune of 1871, Gould (1991) underscored the importance of examining multiple, partially overlapping networks in explaining the insurgents' solidarity and commitment. He found that the "importance of neighborhood identity and the patterns of arrests showed that pre-existing social ties among neighbors and organizational ties formed by the National Guard worked together to maintain solidarity in the insurgent ranks. . . . Cross-neighborhood solidarity could not have emerged in the absence of enlistment overlaps that linked each residential area with Guard units in other areas" (p. 727). Applied to organizational contexts Gould's findings suggest that collective action is less likely to succeed if the informal networks are structured so as to be either isomorphic with preexisting formal ties, or if they "completely cut across pre-existing networks" (p. 728). From a MTML perspective, this suggests that multiplexity would serve as a generative mechanism for collective action networks.

Knoke (1990, p. 5) examined the determinants of member participation and commitment among 8,746 respondents from 35 "collective action organizations," professional associations, recreational clubs, and women's associations. He discovered that "member's involvements in their collective action organizations are enhanced by extensive communication networks that plug them into the thick of policy discussions, apart from whatever degree of interest they may have in particular policy issues" (p. 185). At the interorganizational level, Laumann, Knoke, and Kim (1985) found that health organizations central in their industry's communication networks were more involved in mobilizing efforts on national policy issues affecting their domain. However, this relationship did not hold up among organizations in the energy industry. Laumann et al. (1985) concluded that centrality in a communication network was more important in predicting collective action in industries that were less institutionalized. Thus, centrality might serve in a MTML model as a generative mechanism to create network realizations in less institutionalized industries but not in more institutionalized ones. If both types of industries were included in such a study, level of institutionalization could be included as an attribute of the firms, thus enabling it to be treated as a generative mechanism in the MTML model.

Collective Action and the Adoption of Innovations

Theories of collective action have also been used to examine the adoption of new interactive communication technologies (Markus, 1990; Rafaeli & LaRose, 1993). Valente (1995, 1996) has examined the effect of "threshold" (Granovetter, 1978) on adoption behavior. The *threshold* is defined as the number of other adopters that must be present in a person's network before the person decides to adopt. The threshold levels of individuals determine whether the group as a whole can achieve the critical mass necessary for rapid and widespread collective action. Rice, Grant, Schmitz, and Torobin (1990) examined the role of critical mass in predicting the adoption of an electronic mail system at a decentralized federal agency. They found that individuals' decisions to adopt the system were contingent on the decisions of others with whom they reported high levels of task interdependence. Further, individuals' adoption decisions were influenced by the extent to which they valued the potential communication with others who were likely to be accessible via the new system. Gurbaxani (1990) used an adoption model based on critical mass theory to predict with considerable accuracy university adoption of the BITNET computer network. At the interorganizational level studies on governmental and nonprofit organizations have examined the role of network ties in overcoming obstacles to collective action (Mizruchi & Galaskiewicz, 1994; Rogers & Whetten, 1982; Turk, 1977).

Extensions to Collective Action Theory

The interest in examining the emergence of networks from a collective action perspective is relatively recent. It has been used persuasively to address issues of mobilization and the adoption of innovation. However, unlike some other mechanisms discussed in this book, the theoretical developments in this area have not been well complemented by empirical evidence. Scholars have proposed mathematical models, and some have carried out simulations. However, few of these efforts have been empirically validated.

In addition to the need for more empirical research, there are also some conceptual issues that continue to be advanced. First, the conceptualization of information technologies, such as discretionary databases, as public goods (Fulk et al, 1996) suggests that collective action theories can offer a more sophisticated explanation of the emergence of organizational networks, extending their present use to study the adoption of technologies in organizations. Discretionary databases are the message repositories that link knowledge suppliers and consumers, thereby creating connective and communal networks of individuals who share knowledge domains.

Second, in addition to the utility of a collective action perspective to study the adoption of technology-based public goods, Lessig (2001) argues that it also enables, and can possibly constrain, the future development of such public goods. Using the brief, but tumultuous, history of the Internet, Lessig (2001) notes that in its early days, the design of the Internet "Commons" occurred at three layers—content, code, and physical—which fostered further creativity and innovative development of these three layers. However in recent years, Lessig cautions, some of this creativity and innovation has been directed toward the development of an architecture at all three levels that is not conducive to further creative development of the Commons. His example underscores the paradox that when the public good is itself a network, networks designed to maximize short-terms benefits of collective action might intentionally or otherwise impede the sustainability of collection action in the network over the long term.

Third, there is potential for the application of network approaches to the conceptualization of free-riding and its role in collective action. Collective action by groups is based on an underlying premise of social control. Homans's (1974) cohesion-compliance hypothesis predicts that group members are able to enforce social control on one another by exchanging peer approval for compliance with group obligations. Flache and Macy (1996) argue that under some circumstances members may choose to offer peer approval in exchange for peer approval rather than compliance from others. Using computer simulations of groups' networks, they observed that in these situations groups might reach a high level of cohesion that is not accompanied by a higher level of compliance or better group performance. Contrary to Homans's cohesion-compliance hypothesis, Flache and Macy (1996) concluded that "peer pressure can be an effective instrument for blocking compliance, especially in groups in which the cost of compliance is high relative to the value of approval" (p. 29). Oliver (1980) describes this phenomenon, where social control is directed toward the maintenance of interpersonal relationships at the expense of compliance with group obligations, as the "second-order free-rider problem."

Theoretical Mechanisms of Mutual-Interest and Collective Action

Like theories of self-interest discussed in the first half of this chapter, theories of mutual interest and collective action are also based on an economic calculus. However, unlike theories of self-interest, the calculus here seeks to jointly maximize the interest of the collective rather than those of the individual. As discussed in the preceding section, theories of collective action seek to explain the conditions under which actors will be sufficiently mobilized to contribute to a collective public good.

Let us define $R1_{ij}$ as the relation indicating the contribution that actor i will make toward a public good, j. In this network, the actors can be either one or more human agents (that is, individuals or aggregates of individuals) and one or more nonhuman agents (that is public goods, such as databases). The attribute $A1i$ is used to defined a node as either a human (say, a value of 1) or nonhuman agent (say, a value of 0). If actor i is a human agent and j is a nonhuman agent, let us define $R2_{ij}$ as the value that actor i ascribes to this public good. If this public good were a database, as discussed in the preceding section, $R2_{ij}$ would depend on how useful and unique this database was to actor i. Of course the value of the public good, $R2_{ij}$, would itself be a function of the total provision of the public good. If the public good were a database, the provision of the public good would indicate the completeness, accuracy, and currency of this database. Hence, the provision of the public good could be represented as some function of $\Sigma R1_{kj}$, the sum of the contributions by all human agents k to the public good, j. Finally, in making this contribution toward a public good j, actor i will incur certain costs, $R3_{ij}$. Presumably, the costs of actor i's contribution, $R3_{ij}$, will be offset by the potential benefits that actor i can gain from the public good. Adapting Marwell and Oliver's (1993) production function, if actor i is a human agent and actor j is a nonhuman agent, the theoretical mechanism for collective action could be represented as:

$$R1_{ij} = R2_{ij}[\Sigma_k R1_{kj}] - R3_{ij} \tag{7}$$

That is, actor i's contribution to a public good is based on the net difference between the value of the public good to actor i (which in turn is a function of actor i's perceived provision of the public good, j) less the costs incurred by the actor in contributing to the public good. This network mechanism describes the relation of each human agent to a nonhuman agent based, in part, on a global measure of the relations by human agents to a nonhuman agent.

It should be evident from the preceding section that equation 7 represents the classical theoretical mechanism posited by the theory of collective action. However, as was also previously discussed, this classical perspective was premised on the flawed assumption that communication did not occur among the human agents. Let us define $R4_{ij}$ as a communication relation among human agents, that is, $R4_{ij}$ takes on a value of 0 if either actor i or actor j is a nonhuman agent. Based on our earlier definition of the attribute A1, indicating an agent as human or nonhuman, $R4_{ij}$ is valid only when $(A1_i)(A1_j) = 1$. Then, a first response to this flawed assumption, as discussed in the previous section, would be to modify the theoretical mechanisms thus:

$$R1_{ij} = \{R2_{ij}[\Sigma_k R1_{kj}] - R3_{ij}\} * (NC[R4]) \tag{8}$$

where NC[R4] refers to a global property of the communication network, R4, such as its network centralization. That is, the contribution by actor i to the public good is moderated by the overall centralization of the communication network among the human agents. All else being equal, an actor is more likely to contribute to the public good if the actor is part of a more centralized communication network.

Summary

The second half of this chapter has explored the logic of two collective action theories with an emphasis on the communication networks that comprise the collective. Public goods theory demonstrated that network connectedness influences who contributes to the creation and or maintenance of public goods, including the communication public goods of connectivity and communality. People who are resource rich, who have significant interests in seeing the good realized, and who have extensive ties to others who have similar interests and resources are the ideal targets for communication campaigns by people who wish to mobilize collective goods. An important tie between self-interest and mutual-interest theories arises in the case of communication dilemmas. These occur when contributing to the collective good is at odds with self-interest, as may occur in contributing to a discretionary database. The resolution to communication dilemmas is a public goods transformation that aligns individual interests with collective ones.

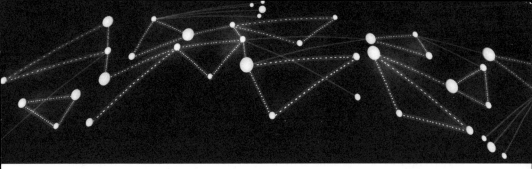

6

Contagion, Semantic, and Cognitive Theories

This chapter reviews theory and research that seeks to explain the emergence of communication networks based on individuals' cognitions about other people and the relations among those individuals. *Contagion* theories seek to explain networks as conduits for "infectious" attitudes and behavior. *Semantic* theories attempt explanations on the basis of networks that map similarities among individuals' interpretations. Theories of *cognitive social structures* examine cognitions regarding "who knows who" and "who knows who knows who," while theories of *cognitive knowledge structures* examine cognitions of "who knows what" and "who knows who knows what." Finally, *cognitive consistency* theories explain how networks are understood on the basis of individuals' cognitions of consistency or balance in their networks. The remainder of this chapter discusses each of these areas and their extensions.

Contagion Theories

Contagion theories are based on the assumption that the opportunities for contact provided by communication networks serve as a mechanism that exposes people, groups, and organizations to information, attitudinal messages, and the behavior of others (Burt, 1980, 1987; Contractor & Eisenberg,

1990). This exposure increases the likelihood that network members will develop beliefs, assumptions, and attitudes that are similar to those of others in their network (Carley, 1991; Carley & Kaufer, 1993). The contagion approach seeks to explain organizational members' knowledge, attitudes, and behavior on the basis of information, attitudes, and behavior of others in the network to whom they are linked. Rogers and Kincaid (1981) refer to this as the *convergence* model of communication.

Theories that are premised on a contagion model, at least in part, include social information processing theory (Fulk, Steinfield, Schmitz, & Power, 1987; Salancik & Pfeffer, 1978), social influence theory (Fulk, Schmitz, & Steinfield, 1990; see also Marsden & Friedkin, 1993), structural theory of action (Burt, 1982), symbolic interactionist perspectives (Trevino, Lengel, & Daft, 1987), mimetic processes exemplified by institutional theories (DiMaggio & Powell, 1983; Meyer & Rowan, 1977), and social cognitive and learning theories (Bandura, 1986). Fulk (1993) notes that these constructivist perspectives "share the core proposition that social and symbolic processes produce patterns of shared cognitions and behaviors that arise from forces well beyond the demands of the straightforward task of information processing in organizations" (p. 924). She also points out that the mechanisms offered by these theories differ not so much because of conflicting premises as because the theories focus on different aspects of the social construction process. As we shall review later, these theories also differ in the level of analysis at which they operate. For instance, while social information processing theory typically explains contagion among individuals, the mimetic processes proposed by institutional theories explain behavior at the interorganizational (or institutional) level.

Theoretical Mechanisms of Contagion

Contagion mechanisms have been used to explain network members' attitudes as well as behavior. Erickson (1988) offers a comprehensive overview of the various theories that address the "relational basis of attitudes" (p. 99). She describes how various network dyadic measures such as frequency, multiplexity, strength, and asymmetry can shape the extent to which others influence individuals in their networks. Moving beyond the dyadic level of network contagion, she also describes cohesion and structural equivalence models that offer alternative, and in some cases complementary, explanations of the contagion process. Contagion by cohesion implies that the attitudes and behaviors of the others to whom they are directly connected influence network members. Contagion by structural equivalence implies that others who have similar structural patterns of relationships within the network influence people.

In its primitive form, contagion mechanisms seek to explain a focal person's attributes, based on the attributes of other people in the network and the relations through which these other individuals' attributes "infect" the attributes of the focal person. As discussed previously, the actors in the network may be individuals, groups, organizations, industries, associations, nations, and so on. Let us say that the focal person is i and each other person is j. The attributes of the actors may be their attitudes, behaviors, or other practices. Each actor i has attributes $A1_i$, $A2_i$, and so on. The relations among the individuals may be advice relations, reporting relations, a more general communication relation, or some surrogate measure of communication such as joint membership in clubs, trade associations, boards of directors, or alliances. Finally, the relations from actor i to actor j are $R1_{ij}$, $R2_{ij}$, and so on.

A contagion mechanism would propose that the value of a focal person's attribute, $A1_i$, is contagiously influenced by the values of the attribute, $A1_j$, of other people in the network. Further, the extent to which the focal person is influenced by each other actor's attribute is determined by the strength of the focal person i's relation, $R1_{ij}$, with each of the other actors, j. In other words, the contagion mechanism would posit that the value of the focal actor i's attribute $A1_i$ is a function of the combined influence of each other actor j's attribute and the relation, $R1_{ij}$, between i and j. The primitive form of the contagion mechanism can then be represented as:

$$A1_i = \text{function } [\Sigma(R1_{ij})(A1_j)] \tag{1}$$

where the value of an attribute for person i is contagiously influenced by the sum of the value of that attribute $A1_j$ for each other person j weighted by person i's relation, $R1_{ij}$, with that actor j.

This primitive representation of the contagion mechanism can then be extended in several ways. First, the value of person i's attribute, $A1_i$, may be contagiously influenced by additional attributes, $A2_j$, $A3_j$, and so on, of other people j. For instance, an actor's satisfaction at work, $A1_i$, may be influenced by the satisfaction, $A1_j$, of other people, j, as well as by their level of expertise, $A2_j$. In this case the contagion mechanism can be represented as:

$$A1_i = \text{function } [\Sigma(R1_{ij})(A1_j) + \Sigma(R1_{ij})(A2_j)] \tag{2}$$

Second, the value of person i's attribute, $A1_i$, may be contagiously influenced by multiple relations such as an advice relationship, $R1_{ij}$, and a reporting relationship $R21_{ij}$. One such contagion mechanism can be represented as:

$$A1_i = \text{function} \left[\sum(R1_{ij})(A1_j) + \sum(R2_{ij})(A2_j) \right] \tag{3}$$

Third, the value of person i's attribute, $A1_i$, may be contagiously influenced by properties of relations such as reciprocity (discussed in chapter 2). For instance, the extent to which actor i's attributes are contagiously influenced by each other agent j may depend on whether an $R1_{ji}$ relation reciprocates the relation, $R1_{ij}$, to that other person. That is, it depends on the values of the $R1_{ij}$ and the $R1_{ji}$ relations. Substantively this would imply that an actor i would be more influenced if the actor has a mutual two-way, rather than a one-way, relationship with another actor j. This contagion mechanism can be represented as:

$$A1_i = \text{function} \left[\sum(R1_{ij})(R1_{ji})(A1_j) \right] \tag{4}$$

While reciprocity is a property of one relation, an agent i's attribute could also be contagiously influenced by the properties of multiple relations, such as multiplexity. For instance, an agent i may be contagiously influenced by other actors if, and only if, they have both task, $R1_{ij}$, and social, $R2_{ij}$, communication relations to these other actors, j. In that case the contagion mechanism will be represented as:

$$A1_i = \text{function} \left[\sum(R1_{ij})(R2_{ij})(A1_j) \right] \tag{5}$$

While the above examples illustrate contagion via cohesion, contagion can also occur via the structural equivalence between each actor i and each other actor j. As defined in chapter 2, structural equivalence is one such measure of the extent to which each person i has similar patterns of one or more relations with each other individual j. Hence unlike cohesion, contagion by structural equivalence posits that each actor i is contagiously influenced by another actor j to the extent that both actors i and j have similar relations to all the other actors in the network. As such, it is a dyadic measure that is based on the two agents' relations with all the agents in the network. The contagion mechanism for structural equivalence can be represented as:

$$A1_i = \text{function} \left[\sum(SE_{ij})(A1_j) \right] \tag{6}$$

where

SE_{ij} is the structural equivalence between actors i and j on one or more relations.

The contagion mechanisms described so far do not take into account a person's resistance or inertia to contagious influences. For instance, consider someone's decision to adopt a new technology. People who are technological novices experiencing a high level of uncertainty may be more likely to be contagiously influenced by other actors than those who have greater confidence in their own judgment. A contagion mechanism that takes into account individual variability in vulnerability can be represented as:

$$A1_i = \text{function} \ [V_i\Sigma(R1_{ij})(A1_j)] \qquad (7)$$

where,

V_i is person i's vulnerability to contagion.

In addition to variations in resistance to contagion, in some cases the effect of contagion may not be realized until a certain threshold level is reached. That is, the social influence of other people, j, may need to reach a certain threshold level before the focal actor i decides to, say, adopt an innovation. Further, this threshold level may be different for different people, that is, some actors may have a lower threshold for adopting a technology than others. A contagion mechanism that incorporates threshold values is:

$$A1_i = \text{function} \ [T_i - \Sigma(R1_{ij})(A1_j)] \qquad (8)$$

where,

T_i is actor i's threshold for changing the value of their attributes, and R and A are relevant relations and attributes, as discussed above.

Empirical Research Using Contagion Mechanisms

An impressive body of empirical research at both the intraorganizational and interorganizational level is based on the contagion mechanism. At the intraorganizational level, studies have proposed a contagion mechanism to explain (1) general workplace attitudes, (2) attitudes toward technologies, and (3) organizational behavior such as turnover and absenteeism. Researchers have also used contagion to explain interorganizational behavior. Each of these topics is reviewed on the following pages. The section concludes with suggestions for extensions of organizational research based on a contagion mechanism.

General workplace attitudes

Several studies have examined the extent to which contagion explains individual attitudes in the workplace. Friedkin's (1984) early research showed that educational policymakers were more likely to perceive agreement with others who were either in the same cohesive social circle or were structurally equivalent. Walker (1985) discovered that members of a computer firm who were structurally equivalent were more likely to report similar cognitions about means-ends relationship of product development. And Rentsch (1990) found that members of an accounting firm who communicated with one another were more likely to share similar interpretations of organizational events.

Goodell, Brown, and Poole (1989) use a structurational argument (Poole & McPhee, 1983) to examine the relationship between communication network links and shared perceptions of organizational climate. Using four waves of observation over a ten-week period from an organizational simulation, they found that members' communication networks were significantly associated with shared perceptions of the organizational climate only at the early stages of organizing (weeks two and four). In another study comparing the cohesion and structural equivalence mechanisms of contagion, Hartman and Johnson (1989, 1990) found that members who were cohesively linked were more likely to have similar levels of commitment to the organization. However, those who were structurally equivalent were more likely to have similar perceptions of role ambiguity in the workplace. Pollock, Whitbred, and Contractor (2000) compared the relative efficacy of three models that seek to explain an individual's satisfaction in the workplace: the job characteristics model (Hackman & Oldham, 1976), the individual dispositions model (Staw & Ross, 1985), and the social information processing model (Salancik & Pfeffer, 1978). Using data from the public works division of a military installation, Pollock et al. (2000) found that employees' satisfaction was significantly predicted only by the social information processing model, that is, by the satisfaction of friends and communication partners in their social networks, but not by the characteristics of their jobs or their individual dispositions.

Attitudes toward technologies

Several researchers have examined the extent to which contagion explains organizational members' attitudes toward technologies. Drawing on social information processing theory (Salancik & Pfeffer, 1978) and social cognitive theory (Bandura, 1986), Fulk and her colleagues (Fulk, Schmitz, & Ryu, 1995; Schmitz & Fulk, 1991) found that organizational members' perceptions and use of an electronic mail system were significantly influenced by the attitudes and use of the members' supervisors and five closest co-workers. Further, Fulk (1993) found that social influence was even more pronounced in more cohesive groups. The attitudes and use of other members in their communication networks significantly influenced individuals' attitudes and use of an electronic mail system. This effect was attenuated, but persisted, even after she controlled for the effect of the work group's attitudes and use on each group member.

Rice and Aydin's (1991) research showed that hospital employees who communicated with one another or shared supervisory-subordinate relationships were more likely to share similar attitudes about a recently introduced information technology. Rice, Grant, Schmitz, and Torobin (1990) found that individuals' use of e-mail in a decentralized federal agency was predicted by the use of the technology by others in their communication network. Further, groups of individuals who communicated more strongly with one another were more likely to share similar e-mail usage patterns.

Using longitudinal data from a federal government agency, Burkhardt (1994) found that individuals' attitudes and use of a recently implemented distributed data processing computer network were significantly influenced by the attitudes and use of others in their communication network. She found that individuals' perceptions of their self-efficacy with (or mastery of) the new technology were significantly influenced by those with whom they had direct communication, which is the theoretical mechanism of contagion by cohesion. However, individuals' general attitudes and use of the technology itself were more influenced by the attitudes and behaviors of those with whom they shared similar communication patterns, that is, contagion by structural equivalence. Burkhardt also found that the contagion effect was higher for individuals who scored higher on a self-monitoring scale.

Extending this line of longitudinal research on contagion effects, Contractor, Seibold, and Heller (1996) conducted a study comparing the evolution of the social influence process in face-to-face and computer-augmented groups. They found that group members initial influence on each others' perceptions of the structures-in-use (i.e., the interaction norms enacted during the meeting) was high in the face-to-face condition, while group members using group decision support systems (GDSS) started out with low levels of social influence on one another. However, the difference between face-to-face and technologically augmented groups was only transient. By their third meeting members in all groups heavily influenced each other's perceptions of the structures-in-use. While the preponderance of research has focused on similarity in attitudes based on contagion, Bovasso (1995) reports results from a process he calls *anticontagion*. In a study of managers at a large multinational high-tech firm, Bovasso (1995, pp. 1430–1431) found that "individuals who perceive themselves as strong leaders are influenced by peers who do not perceive themselves as strong leaders" and vice versa.

BEHAVIOR THROUGH CONTAGION

Several network studies have utilized a contagion explanation for organizational members' behaviors, including voluntary turnover, absenteeism, job-seeking, socialization, and unethical behavior. Krackhardt and Porter (1986) found that employees voluntarily quitting their jobs were more likely to be structurally equivalent to one another than those who remained. However, they found that employees who were absent were more likely to be cohesively connected with one another through friendship ties. They suggested that decisions about turnover were more closely related to individuals' roles in the organization and hence, members were more influenced by others in similar roles. On the other hand, decisions about absenteeism reflected norms in the organizations that were communicated through cohesive friendship ties. In a more recent study, Feeley and Barnett (1996) examined employee turnover at a supermarket and found that both social influence and structural equivalence networks predicted the likelihood of employees leaving the organization. Kilduff (1992) studied graduate business students' job-seeking behavior and found that students' decisions to interview with particular organizations were influenced by the opinions communicated to them by others in their friendship networks. The contagion effect was more pronounced for students who reported being high self-monitors. Zey-Ferrell and Ferrell (1982) reported that employees' self-reported unethical behavior was better predicted by their perceptions of their peer behavior than either their own beliefs or those of top management. Research on organizational socialization (Jablin & Krone, 1987; Sherman, Smith, & Mansfield, 1986) has also identified newcomers' positions in their new communication networks as a predictor of their assimilation into the organization.

The contagion mechanism has also been used to explain behavior at the interorganizational level. Organizations can link to other organizations in many ways. Useem (1983) describes how organizations use director interlocks as a tool to scan their environments. These linkages are important because they provide the opportunity for communication and the exchange of ideas, practices, and values. Both the formal activities surrounding the board meetings and the informal activities and acquaintance ties that are created enable people to discover how things are done in other organizations. In these and similar interorganizational studies the opportunity to communicate afforded by the existence of linkages is viewed as more important than specific message content.

Consistent with Useem's (1983) view, much of the more recent literature examines the mechanisms by which organizations utilize these linkages to transfer organizational practices and structural forms. Davis (1991) found that Fortune 500 corporations were more likely to adopt the "poison pill" strategy to defend against corporate takeovers if their boards had directors from organizations that had already adopted a similar strategy. Haunschild's (1993) research showed that the number and types of corporate acquisitions undertaken by their interlock partners significantly influenced the number and type of takeovers attempted by firms. Likewise, her 1994 research demonstrated that *acquisition premiums* (p. 406), the price that a firm pays to acquire another firm over the market value prior to the takeover announcement, are similar to those that their partner firms paid for their acquisitions. Other research by Palmer, Jennings, and Zhou (1993) has shown that firms are more likely to adopt a multidivisional form when they are linked to corporations that have already adopted that form. Similarly, Burns and Wholey (1993) found that a hospital's decision to adopt a matrix management program was significantly predicted by the adoption decision of other local hospitals with high prestige and visibility. Goes and Park (1997) found that hospitals that were structurally tied to other hospitals in a multihospital system were more likely to adopt innovations, and Westphal, Gulati, and Shortell (1997) found that contagion also explained the adoption of total quality management (TQM) practices in the organization. However, they observed that early adopters of TQM were more likely to use the other early adopters in their medical alliance network to clarify their functional understanding of TQM. The early adopters were therefore more likely to customize the program to their organizational needs. In contrast, late adopters were more likely to seek out other adopters in their alliance network to determine the legitimacy of using TQM. Hence the late adopters were more likely to adopt the TQM program without any customization. Stearns and Mizruchi (1993) found that the type of financing used by a firm, short- versus long-term debt, was influenced by the types of financial institutions to which it was linked by its board of directors, commercial bankers versus representatives of insurance companies. However, the embeddedness of an organization's board of directors has a somewhat counterintuitive influence on the selection of its CEO. Khurana (1997) found that Fortune 500 companies whose boards of directors were well embedded into the system of interlocking directorates were *less* likely to choose an outsider as a CEO because "a high level of embeddedness is likely to constrain actions rather than facilitate them" (p. 17).

Interlocking directorates are only one of several possible mechanisms for linking organizations. Organizations are likely to be linked to bankers, attorneys, accountants, suppliers, and consultants, all of whom serve as conduits for the flow of information between organizations. Basing their arguments on the mimetic processes articulated by institutional theory (DiMaggio & Powell, 1983), Galaskiewicz and Burt (1991) and Galaskiewicz and Wasserman (1989) discovered that contribution officers who were structurally equivalent in an interorganizational corporate network were more likely to give charitable donations to the same nonprofit groups than those who were cohesively linked. Mizruchi (1989, 1992) found that organizations that were structurally equivalent in the interorganizational network were more likely to have similar patterns of political contributions. Baum and Oliver (1991) showed that increased ties to legitimating institutions significantly reduced the likelihood of failure among new organizations. And, in a ten-year study, Goes and Park (1997) found that hospitals linked to their institutional environments through industry and trade associations were more likely to adopt innovations in an effort to gain legitimacy. This effect was even more pronounced when the hospital industry entered a turbulent phase after introduction of two regulatory events in 1983. Interestingly, these findings are similar to those obtained under predictions from exchange and resource dependency theories, though obviously generated by a different theoretical mechanism.

Extensions to Contagion Theories

Contagion theories offer by far the most common theoretical mechanisms for studying the emergence of networks. The notion of a network as a labyrinth of conduits for information flow lends itself to theoretical mechanisms based on contagion. Perhaps because of their preponderance in the network literature, studies based on contagion theories of networks have also been widely criticized. Some of these critics advocate greater specificity in the network mechanisms that facilitate contagion. Others criticize the studies for not taking into account the content of the messages that flow through these networks. In particular, they argue that the content of messages may actually inoculate against contagion. Both of these point to important limitations of current research on contagion and suggest interesting avenues for future research. They are discussed in greater detail below.

While network researchers frequently invoke contagion theories, they often fall short of articulating specific mechanisms and network models by which individuals, groups, and organizations influence each other's actions and behaviors (Contractor & Eisenberg, 1990; Marsden & Friedkin, 1994; Rice, 1993a). There are four recent attempts to articulate mechanisms that make the contagion process more theoretically specific and comprehensive for communication networks.

First, Krackhardt and Brass (1994) note that the contagion processes described by social information processing theory must over time lead to an equilibrium wherein everyone in the network will eventually converge in their attitudes or actions. They note that this conclusion undermines the very premise of social information processing theory that seeks to explain the variation in people's attitudes based on their differential exposure to social information. Krackhardt and Brass (1994) suggest that the *principle of interaction*, which is assumed by contagion theories, needs to be augmented by a second contagion mechanism, the *principle of reflected exclusivity*. The principle of interaction states that greater interaction leads to greater similarity in attitudes. By contrast, the principle of reflected exclusivity states that "the degree of influence person j has on person i's evaluation . . . is inversely proportional to the amount of time person j spends with all others" (Krackhardt & Brass, 1994, p. 219).

Second, Krassa (1988) advocates the inclusion of members' threshold levels in a social influence model. In its simplest form, the threshold is the number of others that people must be influenced by before succumbing (Granovetter, 1978). Individuals' thresholds could be a function of the intensity of their opinion and their aversion to the risk of being socially isolated. Krassa (1988) uses computer simulations of a contagion model to demonstrate the effects of people's threshold distributions on their opinions.

Third, Rice (1993a) has argued that a network contagion model of social influence should also take into consideration the ambiguity of the situation. Drawing on research by Moscovici (1976), Rice (1993a) argues that people are more vulnerable to social influence by contagion when confronted with ambiguous, or novel, situations. Based on this argument, Contractor, Seibold, and Heller (1996) hypothesized that groups using new collaboration technologies (a novel situation) would be more likely to influence each other's perceptions of the medium than groups in a traditional face-to-face meeting. However, they found that social influence was actually greater in face-to-face groups, perhaps because the novelty in this case was associated with the very medium used to socially influence one another.

Fourth, in an attempt to extend the current debate surrounding the relative efficacy of contagion via cohesion versus structural equivalence, Pattison (1994) argued for a closer examination of automorphic or regular equivalence in addition to mechanisms based on contagion by cohesion and structural equivalence. Unlike structural equivalence, which in its strict operationalization is defined as two individuals having identical network links to the same others, regular equivalence is defined as two people having similar patterns of relationships, but not necessarily with the same others (White & Reitz, 1989). Pattison (1994) argues that people who are regularly equivalent are more likely to have similar social cognitions because "cognitive processes may directly involve the individual's perceptions of his or her social locale" (p. 93). In a longitudinal study of students in an undergraduate class, Michaelson and Contractor (1992) found that students who were regularly equivalent were more likely to be perceived as similar by their classmates than those who were structurally equivalent.

To summarize, the network mechanisms implied by contagion theories must be refined to (1) include the principle of reflected exclusivity and thereby avoid an inevitable homogenization of attitudes or behavior; (2) include threshold levels that vary across actors; (3) calibrate the importance of social influence based on the uncertainty of the situation; and (4) consider automorphic or regular equivalence, in addition to cohesion and structural equivalence, as influential mechanisms for contagion.

As mentioned at the start of this section, network scholars using contagion theories focus attention on how actors may be "infected" by the attitudes and behaviors of other actors. Contagion models are hence, ironically, very much like the now discredited *hypodermic needle model* of communication, where mere exposure to messages is seen as "injecting" message attitudes and values into recipients. It is true that in some cases an idea or set of ideas is so powerful that people adopt it en toto. It is also true that people sometimes resist advocated message positions no matter how reasonable or appealing. But these cases are fairly rare. Missing in the contagion model is the typical ebb and flow of messages through networks that typifies human communication. In human interaction messages containing differing ideas, values, and attitudes flow back and forth among people as they negotiate resolutions. The most typical outcome is modifications to the different positions each person held at the outset of the contagion process, modifications that influence both contaminators and the contaminated.

Historically, some theorists argued that the best way to counter message infection was to isolate people from exposure to the infecting message. From a network perspective, this consists of isolating all or part of the network from contact with the infecting part of the network. Of course, as totalitarian governments have learned in recent decades, the proliferation of communication technologies makes this a difficult strategy to implement. Other theorists argued that the most effective strategy is to counterinfect people with intense countermessages. This suggests flooding the network with messages containing counterarguments. This may work in some cases, but certainly not in others.

McGuire (1966) developed an intriguing theory that focuses on how actors may become resistant to contagious messages. Extending the biological analogy of contagion he developed *inoculation theory*. Medical inoculation works by injecting people with small amounts of an infecting agent, often one with reduced virulence, to give the body's natural immune and defense system the opportunity to build up its own resistance. If successful, the body will develop sufficient resistance so that it will reject contagion even from a full-strength infecting agent.

McGuire argued that an analogous process to that of medical inoculation worked with people's responses to contagious messages. If they were exposed to a weakened form of the arguments or persuasive tactics in a message, and perhaps some mild form of counterarguments, they would begin to think of the reasons why the arguments were flawed. Given enough time, they would build their own internal defenses against these infecting arguments. Thus, when they were subsequently exposed to messages that contained these types of arguments, they would be resistant to the attempts to get them to change their attitudes or behavior. In short, they had been inoculated and contagion processes would fail.

Theory and research on message strategies has several implications for contagion theories of networks. First, some parts of the network will receive infecting messages but it is likely that others will not. This suggests that the flow of messages will create subnets, cliques, or groups within the network that are defined by those who receive particular virulent strains of messages and those who do not. Second, being connected to others in the network does not imply that contagion will necessarily occur. Other factors, including the development of resistance via the flow of inoculation messages, come into play that help to determine who will be influenced by contagion processes and who will not. Third, some people in the network may receive inoculation messages while others will not. This suggests that in addition to those who receive infecting messages and those who do not, there is another bifurcation of the network into those who are inoculated and those who are not.

Semantic and Cognitive Theories

The contagion mechanisms discussed in the previous section focused on the extent to which others who were linked to individuals via cohesion or structural equivalence influenced their attitudes and actions. These studies explain attitudes and behavior based on individuals' actual interactions. Researchers have employed four concepts to gain insight into the structure of individuals' cognitions: semantic networks, knowledge structures, cognitive social structures, and cognitive consistency. These areas are discussed in greater detail below.

Semantic Networks

The concept of semantic networks was introduced into the organizational communication literature by Monge and Eisenberg (1987) in response to calls for a more systematic treatment of message content in networks. It should be noted that Monge and Eisenberg's (1987) use of the phrase "semantic networks" is inspired by, but distinct from, its use for over two decades in the cognitive science, social psychology, and artificial intelligence literatures where it refers very specifically to networks generated from texts or other documentary artifacts, where words or ideas are the nodes and the relations exist among those words or ideas. These networks are often generated through automated software programs typically using some artificial intelligence or neural network techniques. This more traditional definition of the term *semantic networks* is illustrated in Carley and her colleagues' text analysis (Carley, 1986, 1997; Kaufer & Carley, 1993), Danowski's (1982) word network analysis of computer bulletin-board messages, and Woelfel and his colleagues' Galileo system and CATPAC analysis (Woelfel & Fink, 1980, Woelfel & Stoyanoff, 1993). More recently, Corman, Kuhn,

McPhee, and Dooley (2002) have developed centering resonance analysis of organizational messages, which they used to analyze the media coverage of key concepts and protagonists associated with the terrorist attacks against the United States on September 11, 2001.

The essential variation Monge and Eisenberg (1987) offered on the more traditional conceptualizations of semantic networks was a focus on the shared interpretations that people have for message content, particularly those messages that comprise important aspects of an organization's culture, such as corporate goals, slogans, myths, and stories (Dunn & Ginsberg, 1986; Fiol, 1989). Monge and Eisenberg (1987) argued that asking people to provide their interpretations of one or more significant communication messages, events, or artifacts could be used to create semantic networks. While traditional semantic networks focused primarily on textual documents, the variation proposed here was on people's interpretations of these texts. Of course, these interpretations could also be considered texts and analyzed using the more traditional semantic networks approaches described above. Monge and Eisenberg (1987), on the other hand, proposed a content analysis of members' responses to provide categories of interpretation. Linkages could then be created between people who share similar interpretations. The resultant network articulation provides a picture of the groups of people who share common understandings, those who have idiosyncratic meanings such as isolates, and those who serve as liaisons and boundary spanners between the various groups.

THEORETICAL MECHANISMS OF SEMANTIC NETWORKS

An early motivation for the study of semantic networks was to disambiguate the relationship between communication and shared understanding. A semantic networks perspective challenges the received view that communication does, or even should, lead to shared interpretations and understanding. The focus therefore is on understanding how other relations among individuals may influence a semantic relation, which is a relation of shared interpretations among people. While contagion models were concerned with the ways in which networks contagiously influence the attributes of actors in the network, semantic network models are concerned with the pattern of these shared attributes. In particular, they are concerned with those attributes of people that index their interpretations.

One must first define a semantic relation, S_{ij}. Consider person i's interpretations of an organization's mission statement. These interpretations could be coded into several categories, M1 (say, quality), M2 (say, profit-ability), and so on. These categories would serve as attributes for each individual. If actor i interpreted the mission as including quality, then actor i's attribute, $M1_i$ would be assigned a value of 1. Further, if actor i did not interpret the mission as including profitability, then $M2_i$ would be 0. Of course, these attributes could take on values other than just zero or one depending on the extent to which actor i considered these attributes to be part of the mission. A semantic relation, S_{ij}, is then defined as the degree to which two people share dissimilar interpretations on one or more such attributes of the mission. That is:

$$S_{ij} = (M1_i - M1_j) + (M2_i - M2_j) + \ldots \quad (9)$$

Of course this measure of dissimilarity in shared interpretations can be converted to provide a measure of similarity. With S_{ij} thus defined, several properties of the semantic network can now be examined. In a semantic network, a densely connected network is one in which the members are closely tied to each other through several shared interpretations. A semantic network clique would represent a collection of people who share common interpretations with one another but not with others outside the clique. Further, an actor who has high degree centrality in the semantic network is one who shares interpretations in common with many other individuals. An actor who has high betweenness centrality in a semantic network shares, at least some, interpretations with other actors who may not directly share those interpretations. For instance, this could be a person who manages multiple interpretations across multiple "interpretive" groups.

The generative mechanisms proposed by a semantic networks perspective posit the extent to which the semantic relations within a network can be explained at the individual, dyadic, and the global levels of analysis. A semantic tie between actors i and j may be explained by nodal attributes of actor i or actor j. As we shall see, research suggests that these attributes could include tenure in the organization or level in the hierarchy. The semantic tie may also be explained at the dyadic level by shared attributes. For instance, two people may be more likely to share interpretations if they are at the same level in the hierarchy or belong to the same gender. Also at the dyadic level, other relations (such as a communication or a reporting relation) between the two individuals may influence the semantic tie. An extension here would include structural equivalence measures based on these other relations. As discussed in the review of empirical research below, similarity in shared interpretations between two agents is explained by the extent to which they are structurally equivalent or have similar patterns of communication (Contractor, Eisenberg, & Monge, 1997). Finally, at the network level, the presence of a semantic tie may be influenced by a global measure of the semantic network. For instance, interpretive theories of "strong culture" (Deal & Kennedy, 1982) would argue that the overall density of the semantic network might influence the likelihood of a semantic tie. These various theoretical mechanisms at the actor, dyad, and global levels can be represented as:

$$S_{ij} = \text{function } [A_i, A_j, (A_i - A_j), R_{ij}, SE(R)_{ij}, \Sigma 2S_{ij}/(N)(N-1)] \qquad (10)$$

where,

A_i and A_j are the attributes of persons i and j,

$A_i - A_j$ represents shared attributes between i and j,

R_{ij} is another relation (such as communication) between persons i and j,

$SE(R)_{ij}$ is the structural equivalence of the communication relation between i and j, and

$\Sigma 2S_{ij}/(N)(N-1)$ is a measure of the density of the semantic network among N people. ΣSij are the observed ties among the N people. And $(N)(N-1)/2$ are the possible ties among N people. Hence, this formula reflects the density of the observed to the possibilities.

EMPIRICAL RESEARCH ON SEMANTIC NETWORKS

With respect to empirical studies of semantic networks, Lievrouw, Rogers, Lowe, and Nadel (1987) used four methods to identify the invisible research colleges among biomedical scientists: (1) cocitation analysis, (2) coword occurrence, (3) interpretive thematic analysis, and (4) network analysis. They concluded that their focus on the content of the networks helped clarify the structure of the invisible colleges. On the basis of communication network patterns alone, all the scientists would have been clustered into one invisible college. However, a closer examination of content helped them identify several invisible colleges, "each of which represents a distinct and identifiable line of research" (p. 246). Note that Lievrouw and colleagues' operationalization of a semantic network was based on coword occurrences, which were more akin to traditional semantic network analytic techniques. Using a similar approach, Kaufer and Carley (1993) identified links between social networks, knowledge networks, and semantic networks using a combination of historical analysis, empirical studies and computer simulations.

In a study of a high-technology firm, a library, and a hospital, Contractor, Eisenberg, and Monge (1997) examined the semantic networks representing the extent to which employees shared interpretations of their organizations' missions. In addition to their actual agreement, employees were also asked to report their perceived agreement, that is, the extent to which they believed others shared their interpretations in the organization. They found that employees at higher levels in the hierarchy were more likely to perceive agreement, even in cases when there was no agreement. However, employees with more tenure in the organization were more likely to have actual agreement, even though they did not perceive that others shared their interpretations of the mission. Contrary to the accepted view that communication builds shared meaning, employees cohesively connected in the communication network were not more likely to agree with their colleagues' interpretations of the organizational mission, even though they perceived agreement. However, employees who were structurally equivalent were more likely to share actual agreement, even though they were not as likely to perceive agreement.

Krackhardt and Kilduff (1990) applied the notion of semantic networks to examine individuals' attributions about others in the network. They asked individuals in an organization to make cultural attributions on seven dimensions about the behaviors of other members in the organization. They found that individuals who were friends were more likely than nonfriends to make similar attributions about other members in the organization. Rice and Danowski (1993) applied the notion of semantic networks to examine individuals' attributions of the appropriation of a voice mail system. They found that individuals who used the system for "voice processing" (i.e., routing and structuring the flow of messages among individuals) characterized their use of the technology in terms that were systematically distinct from those who used the voice mail technology as a substitute for traditional answering machines.

Two studies have used semantic networks to examine variations in national cultures. Jang and Barnett (1994) analyzed the chief operating officers' letters that seventeen Japanese and eighteen U.S. organizations published in the organizations' annual reports to stockholders. They found that the co-occurrence of words in these messages resulted in two distinct clusters for the Japanese and U.S. companies. Further, the words co-occurring in the Japanese annual reports focused on concepts related to organizational operations, while the U.S. documents focused on concepts related to organizational structure. In a study of twelve managers from five European countries, Stohl (1993) examined the cultural variations associated with

managers' interpretation of a key communicative process, worker participation. She found that the semantic network based on shared interpretations of the concept reflected greater connectedness within countries than
between countries. Further, similarities in interpretations about worker
participation were systematically associated with three of Hofstede's (1984)
dimensions of cultural variability across countries. As Stohl (1993, pp. 102–
103) says, these were: (1) the *power distance index*, the extent to which less
powerful people accept inequality in power, (2) the *uncertainty avoidance
index*, the extent to which people avoid uncertainty by relying on strict codes
of behavior, and (3) *individualism*, the extent to which citizens place primary
importance on the needs of the individual rather than the collective.

EXTENSIONS TO SEMANTIC NETWORKS

The theoretical mechanisms of contagion have also been used to explain
the coevolution of communication and semantic networks. Contractor and
Grant (1996) developed a computer simulation of the effects of social contagion in communication and semantic networks that contained varying
levels of initial network density and heterogeneity. They found that the time
required for semantic convergence within groups was positively related to
the density of the communication and semantic networks, inversely related
to the heterogeneity of the communication network, and inversely related
to the individual's inertia against being influenced socially. Significantly,
the initial heterogeneity in the semantic network, an indicator of initial
variation in interpretations, was not a significant predictor of the time required for semantic convergence.

   In a similar endeavor, Carley (1990, 1991) offered a *constructural
theory* of group stability, modeling the parallel cultural and social evolution of a group. Social structure was defined as the distribution of interaction
probabilities, and culture was defined as the distribution of distinct facts.
Carley's (1991) model described a cycle of three events for each group member: "(1) action—exchange information with their partners; (2) adaptation—
acquire the communicated information and update the probabilities of interaction; and then (3) motivation—choose new interaction partners on the
basis of their new probabilities of interaction" (p. 336). Results of computer
simulations showed that these groups did not evolve monotonically toward
greater homogeneity. Instead, they often oscillated through cycles of greater
and lesser cohesiveness. Her simulations also indicated that groups with
"simpler" cultures (i.e., fewer facts to be learned by group members) tended

to stabilize more quickly. Further, those in less homogeneous groups (i.e., where facts were not equally distributed) were less likely to stabilize, since they could form enduring subcultures. One corollary of simulations based on the constructural theory is that the probabilities for two individuals to interact are not symmetric (Carley & Krackhardt, 1996). Further, they validated the simulations' predictions of asymmetric ties in the constructural model using empirical social cognitive network data.

Network Organizations as Knowledge Structures

Kogut, Shan, and Walker (1993) propose a complementary view of semantic networks as meaning structures, arguing that it is useful to view interorganizational networks as structures of knowledge. Organizations seek out other organizations because they want to establish some form of relationship. But to do so, they must first find at least some of the other organizations that are also interested in entering into the relationship with them and choose among the alternatives. This means they must acquire information about the other organization and compare it with information from other organizations. Often, in searching for partners, organizations begin close to home or on the basis of recommendations from others with whom they are already linked. Over time, this searching process builds up a knowledge base about the skills, competencies, trustworthiness and other capabilities of the organizations.

Once organizations choose partners, however, they tend to spend less time seeking other partners. As Kogut, Shan, and Walker (1993) say, "because information is determined by previous relations and in turn influences the subsequent propensity to do more relations, the structure of the network tends to replicate itself over time. The early history of cooperation tends to lock in subsequent cooperation" (p. 70). Further, they observe that "the replication of the network is a statement of the tendency of learning to decline with time. The structure of the network is a limiting constraint on how much new learning can be achieved. . . . But when viewed from the perspective of the evolution of networks, there is a tendency for old lessons to be retaught" (p. 71).

Powell, Koput, and Smith-Doerr (1996) argue that learning networks are particularly important in industries where there is rapid technological development, knowledge is complex, and expertise is distributed around many organizations. Using data collected on 225 firms over four years, they found strong evidence for increasing levels of interorganizational communication and collaboration in the biotechnology industry, including increases in ties and network density. In a study of two new biotechnology firms (NBFs), Liebeskind, Oliver, Zucker, and Brewer (1996, p. 428) documented how they used social networks to "source their most critical input—scientific knowledge." They found that "almost none of the individual-level exchanges of knowledge through research collaboration involved organizations with which either NBF had a market agreement." (p. 439). The lack of market-based contractual arrangements increased their flexibility to create and dissolve networks as well as adapt strategically to evolving research interests.

Bovasso (1992) used four network measures of an organization's structure—density, range, prominence, and elitism—to examine the changes that resulted when three high-technology, knowledge intensive firms on three continents were merged by the parent corporation to create a single networked organization. In the newly formed networked organization, Bovasso (1992) found support for the emergence of a structural convergence, with geographic divisions and hierarchical levels having a smaller impact on members' involvement in the influence of ideas and control of resources. More specifically, geographical and hierarchical differences in prominence, elitism, and density scores between middle and upper management in the three firms were reduced.

Cognitive Social Structures

Several researchers (Corman & Scott, 1994; Krackhardt, 1987) have sought to distinguish people's cognitions of social structures from their actual, observed communication networks. This line of research was precipitated by a series of studies in the early 1980s questioning the ability of informants to accurately report their own communication network patterns (Bernard, Killworth, & Cronenfeld, 1984; Bernard, Killworth, & Sailer, 1980, 1982; Freeman, Romney, & Freeman, 1987). Their results underscored the problematic nature of collecting self-report measures of communication network data if the underlying theory being tested was based on the assumption that individuals' attitudes and behavior were shaped by their actual communication networks. However, as Richards (1985) argued, the differences between self-reported and observed network data is problematic only if the underlying theoretical construct being measured was actual communication behavior (see also, Marsden, 1990). In fact, Richards (1985) notes that many social and psychological theories are based on individuals' perceptions—an assertion well captured by W. I. Thomas's observation that "perceptions are real in their consequences even if they do not map one-to-one onto observed behaviors" (Krackhardt, 1987, p. 128; Pattison, 1994). For researchers drawing on such social and psychological theories, a discrepancy between observed and self-reported measures would suggest a measurement error in using data about observed communication.

Krackhardt (1987) developed the concept of *cognitive social structures* (CSS) to characterize individuals' perceptions of the social networks. Cognitive social structures assume the status of socially shared, structural, "taken-for-granted facts" (Barley, 1990, p. 67) by individuals about the predictable and recurrent interactions among individuals in the network, even if these cognitions are at variance with the actual communication. Krackhardt (1987) aggregated individuals' cognitive social structures to estimate a *consensual cognitive social structure*, in which a link existed between two individuals if others in the network perceived this tie, irrespective of whether it was acknowledged by either of the people in the dyad. As such, a link in the consensual cognitive social structure indexed a common adage: it is not who you know, but who others think you know.

GENERATIVE MECHANISMS BASED ON COGNITIVE SOCIAL STRUCTURES

Traditional network structures index a relation, R_{ij}, from person i to person j. This relation is typically based on i's self-reported relation to j. However, a *cognitive social relation*, R_{ijk}, is actor k's cognitive perception of the relation from any actor i to any other actor j. *Consensus* in cognitive social structures exists when a preponderance of people, k, agree on the presence or absence of a relation between actors i and j. Preponderance is typically, but not necessarily, defined as at least half of the network members, k. *Accuracy* in cognitive social structures exist when k's perception of the relation from actor i to actor j is similar to what i reports is the relation to j.

Theories of cognitive social structures identify mechanisms that explain why a person infers a relation between any two other people in the network. As a corollary, theories of cognitive structures also identify mechanisms that explain consensus or accuracy in cognitive social structures. The mechanisms posited by theories of cognitive social structures are based on the actors' attributes as well as their relations with others in the network.

Individuals' *attributes*, such as their level in the hierarchy or their tenure in the organization, may influence their perceptions of who knows who in the network. This occurs, for instance, because people higher in the hierarchy may be in a better position to chart the organization's network. Additionally, actors who have a longer tenure in the organization may have more of an opportunity to assess the pattern of relations among the other actors in the organization.

In addition, the actor's *relations* with others in the network, measured at multiple levels, also influence their cognitive social structure. At the *nodal* level, the centrality of actors will influence their perception of the network. Further, actors with high centrality may be more likely to have accurate perceptions of the social structure. This happens because they are better connected, directly or indirectly, with others in the network and hence have a "bird's eye" view of the overall social network. Actors who are on the periphery of the network, or who are isolates, will have less accurate as well as dissimilar cognitive social structures.

At the *dyadic* level, person k's perceptions of the relation between i and j will be influenced by person k's dyadic relations with i and j. For instance, person k's perception of a communication relation between i and j may be informed by k's communication relation with those two individuals. It follows, therefore, that actors who have ties to one another will tend to have similar (consensual) views of the overall social network. Thus, communication between people may lead to a shared perception of the overall social structure. Further, one can argue that people who are structurally equivalent may also have similar cognitive social structures by virtue of having similar patterns of communication with all others in the network. It is interesting to note that both of these explanations at the dyadic level can be considered as special cases of the contagion mechanisms discussed earlier in the chapter. In this case the people that comprise the dyad are contagiously influencing each other's perceptions of the cognitive social structure.

Also, at the dyadic level actor k's perception of a relation from actor i to actor j may also be influenced by k's other relations, say proximity, to i and j. Hence, people who are tied by other relations, such as proximity, may also have similar cognitive social structures. Proximity between two people offers them a similar vantage point to observe the overall network.

At the *global* level, people who are densely connected with one another are more likely to have similar and accurate perceptions of relations among other actors within their network. As we shall see in the empirical research reviewed below, many of these mechanisms have been studied, though typically they have been examined independently of one another. However, the MTML approach advocated in this book enables these mechanisms to be explored together, which can be represented, for instance, as:

$$R1_{ijk} = \text{function} \left[A_k, NC(R1)_k, R1_{ki}, R1_{kj}, R2_{ki}, R2_{kj}, \Sigma 2R1_{ij}/(N)(N-1) \right] \quad (11)$$

where,

A_k is person k's attribute,

$NC(R1)_k$ is k's network centrality,

$R1_{ki}$ and $R2_{ki}$ are person k's relations, R1 and R2, with i,

$R1_{kj}$ and $R2_{kj}$ are k's relations, R1 and R2, with person j, and

$\Sigma 2R1_{ij}/(N)(N-1)$ is the network density.

EMPIRICAL RESEARCH BASED ON COGNITIVE SOCIAL STRUCTURES

Several empirical studies have demonstrated the explanatory power of the cognitive social structure concept. Krackhardt (1987) found that managers in a high-technology entrepreneurial firm who were deemed as highly central (betweenness) in the consensual cognitive social structure were significantly more likely to be able to reconstruct accurately the "actual" advice network reported by the people involved. Krackhardt (1990) also found that the perceived influence of organizational members was significantly associated with their ability to estimate the consensual cognitive social structure in terms of advice relationships. Krackhardt's (1992) research chronicled how a union's inability to accurately assess the organization's social structure led to their failure in organizing employees. Further, Kilduff and Krackhardt (1994) demonstrated that individuals' reputations in the organization were more closely associated with their centrality in the consensual cognitive structure than in the actual communication network based on the self-reports of the people involved. Finally, Heald, Contractor, Koehly, and Wasserman (1998) found that individuals of the same gender, in the same department, and in a supervisor-subordinate relationship were more likely to share similar cognitive social structures. Those individuals who were linked in acquaintance and communication networks were also more likely to share similar cognitive social structures.

EXTENSIONS TO COGNITIVE SOCIAL STRUCTURES

The conceptual and empirical work on cognitive social structures have moved the initial debate about differences between actual and perceived communication from the methodological and measurement domain to a substantive exploration of the ways in which actual and perceived communication enable and constrain each other. Corman and Scott (1994) deployed Giddens's (1984) structuration theory to argue that three modalities explain the recursive relationships between observable communication and cognitive social structures: reticulation, activation, and enactment. "Reticulation denotes the duality in which perceived communication relationships are produced and reproduced in observable communication behavior. Activation represents the duality of activity foci in the structural domain with joint activity in the interaction domain. . . . Enactment relates coding conventions in the structural domain to triggering events in the interaction domain" (Corman, 1997, p. 69). They refer to this perspective as the *latent network* of perceived communication relationships.

Research on cognitive social structures has taken on additional currency with the advent of virtual organizations supported by information and communication technologies. In traditional organizations, individuals who are physically colocated have several opportunities to observe face-to-face interactions, and thereby shape their perceptions and social cognitions (Brewer, 1995) of the organization's social structures. The pervasiveness of electronic communication media in virtual organizations makes it increasingly difficult for individuals to discern social structures. Consequently, organizational members have significant problems accurately determining "Who knows who?" and "Who knows who knows who?" Ironically, information technologies that are responsible for triggering this problem can also be used to overcome these obstacles. Because information transacted over electronic media such as the web can be stored in digital form, a new generation of software called *collaborative filters* or *communityware* has emerged (Contractor, 1997; Contractor, Zink, & Chan, 1998; Kautz, Selman, & Shah, 1997; Nardi et al., 2002; Nishida, Takeda, Iwazume, Maeda, & Takaai, 1998). These communityware technologies can be used to make visible the organization's virtual social and knowledge structures. One web-based tool, IKNOW (Inquiring Knowledge Networks On the Web, developed at the University of Illinois at Urbana-Champaign by Contractor, O'Keefe, & Jones, 1997) generates visual representations of these social and knowledge networks based on individuals' interests, relationships, and the structure and content of their electronically stored information such as web pages. They can assist individuals in searching the organization's databases to automatically answer questions about the organization's knowledge network, that is, "Who knows what?" as well as questions about the organization's cognitive knowledge networks, that is, "Who knows who knows what?" within the organization. The use of these kinds of tools is likely to have a leveling effect on the organization's cognitive social structure, because they can potentially undermine the perceived centrality of those individuals in the organization who are viewed as important resources about the organization's social and knowledge networks.

Contractor and Bishop (2000) show how these communityware technologies can also be used to augment cognitive knowledge networks in an interorganizational context. They described a network of organizations supporting low-income communities in the Champaign-Urbana area in East-Central Illinois. The nodes in this network were local, state, and nonprofit agencies such as the local offices of the Health and Human Services, Planned Parenthood, the Urban League, United Negro College Fund, Land of Lincoln Legal Assistance, and the Shelter for Battered Women. Each organization provided their area of service (financial aid, education, legal assistance, etc.), the target groups (young children, the aged, single women, etc.), their prior collaborations with one another, as well as the resources for which they had the greatest need. The Prairie-KNOW software augmented their prior cognitive knowledge networks about one another, thereby facilitating the development of novel and creative multiorganizational network alliances to better serve the target communities.

Transactive memory theory, discussed next, provides a theoretical basis for extending explanations of cognitive social structures—"who knows who?" and "who knows who knows who?"—to the realm of cognitive knowledge networks—"who knows what?" and "who knows who knows what?"

Cognitive Knowledge Networks
and Transactive Memory Theory

Knowledge networks are distributed repositories of knowledge elements from a larger knowledge domain that are tied together by knowledge linkages within and between organizations. As discussed in chapter 3, the nodes that contain the knowledge can be human or nonhuman agents such as people, databases, avatars, webbots, computer files, or other forms of knowledge repositories.

The interesting phenomena in knowledge networks are the possible media for transmitting knowledge elements from one node in the network to another, the flows of information that occur, and the levels of knowledge that exist in each repository. As mentioned briefly in chapter 3, *cognitive knowledge networks* are the perceptions that people have of the knowledge networks in which they are involved. These perceptions reflect at some level of accuracy the knowledge elements possessed by the people and other repositories in the network as well as the relational ties between the knowledge repositories throughout the network (Cross & Baird, 2000; Cross, Nohria, & Parker, 2002; Cross, Parker, Prusak, & Borgatti, 2001; Heald, Contractor, Koehly, & Wasserman, 1998; Pattison 1994).

GENERATIVE MECHANISMS BASED ON COGNITIVE KNOWLEDGE NETWORKS

The *theory of transactive memory* explains how interdependent people within a knowledge network, each with their own set of skills and expertise, develop cognitive knowledge networks that help them identify the skills and expertise of others in the network (Hollingshead, 2000; Moreland, 1999; Moreland & Argote, in press; Wegner, 1987, 1995). These transactive memory systems facilitate the flows of knowledge among actors within the network, thereby reducing the need for each actor to possess skills or expertise available elsewhere in the knowledge network. As discussed elsewhere, networks can be composed of human and nonhuman entities at various levels, such as individuals or groups within and among organizations.

Consider a network where each individual is required to accomplish a set of tasks. The tasks may require multiple areas of expertise that they may not individually possess and hence requires them to be interdependent with others in the network. Further each person is exposed to new information about areas that may not necessarily be in their areas of expertise. Palazzolo, Serb, She, Su, and Contractor (2001) developed a network formulation of the theoretical mechanisms of transactive memory theory (see equations 12, 13, and 14). They begin by noting that the theory of transactive memory identifies four interrelated processes by which people in a network develop transactive memory systems: expertise recognition, retrieval coordination, directory updating, and information allocation. Further, the theory identifies specific generative mechanisms for each of these processes.

Expertise recognition is the process by which people identify others in the network who have expertise in various topics, say X and Y. As such, it represents an individual's response to "who knows what?" This expertise recognition may be based on stereotypes of what others "should" know. For instance, a person operating on the basis of stereotypes may infer that an Asian actor in the network would be highly proficient in computer programming. Expertise recognition on the basis of stereotyping is especially likely when the actors do not know or communicate with one another. In other instances, individuals' expertise recognition may also be informed by their actual expertise. They may learn about this by interacting directly or indirectly with others in the network. In network terminology, expertise recognition can be defined as a relation, ERX_{ij}, which indicates person i's perception of person j's level of expertise on a particular topic, say, X. The actual expertise of j, which is an actor attribute, would be EX_j. Likewise, a second relation, ERY_{ij}, would indicate i's perception of j's actual level of expertise on topic Y, EY_j.

Retrieval coordination is the process by which people confronted with a task for which they do not possess all the necessary skills coordinate the retrieval of information from among the experts they have identified in the expertise recognition process. Retrieval coordination is distinct from expertise recognition because an actor may identify (or recognize) several other actors with expertise. The decision on whom to approach may additionally be influenced by preexisting communication relations among these people. In network parlance, RCX_{ij} would indicate i's effort to retrieve information about topic X from j. The relation RCX_{ij} could be activated when person i, receives $TaskX_i$, a task requiring expertise in topic X on which i is not an expert but perceives j to be an expert.

Directory updating is the process by which people update their directories of "who knows what?" For instance, person i may, as a result of coordinating retrieval of information from j, upgrade (or downgrade) her or his perception of actor j's expertise in a certain area. Alternatively, actor i may learn through communication with actor j or other actors, k, about actor j's expertise in a certain area. The end result of the directory updating process is a change in value of their expertise recognition relation (say, ERX_{ij} or ERY_{ij}) with person j.

Finally, *information allocation* is the process by which individuals who receive information outside their areas of expertise determine who else in the network would find that information relevant to their respective areas of expertise. For instance, person i may receive $InfX_i$, information about a topic X, that is outside her or his area of expertise. However, i may be aware that j has expertise on topic X and hence might find that information relevant. Therefore, person i might choose to allocate that information to j. The relation, AX_{ij} indexes i's effort to allocate information on topic X to j.

The processes that describe the development of a transactive memory system, each with their own generative mechanisms can be represented as:

$$ERX_{ij} = \text{function } [A_j, EX_j, C_{ij}, \Sigma(C_{ik})(ERX_{kj})] \tag{12}$$

$$RCX_{ij} = \text{function } [TaskX_i, (ERX_{ij} - EX_i), C_{ij}] \tag{13}$$

$$CAX_{ij} = \text{function } [ERX_{ij}, C_{ij}, InfX_i] \tag{14}$$

where

ERX$_{ij}$ is person i's recognition of person j's expertise on topic X,

A$_j$ is some attribute of j,

EX$_j$ is j's actual expertise on topic X,

C$_{ij}$ is the communication from i to j,

Σ(C$_{ik}$)(ERX$_{kj}$) is the sum of actor i's communication with other actors, k, weighted by those others' recognition of j's expertise on X,

RCX$_{ij}$ is actor i's effort to coordinate retrieval of information of topic X from actor j,

TaskX$_i$ is a task that actor i has requiring expertise on topic X,

(ERX$_{ij}$ – EX$_i$) is the difference between actor i's expertise on topic X and actor's i's recognition of actor j's expertise on topic X,

CAX$_{ij}$ is actor i's attempt to allocate information on topic X to actor j, and

InfX$_i$ is the information i receives on topic X.

As we shall see in the discussion of empirical research that follows, transactive memory theory advocates that a well-developed transactive memory system has two requirements: First, knowledge must be well *differentiated* within the network. That is, different people develop expertise in different areas, thereby reducing the load on individuals to develop expertise in all areas. Second, people must be *accurate* in their recognition of expertise among the various actors in the network. When confronted with tasks or provided information in areas outside their own expertise, actors should be capable of retrieving and allocating that information efficiently with the appropriate others in the network.

The generative mechanisms of transactive memory discussed in this section involve only attributes and relations at the dyadic level. However, the theory posits that these generative mechanisms can lead to a well-developed transactive memory system that has emergent properties, such as knowledge differentiation, which are measured at the global level.

EMPIRICAL RESEARCH ON COGNITIVE KNOWLEDGE STRUCTURES

Transactive memory is the specialized collective division of labor with respect to the encoding, storage, and retrieval of information from different substantive knowledge domains that develop during the course of work relationships (Hollingshead, 1998a, b, 2000; Moreland, 1999; Wegner, 1987, 1995). Members of work groups and organizations become specialists in some knowledge domains but not others; and all members come to expect each particular member to be able to access information in appropriate domains. An important finding in the transactive memory literature is that learning in knowledge networks can be affected by individuals' perceptions of others' relative expertise, that is, by their cognitive knowledge networks. Individuals tend to focus on learning information in their own areas of relative expertise and expect others to do the same (Hollingshead, 1998b; Hollingshead, 2000; Wegner, Erber, & Raymond, 1991). At the same time, they must develop their own view of "who they think knows what" in order to connect with those whose knowledge they need. This division of cognitive labor reduces the amount of information for which each individual is responsible, yet provides all members access to a larger pool of information across knowledge domains. When one person needs information in another's area of expertise, they can simply ask for it rather than spend time and energy learning it on their own.

Members specialize in different knowledge domains based on their relative expertise, skills or experiences, formal assignment (e.g., by a high status member), or negotiated agreements with other members. Members develop their cognitive knowledge networks, that is, what they think others actually know or should know, through both formal and informal channels. Communication often provides the basis for learning about others' expertise, and it is important for coordinating who will learn what (Hollingshead, 1998a, 1998b; Moreland, Argote & Krishnan, 1996). Members can learn informally who is the relative expert across knowledge domains through shared experiences and conversations with other members (Hollingshead, 1998c; Wegner, 1987). Members can also learn what other members know or should know more explicitly through instruction from other people, such as a supervisor, or from procedures in the form of documents, manuals, or other codified reference materials (Hollingshead, 2000; Moreland, 1999). Over time, members gain responsibility for the encoding, storage, and retrieval of information in different domains. Thus, the transactive memory system becomes more efficient over time, which means that knowledge becomes more differentiated and less redundant among individuals in the system. Many studies have empirically demonstrated that transactive memory systems can have a positive impact on group decision making and group performance (e.g., Cicourel, 1990; Hollingshead, 1998a, 1998b, 1998c; Hollingshead, 2000; Liang, Moreland, & Argote, 1995; Littlepage, Robison, & Reddington, 1997; Moreland, Argote, & Krishnan, 1996; Stasser, Stewart, & Wittenbaum, 1995; Wegner et al., 1991).

Recent work on transactive memory has employed a computer metaphor to explore the extent to which information processing in a computer network resembles that of cooperative memory systems used by human groups. As Wegner (1995) states, "The computer model shows us that getting organized (directory updating), channeling information to the right places (information allocation), and having a strategy for getting it back (retrieval coordination) are all things we must think about to link computer memories. And as we have seen, there is evidence that these same tasks arise and must be undertaken when humans remember in groups. To the degree that human groups do solve these problems, it appears that their group memory structures develop and become capable of memory feats far beyond those that might be accomplished by any individual" (p. 336).

EXTENSIONS TO TRANSACTIVE MEMORY THEORY

Contractor, Carley, Levitt, Monge, Wasserman, Bar, Fulk, Hollingshead, and Kunz (1998) argued that network perspectives offer a useful approach to extend Wegner's (1995) model of transactive memory systems as a computer network. Communication networks influence the degree of knowledge differentiation among members and the accuracy of their cognitive knowledge networks. Their arguments were based on observations of how people in organizations use intranets as a medium to learn about knowledge networks. Intranets serve many functions in the transactive organizational knowledge system. They serve as repositories for unique knowledge that people possess. They offer a means by which people can learn about the knowledge and expertise of other people in the system. Intranets can provide listings about each person's expertise and job responsibilities, and may also provide search engines that can assist in identifying information or the likely holders of it. They can describe the routines and procedures that people should follow to obtain knowledge they need to do their work. People can also evaluate the topics and quality of information contributed to intranets by others to infer what others know.

In summary, transactive memory theory demonstrates that domains of knowledge are distributed throughout human and technical repositories in knowledge networks. People negotiate their own information expertise, and rely on others in the network to develop and maintain complementary knowledge, thereby reducing the information burden on all. Participation in the network requires that people share information so that it flows freely from point to point in the network.

Cognitive Consistency

Like the semantic networks and cognitive social and knowledge structures discussed above, consistency theories focus on members' cognitions. However, in this case the explanatory mechanism underscores individuals' aspirations for consistency in their cognitions. When applied to organizational communication networks, consistency theories seek to explain the extent to which a drive for consistency is manifest in people's networks and attitudes. Members' attitudes are viewed as a function of the balance in their networks rather than alternative mechanisms such as contagion. Heider's (1958) balance theory posited that if two individuals were friends, they should have similar evaluations of an object. This model was extended and mathematically formulated by Harary, Norman, and Cartwright (1965), and later by Davis and Leinhardt (1972) and Holland and Leinhardt (1975), who argued that the object could be a third person in a communication network. If the two individuals did not consistently evaluate the third person, they would experience a state of discomfort, and would strive to reduce this cognitive inconsistency by altering their evaluations of either the third person or their own friendship. They extended this line of argument to all possible triads in a network. Researchers have examined the effects of cognitive consistency on both attitudes and behavior.

GENERATIVE MECHANISMS FOR CONSISTENCY THEORIES

The generative mechanism for cognitive consistency theory is premised on a relatively simple, compelling, and yet strikingly underutilized concept at the triadic level, transitivity. As defined in chapter 2, transitivity measures the extent to which person i has a direct relation to person j, while also having indirect relations to j via several intermediary people, k. Thus a triad of three actors (i, j, k) is transitive if actor i has a tie to actor j, i has a tie to k, and k has a tie to j. If the ties are nondirectional, then a triad is transitive if the three actors have ties to one another. Any actor i can be embedded in several transitive triads involving other actors, j and k. In fact, in a network of size N each actor i can be involved via N-2 transitive triads with each other actor j. The generative mechanism posited by cognitive consistency is that the number of transitive triads in which they are embedded influences an actor's attributes. Thus, as we shall see below, according to cognitive consistency theory, an individual's satisfaction at work is influenced by the extent to which the individual is embedded in a large number of transitive triad relations. If the relation is a friendship relation, cognitive consistency theory argues that individuals are satisfied when their friends are friends with one another. The generative mechanisms for cognitive consistency can be represented as:

$$A_i = \text{function } [\Sigma\Sigma(R_{ij})(R_{jk})(R_{ik})] \tag{15}$$

where

A_i is an attribute of actor i, and

R_{ij}, R_{jk}, and R_{ik} indicate the presence (or absence) of relations from actor i to actor j, actor j to actor k, and actor i to actor k respectively.

If any one of these relations are absent the product of the three terms is zero. The second of the Σ signs indicates that for each pair of actors i and j one must sum the transitivity across all other actors k. The first of the Σ signs indicates that for each actor i one must sum the transitivity across all other actors j.

It must be noted that this mechanism is analytically and substantially distinct from a contagion network mechanism discussed earlier in this chapter. Analytically, they both seek to explain phenomena at the actor level. However, the contagion network mechanism offers explanations primarily at the dyadic level while cognitive consistency focuses on the triadic level of analysis. Substantively, in a contagion network mechanism, the individual attributes are directly influenced by those of other individuals weighted by the focal person's relations with these others. In contrast, according to a cognitive consistency network mechanism, the attributes of an actor are not influenced by the attributes of others. Instead, the focal actor's attributes are solely influenced by the configuration of triadic relations it has with other actors. It is evident, given the example used here, that the contagion and cognitive consistency network mechanisms offer very different explanations for how the network may influence an individual's satisfaction.

THE EFFECT OF COGNITIVE CONSISTENCY ON ATTITUDES

Consistency theories have played an important role in clarifying an earlier debate about the relationship between involvement in communication networks and work attitudes such as job satisfaction and organizational commitment. Early studies (e.g., Brass, 1981; Eisenberg, Monge, & Miller, 1984; Roberts & O'Reilly, 1979) reported contradictory and inconsistent findings about the extent to which individuals who were well-connected, integrated, or central in their communication networks were more likely to be satisfied and committed to their organizations. Consistency theories suggest that it is not the centrality or number of links in individuals' networks but the perceived balance within the network that influences level of satisfaction and commitment. Krackhardt and Kilduff (1990) found that individuals' job satisfaction scores were predicted by the extent to which they agreed with their friends on cultural attributions about other members in the network. Kilduff and Krackhardt (1993) found that individuals who were highly central in the friendship network were less satisfied than others who were less central; however, those who saw their friendship networks in balance (they call it "schema consistent") were more likely to be satisfied and committed. In a study of three organizations (described earlier in the section on "Semantic Networks"), Contractor, Eisenberg, and Monge (1996) also found that the extent to which employees shared common interpretations of their organization's mission had no direct bearing on their level of satisfaction or organizational commitment. However, those who perceived greater agreement with others' interpretations were more likely to be satisfied and committed. Barnett and Jang (1994), while not explicitly invoking consistency theories, found that members of a police organization who were central and connected in their communication networks were more likely to perceive their views of salient organizational concepts as being consistent with those of others. Researchers have used network concepts of transitivity to operationalize the effect of balance in the network.

THE EFFECT OF COGNITIVE CONSISTENCY ON BEHAVIOR

Consistency theories have also been related to the behavior of organizational members. Krackhardt and Porter (1985) found that friends of those who voluntarily left an organization were no longer exposed to their former co-workers' unhappiness and were therefore able to restore their previous perceived balance; as a result they reported greater levels of satisfaction following the departure of these friends from the organization. Brass, Butterfield, and Skaggs (1995) argued that the need for balance among three people can also influence the likelihood of unethical behavior. "The addition of the third party with strong ties to both other actors will act as a major constraint on unethical behavior when the two actors are only weakly connected" (p. 7). Further, they proposed that the likelihood of unethical behavior is least likely to occur when all three people are connected by strong ties (i.e., a Simmelian triad, Krackhardt, 1992).

The deployment of consistency theories to explain organizational phenomena is relatively recent. Conceptually and analytically, it challenges network researchers to move from the dyad to the triad as the smallest unit of analysis. As the examples above indicate, it has the potential of resolving many of the inconsistent results in network studies that use the dyad as the primary unit of analysis.

Like the other cognitive theories discussed in the previous section, consistency theories have also been utilized to address the ongoing debate about differences between actual and perceived communication. Freeman (1992) suggested that consistency theories offer a systematic explanation for differences between actual and self-report data on communication. He argued that individuals' needs to perceive balance in observed communication networks help explain some of the errors they make in recalling communication patterns. Using experimental data collected by De Soto (1960), Freeman found that a large proportion of the errors in subjects' recall of networks could be attributed to their propensity to "correct" intransitivity, a network indicator of imbalance, in the observed network.

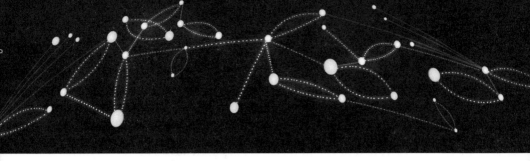

7

Exchange and Dependency Theories

Extensive research has been conducted that seeks to explain the emergence of networks based on exchange and dependency mechanisms. Social exchange theory, originally developed by Homans (1950, 1974) and Blau (1964), seeks to explain human action by a calculus of exchange of material or information resources. In its original formulation, social exchange theory attempted to explain the likelihood of a dyadic relationship based on the supply and demand of resources that each member of the dyad had to offer. Emerson (1962, 1972a, 1972b) extended this original formulation beyond the dyad, arguing that in order to examine the potential of exchange and power-dependence relationships, it was critical to examine the larger network within which the dyad was embedded. Since then several scholars have developed this perspective into what is now commonly referred to as network exchange theory (Bienenstock & Bonacich, 1992, 1997; Cook, 1977, 1982; Cook & Whitmeyer, 1992; Cook & Yamagishi, 1992; Markovsky, Willer, & Patton, 1988; Skvoretz & Willer, 1993; Willer & Skvortez, 1997; Yamagishi, Gillmore, & Cook, 1988).

Network exchange theory posits that the bargaining power of individuals is a function of the extent to which they are vulnerable to exclusion from communication and other exchanges within the network. The argument is that individuals forge network links on the basis of their analysis of the relative costs and returns in exchanging their investments with others in the network. This is in contrast with theories of self-interest where actors seek to maximize their individual investments independent of its exchange value. Likewise, individuals maintain links based on the frequency, the uncertainty, and the continuing investments to sustain the interaction. Location in the network may confer on some people an advantage over others in engaging in exchange relationships. Aldrich (1982) notes that this argument is at the core of several theories dealing with social exchange as well as resource dependence theories. Within organizations, network researchers have proposed a social exchange mechanism for the study of (1) power, (2) leadership, and (3) trust and ethical behavior. At the interorganizational level, researchers have (1) tested resource dependence theory, (2) examined the composition of corporate elites and interlocking board of directorates, and (3) sought to explain the creation, maintenance, and dissolution of interorganizational links. In the following section we discuss the theoretical mechanisms postulated in social exchange and resource dependency processes within and among organizations. In subsequent sections we examine relevant network research that explores these two theories. The chapter concludes with proposed extensions to the study of organizational networks from a social exchange perspective.

Theoretical Mechanisms of Social Exchange and Resource Dependency

In its primitive form, theories of social exchange seek to explain how people create, maintain, and dissolve network linkages on the basis of resources and attributes they possess and need as well as the resources that others in their networks possess and need. Hence the development of a communication relation, C_{ij}, between two people, i and j, can be represented as:

$$C_{ij} = \text{function} \left[(R1_i - R1_j)(R2_j - R2_i) \right] \qquad (1)$$

where

$R1_i$ and $R1_j$ are the resources, on item 1, available to person i and needed by person j,

$R2_i$ and $R2_j$ are the resources, on item 2, needed by i and available to j.

Thus, a communication relation between two people is prompted if there is a potential for exchange in resources between them. According to social exchange theory, this discrepancy in resource needs is a necessary, but not sufficient, condition for the realization of a network tie. For instance, there may be several individuals, j, who can provide actor i with the necessary resources. In such cases, actor i seeks to forge links with specific actors, j, so as to minimize their dependence on other actors, j. This calculus implies that people will choose to forge links that will reduce their dependence or increase their power or centrality in the network. Alternatively, actors who have higher betweenness centrality will be in a better position to create new exchange links with others. This can be represented as:

$$C_{ij} = \text{function } [(R1_i - R1_j)(R2_j - R2_i)(\text{Betweenness Centrality}_i)] \qquad (2)$$

Since each of the people in the network will be seeking to pursue the same strategy, not all attempts at initiating an exchange relation will be reciprocated. A social exchange will only occur if both individuals, i and j, mutually recognize the merits of the relationship. Thus a mutually acceptable social exchange relationship, SE_{ij}, can be represented as:

$$SE_{ij} = (C_{ij})(C_{ji}) \qquad (3)$$

where, C_{ij} is described in equation 2 and C_{ji} can be represented as:

$$C_{ji} = \text{function } [(R1_j - R1_i)(R2_i - R2_j)(\text{Betweenness Centrality}_j)] \qquad (4)$$

As a result, ceteris paribus, the system of equations 2 through 4 will result in the emergence of an equilibrium state where people will develop stable exchange relations with others depending on their relative centrality in the network.

Finally, the creation of exchange relations could also be a function of other relations in the network. As we shall describe later, a strong trust relation between two people could serve as an important influence on the development of a social exchange relation. The influence of an additional, say, trust relation T_{ij}, on the social exchange relation could be represented as:

$$SE_{ij} = (C_{ij})(C_{ji})(T_{ij})(T_{ji}) \qquad (5)$$

where T_{ij} and T_{ji} is the trust that persons i and j have in one another. As we shall discuss below, in some cases, the trust relation may be influenced by third parties, k, that is, the trust between two network members, i and j, may be derived from their trust ties to all "third-party" members, k.

The above discussion illustrates the generative mechanisms of social exchange on the basis of only two types of resources, R1 and R2, and two types of relations, communication, C_{ij}, and trust, T_{ij}. In reality, the number of resources that are possessed and can be potentially exchanged among the members of a network could be very varied—money, raw materials, finished goods, information, and so on. Likewise, the members could also be enmeshed in a number of relations with others in the network. These could include instrumental ties, social ties, interlocking boards of directors, and perhaps most significantly, prior exchange relations. The mechanisms described here, and illustrated in equations 1 through 5, can be appropriately scaled to account for additional resources and relations. The mechanisms outlined above are well illustrated in the empirical findings discussed below.

Empirical Research Using Exchange Mechanisms

Power

Social exchange theory has been used to examine the power that ensues from a structural position. In terms of exchange theory, power is defined as a function of dependence on others in the network. Location in the communication network is associated with greater power to the extent it offers greater access to valued material and informational resources. Specifically, people, groups, and organizations have power to the extent that they have access to alternate sources of a valued resource, and the extent to which they control resources valued by others in the network (Emerson, 1962). In a series of experimental and simulation studies, Cook and her colleagues (Cook & Emerson, 1978; Cook, Emerson, Gillmore & Yamagishi, 1983) found evidence to support a power-dependence relationship. Carroll and Teo (1996) found that in order to increase their resources, organizational managers were more motivated than nonmanagers to have larger core discussion networks and to create more communication links outside the organization by memberships in clubs and societies. In her study of interorganizational social services, Alter (1990) found that the existence of a centralized, dominant core agency reduced the level of conflict and competition between service organizations and improved their level of cooperation. However, Hoffman, Stearns, and Shrader (1990) found that organizational centrality in four multiplex interorganizational networks depended on the nature of the network.

Several studies have equated network centrality with different sources of power. Brass (1984) suggested two measures of centrality that reflect different dimensions of power. Closeness, the extent to which people, groups, and organizations can reach all others in a network through a minimum of intermediaries, corresponds to the "access of resources" dimension of power (Sabidussi, 1966). Betweenness, the extent to which a network member lies between others not directly connected, corresponds to the "control of resources" dimension of power (Freeman, 1977, 1979). Brass (1984, 1985a) showed that both measures of centrality correlated with reputational measures of power. Further, Brass (1984, 1985a) found that employees with high scores on network indicators of power were more likely to be promoted to supervisory positions, and Burkhardt and Brass (1990) discovered that early adopters of a new technology increased their power. Ibarra (1993a) found that centrality in the informal network was at least as important as the formal hierarchical network in predicting power; Krackhardt (1990) reported similar results for advice and friendship networks. Interestingly, Brass and Burkhardt's (1992) research revealed that measures of centrality at the departmental level were more strongly related to several indices of power than measures at the subunit or the organizational levels.

Leadership

The success of network formulations to predict power has prompted some scholars to suggest its use in extending theories of leadership such as Graen's (1976) *leader-member-exchange theory* (Krackhardt & Brass, 1994) and *attribution theories* of leadership (McElroy & Shrader, 1986). Fernandez (1991) found that the effects of informal communication networks on perceptions of leadership were different in three types of organizations. Specifically, he found that informal communication predicted perceptions of leadership most strongly in a participatory organization, a telephone-counseling center, only weakly in a professional organization, a public finance department of a large investment bank, and not at all in the hierarchical organization, a metallurgical firm.

Trust and Ethical Behavior

Researchers have also used social exchange theory to study the development and utility of trust in organizational and interorganizational networks. As Burt and Knez (1996) note, "trust is committing to an exchange before you know how the other person will reciprocate" (p. 69). In a study of managers in a large high-technology firm, they found that the communication networks in which two individuals were embedded predicted the probability of a trust relationship between them. In particular, the trust between two individuals in close contact was high if other members in the organizations indirectly connected the two members to one another. Further, the *dis*trust between two individuals who were not in close contact was further attenuated if other members in the organization indirectly connected them to one another. This research indicates that indirect communication linkages reinforce trust and distrust relations between people. Labianca, Brass, and Gray (1998) also reported a similar *amplification effect*. They suggest that the amplification effect occurs because the secondhand information transmitted by indirect communication linkages "may be more polarized or exaggerated (either positively or negatively) than firsthand information" (p. 64), as grapevine (rumor) studies have found (e.g., DeFleur & Cronin, 1991; Schachter & Burdick, 1955).

In a study involving trust as measured via friendship networks, Krackhardt and Stern (1988) found that a relatively higher proportion of interunit (as compared to intraunit) friendship ties was particularly helpful to organizations coping with crisis conditions. In this case, the high level of trust was seen as a prerequisite for the increased interunit coordination required during a period of high uncertainty and the ensuing potential conflict. Larson's (1992) study of entrepreneurial firms indicated that trust as well as shared reciprocity norms, close personal relations, and reputation determined with whom and how exchanges occurred.

Researchers examining ethical behavior in organizations also deploy the exchange mechanism. Brass, Butterfield, and Skaggs (1995) suggest that networks could also offer an explanation for the likelihood of unethical behavior in a dyad since the connectedness of people is highly related to their observability. Brass et al. (1995) propose that "the strength of the relationship between two actors will be positively related to the opportunity to act in an unethical manner, but negatively related to the motivation to act unethically. Frequency and trust provide increased opportunity, but intimacy and empathy decrease the motivation" (p. 6).

Resource Dependency Theory and Power in Interorganizational Networks

In his now classic article, Benson (1975) defined interorganizational networks as a *political economy*. By this he meant that interorganizational communication and exchange networks were the mechanisms by which organizations acquired and dispensed scarce resources, thus creating and perpetuating a system of power relations. Organizations were viewed as dependent on their positions in the network, which subsequently influenced their ability to control the flow of scarce resources.

Pfeffer and Salancik (1978) drew on Benson's work on political economy and social exchange mechanisms (Emerson, 1962, 1972a, 1972b) to formulate resource dependency theory. This theory argues that organizations structure their resource linkages in order to buffer themselves from the organization's environment (Pfeffer & Salancik, 1978). In particular, they identify two mechanisms that organizations can use toward this end. First, by *network extension* organizations can seek to increase the number of exchange alternatives by creating new network links. Second, by *network consolidation* they can decrease the number of exchange alternatives for others by forming a coalition with other resource providers. These counterbalancing mechanisms provide an explanation for the stability of exchange relationships and potential redistribution of power among the individuals. Burt (1991) developed a measure of equilibrium to assess the likelihood that network members have the resources to reconfigure their exchange networks and thereby the distribution of power.

A major tenet of resource dependency theory is that organizations tend to avoid interorganizational linkages that limit their decision making and other forms of autonomy. Oliver (1991; see also Oliver, 1990) tested this assumption across five relational types that ranged from highest to lowest levels of autonomy: personal meetings, resource transfers, board interlocks, joint programs, and written contracts. Surprisingly, she found no evidence that linkages which implied greater loss of autonomy led to lower likelihood of establishing the relationship.

A substantial body of empirical research draws on a resource dependence framework to study the pattern of interorganizational networks. These studies examine a wide variety of resource relationships, including money, material, information, and messages. However, the focus of these relationships is more concerned with the pattern of relationships than their content; thus, the majority of resource dependency research is conducted from a positional perspective. In some of the earlier studies in this area, Laumann and Pappi (1976) and Galaskiewicz (1979) reported that organizations that were more central in their networks had greater reputational influence. In a broad-based study assessing the power of the U.S. labor force, Wallace, Griffin, and Rubin (1989) discovered that the labor force in industries that were more central in the network of interindustry transactions were more likely to receive higher wages than the labor force in peripheral industries. Gerlach's (1992) study of the Japanese corporate network, including intercorporate *keiretsu* groupings, found strong evidence of the centrality of financial institutions in these networks and their resultant ability to control the capital allocation process (see also Lincoln, Gerlach, & Takahashi, 1992). However, in a study of health systems, Oliver and Montgomery (1996, p. 771) observed that "the organization with greatest influence within the system (because of its ability to allocate funds) may not be the organization that takes the largest role in terms of coordinating routine contacts," such as client referrals.

Two studies show the impact of resource exchange on effectiveness. Miner, Amburgey, and Stearns's (1990) research on 1,011 newspaper publishers in Finland from 1771 to 1963, found that publishers with a greater number of interorganizational resource linkages, typically to political parties, had a higher overall success rate. Goes and Park (1997) found that "a greater volume of [resource] exchanges between hospitals increases the likelihood that innovation will spread between them" (p. 771).

Provan and Milward (1995) reported research designed to extend resource dependency theory by focusing on the effectiveness of the entire interorganizational network (see also Provan, 1983) rather than the antecedents and outcomes of individual organizations. Further, they pointed out that how well individual organizations perform is less important than how the interorganizational network as a whole performs. Studying the mental health care delivery system in four cities, they found that networks with a centralized decision-making agency were more effective than networks in which decision making was widely dispersed across agencies. Their data also suggested that the relationship between network structure and network effectiveness is influenced by the existence of a relatively munificent environment and the degree to which the overall network is stable.

Corporate Elites and Interlocking Boards of Directors

Corporate elites and networks created by linkages among people who serve on multiple corporate boards are areas that have received considerable research attention in interorganizational relations. As Knoke (1993) indicated, "A power elite is established at the intersection of three social formations: a class-conscious upper social class of wealth-holders, interlocked directors of major corporations, and a policy-planning network of foundations, research institutes, and nonpartisan organizations" (p. 26). Useem's (1983) classic study argued that these overlapping networks of friendship, ownership, membership, and directorship produced a core set of individuals, or *inner circle*, which wields enormous power. Knoke (1993) explained that because its members simultaneously hold multiple directorships, the core can act politically in the interests of the class, which transcend the parochial concerns of its individual firms" (p. 26). Consistent with this view, Romo and Anheier (1996) found evidence that a core group of elites explained the emergence and institutionalization of consortia for private development organizations in Nigeria and Senegal. Studies have also shown that individuals who were more centrally located in the interlocking board of directors were also more likely to play a leadership role in cultural, philanthropic, and policy-making organizations (Domhoff, 1983; Mizruchi & Galaskiewicz, 1994; Ogliastri & Davila, 1987; Ratcliff, Gallagher, & Ratcliff, 1979; Useem, 1980).

Historically, the focus of interlocking directorate research has been on corporate control. However, Mintz and Schwartz (1985) argued that "the most compelling interpretation of the overall network created by the collection of individual reasons for and response to director recruitment is a general communication system" (p. 141). In fact, as Mizruchi (1996) contends, "the emphasis on interlocks has moved increasingly toward their value as a communication mechanism rather than as a mechanism of control" (p. 284).

Creation, Maintenance, Dissolution, and Reconstitution of Interfirm Links

Studies have also deployed a resource dependence framework to explain the creation of links in interorganizational networks. Mizruchi and Stearns (1988) found two general factors that explained the addition of new financial members to an organization's board of directors. Under favorable economic conditions, when capital demand and supply are increasing, organizations initiate links with financial institutions through their board of directors to co-opt these institutions' financial and informational resources. However, during unfavorable economic conditions, including contractions in the business cycle, lower solvency, and lower profitability, it is the financial institutions that infiltrate companies' boards of directors to protect their investments. This finding is qualified by Boyd's (1990) research that showed high performing firms responded to resource scarcity and competitive uncertainty by decreasing the number of their directors but increasing the density of their linkages with other firms. Mizruchi (1996) argued that a number of other factors also affect the creation of interlocking directorates.

These include creating legitimacy for the firm, advancing the careers of those who serve as directors, and fostering the social cohesion of the corporate upper class.

Palmer, Friedland, and Singh (1986) used resource dependency theory to hypothesize the conditions under which a broken interlock tie between two organizations (due to death, retirement, etc.) would be reconstituted. They found that interlock ties were likely to be reconstituted if the departing member represented an organization with which the focal organization had (1) formal coordination, such as long term contracts or joint ventures, (2) direct business ties, or (3) headquarters that were physically proximate.

Larson (1992) demonstrated that firms tend to enter repeated alliances with each other; thus, dependencies tend to generate further dependencies. Gulati's (1995) research showed that the information provided by both direct and indirect ties of prior alliances established the basis for the formation of additional alliances. However, his research also showed that as the benefits of linking with specific others declined over time organizations looked for new alliances. Of course, as Baum and Oliver (1992) noted, there is a carrying capacity to alliances in that most organizations can successfully support only a limited number of connections and many firms fear the overdependence that too many ties might bring.

Seabright, Levinthal, and Fichman (1992) theorized that reductions in the resource fit between organizations would lead to pressures to dissolve interorganizational relations while increases in personal and structural attachments would counter those pressures and lead to continued relations. Their results supported the hypotheses but also showed that personal and structural attachments attenuated the firms' likelihood of dissolving ties under conditions of reduced fit. This finding underscores the importance of established communication and social attachments in maintaining interorganizational relations beyond the point where a strict exchange or resource dependency perspective would predict that they would dissolve, even at times when it might be disadvantageous to maintain them. Overall, however, Mizruchi's (1996) review of the research literature on corporate interlocks led him to conclude that "although the findings have been mixed, on balance they support the view that interlocks are associated with interfirm resource dependence" (p. 274).

The research on interlocking directorates assumes that each organization is a separate entity tied together at the top by corporate elites. While interest continues in interlocking directorates, a new field of research has developed over the past decade that focuses on an emergent organizational form, network organizations. This perspective relaxes these two assumptions of separate entities and executive ties only. We explore this new area in the next section.

Network Organizations

Network organizations are comprised of a collection of organizations along with the linkages that tie them to each other, often organized around a focal organization. There are numerous variations on the network organizational form, including joint partnerships, strategic alliances, cartels, R&D consortia, and a host of others.

The theoretical mechanisms that generate most network organizations are exchange and dependency relations. Rather than being organized around market or hierarchical principles, network organizations are created out of complex webs of exchange and dependency relations among multiple organizations. In a sense, the network organization becomes a supraorganization whose primary function is linking many organizations together and coordinating their activities. Unlike interlocking directorates, the network ties usually occur throughout the entire organization rather than only at the top, and the separate organizations often give up some or all of their individual autonomy to become a part of the new network organization.

Miles and Snow (1992) observe that network organizations differ from their predecessors (functional, multidivisional, and matrix forms) in four important ways. First, rather than subsume all aspects of production within a single hierarchical organization they attempt to create a set of relations and communication networks among several firms, each of which contributes to the value of the product or service. Second, networks are based on a combination of market mechanisms and informal communication relations. As they say, "The various components of the network recognize their interdependence and are willing to share information, cooperate with each other, and customize their product or service—all to maintain their position within the network" (p. 55). Third, members of networks are often assumed to take a proactive role in improving the final product or service, rather than merely fulfilling contractual obligations. Finally, a number of industries are beginning to form network organizations along the lines of the Japanese *keiretsu*, which links together producers, suppliers, and financial institutions into fairly stable patterns of relations.

Poole (1999) argues that new organizational forms, including network organizations, are constituted out of six essential qualities. These are:

1. The use of information technology to integrate across organizational functions.
2. Flexible, modular organizational structures which can be readily reconfigured as new projects, demands, or problems arise.
3. Use of information technology to coordinate geographically dispersed units and members.
4. Team-based work organization, which emphasizes autonomy and self-management.
5. Relatively flat hierarchies and reliance on horizontal coordination among units and personnel.
6. Use of intra- and inter-organizational markets to mediate transactions such as the assignment and hiring of personnel for projects and the formation of interorganizational networks. (pp. 454–555)

In today's world, nearly all organizations are embedded to some extent in an emergent interorganizational communication network. For example, most economic institutions are linked together in *value chains* (Porter, 1980) or "value constellations" (Norman & Ramirez, 1993) where each receives a partially finished product from an "upstream organization," adds its contribution, and then delivers it to the next "downstream organization" for its contribution. Similarly, educational institutions typically relate to other educational institutions in a chain from preschool to postgraduate education. And, religious organizations are frequently affiliated with coalitions of other like-minded religious groups. Of course, all must deal with the taxation authorities of federal, state, and local governments.

In one sense, network organizations create what have come to be called *boundary-less organizations* (Cross, Yan, & Louis, 2000; Nohria & Berkley, 1994). Where one organization begins and the other ends is no longer clear. Organizations come to share knowledge, goals, resources, personnel, and finances, usually with highly sophisticated communication technology (Monge & Fulk, 1998). To accomplish this they must establish collaborative work arrangements, since that is the only way to transfer embedded knowledge.

Ghoshal and Bartlett (1990) argued that multinational corporations (MNCs) have traditionally been viewed as an intraorganizational network, in many ways not different from traditional national companies. Each satellite, subsidiary, or foreign partner has been seen as directly connected to the home corporate office, thus tying the MNC into an integrated hub-and-spoke structural whole. However, they point out that this view of the MNC fails to take into account the extended networks in which each of the subsidiaries is embedded. These national, regional, and competing global networks require a reconceptualization of MNCs as network organizations.

Limitations of Network Organizations

A number of authors have pointed out that network organizations have a number of limitations. Miles and Snow (1992) observe that network organizations contain the vestigial weaknesses of their predecessors, the functional, multidivisional, and matrix forms. To the extent that parts of these prior forms remain in the network organization, the new form retains their prior limitations. Krackhardt (1994) identifies four potential constraints on communication and other networks. The first he calls the "Law of N-Squared," which simply notes that the number of potential links in a network organization increases geometrically with the number of people. In fact, it grows so quickly that the number of people to which each person could be linked quickly exceeds everyone's communication capacity. The second constraint is "The Law of Propinquity," a rather consistent empirical finding that "the probably of two people communicating is inversely proportional to the distance between them" (p. 213). Though numerous communication technologies have been designed to overcome this phenomenon, Krackhardt argues that the tendency remains and is difficult for people to overcome. The third constraint he identifies is the "Iron Law of Oligarchy," which is the tendency for groups and social systems, even fervently democratic ones, to end up under the control of a few people. Finally, Krackhardt (1994) notes the potential problem of overembeddedness. He observes that "people as a matter of habit and preference are likely to seek out their old standbys, the people they have grown to trust, the people they always go to and depend on, to deal with new problems, even though they may not be the ones best able to address these problems" (p. 220).

Poole (1999) also points to several human problems that stem from the tightly coupled technology but fluid management philosophies on which most network organizations are built. Poole (1999) notes that foremost among these problems are maintaining a sense of mission, commitment, loyalty, and trust, and dealing with increased levels of work stress and burnout.

Extensions to Exchange and Dependency Theories

While some variation exists across different studies, the preponderance of evidence suggests that many inter- and intraorganizational communication networks are created and maintained on the basis of exchange mechanisms. Further, as people and organizations find their exchanges no longer rewarding, or as new or competitive others offer better bargains in the exchange, linkages begin to dissolve.

Despite its intellectual roots in the study of interpersonal relationships, exchange and dependency theories have been more extensively deployed in the study of interorganizational networks, often within the context of resource dependency theory, than intraorganizational networks. Much of the intraorganizational research reviewed above, while premised in a social exchange perspective, does not invoke the theory explicitly. Further, in areas such as leadership, trust, and ethical behavior, the studies so far are more illustrative then programmatic attempts at applying social exchange theory. X-Net, a computer simulation tool developed by Markovsky (1995) should help researchers explore the emergence of networks in terms of different rules of exchange and varied resources. Researchers have also proposed integrating network exchange theory with rational choice theory (Markovsky, 1997) and identity theory (Burke, 1997), and a general theoretical method called E-state structuralism (Skvoretz & Fararo, 1996; Skvoretz & Faust, 1996) that integrates research on expectation states theory (Berger, Cohen, & Zelditch, 1966) with network exchange theory. Expectation states theory argues that a person's "behavior towards social objects depends on postulated and unobservable states of relational orientations to objects, E-states for short" (Skvoretz & Fararo, 1996, p. 1370). The social objects toward which individuals orient are the networks of ties among the individuals. E-state models specify "how the state of this network, i.e. the number and nature of the ties linking actors, changes over time as individuals interact" (Skvoretz & Fararo, 1996, p. 1370).

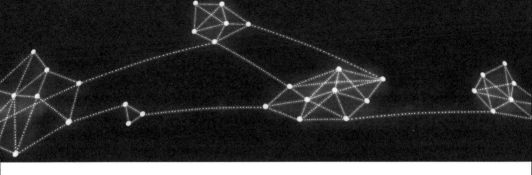

8

Homophily, Proximity, and Social Support Theories

This chapter discusses three families of theoretical mechanisms—homophily, proximity (physical and electronic), and social support—that have been identified by social scientists as important motivations for why we create, maintain, dissolve, and reconstitute our communication networks. While much of this research is conducted in nonorganizational settings, this chapter focuses on the theory and research that we consider to be most germane to communication and other organizational networks.

Homophily

Several researchers have attempted to explain communication networks on the basis of *homophily*, that is, the selection of others who are similar. Brass (1995a, p. 51) notes that "similarity is thought to ease communication, increase predictability of behavior, and foster trust and reciprocity." Homophily has been studied on the basis of similarity in age, gender, education, prestige, social class, tenure, and occupation (Carley, 1991; Coleman, 1957; Ibarra, 1993b, 1995; Laumann, 1966; Marsden, 1988; McPherson & Smith-Lovin, 1987).

Several lines of reasoning provide support for the homophily hypothesis. These fall into two general categories: the *similarity-attraction hypothesis*

(Byrne, 1971) and the *theory of self-categorization* (Turner, 1987). The similarity-attraction hypothesis is exemplified in the work of Heider (1958) who posited that homophily reduces the psychological discomfort that may arise from cognitive or emotional inconsistency. Similarly, Sherif (1958) suggested that individuals were more likely to select similar others because by doing so they reduce the potential areas of conflict in the relationship. The theory of self-categorization (Turner & Oakes, 1986) suggests that individuals define their social identity through a process of self-categorization during which they classify themselves and others using categories such as age, race, gender. Schachter (1959) argued that similarity provided individuals with a basis for legitimizing their own social identity. The manner in which individuals categorize themselves influences the extent to which they associate with others who are seen as falling into the same category.

Theoretical Mechanisms of Homophily

It is easy to see that the theoretical mechanism by which homophily influences the likelihood of a communication relation is based on the similarity among specific attributes of the actors. Consider, C_{ij} as the communication relation between two actors i and j. Further, consider $A1_i$ and $A2_i$ as representing two attributes, say gender and tenure in the organization, possessed by actor i. A homophily mechanism would posit that the likelihood of communication between actor i and j would be positively influenced if both actors i and j were of the same gender or had similar tenure in the organization. The homophily mechanisms for these two attributes would be represented as:

$$C_{ij} = \text{function } [(A1_i) - (A1_j)] \tag{1}$$

$$C_{ij} = \text{function } [(A2_i) - (A2_j)] \tag{2}$$

In both equations, the function is negative (or inverse) because the difference in values of the attributes for the two actors would indicate dissimilarity in gender and this would reduce the likelihood of communication.

An extension of this approach would be to consider collectively the likelihood of homophily across multiple attributes. For instance, one may posit that the likelihood of communication is substantially higher only when the two actors are of the same gender *and* have similar tenure. In such cases, the mechanism may be represented as:

$$C_{ij} = \text{function } [\{(A1_i) - (A1_j)\}\{(A2_i) - (A2_j)\}] \tag{3}$$

Here again the function specified is a negative or inverse relationship. In this case, the likelihood of communication increases only when the two actors have the same or similar values for both of the attributes specified.

Empirical Research Using Homophily Mechanisms

A substantial body of organizational demography research is premised on homophily mechanisms. In addition, several studies have focused specifically on gender homophily. Each of these two areas is reviewed below.

GENERAL DEMOGRAPHIC HOMOPHILY

The increased workforce diversity in contemporary organizations has seen a rise in the creation of heterogeneous work groups that complicate individuals' desires for homophily. Several studies have examined the extent to which individuals' predilection for homophily structures organizational networks. Zenger and Lawrence (1989) found that technical communication among researchers in a high-technology firm was related to their age and tenure distribution. Studies by O'Reilly and colleagues (Tsui, Egan, & O'Reilly, 1992; Tsui & O'Reilly, 1989; Wagner, Pfeffer, & O'Reilly, 1984) found that differences in age among employees hindered communication and social integration and resulted in lower commitment and greater turnover among employees.

Basing their arguments on the principle of homophily, Liedka (1991) studied the age and education distribution of members recruited to join voluntary organizations such as youth groups, farm organizations, and sports clubs. Using data collected in the 1985 and 1986 General Social Survey, he found results at the aggregate level, suggesting that members of voluntary organizations were more likely to persuade others similar to their age and education to join the organization. He also found that when people in the same age groups were more densely connected, they were more likely to be represented in voluntary organizations. At the interorganizational level, Galaskiewicz (1979) and Schermerhorn (1977) found that interorganizational links were more likely to occur among individuals who perceived similarity in religion, age, ethnicity, and professional affiliations.

GENDER HOMOPHILY

Considerable research has examined the effect of *gender homophily* on organizational networks. Lincoln and Miller (1979) found that similarities in sex and race of organizational employees were significant predictors of their ties in a friendship network. Brass's (1985b) research indicated that communication networks in an organization were largely clustered by gender.

Several studies have examined the effects of gender homophily on friendship. For instance, Leenders (1996) discovered that gender was a more influential predictor of enduring friendship ties than proximity. In a study of thirty-six female and forty-five male senior managers in two New York state government bureaucracies, Moore (1992, p. 53) found that "half of the advice cliques and nearly that proportion of cliques in the friendship network contain men only." Ibarra's (1992) research of an advertising agency revealed that even though women reported task-related communication and advice influence ties with men, they were more likely to select other women in their social support and friendship networks. Men, on the other hand, were more likely to have instrumental as well as noninstrumental ties with other men. She pointed out that the constraints of social exchange (see chapter 7) and the resulting need to be connected with the organization's predominantly male power base often force women to forgo their propensity for homophily in terms of their instrumental relationships.

Some aspects of culture bear on the preceding results. For example, contrary to other findings, research by Crombie and Birley (1992) showed that the network of contacts among female entrepreneurs in Ireland was not different from that of men in terms of size, diversity, density, and effectiveness. Perhaps the reason for this result is that the people in this study were entrepreneurs. However, the women tended to be younger, owners of smaller businesses that had been established for shorter periods of time, and less involved in traditional exterior activities such as belonging to civic organizations. Women also tended to rely on men and women for advice while men consulted largely with other men. In similar fashion, Ethington, Johnson, Marshall, Meyer, and Chang (1996) studied two organizations with different gender ratios. They found that men and women were equally integrated into and prominent in each others' networks in an organization that had an equal ratio of men and women and an equal gender distribution in the power hierarchy. However, in an organization that had a 75 percent to 25 percent female-to-male ratio, the networks were more segregated and women were more prominent.

Extensions to Theories of Homophily

Communication scholars have maintained an enduring interest in the principle of homophily as a theoretical mechanism to explain the emergence of networks. In response to the ongoing focus on workforce diversity, they have invoked this mechanism in the study of gender and race issues. The principle of homophily has also been suggested as a network mechanism that is relevant to researchers interested in the social comparison processes used by individuals to make assessments, for instance, about their perceptions of equity in the workplace. According to equity theory (Adams, 1965), individuals' motivations are a direct function of the extent to which their input (i.e., efforts) to output (i.e., rewards) ratios are commensurate with those of relevant others. *Social comparison theory* (Festinger, 1954) suggests that these relevant others are selected on the basis of being similar, or homophilous, in salient respects. Likewise, *social identity theory* (Turner & Oakes, 1989) proposes that these relevant others are those who are seen as sharing the same "social identity" as the focal person. Krackhardt and Brass (1994) suggest that the selection of relevant others is constrained and enabled by the networks in which individuals are embedded. Individuals could select as relevant others those with whom they have close communication ties (i.e., a cohesion mechanism) or with others who they see as having similar roles (i.e., a structurally equivalent mechanism).

Several scholars have urged that similarity of personality characteristics be used to explain involvement in communication networks (Brass, 1995a; Tosi, 1992). McPhee and Corman (1995) adopted a similar perspective in an article that drew on Feld's (1981) *activity focus theory* to argue that interaction is more likely to occur among individuals who share similar foci, including being involved in the same activities. They found limited support for their hypotheses in a study of church members, suggesting the need for further research.

Theories of Physical Proximity

A number of researchers have sought to explain communication networks on the basis of *physical proximity* (Corman, 1990; Johnson, 1992). Proximity facilitates the likelihood of communication by increasing the probability that individuals will meet and interact (Festinger, Schachter, & Back, 1950; Korzenny & Bauer, 1981; Monge, Rothman, Eisenberg, Miller, & Kirstie, 1985). If these interactions were to occur, they would allow individuals the opportunity to explore the extent to which they have common interests and shared beliefs (Homans, 1950).

Theoretical Mechanisms on Physical Proximity

The theoretical mechanisms whereby physical proximity influences the communication network are relatively simple. Let us say the focal person is i and each other individual is j. The communication relation from actor i to actor j is given by C_{ij}. The physical distance between i and j is given by D_{ij}. Hence the basic mechanism posits that:

$$C_{ij} = \text{function } [1/(D_{ij})] \tag{4}$$

This is clearly an inverse function. That is, as the distance D_{ij} increases the probability of communication decreases. Further, as will be discussed in the empirical research below, the effect of proximity on communication is not a linear function. That is, as the distance between two actors is increased twofold, the likelihood of communication is reduced by more than half. Hence the function is more accurately described as:

$$C_{ij} = \text{function } [1/(D_{ij})]^x \tag{5}$$

where the exponent, x, is a value greater than 1. If $x = 2$, the mechanism specified would posit that as distance between two actors, D_{ij}, doubles, the likelihood of communication, C_{ij}, is reduced by a quarter.

Empirical Research on Physical Proximity

Early research in organizational settings indicated that the frequency of face-to-face dyadic communication drops precipitously after the first 75–100 feet (Allen, 1970; Conrath, 1973). Zahn's (1991) more recent research also demonstrated that increased physical distance between offices, chain-of-command, and status led to decreased probability of communication. Likewise, Van den Bulte and Moenaert (1998) found that communication among R&D teams was enhanced after they were colocated. Therefore, individuals who are not proximate are deprived of the opportunity to explore these common interests and are hence less likely to initiate communication links. As such, physical or electronic proximity is a necessary but not sufficient condition for enabling network links. Dramatic evidence of the influence of physical proximity is available in the physical dislocation of 817 employees of the

Olivetti factory in Naples following 1983–1984 earthquakes. Bland et al. (1997) report that employees who were permanently relocated rather than evacuated only temporarily reported the highest distress levels due to the disruption in their social networks. Rice (1993a) notes that physical proximity may also facilitate contagion (see chapter 6) by exposing spatially colocated individuals to the same ambient stimuli. Rice and Aydin (1991) found modest evidence of the role played by physical proximity on employees' attitudes toward a new information system. At the interorganizational level, Palmer et al. (1986) found that interlock ties were more likely to be reconstituted if departing members represented organizations whose headquarters were physically proximate to that of focal organizations.

Theories of Electronic Proximity

In the past decade there has been considerable and growing interest in the intersection between computer networks and social networks. Many have argued that network analysis is an especially appropriate framework for investigating this intersection (Contractor & Eisenberg, 1990; Haythornthwaite, 1996; Rice, 1994b; Wellman, 2001). In light of the digital revolution, and the consequent blurring of distinctions between telecommunication and computing technologies, these technological networks span virtually all new communication technologies, including wireless mobile devices, instant messenger programs, short-messaging services, pagers, and videophones. At a metatheoretical level, the research and debate has largely focused on the extent to which these new media substitute, enlarge, or reconfigure preexisting communication networks. The new media offer various affordances (Contractor & Bishop, 2000; Gaver, 1996; Norman, 1999; Wellman, 2000)—cheaper and greater bandwidth; portability; embedded, pervasive, and ubiquitous computing; telepresence; and personalization of agents or networks (e.g., "buddy lists" in Instant Messenger programs). This poses questions about the potential of new media (1) to *substitute* for the older media we used to sustain our communication networks, (2) to *enlarge* (or supplement) our communication networks via older media, and (3) to *reconfigure* our communication networks—the number, diversity, proximity, and frequency of the people with whom we communicate. These research questions are motivated by a general public desire to find out if the Internet is making society in general, and the workplace in particular, more or less mobile, global, networked, centralized, or democratic. In addition to individual researchers, and partly in response to public curiosity, the National

Geographic Society (Wellman, Quan Haase, Witte, & Hampton, 2001) and the Pew Internet and American Life Project (Horrigan & Rainie, 2002) have organized large national and international studies to investigate these questions.

Theoretical Mechanisms of Electronic Proximity

The theoretical mechanisms in the previous section specifying the influence of electronic proximity on communication networks were conceptualized at three levels: substitution, enlargement, and reconfiguration. They can be further conceptualized in terms of (i) the communication relations CX_{ij}, CY_{ij}, CZ_{ij}, among the actors based on their use of specific communication media, say X (email), Y (video-conferencing), Z (instant messaging), and (ii) the attributes of the actor i, AX_i, AY_i, AZ_i, reflecting their use of the specific communication technologies X, Y, and Z. For instance, AX_i would be 7 if, on a scale of 1 to 7, actor i extensively used communication medium X, and AY_i would be 3 if actor i was only a moderate user of medium Y.

Hence, as a baseline requirement, the communication via medium X between two actors i and j would require that each actor had adopted the technology X. Therefore:

$$CX_{ij} = \text{function } [(AX_i)(AX_j)] \tag{6}$$

A *substitution mechanism* would posit that communication between actors i and j using X would be reduced if both actors i and j also had access to another communication medium, Y. For instance, if two actors had access to videoconferencing (Y), this would substitute for, and thereby reduce their communication via e-mail (X). This mechanism would be represented as:

$$CX_{ij} = \text{function } [(AX_i)(AX_j)/(AY_i)(AY_j)] \tag{7}$$

An *enlargement mechanism* would posit that communication between actors i and j using medium X would augment their communication using medium Y. For instance, actors may use e-mail (X) to schedule video-conferences (Y). This mechanism would be represented as:

$$CY_{ij} = \text{function } [(AX_i)(AX_j) + (AY_i)(AY_j)] \tag{8}$$

Finally, a *reconfiguration mechanism* would posit that communication between i and j using medium Z would reconfigure their relationships with other actors using media Z as well as X, for instance, if actor i decided to adopt instant messaging (Z). This adoption may facilitate communication with other actors, j, using instant messaging. Given the additional invest-ment in time and resources associated with this adoption, actor i's use of communication medium X may be diminished thereby reducing and recon-figuring their extant communication network with other actors, via medium X. This reconfiguration mechanism would be represented by:

$$CZ_{ij} = \text{function } [(AZi)(AZj)] \tag{9}$$

$$CX_{ij} = \text{function } [(AX_i)(AX_j) - \Sigma CZ_{ik}] \tag{10}$$

where CZ_{ij}, the communication relation via medium Z between actors i and j is influenced by the use of the medium Z by actors i and j, and CX_{ij}, the communication relation via medium X between actor i and actor j is posi-tively influenced by the use of medium X by actor i and actor j, but nega-tively influenced by the sum of actor i's communication via medium Z with all other actors, k.

Empirical Research on Electronic Propinquity

The effects of new communication technologies on the creation and modi-fication of social networks are well documented (Barnett & Salisbury, in press; Haythornthwaite & Wellman, 2001; Kraut, Patterson, Lundmark, Kiesler, Mukopadhyay, & Scherlis,1998; Rice, 1994b; Wellman, Quan Haase, Witte, & Hampton, 2001; Wellman, Salaff, Dimitrova, Garton, Gulia, and Haythornthwaite, 1996; for comprehensive recent reviews, see DiMaggio, Hargittai, Neuman, & Robinson, 2001; O'Mahony, & Barley, 1999). Many, but not all, of these studies use social network methods. And many, but not all, of these studies examine organizational communication (as distinct from other personal communication) relations.

The general conclusions of the empirical research are that new media are simultaneously substituting, enlarging, and reconfiguring our commu-nication networks. The specific instantiations to be found in individual stud-ies are more likely explained by other contextual factors rather than sim-ply the introduction of the technology. In some cases, the new media makes us more mobile while in other cases it eliminates the need for travel. In some cases it increases our off-line affiliations while in other instances it decreases them. It helps increase our global reach but also strengthens local communi-ties and geographically distributed, but culturally contiguous, "diasporas." It can lead to greater centralization in some organizations, but also under-mines centralization in others. It can decrease social isolation in some contexts, but in other contexts can endorse the claim that we are increasingly "bowling alone" (Putnam, 2000).

The conflicting findings have further fueled an enduring and fundamental intellectual tension between, what at two extremes, constitute the "technological imperative" and the "organizational imperative" (Markus & Robey, 1988). Research from a *technological imperative* seeks to find changes in organizations resulting from changes in the technology. Scholarship from an *organizational imperative* seeks to explain changes in the use of technology based on organizational constraints. The research on new media reviewed above has been predominantly from the technological imperative perspective. Throughout history, the introduction of new communication technologies has prompted proponents of the technological imperative (or, in its more extreme form, technological determinism) to investigate the effects of these technologies on the processes of organizing.

Fischer (1992) offers a very insightful and historical critique of these approaches to the study of one of the most successful communication technologies of the twentieth century, the telephone. The advent of the telephone prompted many to examine whether increased centralization or decentralization in the workplace would result. As Pool, Decker, Dizard, Israel, Rubin, and Weinstein (1977) document extensively, the introduction of the telephone facilitated an increase in centralization (the development of offices in high-rise buildings downtown) and an increase in decentralization (the development of suburban offices). Tehranian (1990) termed this phenomenon the *dual effects hypothesis*: technologies have opposite effects at the same time and in spite of each other. The likelihood that one effect is more prominent depends less on the technology and more on other social and organizational contingencies.

More recently, in the 1980s, undaunted by the lessons learned from the introduction of the telephone, the introduction of e-mail in organizations prompted similar research questions about its impact on centralization in organizations. After a decade of active research, the results mirrored the dual effects found in the case of the telephone (Rice, 1994). The advent of the Internet and the Web has unleashed a new spate of research in the same tradition and scholars are arriving at the similar inconclusive results. For instance, contrary to conventional wisdom that the new network forms of organizing should be less centralized, Ahuja and Carley (1999) found that these forms of organizing often exhibited very high levels of centralization and hierarchy in the communication network. Indeed, in a recent review, O'Mahony and Barley (1999, pp. 143–145) note that the empirical research is inconclusive on "whether information technologies further centralization or decentralization" and appear to depend on management contingencies. Less intuitive, but just as evident, are the effects of new technologies in preserving old communication structures. In a study of three sectors (the book trade, magazine and newspaper trade, and the newsprint suppliers) of the publishing industry in the United Kingdom, Spinardi, Graham, and Williams (1996) found that the introduction of electronic data interchange (EDI) consolidated and further embedded existing interorganizational relationships, thereby preventing business process reengineering.

Extensions to Theories of Physical and Electronic Proximity

The proliferation of information technologies in the workplace capable of transcending geographical obstacles has renewed interest in the relative effects of physical and electronic proximity and their interaction with communication patterns (Kraut, Egido, & Galegher, 1990; Steinfield & Fulk, 1990). Fulk and Boyd (1991) underscored the potential of network analysis "to test the situational moderating effect of geographic distance on media choice" (p. 433). Corman (1996) suggested that *cellular automata models* are particularly appropriate for studying the effects of physical proximity on communication networks. Cellular automata models can be used to study the collective and dynamic effects of proximity on the overall communication network when individuals in the network apply theoretically derived rules about creating, maintaining, or dissolving links with their "local," that is, proximate, network neighbors (Contractor, 1999).

The recurrence of studies from a technological imperative perspective with each new cycle of technological innovation suggest an abiding, albeit perhaps naïve, desire to seek simple, univalent, and unidirectional organizational effects of new media. However, alongside the substantial amount of research based on a technological imperative, and partly in response to it, there is a growing body of theorizing and research that embraces the emergent perspective (Markus & Robey, 1988). The *emergent perspective* seeks to strike a balance by acknowledging the role of technological affordances in triggering or facilitating some organizational processes but also explicitly incorporating the organizational imperatives that might moderate the influence of these technological affordances (Monge & Contractor, 2001). Theories based on an emergent perspective seek to understand the complex, adaptive, recursive, self-organizing patterns that emerge by examining the interrelationships between the genres and use of new media on the one hand and organizing structures and norms on the other hand (Arrow, McGrath, & Berdahl, 2000; DeSanctis & Fulk, 2000; DeSanctis, & Poole, 1994; Hollingshead & Contractor, 2002; Jackson, Poole, & Kuhn, 2002; Orlikowski, 1992; Yates, 1989). While many of these theoretical perspectives are cognizant and sympathetic to the role of social networks, they do not explicitly offer network mechanisms as part of their explanatory frameworks.

More generally, we believe that the intersection of computer networks and organizational communication networks are most usefully framed in terms of a multitheoretical model where the technological imperative theories deployed by the research cited earlier in this section is considered in conjunction with other theoretical mechanisms presented in other chapters of this book. One instructive example of this approach can be found in the research on media selection. Early research (Daft & Lengel, 1986; Short, Williams, & Christie, 1976) on media selection theorized that an individual's use of a specific communication channel would be determined by matching the *richness* of the information to be processed with the richness afforded by a particular medium. For communication tasks like negotiation that require a high degree of richness (defined as, among other factors, feedback, multiple cues, language variety), individuals will use a rich medium such as face-to-face or video-conferencing. On the other hand, for communication tasks that require a low degree of richness, such as finding out a flight schedule, individuals will prefer to access a leaner medium, for example, a written document. This explanation seeks to explain media use based solely on the affordances they offer.

However, in response to a lack of strong empirical support, Fulk, Schmitz, and Steinfield (1990) advocated a social influence model for technology use. The selection of a particular communication technology, they argued, is at least in part influenced by the selection of communication technologies by others in the individuals' social networks. Contractor and Eisenberg (1990) advanced this argument by positing that it was important for those considering the adoption of new communication technologies to anticipate their recursive consequences. These communication networks might be undermined or reinforced by the individuals' uses of the technology to develop new ties. As discussed in chapter 6, this explains the creation of communication technology links on the basis of a contagion mechanism.

Likewise, Markus (1990) argued that the decision to use a communication technology was predicated on the collective decision of at least a critical mass of other users in the individual's social network. For instance, the likelihood of an individual's use of an instant messenger (IM) application will be greatly enhanced once a critical mass of the individual's "buddies" has also signed up for that IM application. As discussed in chapter 5, this explanation relies on the logic of collection action (or mutual interests). This example illustrates the merits of explaining the creation of technologically mediated communication links on the basis of multiple theories. The affordances offered by the medium may be a necessary, but not sufficient, condition for its use. Other theoretical mechanisms, such as contagion and collective action, must be considered—in conjunction with technological affordances—in order to explain the creation, maintenance, dissolution, and reconstitution of communication networks.

Another example of this approach would be an extension to the work on coordination theory (Crowston, 1997; Malone & Crowston, 1992; Malone & Rockart, 1991). *Coordination theory* is explicitly concerned with the ways in which technology offers affordances that can be used to reduce the cost of coordination. Coordination costs are a key mechanism in transaction cost economics (TCE) theory to explain the emergence of network ties based on self-interest. Hence, one multitheoretical model would consider the emergence of technologically mediated communication network linkages based on the logic of TCE, where the coordination costs associated with the communication medium would be derived from the principles of coordination theory.

Social Support Theories

Interest in social support networks can be traced back to Durkheim's (1897–1977) groundbreaking work on the impact of solidarity and social integration on mental health. A social support explanation focuses on the ways in which communication networks help organizational members to cope with stress. Wellman (1992) and others have adopted this framework in their study of social support networks. Their research is largely based on the premise that social networks play a *buffering role* in the effects of stress on mental well-being (Berkman & Syme, 1979; Hall & Wellman, 1985).

Two general mechanisms exist by which social networks buffer the effects of stress. First, an individual in a dense social support network is offered increased social support in the form of resources and sociability. Lin and Ensel's (1989) research produced evidence that strong ties in the support network provided social resources that helped buffer both social and psychological stress. Second, Kadushin (1983) argued that social support can also be provided by less dense social circles. *Social circles* (Simmel, 1955) are networks in which membership is based on common characteristics or interests. Membership in a social circle can help provide social support "by (1) conveying immunity through leading the members to a better understanding of their problems, (2) being a resource for help, or (3) mobilizing resources" (Kadushin, 1983, p. 191).

Theoretical Mechanisms for Social Support

The theoretical and empirical literature on social support suggests several influences on the social support, SS_i, available to person i, some of which are relational. Other influences rely on attributes of person i and other people j in the network. In its most primitive form the social support for person i is increased if the individual is densely connected via communication ties, C_{ij}, with all other js. Thus:

$$SS_i = \text{function } [\Sigma C_{ij}] \tag{11}$$

However, a somewhat more sophisticated explanation suggests that social support is only enhanced when others in the communication network share common interests, say A, and thereby a common understanding of their problems. An example would be a common interest and understanding of the problems confronting, say, nursing. In this case, the mechanism would be represented as:

$$SS_i = \text{function } [\Sigma(C_{ij})(A_i)(A_j)] \tag{12}$$

Here, the amount of social support available to person i would be the sum of their communication with all other people j weighted by the degree to which they share common interest in attribute A.

A second mechanism proposed above would also include the material resources (MR) and informational resources (IR) that actors j may be able to offer actor i as part of their social support. The mechanism represented in equation 12 would be expanded thus:

$$SS_i = \text{function } [\Sigma(C_{ij})(A_i)(A_j) + \Sigma(C_{ij})(MR_j) + \Sigma(C_{ij})(IR_j)] \tag{13}$$

Finally, the third mechanism reviewed above suggests that the social support to an individual i may be influenced by the ability of other people, j, in their network to mobilize additional resources. There are multiple ways to operationalize actor j's ability to mobilize resources. For instance, a person j who is well connected to others (i.e., high degree centrality) may be in a better position to mobilize resources than a less well-connected individual. The mechanism represented in equation 13 would be expanded thus:

$$SS_i = \text{function } [\Sigma(C_{ij})(A_i)(A_j) + \Sigma(C_{ij})(MR_j)(\Sigma C_{jk}) \qquad (14)$$
$$+ \Sigma(C_{ij})(IR_j)(\Sigma C_{jk})]$$

where ΣC_{jk} represents the degree of centrality of person j among all other people, k, in the network.

Empirical Research Using Social Support Mechanisms

A substantial amount of research exists on the role of networks in providing social support in various nonorganizational contexts, such as families, communities, and neighborhoods (for reviews, see O'Reilly, 1988; Walker, Wasserman, & Wellman, 1994). In a classic longitudinal study of residents in a northern California county, Berkman and Syme (1979) found that respondents "who lacked social and community ties were more likely to die in the follow-up period than those with more extensive contacts" (p. 186). Berkman (1985) found that individuals with fewer social support contacts via marriage, friends, relatives, church memberships, and associations had a higher mortality rate.

Researchers (Barrera & Ainlay, 1983; Cutrona & Russell, 1990; Wellman & Wortley, 1989, 1990) have identified four dimensions of social support, including emotional aid, material aid (goods, money, and services), information, and companionship. Considerable empirical evidence demonstrates that individuals cannot rely on a single network link, except to their parents or children, to provide all four dimensions of social support. A study by Wellman and Wortley (1989, 1990) of a community in southern Ontario, Canada, found that individuals' specific network ties provided either emotional aid or material aid, but not both. Additionally, studies have found that women are more likely to offer emotional aid then men (Campbell & Lee, 1990).

Remarkably few studies have examined networks of social support in organizational contexts even though several scholars have underscored the need for research in this area (Bass & Stein, 1997). For example, Langford, Bowsher, Maloney, and Lillis (1997) proposed the examination of networks to study social support in nursing environments such as hospitals and nursing homes. A comparison of six hospital units by Albrecht and Ropp (1982) found that the volume and tone of interaction in the surgical unit's communication network improved their ability to cope with chronic pressures and stress. In one of the few studies of social support networks in organizations, Cummings (1997) found that individuals who reported receiving greater social support from their networks were more likely to generate radical (i.e., frame-breaking) innovation.

Hurlbert (1991) used egocentric network data for a sample of respondents from the 1985 General Social Survey (the first national sample containing network data) to examine the effect of kin and co-worker networks on stress, as measured by individuals' job satisfaction. She argued that individuals' networks may (a) provide resources to decrease the level of stress created by job conditions, or (b) provide support thereby helping the individual cope with job stress. She found that membership in a co-worker social circle was positively associated with job satisfaction, even after controlling for other social and demographic variables. The effect on job satisfaction was even higher if the co-workers were highly educated, suggesting that they were able to offer additional instrumental resources. However, Hurlbert (1991) also found that for individuals who were in blue-collar jobs or those with low security, "kin-centered networks may exacerbate, rather than ameliorate, negative job conditions" (p. 426). Consistent with this latter finding, Ray (1991) and Ray and Miller (1991) found that individuals who were highly involved in networks offering social support to friends and co-workers were more likely to report high levels of emotional exhaustion. The negative effects of the network on individuals were also reported in a longitudinal study of relatively well-functioning older men and women. Seeman, Bruce, and McAvay (1996) found that men who had larger instrumental support networks were more likely to report the onset of daily living disabilities. They speculated that these results may reflect "the consequences of greater reliance on others, a behavior pattern which may, over time, erode the recipient's confidence in their [sic] ability to do things independently" (pp. 197–198).

At the interorganizational level, Eisenberg and Swanson (1996) noted that Connecticut's Healthy Start program served an important social support role for pregnant women by serving as referral to hospitals and agencies. Zinger, Blanco, Zanibbi, and Mount (1996) reported that Canadian small businesses relied more heavily on an informal support network than government programs. Paterniti, Chellini, Sacchetti, and Tognelli (1996) described how an Italian rehabilitation center for schizophrenic patients successfully created network links with other organizations to reflect "the social network that surrounds the patient and from which he [sic] has come" (p. 86).

Extensions to Social Support Theories

The amount of research on social support networks has increased substantially in the past few years. Some of these changes are perhaps motivated by changes in the organizational landscape, such as the increase in outsourcing, telecommuting, job retraining for displaced workers (Davies, 1996), and small business start-ups (Zinger et al., 1996). All of these activities often serve to isolate the individual worker from the institutional support structures of traditional organizations. Hence, there is greater salience today for improving our understanding of the role of social support mechanisms in the emergence of networks.

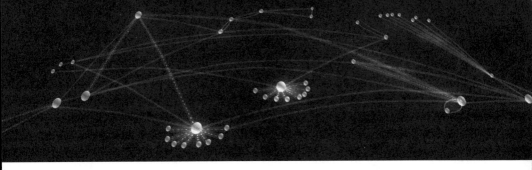

9

Evolutionary and Coevolutionary Theories

> Eighteenth-century science, following the Newtonian
> revolution, has been characterized as developing the sciences
> of organized complexity, nineteenth-century science, via
> statistical mechanics, as focusing on disorganized complexity,
> and twentieth- and twenty-first-century science as
> confronting organized complexity.... Living systems—
> organisms, communities, coevolving ecosystems—are the
> paramount examples of organized complexity. (Kauffman,
> *The Origins of Order*)

Chapter 3 discussed the emergence of communication networks from the
perspective of complexity theory. Specifically, we described complexity as
a network of agents, each with a set of attributes, who follow rules of interaction, which produces emergent structure. Complexity arose from the fact
that there were numerous agents with extensive relations. Some complex
systems but by no means all, we argued, were self-organizing, meaning that
they created and sustained internal structure in response to the flow of
matter and energy around them. Some readers, particularly those with some
familiarity with the complex adaptive systems literature, may have noticed
that the discussion of complexity in chapter 3 did not include processes of
adaptation, evolution, or coevolution. The reason for this is that it is pos-

sible to view these as theoretical mechanisms that operate in at least some complex, self-organizing systems, though not necessarily all. Thus, we have chosen to treat adaptation and the coevolutionary perspective as theoretical mechanisms in the same manner as the other theoretical mechanisms we have examined in chapters 5 through 8. In the present chapter we examine adaptive and coevolutionary processes as the basis for building MTML models of emergent communication networks that form the basis for organizational populations and communities.

Evolutionary Theory and Population Ecology

Modern interest in evolutionary theory as a basis for studying human social processes can be traced to the work of Amos Hawley (1950, 1968, 1986). Much of the interest in applying this perspective to studying organizational structures is credited to Donald Campbell (1965, 1974). Over much of his professional life Campbell explored the application of evolutionary theory to a wide array of sociocultural processes, including organizations (Baum & McKelvey, 1999). Campbell is perhaps best known throughout the social sciences for his work on experimental and quasi-experimental design (Campbell and Stanley, 1966; Cook & Campbell, 1980) and multimethod triangulation (Campbell & Fiske, 1959). Nonetheless, McKelvey and Baum (1999) point to Campbell's enormous influence in organizational science via the early work of Aldrich (1972) on organizational boundaries, Weick's (1979) formulation of an *evolutionary model of organizing*, Hannan and Freeman's (1977, 1983) development of *population ecology theory* (and inertial theory), McKelvey's (1982) work on *organizational taxonomies*, and Nelson and Winter's (1982) *evolutionary theory of economics*.

As an extensive review by Baum (1996) amply demonstrates, much organizational research has been conducted in the past two decades to test the various forms of evolutionary theory listed in the previous paragraph. We reproduce table 1 from Baum's (1996) chapter here and highlight its key findings (see table 9.1).

Baum organizes this corpus of work into three key areas: Demographic processes, ecological processes, and environmental processes. Typical research on *demographic processes* looks at the liability (advantage) of age and size, showing competitive advantage to older, established organizations as well as to larger ones (Freeman & Hannan, 1983). Research on *ecological processes* has concentrated on niche width dynamics, population dynamics, density dependence, and community interdependence. *Niche width* research

Table 9.1
Major Ecological Approaches to Organizational Founding and Failure (from Baum, 1996)

	Key Variables	Key Predictions	Key References
Demographic Processes			
Age dependence	Organizational age	Liability of newness: organizational failure rates decline with age as roles and routines are mastered, and links with external constituents established	Freeman et al., 1983
		Liability of adolescence: organizational failure rates rise with initial increases in age, reach a peak when initial buffering resource endowments are depleted, then decline with further increases in age	Bruderl and Schussler, 1990; Fichman and Levinthal, 1991
		Liability of obsolescence: organizations' failure rates increase with age as their original fit with the environment erodes	Baum, 1989a; Ingram, 1993; Ranger-Moore, 1991; Barron et al., 1994
Size dependence	Organizational size	Liability of smallness: organizational failure rates decline with size which buffers organizations from threats to survival	Freeman et al., 1983
Ecological Processes			
Niche-width dynamics	Specialist strategy	Specialists exploit a narrow range of resources and are favored in fine-grained and concentrated environments	Freeman and Hannan, 1983, 1987; Carroll, 1985
	Generalist strategy	Generalists tolerate widely varying environmental conditions and are favored in coarse-grained, high-variability environments	

(continued)

Table 9.1
(continued)

	Key Variables	Key Predictions	Key References
Ecological Processes			
Population dynamics	Prior foundings	Initial increases in prior foundings signal opportunity, stimulating new foundings, but further increases create competition for resources, suppressing new foundings. Increases in prior foundings that signal organizational differentiation lower the failure rate	Carroll and Delacroix, 1982; Delacroix and Carroll 1983; Delacroix et al., 1989
	Prior failures	Initial increases in prior deaths free up resources, stimulating new foundings, but further increases signal a hostile environment suppressing new foundings. Resources freed up by prior deaths lower the failure rate	
Density dependence	Population density (i.e., a number of organizations in a population)	Initial increases in density increase the institutional legitimacy of a population, increasing foundings and lowering failures, but further increases produce competition, suppressing foundings and increasing failures	Hannan and Freeman, 1987; 1988; 1989; Hannan and Carroll, 1992
Community interdependence	Population density	Examines cross-population density effects. Competitive (mutualistic) populations suppress (stimulate) each other's founding rates and raise (lower) each other's failure rates	Hannan and Freeman, 1987; 1988; Barnett, 1990; Brittain, 1994

Environmental Processes

		References
Institutional processes		
	Political turmoil	Political turmoil affects patterns of founding and failure by shifting social alignments, disrupting established relationships between organizations and resources, and freeing resources for use by new organizations	Carroll and Delacroix, 1982; Delacroix and Carroll, 1983; Carroll and Huo, 1986
	Government regulation	Government policies affect patterns of founding and failure by, for example, enhancing legitimacy, stimulating demand, providing subsidies, and regulating competition	Tucker et al., 1990a; Baum and Oliver, 1992; Barnett and Carroll, 1993
	Institutional linkages	Linkages to legitimated community and public institutions confer legitimacy and resources on organizations, lowering the failure rate	Singh et al., 1986b; Baum and Oliver, 1991
Technological processes		
	Technology cycles	Technology cycles affect patterns of founding and failure by, for example, changing the relative importance of various resources, creating opportunities to establish new competitive positions, and rendering competencies of existing organizations obsolete	Tushman and Anderson, 1986; Anderson, 1988; Suárez and Utterback, 1992

examines the amount of environmental resources available to organizations and the adaptation strategies they pursue as a function of being in wide or narrow niches. Carroll's (1985) work and others show that firms with wide niches typically adopt a *generalist strategy* while those in narrow niches adopt a *specialist strategy*. *Density dependence* focuses on the number of organizations in a population and the capacity of the environment to support that number. Research by Delacroix and Carroll (1983) and by Hannan and Carroll (1992) show that as a population invades new resource niches they typically thrive until new arrivals reduce the level of resources available and makes survival more difficult for all. *Community interdependence* "examines cross-population density effects" (Baum, 1996, p. 80), including symbiosis and competition (see Barnett, 1990; Brittain, 1994).

The third category in Baum's (1996) summary is *environmental processes*. These include institutional processes such as political upheaval (Carroll & Huo, 1986), governmental regulation (Barnett & Carroll, 1993), and institutional linkages (Baum & Oliver, 1991). Environmental processes also include technological processes, which refers to the effects of new technologies on creation of new firms, of changing structures in older ones, and impacting on survival rates (Anderson, 1988; Tushman & Anderson, 1986). While we review a number of these studies in greater detail later in the chapter, it is important to emphasize at this point an observation made by DiMaggio (1994), specifically, that relatively little of this work has focused on the networks among the members of a population or the networks that tie together different populations. As he says, this provides new and important opportunities for reconceptualizing evolutionary theory and conducting empirical research that incorporates networks.

In this chapter we examine evolutionary and coevolutionary theory as applied to communication and other networks. In the next section we examine the basic mechanisms for change and stability postulated by evolutionary theory. In the subsequent section we return to the issue of organizational forms discussed earlier in the book, but this time apply them to the notion of organizational populations. This leads naturally to a critique of the population ecology perspective and to a discussion of community, community ecology, and the issues surrounding coevolution. We then examine one network-based theory of evolution, Kauffman's NK model, where N represents the number of nodes in the population and K the number of epistatic linkages among the nodes, that is, the genetic network. After revisiting the issue of complexity raised in the third chapter, we explore Kauffman's work extended to the coevolutionary case, his NK(C) model, where N and K are as before but C represents linkages among members of different populations. Along with Astley (1985), Baum and Singh (1994), and others, we see evolutionary and coevolutionary processes unfolding in communities of organizational populations that inhabit environmental niches that contain resources. The members of the various populations are tied together to greater or lesser degrees by networks of competitive and symbiotic relations that foster their own efforts to acquire resources as well as the collective good of the community. Ultimately, one or more of these coevolutionary processes fail and the community collapses, making it possible for the entire process to begin anew.

Variation, Selection, and Retention

Evolutionary systems are built on the basis of three fundamental processes. These are variation, selection, and retention. In this first section we review these three basic components of evolutionary theory. Later, we explore how they operate on grander scales.

Organizations are typically "created" on the basis of elementary components or building blocks. Nelson and Winter (1982) argued that these fundamental components are routines and established sets of activities sometimes called *communities of practice* (see also Brown & Duguid, 1991). McKelvey (1982) called the elementary building blocks "comps" or the *competencies* that represent the organizations' skills and capabilities. Aldrich (1999) observed that in practice elemental routines and competencies are often *bundled* into larger routines and competencies. Rao and Singh (1999) suggested that these should be sorted into *core and peripheral competencies* and identified—"goals, authority relations, technologies, and markets" (p. 66)—as the four core organizational competencies. These four core competencies are arranged in somewhat of a hierarchy with goals being the most central and hardest to change and markets the least central and easiest to change. They label all other competencies beyond these four as peripheral, so a competency like advertising would be seen as peripheral rather than core.

The source of evolutionary change is *variation*. The counterpart to variation is *stability*. Both are important. Forces, often random, introduce change; existing practices, representing *inertia*, resist change (Hannan & Freeman, 1977, 1984). Evolution explores the constant tension between these two pressures: how organizations with sets of routines, activities, and traits turn into organizations with different routines, activity sets, and traits . . . or fail to do so. Journalistic organizations develop routines for creating news stories. Hospitals and physicians develop competencies or competency sets for diagnosing and treating illnesses. Steel mills develop routines for converting ore or scrap into rolls of steel. If routines and activities are the various knowledge, physical skills, and other competencies that organizations employ to create and deliver products and services (Nelson & Winter, 1982), then variations comprise the set of other possible competencies that organizations could develop or acquire. These variations are typically made up of new combinations or rearrangements of existing or prior routines and competencies. For example, new treatment regimes are typically developed when new drugs are approved for treating patients. Often the new practices are variations on prior ones that incorporate the new modifications required by the new drug.

In the organizational sciences, it is typical to distinguish two types of variations: "blind" and "intentional" (Aldrich, 1999, pp. 23–25). Both are considered important in organizational processes. *Blind variations* are like random biological mutations that occur largely by chance. Without planning, people stumble on alternative ways of doing things. Accidents happen that prove to be fortuitous. A routine gets disrupted and in coping with the anomaly people discover ways to improve the process. New people join organizations and introduce new alternatives to existing routines (March, 1994). Events happen to organizations and their environments to which they must respond. These include things like technological inventions, governmental regulations, degradation of environmental niches, and new entrants into the competitive field. In responding to these events they typically, though not always, have the opportunity to broaden their knowledge and capabilities, that is, to learn from the challenges facing them (Miner, 1994).

Intentional variations are the actions that people take in trying to solve problems. Entrepreneurs invest extensive energy in developing new organizations capable of generating innovative products and services (Aldrich, 1999). Research and development departments in existing organizations actively seek innovations, new variations on old themes designed to improve existing practices. They also try to invent new products and services, ones that have not been known before. *Trial and error learning* is at the heart of most intentional variations. "Trials are variations in the established way of doing things" (Romanelli, 1999, p. 80), and thus, provide possible solutions which people employ to address problems that arise in routines and competencies. People use experiments, hunches, bench marking, imitation of other organizational practices, consultants, and creative exploration to find alternatives by which to solve problems. March (1991) calls this type of organizational learning *exploration*, where organizations actively pursue new ways of knowing. He contrasts this with *exploitation* where organizations seek to get the most out of known and established practices. Thus, most organizations operate on the basis of both blind and intentional variation (Nelson & Winter, 1982).

Selection is the second fundamental evolutionary process. Selection processes operate on variations to choose some over others, thus, of course, also rejecting the variations not chosen. Selection typically operates through a set of criteria that attempt to optimize benefit and minimize harm. "Selection criteria are set through the operation of market forces, competitive pressures, the logic of internal structuring, conformity to institutionalized norms, and other forces" (Aldrich, 1999, p. 26). This is not to say that harmful variations are never selected. Indeed, they are, since it is not possible for people or organizations to know in advance whether selected variations will, in fact, improve organizational fitness (Romanelli, 1999). Some of these selection devices, such as choice of organizational structure and strategy, are within the control of organizational managers and permit people to make conscious choices among alternatives. Other selection devices, like the appearance of new technologies or the formation of new government regulations, occur in the organization's environment and are beyond its control. Nonetheless, organizations generally make every effort to select alternatives that they believe will benefit them and to respond to organizational variations that they cannot control. Processes that lead to selection of variations include *interorganizational imitation* (Miner & Raghavan, 1999), *mimetic learning* (Mezias & Lant, 1994), and *vicarious learning* (Delacroix & Rao, 1994; DiMaggio & Powell, 1983) in which organizations copy or borrow (Campbell, 1969) what they perceive as the successful practices of other organizations, thus introducing new variations into their own communities of practice. Miner and Raghavan (1999) observe that "repeated interorganizational imitation acts as a *selection engine* to change the nature and mix of routines enacted in a population of organizations" (p. 35, italics added).

Retention is the third part of the evolutionary system. A *retention mechanism* (Aldrich, 1999, p. 30) is the process by which a selected variation becomes an integral part of the organization, an accepted routine, an innovative competency, or a new trait. Thus, the new variation becomes part of the standard ways of doing things in the organization, part of the community of practice. The new variation replaces the old procedure or is added as a new competency to the activity set. Most of these innovations are rather small, incremental changes designed primarily to improve internal performance and functioning. Other innovations may be more radical (Tushman

& Romanelli, 1985), seeking to change the fundamental form of operation of the organization. These new *radical variations* help to create significant new organizational capabilities, and as they are retained, they help to create new organizational forms as well as stabilize and preserve them. However, as Miner (1994) points out, organizations need to walk a delicate line in selecting and retaining organizational variation. Selection-retention mechanisms that are resistant to selecting and retaining new variations tend to preserve the status quo, and therefore, may prevent the organization from evolving sufficiently to survive. For example, Miner describes how some organizations selected disc-based video systems rather than tape-based alternatives for video conferencing. Market forces eventually selected the tape system as the "dominant design," but many organizations were reluctant to convert from disc to tape because of their sunk costs in the former, thus lowering their likelihood of survival. On the other hand, innovation creates its own liability in that it "prevents the system from harvesting the value of prior innovation" (p. 80). In fact, "the crucial concept underlying the retention process is that of consistency" (p. 80). Thus, organizations must *standardize* or *routinize* newly retained variations in order to operate effectively.

Environmental Niches and Resources

All organizations require *resources* in order to operate (Levinthal, 1994). These include people and their talents—including knowledge, skills, and abilities—financial resources, and raw materials from which to manufacture products. Many of these resources exist in the *niches* or parts of the environment that organizations inhabit (Hannan & Freeman, 1977). Niches can be defined in a wide variety of ways, but all are relevant to the resources they contain and the ability of these resources to support organizational communities. Some niches are defined geographically, in the sense that they exist in some places and not others, such as coal, oil, and diamond fields. Others pertain to knowledge resources, such as new biotechnology firms that have historically located near major universities where much of the original basic research is conducted and where highly skilled employees are available. Some niches are munificent in that they contain abundant resources (Astley, 1985)—many skilled people, plentiful raw materials, favorable tax incentives, while others have only scarce resources—few skilled people, scarce raw materials, and high taxation, to name the most common debits. In either case, niches are comprised of a finite set of resources, which

Hannan and Freeman (1978) describe as the *carrying capacity* of the niche (p. 940; see also Hawley, 1950).

When niches are resource rich, organizations rarely compete, as competition is costly and unnecessary if resources are easy to acquire (Astley, 1985). However, resource rich niches attract other members of the population as well as members of other populations in the community, thus increasing the density of the populations inhabiting the niche (Hannan & Freeman, 1984; as discussed in the next section, populations are identified by their form and function and are also called species; see Hawley, 1986). As population density in the niche increases, resources begin to dwindle as other members consume them. As resources become more difficult to acquire, the members of the population (and in community contexts, other species) begin to compete more intensely. Hannan and Freeman (1977) articulated a density-dependent argument to account for the outcomes of this phenomenon. The argument specifies, and considerable research has shown, that an inverted U-shaped curve describes the relationship between niche density and organizational success (e.g., Delacroix, Swaminathan, & Solt, 1989). Specifically, organizations in a population that move into new, less dense niches tend to thrive, but as additional organizations join the niche, density increases toward the carrying capacity of the niche. As density approaches the carrying capacity, organizations begin to falter, leading eventually to a decline in the entire organizational population.

It is important to point out here that the notion of density in population ecology refers primarily to the number of members of a population, or the number of members of several populations, that inhabit a given niche. As Hannan and Freeman (1977, 1984) use the term, it does *not* refer to the level of connectedness among the inhabitants of the niche, either within a given population or among members of all populations. However, Hawley (1986) points out that "even at the simple organizational level" populations are "organized as a network of relations among species, that is, an ecosystem. It would seem clear, therefore, that the dynamic potential combined with the niche structure of the system constitute it as the selective agent" (p. 56). And, as was noted earlier in the chapter, DiMaggio (1994) also emphasized the fact that population ecology would be significantly improved both theoretically and empirically by incorporation of the network of relations within organizational members of populations and community niches.

While the density-dependence argument provides an important explanation for the size of organizational populations, Brittain and Freeman (1980) have argued that there are a host of other *density independent* environmental factors that influence organizational growth and decline. These include finances, technological changes, and government relations, to name but a few (Brittain, 1994). Of course, other populations of organizations also inhabit these niches and compete for some of the same or similar resources. Thus, all the species relevant to a specific niche must be considered in an analysis of any niche and its carrying capacity.

Organizational Forms and Populations

Few social scientists are accustomed to thinking in terms of *populations*. Most focus their scholarly attention on individual units of analysis such as the person, the single group, and the individual organization. But biologists in general, and those social scientists who have adopted an ecological or community ecology framework are rarely interested in single units of analysis. Instead, they tend to theorize about entire populations and conduct research at either the *population or the community level* (Aldrich, 1999).

Evolutionists typically define populations by their *organizational forms* (McKelvey, 1982). In chapter 1 we defined organizational forms as communication networks and other structures that share common features across a large set of organizations (pp. 1–20; see also Romanelli, 1991, pp. 81–82). Carroll and Hannan (2000) argue that *identity* also constitutes an important aspect of form. Organizations share identities to the extent that people inside the boundaries recognize that particular configurations of properties exist and those outside the organization confer legitimacy on those characteristics and processes (McKendrick & Carroll, 2001). Other organizations that share these unique configurations of characteristics would be considered to be part of the same population. Carroll and Hannan (2000) give the example of microbreweries and brewpubs, which specialize in making stouts and ales and compete with each other in a specialized niche generally apart from the mass producer beer companies. These microbreweries, which have grown enormously in popularity over the past decade, see themselves as specialists that appeal to beer connoisseurs, and the mass producers generally identify them this way also. A number of organizational populations have been extensively studied in the organizational literature recently, including the semiconductor industry (Podolny, Stuart, & Hannan, 1996), the wine industry (Delacroix, Swaminathan, & Solt, 1989), the newspaper industry, microbreweries, children's television program organizations (Bryant, 2002), credit unions (Barron, West, & Hannan, 1994), banks (Barnett,

Greve, & Park, 1994), and nongovernmental AIDS organizations (Shumate, 2002), to name but a few.

Interest in organizational forms and populations raises questions about how organizations come into existence, how they attain *fitness* and *survive* (Hannan & Freeman, 1977), the conditions that lead to their *demise*, and their eventual *re-creation or replacement* by successors (Aldrich, 1999). For example, Barnett and Carroll (1987) studied the transformation of the American telephone industry at the beginning of the nineteenth century by exploring two different organizational forms, the *mutualists* and the *commercialists*. Of course, there were no telephone companies of any form until after the telephone was invented and showed potential as a commercial product or service. As they began to develop, they took two different routes. Mutualists were organized into small, rurally based consumer cooperatives, loosely organized and without much central leadership who tried "to provide telephone service without regard for profitability" (p. 3). Commercialists were larger, city based, centrally organized for-profit organizations represented primarily by the early forms of the Bell System.

Contrary to what people might think today, mutualist companies vastly outnumbered commercialists at the turn of the twentieth century, by a factor of almost ten to one (at least in the regions of the country that Barnett studied). Though these companies cooperated in order to transmit telephone calls among their separate systems, they also competed for customers. In fact, fierce competition for customers between 1900 and 1917 enabled the commercialists to buy out all of the mutualist forms and integrate them into the commercialist form. In less than twenty years the mutualist cooperative form disappeared as an organizational population. Barnett and Carroll (1987) provide a number of explanations for the demise of the mutualist form, including organizational size (mutualists tended to be smaller), geography (country versus city), and technology (the two forms tended to use different transmission technologies).

By examining the entire population of telephone companies, Barnett and Carroll (1984; see also Barnett, 1994) were able to show how evolutionary processes led to the selection of one variation in the population over another. Variation existed in the nature of the two forms, commercialist and mutualists. Commercialists were selected over mutualists by a variety of density dependent and density independent factors. Both cooperation and competition processes occurred, throughout overlapping city and country realms of the niche. Eventually, competition in one realm led to the demise of one form, the presumably less fit mutualist, and the retention of the other, the commercialist. These evolutionary processes led to a fundamental alteration in the population of telephone companies. Of course, most of this analysis is focused on the early years of the American telephony industry in which these processes essentially led to AT&T acquiring a monopoly. Ironically, a continuing study of this population up to the present time would reveal the reversal of this monopoly. Not only was AT&T split into several different competing companies but a new wave of competition emerged from new entrants to the population.

Organizational Change

Evolutionary theory addresses fundamental issues of change. An interesting debate has ensued between two competing perspectives on organizational change. Hannan and Freeman (1978), representing the population ecology perspective, observe that most organizations experience extensive inertia and consequently have considerable difficulty adapting to changes in their environments. This inertia stems from "internal structural arrangements and environmental constraints" (p. 931). Yet, they look at the variety of organizational forms and ask the question, "why are there so many kinds of organizations" (p. 936)? Citing Hawley (1968), Hannan and Freeman (1977) postulate that a principle of *isomorphism* (pp. 938–939) leads organizations to match the characteristics of the environments in which they exist. In short, environmental diversity begets organizational and population diversity. (The principle of isomorphism shares much in common with Emery and Trist's 1965 work on the causal texture of organizational environments, which specified that different types of organizational environments placed different types of demands on organizations to which they must respond in order to survive.)

DiMaggio and Powell (1983), on the other hand, representing the neoinstitutional perspective, look at the same evidence but raise the opposite challenge: "why there is such startling homogeneity of organizational forms and practices" (p. 148). DiMaggio and Powell also invoke the principle of isomorphism as a source of change, but they argue that neoinstitutional processes work within populations so that other organizations become the source of change rather than the environment. DiMaggio and Powell identify three powerful institutional sources for change: "(1) *coercive* isomorphism that stems from political influence and the problem of legitimacy, (2) *mimetic* isomorphism resulting from standard responses to uncertainty, and (3) *normative* isomorphism associated with professionalism" (p. 150, italics in the original). As we discussed in chapter 6, extensive research has been conducted on mimetic and other imitative processes, which can usefully inform this aspect of evolutionary theory. For example, Baum and Oliver's (1991) work shows that new organizations lowered their likelihood of failure by increasing their communication ties to networks of legitimizing organizations in their populations and imitating their practices.

Critique of the Population Ecology Perspective

The focus on evolutionary processes in organizational populations is a genuinely significant contribution to the study of organizations and networks (McKelvey, 1999a, b). Despite these contributions, a number of issues can be raised with the population ecology approach that focuses primarily on single populations. First, it is important to remember that evolutionary theory is inherently multilevel and heterarchical (Baum & Singh, 1994; Rosenkopf & Nerkar, 1999). In the natural realm, this applies throughout the range of all living things, beginning at the genetic level and continuing to the level of the entire planet as an ecosystem of communities of living populations (Kauffman, 1995). Applied to organizations and networks, evolutionary theory also covers a multilevel heterarchy that ranges from the individual entrepreneur (Aldrich & Kenworthy, 1999) or organizational manager (Burgelman & Mittman, 1994) to the level of the ecosystem network that ties together interacting communities (Baum & Singh, 1994) comprised of multiple organizational populations (Brittain, 1994). Thus, a valid conception of evolution must encompass all the populations and niches that comprise the ecosystem network, not just single populations (Hawley, 1986). Of course, it may not be feasible to examine all levels simultaneously. Numerous studies investigate entrepreneurial and managerial activity within organizations (see, e.g., Campbell, 1994; Miner, 1994). Others study organizational processes such as mimetic change with populations (Mezias & Lant, 1994). Yet others examine the interplay between populations within communities (Barnett, 1994; Ruef, 2000; Van de Ven & Grazman, 1999). Finally, though difficult, several studies do attempt to explore multilevel hypotheses. For example, Rosenkopf and Nerkar (1999) examined the coevolution of component, products, and organizational systems within and across hierarchical levels in optical disc technology. And Baum (1999) used Kauffman's NK(C) model (described in the next section) to explore the coevolutionary competition between lower level parts of organizations, like work groups, and the organization as a whole. Their results showed that lower-level parts of the organization "typically out-evolve those at higher levels" (p. 132), thus leading to conflict between the more agile parts and the more stable whole. And as Campbell (1994) said in his study of individual and face-to-face selection mechanisms: "My basic assumption is one of potential conflict between (1) the interests of the firm per se and interests of each individual at every level of the organization; (2) the interests of one person and his or her colleagues at every level in the organization, (3) organizational levels within the organization; and (4) face-to-face groups within the organization" (p. 33). As these diverse examples amply illustrate, future researchers must be careful to specify which part of the entire ecological system they are studying—variation, selection, and retention within individual organizations, within populations of organizations, or within the ecological community comprised of multiple populations of organizations—and where possible, to make their inquiries as inclusive as possible.

Second, Astley (1985) criticizes population ecology on its conception of change. The population ecology perspective, he notes, is change by *phyletic gradualism*. This concept refers to "the gradual one-by-one selection of population members within single lines of descent, or lineages" (p. 225). This principle does produce change, but only from within the population itself, and only from those variations that are capable of being selected, retained, and transmitted to others in the population, thus improving the population overall. When the actual or potential variations within organizations begin to decline, evolutionary processes slow down, thus leading to increased inertia and lowering the likelihood of survival.

The alternative to gradualism is *punctuated equilibrium*. This perspective conceives of change as long periods of relative stability that are interrupted by rapid, abrupt amounts of change. As Astley (1985) says, evolution "moves with an episodic, not gradual tempo" (p. 230). Tushman and Romanelli (1985) view this process as sets of internal and external inconsistencies pitting pressures for change against pressures for inertia. Often, new technologies and inventions create the stimulus for massive organizational change, or provide the basis for creating new populations of organizations. For example, Van de Ven and Grazman (1999) explored the 140-year genealogies of four major health care organizations and identified three to five major events during these organizational histories that led either to significant organizational reorientation or to the creation of new organizational lineages.

Finally, Astley (1985) criticizes population ecology for failing to account for the emergence of new organizational forms and new organizational populations. "Instead of replacing their ancestors through a steady process of transformation, new populations diverge to coexist alongside their ancestors until the latter are suddenly extinguished" (p. 230). Rosenkopf and Tushman (1994) point to a variety of major technological factors and radical innovations that make it difficult for existing organizations to cope with the new demands imposed by the new technologies. Younger, more nimble organizations are the ones typically most capable of dealing with new technologies. Thus, organizations that spin off from older organizations or those that are started by *nascent entrepreneurs* are those that are most likely to create new organizational forms (Aldrich, 1999).

Community Ecology and Coevolution

Community ecology or coevolution examines multiple populations of differing organizations as well as the various niches in which they occur. As indicated above, organizations must typically compete with others in their own populations to acquire the resources they need to survive in their selected environments. For example, Barnett (1990) studied the competition among the members of the population of the telephone companies in Pennsylvania from 1879 to 1934, until one company AT&T dominated the market. And Staber (1989) studied the emergence of worker and consumer co-ops, showing how they competed for customer loyalty. But internal competition is not the only challenge that populations face. They must deal with the members of other populations that coexist in their niche. For example, Haveman (1992) studied the competition between banks and savings and loan associations for customers and their funds under changing regulatory conditions. And Carroll and Swaminathan (1992) examined the emergence of microbreweries and brewpubs who competed to some extent with the mass producers. Often organizations must compete, but under some conditions organizations from different populations can also *cooperate*, seeking mutually beneficial outcomes, a fact that Kauffman (1995, p. 215) says is much more commonly recognized now than in earlier theorizing. Aldrich (1999, citing Hawley, 1950) argues that two types of interdependence drive community dynamics: commensalism and symbiosis. "*Commensalism* refers to competition and cooperation between similar units, whereas *symbiosis* refers to mutual interdependence between dissimilar units" (p. 298, italics in the original). Thus, in large part, relations both within and among populations govern communities. The first relation is the degree to which similar populations in the same niches compete or cooperate and the second is the degree to which different populations in the same or different niches support each other.

Definitions of Community

An important issue that has arisen with regard to community ecology is how to define a community (Aldrich, 1999; DiMaggio, 1994). Hawley's (1950) original sociological work on community ecology focuses relationships within geographically and temporally bound communities. As community ecology has been refitted for organizational scholarship, the definitions of community have taken a more functional approach (Ruef, 2000). That is not to say, however, that organizational scholars completely agree on how community should be defined, operationalized, or analyzed. Astley's (1985) organizational model of community focuses on the technology-based interrelationships between populations. Barnett and colleagues (Barnett, 1994; Barnett & Carroll, 1987; Barnett, Mischke, & Ocasio, 2000) define community on the basis of commensalist and symbiotic relationships between organizations. Hannan and Carroll (1995) broaden the scope of this definition, asserting that community "refers to the broader set of organizational populations whose interactions have a systemic character, often caused by functional differentiation" (p. 30). Rosenkopf and Tushman (1994) add that context is important, in their case the technological context. Aldrich (1999) and Ruef (2000) add that the populations in a community should be organized around a "core," whether it be technological, normative, functional, or legal-regulatory. Ruef (2000) goes about organizing his community of health care populations by focusing on four main functions of the health care field. Aldrich (1999) makes sure to maintain an evolutionary bent to his characterization of community, proffering this succinct definition: "An organizational community is a set of coevolving organizational populations joined by ties of commensalism and symbiosis through their orientation to a common technology, normative order, or legal-regulatory regime" (p. 301).

As we saw in chapter 7 on resource exchange and dependency theory, resources are highly important for organizational survival. However, unlike the logic of those theoretical mechanisms, which focused on cooperative exchange and or mutual dependence, evolutionary theory clearly emphasizes competition and cooperation among organizational populations for scarce resources that exist in their mutual environments. While "survival of the fittest" usually implies the demise of the less fit, survival of the mutually fit implies being the fittest.

As indicated above, Astley (1985) argues that communities operate as "functionally integrated systems of interacting populations" (p. 232). When this happens, he says, they begin to attain a level of *closure* in which the populations "begin to function mainly by exchanging resources with each other rather than directly with the environment" (p. 234). Clearly, this is a process of increasing internal network interdependence among members of different populations as they provide each other with the resources they need and depend for less on the external environment. Many evolutionists would argue that populations strive to become less dependent on their environments. But is this a good thing?

Barnett (1994) warns that "if the structure is poorly coordinated . . . the fitness of the entire community is reduced" (p. 351). Equally important, Astley (1985) argues that network limits apply. A community can only attain a certain size, "after which the complexity of its internal relationships can no longer increase without reducing the community's effectiveness as a functional unit." And, perhaps most important, Astley claims, "The growth of internal complexity accompanying system closure fosters a stabilization of communities but also sets them up for eventual collapse" (p. 236). When communities collapse, what is left of their resources remains in the niche, some of which is recycled by new and emerging populations as the next wave of community begins to develop (Aldrich, 1999).

The community ecological perspective is inherently a multilevel, coevolutionary model of organizational change. It subsumes the population ecology perspective, adds community-level evolutionary mechanisms, and bridges the conceptual gap between the population level and the environment (Aldrich, 1999; Astley, 1985; Barnett, 1994; Ruef, 2000). Barnett and Carroll (1987) point out that this multilevel property can be seen in that "organizational interdependence can exist at several levels: between individual organizations, between populations of organizations, and between communities of organizations" (p. 100).

At the population level of analysis, the relative enactment of competitive and mutual relationships varies over the life cycle of the population. The early entrepreneurs and entrants into a population lay claims on the *open environmental space* (Astley, 1985, pp. 233–234) and its available resources. Because the supply of resources in this space, or niche, is greater than the demand by the nascent organizations, there is no need for competition (Astley, 1985). However, as more organizations enter the population, the demand for resources exceeds the supply, and competition for these resources ensues. As these organizations begin to compete, they also form the beginnings of interrelationships that establish the need for and creation of the community. The commensalist mechanisms of mutualism and competition, interdependence due to similarities, and symbiosis, interdependence due to differences, are functions of the needs of that community (Hawley, 1950, 1986). As the organizations within these populations become more interdependent, areas of need for the community are filled either by outside populations, who then enter the community, or are filled by spin-off populations (Hawley, 1950, 1986).

Mutualistic, competitive, and symbiotic relationships, therefore, form the basis for the emergence of communities. The community, in turn, is the regulator of open spaces (Astley, 1985) and functions as a buffer between the incorporated populations and the environment, especially with regard to resources (which will be described in more detail below). As the changes in the environment restrict or free up resources for the population, the community helps to redistribute the resources based on the changes caused by the environment. In this way, populations that would normally have become extinct because of the sudden exhaustion of vital resources due to changes in the environment will instead rely on the resources contained within the community. In essence, the whole of the community becomes much greater than the sum of its parts, and the benefits to populations of creating such communities may far outweigh the costs.

Survival is therefore "easier" for organizations that are part of a community, not just a population. The community buffers the constraints of the environment, by allowing for a certain amount of self-sufficiency (Barnett, 1994; Hawley, 1950, 1986). Inclusion in such a community is especially important for populations on whom the environment places strict or numerous constraints. In such situations, the community can act as a buffer from these constraints and increase the number and amount of resources to which the population and its members have access.

Summary

At its core, evolutionary theory is fundamentally a theory of change, though this process always works out in the context of inertia. Since the evolutionary mechanism operates primarily to select changes that improve the survival of the species, it can also be viewed as a theory "for development with improvement" (Romanelli, 1999, p. 80; Kauffman, 1995). The evolutionary model is often summarized by its three basic components as variation, selection, and retention, though competition and cooperation are also core processes (McKelvey, 1997). Variation occurs both randomly and intentionally in the real world, though even intentional variations are often blind in that it is impossible to know the outcome of the variation in advance. Some of these variations are beneficial to organizations in that they make them stronger competitors while other variations are harmful, making these less fortunate organizations less fit to compete and therefore to survive. At all levels, evolutionary processes favor organizations with advantageous traits. Thus, organizations typically attempt to select beneficial traits that improve their fit with their environment and therefore their chances of survival. Retention typically occurs by making the change an integral part of internal organizing or by propagation through spin offs or other reproduction methods such as new start-ups. Thus, new organizational competencies and traits percolate through populations and new organizational forms are created. Harmful variations are also sometimes selected, but these are typically "deselected" or not retained after their harmfulness is determined. Unfortunately, this discovery is sometimes made too late to save an organization or population. All these processes occur in the context of extensive competition for the resources that exist in the populations' environmental niches and larger communities and ecosystems (Aldrich, 1979, 1999; McKelvey, 1982, 1997, 1999a, b). In these larger communities, mutualism and symbiosis become important processes as members of populations—as well as entire populations—develop networks of relations with each other. These internal community network structures begin to replace external dependencies, leading to increasingly higher internal complexity. Ironically, as communities increase their internal structural connections, they buffer themselves from the environment, thus extending their own lives, but they also sow the seeds of their own demise, for a complexity threshold exists that limits functional integration (Astley, 1985).

Thus, in coevolutionary theory we see multilevel theoretical mechanisms that lead to the creation, maintenance, dissolution, and eventual re-creation of communication and other networks within organizations, within the members of organizational populations, and among the organizational populations that comprise ecological communities. In the remaining sections of this chapter we examine in greater detail one specific network-based model of complex, self-organized coevolution, Stuart Kauffman's (1993) NK and NK(C) models.

Evolutionary Theory and Kauffman's NK Model of Rugged Fitness Landscapes

Kauffman (1993) developed a theory of evolution and coevolution that he called the NK and the NK(C) models. Although it was originally formulated to explain the origins of life on earth, it provides a comprehensive theory of how complex systems self-organize and coevolve with their environments. Though its roots are in biology, the theory has recently been applied to a number of other contexts. Kauffman (1995, p. 10) himself used it to explore the coevolution of human artifacts and technologies. Applications in the organization sciences include Baum's (1999) study of part-whole competition, Carroll and Burton's (1999) study of complex communication networks, McKelvey's (1999a) study of value chain competitive advantage strategies, and Levinthal and Warglien's (1999) study of fitness landscapes in organization design. The theory is particularly relevant to the topic of this book because it is inherently a network theory that examines the level of connectivity as a driving force in evolutionary and coevolutionary processes. In this section we describe Kauffman's NK model of evolutionary fitness landscapes. This provides the necessary background for exploring the coevolutionary NK(C) model, which we examine in the following section.

In biology, evolution is traditionally thought to operate at the level of *genes* because genes control the traits of organisms. Each population or species has its own unique set of traits, like internal or external skeletons, hair or feathers, feet or fins, and so on. Thus, each species contains it own unique set of genes or gene pool. In this chapter we use the terms genes and traits relatively interchangeably, though in biology genes are viewed as creating traits. Populations of organizations are viewed as having traits though generated by people not genes. Populations of organizations have similar organizational structures, specific competencies, and routines for processing raw materials or providing services, and so on. Likewise, the individual members of each population have unique configurations of that species' genes called the *genotype* (Kauffman, 1993, p. 40). *Genotype space*, or *trait space*, is the collection of all possible genotypes and thus represents the various combinations of characteristics or traits that any individual in the species can have. For example, McKelvey (1999a) lists a number of organizational traits that he calls "value chain competencies" (p. 296) that all computer notebook manufacturers must possess to some degree. These include efficient chip utilization, disk technology, battery technology, mouse technology, heat dissipation, and a number of others. Each organization in the population of notebook manufactures must have these traits or competencies, though each is likely to have different amounts of each. Thus, the genotype space of the population of computer notebook manufacturers includes genotypes that are very similar to other genotypes, and in the limit may differ from others by only one or at most a few traits. Other genotypes in the space are considerably different from each other. Genotype space is so conceived that each genotype is viewed as closest to those that are most similar and farthest away from those that are most different. Kauffman characterizes the dimensionality of the space by "D," by which he means "the number of directions in which each genotype can change to another neighboring genotype by a minimal alteration" (p. 41).

In Kauffman's theory, N refers to the number of genes and K refers to the number of epistatic connections between the genes. An *epistatic linkage* is one in which a given gene or trait is dependent on other genes or traits (p. 40). If no epistatic links exist, each gene is free to vary independently of the other genes. If epistatic links exist, they impose constraints on the mutability and adaptability of the linked traits. Viewed in this fashion, K is a measure of the complexity of relations among the parts that comprise the system.

Boolean Networks

It should be obvious that the collection of traits and the epistatic linkages among them constitutes a network. Indeed, Kauffman represents the N traits and the K linkages as dynamic Boolean networks. "Boolean networks are systems of binary variables, each with two possible states of activity (on and off), coupled to one another such that the activity of each element is governed by the *prior activity* of some elements according to a Boolean switching function" (p. 182, italics added). Each node in a dynamic Boolean network receives input from its epistatic links. Each input prescribes the behavior of the receiving node at the next moment in time, switching it from on to off or vice versa. Since nodes may be linked to and therefore receive inputs from more than one other node, a switching function specifies the behavior of the receiving node as a combination of the inputs (pp. 188–191). Thus, epistatic links are conceived as constraints in the network. As shown in figure 9.1, there are sixteen different Boolean functions for K = 2 (McKelvey, 1999a, p. 308).

Figure 9.1
Sixteen Boolean Functions for K = 2. Source: F. F. Soulie, Y. Robert, & M. Tchuente, *Automata Networks in Computer Science*, 1987, Princeton University Press. Reprinted by permission of Princeton University Press.

Fitness Landscapes

Kauffman employs the notion of a *fitness landscape* to describe the evolutionary behavior of a population. (Kaufmann, 1993, attributes this framework to Sewell Wright 1931, 1932; see p. 33) The fitness landscape represents the level of fitness of each possible genotype in genotype space or of each trait in trait space. Fitness can be viewed as the ability of a particular genotype to survive. Fitness values are assigned to each gene or trait, and the fitness of the genotype is seen as simply the average of all the traits that make up the genotype (p. 42). Genotype combinations that are more likely to survive than others are viewed as *fitter*.

   Assigning a fitness value to each possible genotype generates a fitness landscape across the trait space. This creates a topography showing the fitness of all possible combinations of genetic traits. Biologically, fitness is often conceived as the ability of a population to reproduce a particular set of genetic traits or characteristics (p. 33), though Kauffman says that it can refer to "the measurable capacity . . . to carry out some defined functions" (p. 121). In the organizational context, we can also think of fitness as profitability, productivity, or any other measure of "success" (Levinthal, 2001; Levinthal & Warglein, 1999; McKelvey, 1999a, b).

A species or population is viewed as distributed across this fitness or success landscape according to the particular configuration of genotypes that its members possess. All those individuals with the same genotype are located at the same place on the fitness topography (p. 34). Evolution is viewed as a process in which populations collectively attempt to optimize their fitness by finding, selecting, and retaining the best genotypes, a process that Kaufmann calls an *adaptive walk* (p. 210) or *hill-climbing process* (pp. 33–34). "Mutations move an individual, or its offspring, to neighboring points in the space, representing neighboring genotypes. Selection is reflected in differential reproduction by individuals with different fitness values. Therefore, over time the cluster of individuals representing the population will flow over the fitness landscape" (p. 34).

The fitness landscapes just described contain *local optima* or hills representing genotypes that are fitter and local minima or valleys representing those genotypes that are less fit (p. 45). Kauffman argues that the ability of a population to evolve depends on the nature of the fitness landscape. Landscapes can vary from very *smooth* to *maximally rugged* (p. 45). If all the genotypes in the genotype space have similar fitness levels, the landscape is smooth, and adjacent locations are highly correlated to each other. If adjacent genotypes have very different fitness levels, the landscape is very rugged, and there is very little correlation between adjacent locations. Kauffman calls this the *correlation structure* of the landscape (p. 45). Where correlations are high, knowledge of surrounding locations is easy to acquire from the present locations, and it is easy to move to better locations. By contrast, where the landscape is rugged and the correlation is low, it is difficult to extract information about adjacencies and equally difficult to move to better locations.

It turns out that the parameters of the NK model correspond to the nature of the landscape. Remember that K is the number of epistatic links among the N traits in the model. K can vary between 0, meaning that there are no constraining connections between traits in the system, and $N - 1$, implying that each trait is linked to and constrained by each of the other $N - 1$ traits. When K = 0, there are no epistatic connections among the traits, and thus, each is free to adapt independently of all the others; there are no constraints on the adaptability of the population. Kauffman shows that the fitness values of adjacent locations on this landscape are highly correlated and the landscape as a whole contains a single *global optima* (pp. 45–46). Over time and successive generations all members of the species will search their local one-mutant neighborhoods for superior genotypes and select those that are fitter, in essence mutating by adopting those genotypes as their own. Ultimately, the entire population will engage in adaptive hill-climbing walks throughout the trait space that hone in on one best location on that particular fitness landscape, that is, the most successful combination of traits, the best genotype (pp. 45–46). Kauffman points out, however, that even though the entire population reaches the optima, other landscapes may be superior in that they have better optima. The correlation structure of the landscape and the complexity of the hill-climbing process suggest two things. First, landscapes may change over time, so that a population's landscape may improve or deteriorate. Second, different populations will have different landscapes, which carries the implication that some populations have higher fitness potential than others.

At the other end of the continuum, the landscape created by $K = N - 1$ epistatic linkages is fully random (pp. 46–47). There is no correlation between adjacent locations in the genotype or trait space, and the system is maximally constrained. Rather than one global maximum the landscape is likely to display many local optima though, ironically, few genotypes can climb them (pp. 47–52). Kauffman calls this a *complexity catastrophe* where "conflicting constraints in complex systems limit the optimization of function possible" (pp. 46, 52–54; see also McKelvey, 1999a, b).

Obviously, there are a number of other values for the K and N parameters between these two anchors, $K = 0$ and $K = N - 1$. Kauffman created a series of NK computer simulations to explore the various combinations. Each combination generates a different fitness landscape and thus the set of combinations generates a family of *tunable fitness landscapes* (pp. 54–60, 231), that is, landscapes that vary with changes in the parameters. Though the simulations generate a number of interesting findings, perhaps the most important is that optimal landscapes are generated by small levels of K relative to N, such as $K = 2, 3, 4$, etc. (p. 223). These levels of K are even better than $K = 0$. What this implies is that small amounts of connectivity among the characteristics of a system improve its overall ability to evolve and survive. Too much connectivity leads to complexity catastrophe. As McKelvey (1999b) explains, a catastrophe occurs "because complexity acts to thwart the selectionist process, thereby stopping progression toward improved fitness" (p. 286). In a sense, this phenomena is similar to Astley's (1985) observation that too much increased network density in the community of organizational populations leads to its eventual demise by making it too dependent on internal resources and not sufficiently externally connected.

Kauffman also notes that populations occasionally change in dramatic, discontinuous ways rather than in incremental or minimalist one-mutant steps (p. 69). These *frame-shift mutations* are called *long-jump adaptations* and generate change in several traits simultaneously (pp. 70–74). Though long-jump variations can introduce significant organizational change, they are also subject to complexity catastrophe (p. 72). This type of change is similar to the punctuated equilibrium perspective discussed earlier in the chapter (Astley, 1985; Tushman & Romanelli, 1985).

Self-Organization

In chapter 3 we discussed the notion of self-organizing from the perspective of agent-based modeling. Agents in a network interacted with each other according to a set of rules out of which dynamic networks emerged. Self-organization or autocatalysis also plays an important role in Kauffman's theory of evolution. *Catalysis* refers to a process by which agents facilitate or speed up reactions or interactions among other agents (p. 298; Kauffman, 1995, p. 49). *Autocatalysis*, or a "collectively autocatalytic system," is one in which agents "speed up the very reactions by which they themselves are formed, A makes B; B makes C; C makes A again" (Kauffman, 1995, p. 49). This cyclical network property creates systems that are "self-maintaining and self-reproducing," given sufficient input of matter and energy from their environments (1995, p. 50).

These ideas can be extended to networks of agents, as indicated in figure 9.2. Of particular importance is the idea that "connective properties of random graphs exhibit very sudden transitions—in effect, 'phase transitions'" as a function of the ratio of the number of nodes, N, to the number of edges, E (Kauffman, 1993, p. 307). As the figure shows, when the E/N ratio is low, most nodes are isolated and the graph is largely disconnected. As the E/N ratio increases but remains below .5, the number and size of the components in the network increases but the elements are still relatively disconnected. When E/N passes the .5 threshold, the graph suddenly shifts to one large component that contains most of the nodes, leaving relatively few isolates. This vast web is the *phase transition* of the network and represents a qualitative shift in the nature of the network.

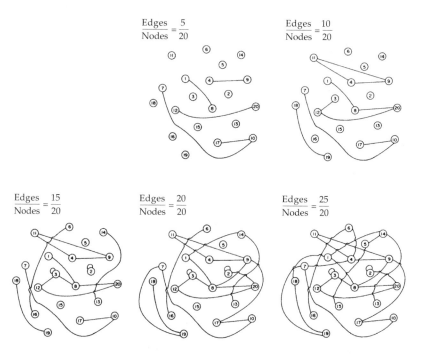

Figure 9.2

Random graphs for a fixed number of points N connected at random by an increasing number of edges E. For large values of N as E/N increases past a threshold of 0.5, most points become connected in one gigantic component. As E/N passes 1.0, cycles of all lengths begin to emerge. Source: Stuart A. Kauffman, *The Origins of Order: Self Organization and Selection in Evolution.* Copyright 1993 by Oxford University Press. Used by permission of Oxford University Press.

Kauffman (1993) claims that one important aspect of his work is to incorporate the concept of self-organization into evolutionary studies (pp. 30–31, see also Kauffman, 1995). Darwin's theory of evolution focuses almost exclusively on natural selection (i.e., the processes of variation, selection, and retention described earlier in this chapter) as the sole source of order in the natural world (Kauffman, 1993, p. 10). Natural selection treats the environment as the exclusive organizing agent via its role in selecting and retaining random variations that increase the fit of the population to the environment. But, Kauffman (1993) argues, natural selection should not be the *"sole source or order"* (p. 11, italics in the original) in the world because assigning primacy to environmental forces is too deterministic; it leaves no room for other organizing processes, other sources of order (Kauffman, 1995, pp. 24–25). Kauffman (1993) argued that although Darwinian natural selection is still the predominant source of order, it is not the only source (p.11). Additionally, self-organization and self-organizing systems constitute another order-generating force in the world (Kauffman, 1993, p. 25). In support of this view he identifies a number of circumstances under which spontaneous order emerges from the interactions of components constituting a complex system. And he observed that natural selection has always acted on systems that exhibit spontaneous order (Kauffman, 1993, p. 16). It is important, he concluded, to incorporate "both selection *and* self-organization" (Kauffman, 1995, p. 25, italics in the original) in our models and theories of the world.

Kauffman (1993) observed that random Boolean networks are "a vast family of disordered systems," which, nonetheless, can be grouped into three qualitatively different classes of systems that he calls *regimes* (p. 174). The first class of systems is the ordered regime. The second class is the chaotic regime. And the third class, which constitutes a phase transition between the other two, is called the complex regime. These different regimes contain different organizing conditions, but it is only the complex regime, the transition between chaos and order, that provides the basis for self-organizing.

The first family of Boolean network systems operating across time (remember that nodes in Boolean networks change their values in discrete time steps according to the rules contained in the epistatic linkages tying the system together), the *ordered regime*, is one in which "many elements in the system freeze in fixed states of activity. These frozen elements form a large connected cluster, or *frozen component*, which spans, or *percolates*, across the system and leaves behind isolated islands of unfrozen elements whose activities fluctuate in complex ways" (Kauffman, 1993, p. 174). The second grouping of Boolean network systems behaving across time, the *chaotic regime*, does not contain a

> frozen component. Instead, a connected cluster of unfrozen elements, free to fluctuate in activities, percolates across the system, leaving behind isolated frozen islands. In this chaotic regime, small changes in initial conditions unleash avalanches of changes which propagate to many other unfrozen elements. These avalanches demonstrate that, in the chaotic regime, the dynamics are very sensitive to initial conditions. (p. 174)

The final family of random Boolean networks is the *complex regime*. In it the

> transition from the ordered regime to the chaotic regime constitutes a phase transition, which occurs as a variety of parameters are changed. The transition region, on the edge between order and chaos, is the *complex* regime. Here, the frozen component is just percolating and the unfrozen component just ceasing to percolate, hence breaking up into isolated islands. In this transition region, altering the activity of single unfrozen elements unleashes avalanches of change with a characteristic size distribution having many small and a few large avalanches. (p. 174, italics in the original)

The fact that all possible random Boolean networks can be organized into three families has important implications for self-organizing. In the ordered state, most elements and links are fixed, so self-organization is difficult, if not impossible. In the chaotic state, almost nothing is ordered, so self-organization is also problematic. It is, Kauffman (1993) says, in the third regime, the complex regime, that self-organization is to be found. Here, elements and linkages are neither fixed nor chaotic and so "life evolves toward a regime that is poised between order and chaos" (p. 26). Here, in the transition region between order and chaos, the system is most capable of self-organization and change and least in danger of losing control by going chaotic or rigidifying into fixed order.

Kauffman's (1993) NK model simulates these theoretical findings. Specifically, he shows the when K = N the "ensemble of networks is maximally disordered" (p. 192), and, in fact, this remains the case for large K relative to N. At the other extreme, when K = 1, the system is highly ordered. Between these two extremes of chaos and order lie transition phases to complex regimes. In the NK model these emerge to differing degrees as K changes from 5 down to 2, (pp. 192–193). Thus, self-organization in complex organisms and organizations depends in large part on the complexity of the internal structure of the network.

Coevolutionary Theory and Kauffman's NK(C) Model of Coupled Landscapes

Kauffman (1993) claims that "the true and stunning success of biology reflects the fact that organisms do not merely evolve, they *coevolve* both with other organisms and with a changing abiotic environment" (p. 237; italics in the original). Lewin and Volberda (1997) argue that organizational evolutionary theory has made a similar transition to coevolutionary theory (see also Lewin, Long, & Carroll, 1999). This move shifts the focus from specific organizations and single organizational forms to multiple organizational forms, their mutual environments, and the resources for which they compete, in short, to the level of the community.

As we discussed early in this chapter, in order to survive, a population of firms must adapt to the organizational niches in which they find themselves and compete with each other for scarce resources. Additionally, the notion of coevolution implies that environments change, often by small incremental random events, occasionally by monumental radical events, and sometimes by the individual or collective efforts of organizations in the niche. Coevolution also acknowledges that different species live together in communities or ecosystems, and thus must deal with each other.

As we saw earlier in the previous section, Kauffman's NK theory describes the self-organizing, adaptive behavior of a population of agents as it evolves across the fitness landscape of the population. The NK model addresses the evolution of single populations but does not address the coevolution of multiple populations. To depict the dynamism of coevolutionary systems, Kauffman formulated the NK(C) model that incorporates two new parameters into the process. As before, N stands for the number of genes, traits, or characteristics in each population, and K represents the number of internal epistatic links that constrain each trait. The first new parameter is "S_i" which stands for the specific sets of *species* that are coevolving (p. 244). Each S possesses its own N and K, that is, each population has a set of traits whose values can vary in specific, defined ways among its members and a set of epistatic links that impose constraints among its traits, ranging from 0 to N – 1. The traits in one species need not be the same as in other species and in fact are likely to be different, at least to some extent. The second new parameter is designated as "C," which represents the epistatic linkages between traits in members of the *different* species or populations (p. 244). High values of C indicate that there are extensive epistatic connections among the populations in the community, which implies that at least some of the traits of each population constrain the traits of some of the other populations. Low values indicate minimal connectivity. Just as K represented a measure of internal complexity in each population, C represents a measure of external complexity among populations (p. 244). C in essence connects or "*couples* the NK landscapes of different 'species'" (p. 238, italics in the original). This implies that adaptive changes in each species' landscape influences the landscapes of all the species to which they are connected. Specifically, "adaptive moves by one species deforms the land-scapes of its partners" (p. 238).

Despite this deformation, coupling provides the possibility that the coupled systems may attain a *Nash equilibrium* over time, a condition where "the local optimum of each partner is consistent with the local optimum of all the other partners via the C couplings" (Kauffman, 1993, p. 245). Although not easily attained, Nash equilibria are typically viewed as the best collective solution for interlinked systems, though not necessarily the best for any one partner nor subset of partners. Since coupling affects the fitness of the respective populations, the question arises as to what level of C, connectivity among populations in the community or ecosystem, and what level of S, the number of species (or populations) in the community, leads most quickly to Nash equilibria. Based on extensive NK(C) computer simulations, Kauffman (1993) concluded that "when $K > S \times C$, all the co-evolving partners encounter a Nash equilibrium rapidly. When $K < S \times C$, the coevolving partners do not encounter a Nash equilibrium for a long time" (p. 253). Since K is a measure of complexity within populations, and S and C are measures of complexity between populations in the community, it is clear from Kauffman's results that there is a tradeoff between internal and external complexity. As the number of species (populations), S, and the number of connections among the species, C, increase relative to a fixed level of K in the different populations, communities are less likely to attain equilibrium. Stated differently, the higher the complexity among the members of the populations within the community relative to the complexity within the individual populations, the slower and less likely the community is to reach equilibrium. Interestingly, this finding is similar to Astley's (1985) conclusion described at the end of the first part of this chapter that communities of populations who grow increasingly dependent on each other internally relative to their external environments encounter a complexity limit which triggers the onset of the community's demise.

Theoretical Mechanisms for an Evolutionary NK Model

NK(C) models, like many other models inspired by systems theory, seek to be transdisciplinary and as a result transcend specific levels of analyses or content domains, leading one wag (quoted in Ahouse et al., 1992) to claim that NKC is an acronym for "No Known Content." In this section, we will attempt to apply the theoretical mechanisms of NK(C) to two known content areas among populations of individuals and among populations of organizations. First, we will apply it to the emergence of complex coevolving belief systems (as proposed by Ahouse et al., 1992). Next, we will apply it to complex coevolving strategic practices by organizations that belong to competing retail chains (Chang & Harrington, 2000).

Ahouse et al. (p. 349, 1992) proposed that in studying the emergence of belief systems, the NK(C) model could be interpreted as follows:

1. Each individual (species) has a number of beliefs (genes) which it may or may not hold. The total number of beliefs are [sic] N.
2. An index of cognitive frustration (fitness) can be constructed, based on the level of consistency among the individual's beliefs, and the congruence of those beliefs with those of surrounding individuals.
3. The contribution of cognitive frustration of each belief is contingent upon K other beliefs within that individual, and C other beliefs in each surrounding actor.
4. Each actor may change one belief each round.

Let us suppose that each person, i, has beliefs about three issues represented as three attributes, $A1_i$, $A2_i$, $A3_i$. These three beliefs are (1) attitudes about making products of high quality, (2) attitudes about making products economically, and (3) attitudes about making products using the latest technology. For each individual, each of the three attributes can take values of 0 or 1. A value of 1 would indicate considering that statement a priority and a 0 would indicate not considering that statement to be a priority. In the parlance of NK(C) models, each individual has three genes and therefore N = 3. The collection of genes (in this case, issues) for each individual is called a genotype. So, for example, an individual with a belief system or genotype that has the form (1, 0, 0) would prioritize making products of high quality but not be concerned about doing so economically or about making products using the latest technology.

For each person, the attitudes on these three issues may influence one another by reinforcement or contradiction. For instance, it is possible that an individual's priorities about making a quality product may be difficult to reconcile with a priority about making a product economically. This would be the case of a negative constraint between actor i's attitudes $A1_i$ and $A2_i$. Likewise, it is easy to argue that a negative constraint exists between an actor i's priority for making a product economically, $A2_i$, and a priority for making a product using the latest, potentially expensive technology, $A3_i$. (For our discussion here, we will discount the counterargument that a new technology may offer the possibility to make products more economically.) Additionally, it is reasonable to argue that there is a positive reinforcement between a person's desire to make a quality product, $A1_i$, and make that product using the latest technology, $A3_i$. For instance, if the product is a mobile phone, using a new circuit design technology may help make a higher quality product.

In the NK(C) framework, the potential influences between an individual's genes are called epistatic ties. Since, following the arguments above, each of the three issues (or genes) could influence the other two, the number of epistatic ties (K) on each belief is 2. In general, we can define K_{pqi} as the epistatic constraint for actor i, from gene p_i to gene q_i.

$$K_{pqi} = 1 \text{ if } p \text{ reinforces } q, \text{ and } p_i = q_i, \text{ else } 0 \tag{1}$$

$$K_{pqi} = 1 \text{ if } p \text{ contradicts (or constrains) } q, \text{ and } p_i \neq q_i, \text{ else } 0 \tag{2}$$

$$K_{pqi} = 0 \text{ if } p \text{ neither reinforces or contradicts } q \tag{3}$$

$$K_{pqi} = 1 \text{ if } p \text{ and } q \text{ are the same gene} \tag{4}$$

In the present example, if p were $A1_i$ (quality products) and q was $A2_i$ (cheaper products), since we have argued that $A1_i$ and $A2_i$ contradict one another, the above system of equations would be reduced to:

$$K_{12i} = 1 \text{ if } A1_i \text{ contradicts } A2_i, \text{ and } A1_i \neq A2_i \text{ else } 0 \tag{5}$$

For an individual with a belief system (0,1,0), K_{12i} would be 1 since $A1_i = 0$ and $A2_i = 1$ and hence the two are not equal to each other.

Note that the K_{pq} relation is an intrapersonal network relationship between beliefs held by the individual. As such it is distinct from most of the network relations we have examined thus far in this book. Equations similar to (5) can be derived for relations K_{13i} and K_{23i}. In principle, the K_{pq} ties do not need to be symmetric, that is, A1 can constrain A2 while A2 may not constrain A1. However, in the present scenario the K_{pq} network ties are symmetric, that is, K_{13} is equal to K_{31}.

Of course, contrary to what we have discussed above, one could argue that these three beliefs, A1, A2, and A3, are independent of another, and that individuals' beliefs about any one of them are not likely to be positively or negatively influenced by their beliefs about either of the other two issues. In that case, there are no constraints among the issues and hence the number of ties, K = 0. Further, K_{12i}, K_{13i}, and K_{23i} are also equal to zero for each person i.

As indicated in the previous section, the central mechanism for all NK(C) models, and more generally, evolutionary and coevolutionary theories, is the desire for individuals to improve their fitness by adapting to the environment. It is this search for improved fitness, however one defines it, which distinguishes the generative mechanisms of evolutionary and co-evolutionary theories from the other theoretical mechanisms discussed in the previous chapters of this book. Before discussing how individuals improve their fitness in this system, it is important to define fitness for the system.

In the present example, the fitness for an individual, as proposed above by Ahouse et al. (1992), can be defined as one's *cognitive consistency*. (While Ahouse et al. [1992] offer the term *cognitive frustration*, we prefer to use the term cognitive consistency.") In chapter 6, we discussed an individual's desire to seek cognitive consistency by forging friendship ties with friends of friends. In this case, we consider cognitive consistency *among* an individual's set of beliefs, $A1_i$, $A2_i$, and $A3_i$. For instance, an individual may seek to adopt a positive attitude about A1 (making a quality product) that is cognitively consistent with a negative attitude about A2 (making a product economically) or vice versa. This configuration would reduce the dissonance that individuals would feel if instead they prioritized making a quality product and making it economically. An individual's attitude on each of the three issues contributes to the overall cognitive consistency, or fitness, of the individual. For actor, i, let us define $W(A1_i)$ as the cognitive consistency or fitness contribution based on an individual's attitude about $A1_i$. Individuals' attitude about A1 (quality) would have differing levels of cognitive consistency depending on their attitudes about $A2_i$ (cheap products) and $A3_i$ (latest technology). For example, if individual i gave high priority toward A1 (quality), while simultaneously giving low priority to A2 (economical) and a high priority to A3 (technology), the person would be in a state of high cognitive consistency (1,0,1). And, the individual's positive attitude toward A1 would make a higher contribution, $W(A1_i)$, toward the person's overall cognitive consistency (fitness). However, if the individual gave a high priority toward A1 (quality) while simultaneously giving high priority to A2 (economical) and a low priority to A3 (technology), the person would be in a state of low cognitive consistency (1,1,0) or high cognitive dissonance. In this case, the individual's positive attitude toward A1 would make a lower contribution toward the person's overall cognitive consistency, $W(A1_i)$.

In general, the fitness contribution of a particular gene, p_i, to an individual i's fitness can be denoted as $W(p_i)$ and defined as:

$$W(p_i) = \Sigma(w_q K_{pqi}) \tag{6}$$

the sum of the epistatic constraints, K_{pq}, between p and all genes, q, for individual i, weighted by a parameter, w_q, measuring the significance of that constraint or reinforcement (see Kauffman, 1993, pp. 40–45). For simplicity, and due to lack of a priori knowledge, let us assume that $w_q = 1$ for all q.

The overall fitness of individual i with a particular configuration of genes, is given by:

$$W_i = 1/N \ (\Sigma(Wp_i)) \tag{7}$$

summed across all N genes, p.

In the present example, for individual i, the fitness contributions for $A1_i$, $A2_i$, $A3_i$ is defined as

$$W(A1_i) = K_{11i} + K_{12i} + K_{13i} \tag{8}$$

$$W(A2_i) = K_{21i} + K_{22i} + K_{23i} \tag{9}$$

$$W(A3_i) = K_{31i} + K_{32i} + K_{33i} \tag{10}$$

Taken together, the overall fitness for an individual i, Wi, can then be given as the average contribution of fitness based on the individual's attitudes toward the three issues:

$$W_i = 1/3 \ [W(A1_i) + W(A2_i) + W(A3_i)] \tag{11}$$

In equation (8), $W(A1_i) = 3$ if an individual's belief system, (A1, A2, A3) = (1,0,1) or (0,1,0). These are the only two belief configurations in which the person would have the highest level of cognitive consistency. The fitness contribution is $W(A1_i) = 1$ for the remaining six configurations, (0,0,0), (0,0,1) (0,1,1), (1,0,0), (1,1,0), and (1,1,1).

In a similar fashion one could compute contributions toward *cognitive consistency* fitness based on the individual's attitudes about the remaining two issues, $A2_i$ and $A3_i$. Since the epistatic ties in this particular scenario are symmetric, the fitness contributions of $A2_i$ and $A3_i$ are identical to the $W(A1_i)$. Hence the individuals with belief systems $(A1_i, A2_i, A3_i) = (1,0,1)$ or (0,1,0) have the highest overall fitness ($W_i = 3$), while the overall fitness $W_i = 1$ for individuals with the remaining six belief systems is (0,0,0), (0,0,1) (0,1,1), (1,0,0), (1,1,0), and (1,1,1).

Now that we have defined and computed a measure of fitness in terms of cognitive consistency, let us return to the task of understanding how, according to NK(C) models, individuals can improve their fitness. In the present example, this means each individual seeks to gain higher cognitive consistency. One way in which they can do so is by considering if a change in one of their beliefs may help them achieve higher cognitive consistency. Consider an individual whose belief system is described by (0,0,1), indicating a high priority only for the use of the latest technology. Equation 11 indicated that the overall fitness for this person was 1. Further, consider that at each step or round in the evolutionary process, this person has the option to change or mutate one belief. If the person chose to change A2 (making products economically) from a 0 to 1, the new configuration for this person would change from (0,0,1) to (0, 1, 1). The overall fitness contribution of individual i, as derived in equation 11 would remain 1, the same as it was previously when the belief configuration was (0,0,1). Instead, if the person had chosen to change A1 (making quality products) from 0 to 1, the new configuration for this person would be (1,0,1). As shown in equation 2, the fitness contribution of A1 would move up from 1 to 3. This would be a good choice from an evolutionary standpoint, because the individual had adapted to a higher level of fitness. Substantively, this means the person adopted quality (A1) as a high priority in addition to the use of the latest technology (A3) and hence reached a higher level of cognitive consistency in terms of priorities.

The process by which an individual can make a change to only one belief at each round was referred to in our earlier discussion of NK(C) models as a one-step mutation. Notice that in the case of the person who had the belief system (0,0,1), one-step mutations could lead to one of three possible new belief systems: (0,0,0), (1,0,1), or (0,1,1). As previously indicated, the change from (0,0,1) to (1,0,1) would have improved the fitness of the individual's belief system from 1 to 3. However, the other two possible one-step mutations from (0,0,1) to (0,0,0) or from (0,0,1) to (0,1,1) would have made no difference to the fitness. As discussed in earlier sections the NK(C) landscape is highly correlated to the extent that the fitness values of belief systems that are separated by one-step mutations, such as those discussed here, tend to be similar, which is to say that a landscape is highly correlated if individuals' fitness (or cognitive consistency) do not change dramatically when they make a change in one of their attitudes. It is therefore easy to see why a highly correlated landscape, that is, one where belief systems that are one-step mutations apart, generally have similar fitness values and are called "smooth" landscapes. The fact that, in the present example, one of the one-step mutations—from (0,0,1) to (1,0,1)—changed the fitness abruptly from 1 to 3 indicates a "rugged" feature in the landscape.

Further, we noted earlier that the belief system represented by (1,0,1) had the highest value (3) of all possible fitness values, that is, the highest cognitive consistency. This is the global optima. Notice also that there was a second global optima associated with the belief system (0,1,0) where the fitness value was also 3. Therefore the landscape that we have defined for the emergence of this belief system is somewhat rugged and has two peaks.

This is consistent with our earlier discussions about NK models, because in this case the number of beliefs, N = 3, is not substantially larger than the number of epistatic constraints between the three beliefs, K = 2. Each of the three beliefs is constrained by the other two beliefs.

While the evolutionary processes described here relied on assessing the change in fitness based on a one-step mutation at each round, one could also consider changes in more than one belief at each round. For instance, the individual with the belief system (0,0,1) could in one round consider altering two or even all three beliefs. Changing two beliefs, say A1 and A3, could lead the individual from a (0,0,1) belief system to a (1,0,0) belief system. These multiple changes in each round were referred to earlier in the chapter as frame-shift mutations or long-jump adaptations. These tend to be riskier and less likely to help the individual move to a higher level of fitness (see Kauffman, 1993, pp. 69–72, 212). Indeed, based on the fitness values reported in equation 2, the simultaneous shift in attitudes A1 and A3, from a (0,0,1) belief system to a (1,0,0) belief system does not improve the cognitive consistency fitness of the individual.

As discussed in previous sections, in rugged landscapes it is less likely that a large number of individuals will be able to improve their fitness. The primary goal of NK models is to define the conditions or landscapes under which the *population* of individuals will have the ability to *collectively* improve their cognitive consistency. The results from the NK simulations described in previous sections indicate that this is less likely to occur when the number of epistatic connections or constraints, K, among individuals' beliefs is large in relation to the number of beliefs, N. In situations where the number of constraints that each belief has with other beliefs, K (2 in the present example) is quite large as compared to the total number of beliefs, N (3 in the present example), the landscape is not considered optimal for the collection of individuals to improve their overall fitness level. This knowledge claim regarding effects at the population level based on processes at the individual level is a central focus of NK(C) models in particular, and evolutionary and co-evolutionary theories more generally. However, it is important to keep in mind that many mutations or adaptations, which we have called here changes in the state of the belief system, do not improve overall fitness. In fact, it is entirely possible to move from a higher state of fitness to a lower one, such as moving from a state of cognitive consistency to one of greater dissonance, for example, moving from (1,0,1) to (0,0,0). Evolutionary theory predicts that in the long run only those modifications that improve fitness will be retained in the population. Those that decrease fitness will eventually disappear.

So, what can NK models tells us about improving the overall or collective level of cognitive consistency among our collection of individuals? There are three general strategies that must be explored. First, one can attempt to reduce the K constraints among the various N beliefs. In the present example, this would imply reframing these three priorities among individuals so that individuals did not experience cognitive dissonance when simultaneously considering, say, quality and price as important priories. Another example of this reframing strategy revisits a counterargument we discounted earlier in this section—that a new technology might in some cases offer the possibility to make products more economically. Such counterarguments may help dismantle individuals' preconceived notions that automatically and epistatically link the use of the latest technology to higher costs. However, it is important to note that the strategy does not call for the elimination of all K constraints among the beliefs. Indeed, the NK simulations reported earlier in this chapter indicate that the most optimal landscapes for collections of individuals to improve their cognitive fitness occurs when K is significantly smaller than N, but higher than 0. So in the present example, the strategy would call for reducing some, but not eliminating all, of the constraints between the beliefs.

A second strategy would be to increase the number of beliefs or priorities among the individuals. The landscape would be less rugged if each individual was defined as having a belief system or genotype that had, say, N = 7 beliefs. However it must be stressed that the additional beliefs introduced should not, for the most part, reinforce or contradict one another. If they did, the increase in the number of beliefs, N, would be accompanied by an increase in the number of constraints, K, between these beliefs. And, the N/K ratio would continue to be large. The strategy should therefore be to increase the number of beliefs where each belief was only constrained by, say, K = 2 other beliefs.

The third strategy for seeking an optimal landscape for the collection of individuals to improve their cognitive fitness brings us to the C component of the NK(C) models. So far we have focused on the evolution of the three beliefs, $A1_i$, $A2_i$, and $A3_i$, held by an individual i. The evolution described so far is based on each individual adapting or changing one's beliefs so as to improve cognitive consistency among the three beliefs. We are now ready to explore the extent to which an individual's cognitive consistency is reinforced or contradicted by the beliefs of other actors, j, in the network.

Theoretical Mechanisms for a Coevolutionary NK(C) Model

As described earlier, let us extend the scenario to account for S individuals in the system. Each of the S individuals in the system has a belief system. Further, let us assume that the belief systems of each of these individuals also deal with the same three issues, A1 (quality product), A2 (cheaper product), and A3 (using the latest technology). We can now begin to consider the ways in which one individual's attitude about, say, A1, is constrained or reinforced, by another individual's attitude about A1, A2, or A3. Following the same substantive logic used for examining intrapersonal attitudes earlier in this section, let us assume that each person's attitude about A1 (quality product) is reinforced by other individuals' attitudes about A1, constrained by other individuals' attitudes about A2 (cheaper product), and reinforced by others' attitudes about A3 (using the latest technology). Likewise let us assume that an individual's attitude about A2 (cheaper product) is reinforced by others' views about A2 (cheaper product) and constrained by others' views about A1 (quality product) and A3 (using the latest technology). Finally, let us assume that an individual's attitudes about A3 (using the latest technology) is reinforced by others' attitudes about A1 (quality) and constrained by others' views about A2 (cheaper product).

In our previous presentation using traditional NK(C) parlance, we indicated that S corresponded to the number of species in the community. However, in the present example we use S to refer to the number of other members of the population rather than the number of other species. In the subsequent example of retail chain stores we treat other populations and hence use S consistently with Kauffman's (1993) model to refer to the number of other populations. Kauffman generally assumes that members of a species have the same genotype so that what pertains to one pertains to all. Thus, links within the genotype (population) and links between different genotypes (different populations) are assumed to operate for all members of each population. Before exploring that situation, we wish to apply Kauffman's model to the members of a single population where this assumption may not apply.

As we described earlier, each belief by an individual is influenced by K (two, in our example) other beliefs by that same individual. Further, each belief for a person is influenced by C beliefs by another individual. In the present example $C = 3$ because each of the beliefs A1, A2, and A3 for an individual are influenced by all three beliefs by another individual. Let us define C_{pqij} as the relation between actor i's belief about p, p_i, and actor j's belief about q, q_j.

$C_{pqij} = 1$ if p reinforces q, and $p_i = q_j$, else 0 $\hspace{2cm}$ (12)

$C_{pqij} = 1$ if p contradicts (or constrains) q, and $p_i \neq q_j$, else 0 $\hspace{1cm}$ (13)

$C_{pqij} = 0$ if p neither reinforces or contradicts q $\hspace{2cm}$ (14)

The first step is to posit if a belief, p_i, held by one individual i is likely to be reinforced or constrained by the belief, q_j, of another individual j. As we discussed above, individual i's view about A2 (making products cheaper) contradicts individual j's views about A3 (use of technology). This invokes the use of equation 13 above. If $C_{23ij} = 1$, it implies that actor i's belief about A2 are different from actor j's views about A3.

Note that the belief p for individual i could be the same as the belief q of another individual. That is, one could consider the relationship between individual i's belief about A1 (quality) and individual j's belief about the same issue, A1 (quality). If we were to posit that i's belief about A1 would reinforce j's belief about A1, then we apply equation 12 above. And, $C_{11ij} = 1$ means that both i and j agree about the priority of A1.

Having defined the C relation, we revisit the fitness contributions of any one belief to the overall fitness of the person's belief system. In our discussion of the NK models, equation 6 specified the fitness contributions of any one belief. Equations 8, 9, and 10 applied that general formalism to the present example. Our goal here is to specify the extent to which the fitness contributions of any one belief are further modified by the C_{pqij} links that connect an individual's beliefs to those of another individual. This fitness contribution of each belief specified in equation 6 can be extended as follows:

$$W(p_i) = \Sigma(w_q K_{pqi}) + \Sigma\Sigma(C_{pqij}) \hspace{2cm} (15)$$

where the second term represents the influence of the C ties. The double summation indicates that an individual i's belief about p is being constrained or reinforced by the sum of all q beliefs held by person j, summed across all persons, j.

It is quite unrealistic to believe that all other individuals are influencing each individual in the system. If they were, the system would be in Kauffman's (1993, p. 244) terminology *completely coupled*. It is more realistic to assume that individuals would only be constrained by the views of others with whom they had some social relation. This relation could be a communication relation, a kinship relation, or a reporting relation. If one reduces the number of people whose belief system can influence the belief system of the target individual, equation 15 can be modified thus:

$$W(p_i) = \Sigma(w_q K_{pqi}) + \Sigma\Sigma(C_{pqij})(R_{ij}) \hspace{2cm} (16)$$

where R_{ij} represents the presence of some social relation between individual i and every other individual j. If individual i has no relation with individual j, the second term in equation 16 will drop out and there will be no C influences on individual i's belief system.

Equation 16 is the fitness contribution of one belief, p_i, for individual i. The total fitness of individual i, is given as indicated in equation 7, by:

$$W_i = 1/N \ (\Sigma(Wp_i)) \qquad (17)$$

representing the average fitness contributions across all beliefs held by an individual.

In the present example, for individual i, the fitness contributions for $A1_i$, $A2_i$, $A3_i$ is now an extension to the fitness contributions specified in equations 8, 9, and 10. They are:

$$W(A1_i) = K_{11i} + K_{12i} + K_{13i} + \Sigma \ (C_{11ij}) \ (R_{ij}) + \qquad (18)$$
$$\Sigma \ (C_{12ij}) \ (R_{ij}) + \Sigma \ (C_{13ij}) \ (R_{ij})$$

$$W(A2_i) = K_{21i} + K_{22i} + K_{23i} + \Sigma \ (C_{21ij}) \ (R_{ij}) + \qquad (19)$$
$$\Sigma \ (C_{22ij}) \ (R_{ij}) + \Sigma \ (C_{23ij}) \ (R_{ij})$$

$$W(A3_i) = K_{31i} + K_{32i} + K_{33i} + \Sigma \ (C_{31ij}) \ (R_{ij}) + \qquad (20)$$
$$\Sigma \ (C_{32ij}) \ (R_{ij}) + \Sigma \ (C_{33ij}) \ (R_{ij})$$

The overall fitness contribution for each individual remains, as in equation 11:

$$W_i = 1/3 \ [W(A1_i) + W(A2_i) + W(A3_i)] \qquad (21)$$

Substantively this means that the cognitive consistency fitness for an individual is now influenced not only by the reinforcements or contradictions among the person's own beliefs but also the beliefs of others in the system. As in the previous discussion of NK models, an individual seeks to improve their fitness in this landscape. Let us reconsider the person who had a belief configuration of (0,0,1). This was a person who prioritized using new technology but did not prioritize quality or making cheap products. In the previous scenario, we described how this person could move up the fitness landscape from a fitness score of 1 to a fitness score of 3 by a one-step mutation that would entail the individual embracing quality (A1) as a priority and thereby moving from a (0,0,1) belief configuration to a (1,0,1) configuration. The landscape was defined as somewhat rugged with two global peaks representing the highest fitness scores an individual could achieve. Specifically, if the individual were able to evolve to either the (1,0,1) configuration or the (0,1,0) configuration, he or she would have achieved maximum fitness, that is, complete cognitive consistency among their beliefs. However, adding the C component into the NK models makes the situation much more complicated since an individual's cognitive consistency can now be reinforced or contradicted by the beliefs of other individuals in the system. In order to achieve the highest level of cognitive consistency fitness value an individual must now not only have beliefs that reinforce one another, but also have ties with other individuals whose beliefs reinforce the individual's beliefs. If, at any time, any of these other individuals change their beliefs the focal individual's cognitive consistency will be altered. Hence, unlike the NK models, the fitness landscape for each individual is no longer constant. The individual can no longer be assured that having the belief system (1,0,1) or (0,1,0) will always lead to maximum fitness. Instead, each individual's fitness landscape is constantly changing depending on the beliefs of other individuals with which this individual has ties and their potentially changing beliefs.

Visually, one can consider each individual *trying* to move to a higher level of fitness on a landscape, the slopes, peaks, and basins of which are constantly shifting. These shifts are precipitated by other individuals who are each trying to scale their own fitness landscapes but are confronted by similar shifts in slopes, peaks, and basins induced by others. In essence, the landscapes for each of these individuals are *coupled* to one another. This coupling has the effect that improvements in one landscape may create improvements to other landscapes to which it is coupled but it may also lead to decrements. In the NK models discussed previously, each individual attempted to evolve to a state of higher cognitive fitness on a fixed landscape. In the NK(C) model discussed here, each individual seeks to coevolve to a state of higher fitness on what Kauffman (1993) calls "coupled dancing landscapes" (p. 243). Achieving improved fitness is often made harder by the coupling.

As in the case of the NK models, the primary focus of NK(C) models is not to explain the adaptive walk of a single entity through the fitness landscape. Rather, it is to make knowledge claims about the collective fitness of entities coevolving in the system. As mentioned previously, Kauffman (1993, p. 253) showed that in NK(C) systems, "When $K > S \times C$, all the coevolving partners encounter a Nash equilibrium rapidly. When $K < S \times C$, the coevolving partners do not encounter a Nash equilibrium for a long time." In the present example, $N = 3$, the number of beliefs held by each individual; $K = 2$, the number of constraints between the beliefs held by a single individual; $C = 3$ the number of constraints between one belief held by an individual and the beliefs of any other one individual; and S is the number of people in the system. Let us suppose we were examining the coevolving belief systems among ten employees in a work unit. Then S would be equal to 10 and S X C would be 30. Since K (which is 2) is much less than S X C (which is 30), the coevolving system would not encounter a Nash equilibrium for a long time. Achieving Nash equilibrium is not necessarily a desirable state. A Nash equilibrium for the present example means that each individual has acquired the most cognitively consistent belief configuration that can be achieved *while taking into account* the belief configurations of all other individuals in the system. However, a Nash equilibrium does not mean that each individual is already at the state of highest cognitive consistency that is achievable. A Nash equilibrium simply means that individuals find themselves with a belief system, where an attempt by any one individual to change one belief at a time (referred to earlier as a one-mutant change) will be very unlikely to take them to a state of higher cognitive consistency. Since each individual can aspire to higher states of cognitive consistency the collective fitness of all the individuals in the coevolving system might actually be quite mediocre. So in the present example, one could argue that it is healthy that the coevolving system does not get locked into a less than desirable state of cognitive consistency. It gives individuals the opportunity to coevolve to higher states of cognitive consistency without getting prematurely stuck at a Nash equilibrium before they have had a chance to improve their individual and collective levels of cognitive fitness.

Our example using the NK(C) model to capture coevolving belief systems might be challenged by some who are more familiar with applications of Kauffman's modeling of species that coevolve with other species within a community. It might also appear to be inconsistent with earlier descriptions in this chapter where most of our discussion focused on populations of organizations that have one organizational form coevolving with populations of organizations with another organizational form. We believe that one of the merits of the mathematical formalisms offered by Kauffman's NK(C) models are that they are *scale-free*. For instance, the knowledge claims about the ruggedness of the fitness landscapes and the time to Nash equilibria for coevolving systems rely exclusively on the parameters N, K, C, and S and transcend the content of what constitutes N, K, C, and S. The basic specification is that an entity has N traits, each of which is influenced by links to K other traits possessed by that same entity and by links to C other traits with some or all of a set of S other entities. In Kauffman's work, the entities could be the genotype of species and the N traits could be the genes; the entities could also be genes or strands of DNA and the N traits could be the four *bases* (adenosine, guamine, cytosine, and thymine) in the DNA.

Further, the entities could be proteins, and the N traits could be the amino acids in the protein. In our example above, the entity was an individual, the N traits were the three beliefs of that individual, K was the influences among the individual's three beliefs, and C was the influence of beliefs by other individuals within the set of S individuals.

We could have constructed an alternative model, where the entities were collections of people within the United States, people within Russia, people within Western Europe, and people within the transitional economies (East European countries such as Hungary, Poland, and the Czech Lands). We could then specify N traits that characterize beliefs held by the U.S. population as a collective, and different sets, perhaps, of N beliefs held by people from Russia, Western Europe, and the transitional economies. In this case, K would be the influences *among* the N beliefs held by the U.S. population, the N beliefs among the Russian population, the N beliefs of the Western European population, and the N beliefs among the population of the transitional economies. And, C would represent the influences *between* the beliefs held by the populations of the United States, Russia, Western Europe, and the transitional economies. As suggested by Ahouse et al. (1992), these could be beliefs about the merits of military spending for security, for the overall economy, and for government involvement in domestic social policies. In this case the public opinion of each population would strive to move up their "coupled" fitness landscapes, where fitness would be defined as cognitive consistency or consensus for the populations. This model could then be applied to advance our understanding of the coevolution of public opinion in the United States, Western Europe, and so on, as well as to investigate how critical events like the end of the Cold War changes these coevolving dynamics creating new cleavages in belief systems. The next example we discuss scales up from the individual as entity to the organization as entity. As such, it serves as a bridge between coevolution of individuals' belief systems described in detail above and the coevolution of populations suggested by this example.

Let us consider a model of the coevolution of stores in competing retail chains that serve customers in multiple markets. The Chang and Harrington (2000, in press) model described in this section builds on the general framework of NK(C) but offers some departures from that model. The similarities and departures will be indicated throughout this example. The entities in this model are the retail stores belonging to different retail chains as well as their respective corporate headquarters. A second set of entities is the customers within the markets served by these stores. The N traits possessed by each store is a set of dimensions that defined the store's operations. Unlike the NK(C) model, where each of the N traits was represented either by their absence or presence, Chang and Harrington (2000) allow for the selection of any one from up to a hundred alternative practices for each of the dimensions. Practices could include strategies such as everyday low prices, special short-term sales, fewer product lines, large inventories, and having sales personnel work on commission. The N traits possessed by each of the customers are their ideal store practices. For instance, Chang and Harrington (2000) suggest "people with higher income may incur greater costs, so they would prefer everyday low prices with fewer sales (which avoids having to spend time searching for sales), fewer product lines, and larger inventories (reducing the chances of being out-of-stock of a product and thus creating the need for another trip to the store), and more attentive though more aggressive sales personnel (which might speed up the time spent buying) as might be achieved by having sales personnel work on commission" (p. 1429).

The K in this model would represent the reinforcing and contradicting relationships among the N dimensions that characterized a store's practices or a single customer's ideal practices. For instance, given each store's space constraints, the practices of having fewer product lines may be positively associated with having larger inventories for each product. On the other hand, practices such as special sales would undermine the practice of everyday low prices.

The C in this model would represent the reinforcing and contradicting relationships among the N dimensions that characterized the practices of a store in one retail chain and those that characterized the practices of a store in a competing retail chain. For instance, a retail store might be constrained in its ability to support an "everyday low sales" strategy if a competitive store launched an aggressive special sales event in that market.

The fitness value for a store is defined by its ability to attract customers who then make purchases that are proportional to the similarity between their ideal practices and those offered by the store. Consistent with the theoretical mechanism of evolutionary or coevolutionary theory, at each round a store considers mutations to its existing practices with an eye toward improving its fitness.

Like the NK(C) models, it considers mutations to its practices to see if that change would improve its ability to move up the fitness landscape, that is, improve its ability to get closer to the ideal store practices of its customers. These mutations can affect one or more dimensions simultaneously and hence eschew the one-step mutation typically studied in NK(C) models. Further, since each trait is not simply present or absent, but can take any one of one hundred values, the mutation could be a change from one practice to one of ninety-nine alternative practices. If the selection of one of these alternative practices leads to an improvement in the store's fitness, it is adopted as an innovation.

In a departure from the basic NK(C) model, a retail chain that has adopted a practice that improves its fitness can, in some cases, propose the idea to the retail chain's headquarters as something that may be implemented chainwide. Hence at each round, in addition to examining its own random mutations, each store might also consider some mutations to its practices suggested by the retail chain's headquarters. Further, each store may also, with some probability, replace an existing practice with one that it observes in competing stores within the same market. Finally, a retail chain's headquarters may also with some probability suggest to its stores a practice suggested by a competitive chain's headquarters to its stores.

Chang and Harrington's (2000, in press) model enable them to consider the influence of different organizational forms on the ability of stores to coevolve over a fitness landscape. First, they are interested in examining the influence of centralized versus decentralized organizational forms on stores' ability to navigate the fitness landscape. Second, they are also interested in the extent to which competition (larger number of competing retail chains) may moderate the influence of centralization and decentralization on the fitness landscape. Finally, in addition to stores as entities, this model also included customers as entities. In addition to examining the influence of (de)centralized organizational forms on the stores' ability to adapt to the fitness landscape, Chang and Harrington (2000) also examined the influence of market heterogeneity defined as variations in customers' preferences for ideal store practices.

In a decentralized organizational form, each store has greater discretion to make changes to its practices based on its own mutations overriding those suggested by headquarters. As such it has greater ability to improve its fitness by tailoring its changes to the ideal store practices of its local customer clientele. On the other hand, in a decentralized organizational form, each store has diminished ability to learn from other stores within the chain based on suggestions relayed via the headquarters. "As stores migrate to different parts of the landscape, a new practice uncovered and adopted at one store will be incompatible with the current practices of other stores in the chain. . . . slowing down the rate of [fitness-enhancing] innovation" (Chang & Harrington, 2000, p. 1436). In a centralized organizational form, each store has very little discretion to override any suggested changes in practices made by headquarters. As a result, interstore learning is greatly enhanced.

The results of their simulations revealed that, based on the mechanisms specified above, one would expect that the overall fitness of the population of stores is greater when centralized organizational forms are used under conditions of low market heterogeneity and decentralized organizational forms lead to greater overall fitness under conditions of high market heterogeneity. Further, under conditions of increased interchain rivalry, centralized organizational forms lead to higher overall fitness values.

The extensions from the basic NK(C) model by Chang and Harrington (2000, in press) in this example point to some general observations about the applicability and extensibility of NK(C) models to the study of coevolving networks. Many of these observations are not inconsistent with Kauffman's pioneering efforts in the formulations of these models. Instead, they point to developments that remedy many of the simplifying assumptions to be found in current NK(C) models (Ahouse et al., 1992). First, much of the current work with NK(C) models assumes that the number of K links between the N traits is a constant value. That is, each of the N traits is reinforced or constrained by some constant number of K other traits. This is a very limiting assumption when studying social systems. It is entirely possible that one of the N traits is constrained or reinforced by, say, three other traits, while another one of the N traits is constrained or reinforced by, say, only one other trait. The NK(C) models also make the same assumption in terms of C. In this case, the NK(C) models assume that each trait is influenced by exactly C number of traits among other entities. There is no flexibility to accommodate that one of the N traits may be constrained by more traits in other entities than another. Further, NK(C) models specify the number of other species, S_i, by which a single entity's traits may be constrained or reinforced. This value of S_i could include all other entities, in which case we defined it earlier as a completely coupled system. Or it could specify a smaller subset, S_i, of all the other entities. The number of entities included in this subset, S_i, is the same for all entities and the specific entities are picked at random. In most realistic models of social systems, the number of entities that each entity may be constrained by will vary on a continuum and furthermore the specific entities will not be picked at random. Instead, some other communication or social relation will define them. Finally, in Kauffman's NK(C) models, the fitness contribution by any one trait to the overall fitness is assigned a random number. Clearly, in social systems we have at least an intuitive sense of which traits may contribute more to the overall fitness as compared to other traits.

Summary

In this chapter we have examined evolutionary and coevolutionary theories as they apply to organizational networks. In the first half of the chapter we saw that random or intentional variations occur in the traits or competencies of organizations that exist in larger populations of organizations. Incremental (minor) innovations, mutations, and other variations in practice that are viewed to lead to the competitive fitness of the organization are selected, usually by environmental forces, but sometimes also by internal selectors. Those that prove to be beneficial are transferred to other organizations in the population via a variety of transmission methods such as mimicry and vicarious learning. Eventually, most of the members of the population retain the variation. More radical technological innovations usually require new organizational forms, which are most often created through entrepreneurial start-ups and organizational spin-offs. These new populations often coexist with their predecessors until the latter finally dissolve. All this typically occurs in the context of intense competition among the members of the population for scarce resources that exist in the organizations' niches. Yet niches also contain other populations, which collectively comprise a community. Here different populations both compete and cooperate with each other. Ironically, over time as stronger cooperative structures are built the community encounters a complexity limit beyond which it cannot reach. At this point, the community begins to disintegrate, sometimes slowly, often rapidly, leaving behind the unused resources that can be deployed by a new wave of organizational populations that enters the now vacated niche.

In the second half of the chapter we examined Kauffman's (1993) NK model of evolution on fitness landscapes and its extension, the NK(C) model of coevolution. N represents the nodes of any system conceived as a network and K the links among the nodes. C represents the connections among different populations or species, S, in a community. Thus, the NK(C) network model captures both the internal complexity of populations and the complexity of the symbiotic relations among coevolving populations in the community. These models also attempt to account for organization by natural selection and by self-organization. Both sources of organizational order exist at the transition phase between highly ordered networks and chaotic networks. As with the earlier theoretical chapters in this book, we concluded with a presentation of a MTML network model, this one, of course, specific to coevolutionary theory.

We began this chapter with a quotation from Kauffman. Though somewhat untraditional, we conclude with another.

> The edge-of-chaos image arises in coevolution as well, for as we evolve, so do our competitors; to remain fit, we must adapt to their adaptations. In co-evolving systems, each partner clambers up its fitness landscape toward fitness peaks, even as that landscape is constantly deformed by the adaptive moves of its coevolutionary partners. Strikingly, such coevolving systems also behave in an ordered regime, a chaotic regime, and a transition regime. It is almost spooky that such systems seem to coevolve to the regime at the edge of chaos. As if by an invisible hand, each adapting species acts according to its own selfish advantage, yet the entire system appears magically to evolve to a poised state where, on average, each does as best as can be expected. Yet, as in many of the dynamical systems we will study in this book, each is eventually driven to extinction, despite its own best efforts, by the collective behavior of the system as a whole. (Kauffman, 1995, p. 27)

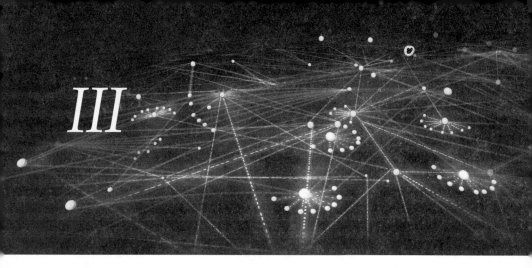

III

Integration

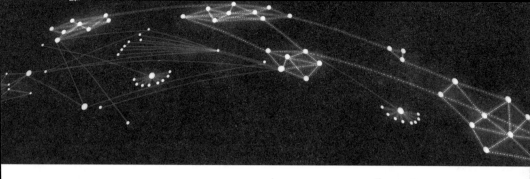

10

Multitheoretical, Multilevel Models of Communication and Other Organizational Networks

The Essential Argument

In this book we have argued for a multitheoretical, multilevel approach to the study of communication and other forms of organizational and social networks. We began by exploring several problems within the existing corpus of network research. We then showed how the MTML model provides a network research strategy that resolves most of these problems. (For ease of presentation, this review of the essential arguments and social theories includes citations only to references that have not been cited in earlier chapters of this book.)

The first problem is the fact that the vast majority of network research is atheoretical. One reason for this is that there are very few explicit theories of social networks. Another reason is that researchers are generally not cognizant of the relational and structural implications inherent in various social theories. Even research that does employ theory typically does so without much attention to the network mechanisms implicit in the theories.

A second problem with network research is that most scholars approach networks from a rather myopic, single-level perspective, which is reflected in the fact that almost all published research operates at a single level of analysis. Thus, they tend to focus on individual features of the network such as density. For the most part, researchers tend to ignore the multiple other components out of which most network configurations are composed, structural components from multiple levels of analysis such as mutuality, transitivity, and network centralization. Employing single levels of analysis is not inherently wrong; it is simply incomplete. Importantly, these components suggest different theoretical mechanisms in the formation, continuation, and eventual reconfiguration of networks. Typically, better explanations come from research that utilizes multiple levels of analysis.

The third problem centers on the fact that most network research focuses on the relatively obvious elementary features of networks such as link density and fails to explore other, more complex properties of networks such as attributes of nodes or multiplex relations. But the members of networks often possess interesting theoretical properties, which help to shape the configurations in which they are embedded, and networks are themselves often tied to other networks. Traditional analyses typically account for relatively simple, surface features of networks and ignore these more subtle and sophisticated structural characteristics inherent in many networks.

The final problem is that most network research tends to use descriptive rather than inferential statistics. The reason for this is that network relations contain inherent dependencies that typically do not exist in traditional attribute data. These dependencies invalidate the assumption of independent observations, which forms the basis for much of the traditional social science research on attributes. Thus, until recently there has not been an arsenal of statistical techniques that network researchers could use to test network hypotheses. Without valid inferential procedures as a basis for generalization, it has seemed prudent to confine one's claims to descriptive statements about the network under observation.

The Multitheoretical, Multilevel Approach

Some solutions we have offered to these four problems center around the multitheoretical, multilevel model. First, the model suggests that network analysts should use a variety of different theories to account for different properties of networks, thereby expanding our explanations and the variance accounted for by those explanations. Second, the MTML model articulates network components that exist at several network levels, from the existence of individual links to characteristics of the network taken as a whole. Third, the MTML model suggests that we can provide better accounts of networks by using a three-tiered analytic approach, which includes attributes of nodes and multiplex or autoregressive networks along with our multilevel network decompositions. Finally, as part of the MTML approach we have described the p^* family of analytic techniques, which addresses the problem of nonindependence inherent in relational data and provides the basis for statistical inference regarding network configurations.

There are a number of reasons that commend the use of multiple theories. First, theorists have yet to develop single, omnibus theories that account for the full array of network characteristics. Until that happens, using multiple theories improves our ability to account for specific network configurations. Second, most theories account for relatively modest amounts of variance in network properties. Using multiple theories enables us to increase the amount of variance we can explain in the networks being studied. Finally, multiple theories provide different prisms through which to explore network configurations, thus providing richer, more textured insights.

The MTML model provides a three-tiered approach to network analysis. The first tier is the decomposition of networks into their potential multilevel components. The second examines the attributes of the nodes. The third explores the role of other networks or the same network at earlier points in time. Not all three tiers need be examined in the same analysis, but a complete analysis will often use all three.

The first analytic tier, network decomposition, consists of identification and assessment of various components of the network. As we explained in chapter 2, greater or lesser degrees of these elementary components comprise networks, which are, for the most part, situated in hierarchical levels. Every network consists of nodes and some level of link density, mutuality, triadic cyclicality and transitivity, cliques properties, and global properties. Every specific network is composed out of a particular configuration of these properties. Further, each of these properties can be explained by one or more social theories. Thus, the first analytic tier consists of theoretical analysis of the network under consideration, examination of possible relevant explanatory theories, and theoretical decomposition of the network into its relevant components explained by those theories.

The second analytic tier, attribute analysis, examines the properties of nodes. Historically, the primary focus of most social science research has been on attributes rather than relations, thus omitting an important dimension of human experience. Historically, the primary focus of network analysis has been on relations, thus minimizing the importance of human attributes. One area of work in network analysis has examined attributes of nodes through blockmodeling, a technique that reconfigures the entire network into subnetworks, each with different values of the attributes, and examines relations within and between blocks. Typically, blockmodeling has been employed to examine the attributes of nodes apart from networks themselves. In the MTML model we advocate examining attributes as one of three analytic tiers. Though nodal attributes can be examined in isolation, in general we recommend that attributes be examined in combination with decomposition of the networks into their elementary components and with other networks. Of course, multiple attributes can be studied as well as the same attributes at multiple points in time.

The third tier of the MTML model is multiplex networks, both other relations in the network and the same relations at previous points in time. It is somewhat surprising that relations have seldom been used to explain other relations, yet multiplex networks—multiple relations on the same set of nodes—are quite rare in the research literature. Our experience is that most network researchers believe that many networks are predictive of other networks, that communication networks, for example, are likely to be highly predictive of friendship networks. Even more obvious is the fact that autoregressive networks—the same network at previous points in time—like other autoregressive processes, are likely to predict current values of the network. But until these relations are demonstrated with empirical research using valid statistical procedures, they remain in the realm of speculation.

The final problem addressed by the MTML approach is the dependency inherent in network data. The p^* family of analytic techniques views every focal network as one possible realization of a very large set of possible network configurations. Each realization is composed of a unique combination of network components, such as mutuality, transitivity, and cyclicality. By conditioning or controlling for the appropriate properties, it is possible to determine whether the level of any given network component exists in the network beyond that which would be expected on the basis of chance alone. This provides a basis for statistical inference about hypothesized network components and thus, a basis for hypothesis tests regarding these components. While p^* techniques are still being developed, as are related approaches, these efforts have provided the foundations for statistical analysis that have long been missing in this area. Since this book has largely focused on the MTML mechanisms for the creation, maintenance, dissolution, and reconstitution of network ties, our description of p^* models has focused primarily on what Robins, Elliott, and Pattison (2001), characterize as *social selection p** models. However, just as important are a second family of *social influence p** models that explain how structural properties of the network at different levels influence the attributes of the individuals (Robins, Pattison, & Elliott, 2001).

In addition to the MTML model and *p** approaches, we have recommended computer simulations as a useful approach to network analysis. Networks are complex entities whose properties are extremely difficult to intuit, even with the help of theory. We described *Blanche*, a multiagent computational modeling environment as one approach to this problem. *Blanche* simulates the three tiers of the MTML model: relations among nodes, attributes of nodes, and the network at earlier points in time. Thus, network simulations can be developed on the basis of network or other social theories and run through multiple iterations. The results of the simulation can be statistically compared to empirical longitudinal data. The simulation can also be used to generate hypotheses about the nature of network configurations at future points in time. When simulations are built on the basis of theory and used in conjunction with real data, they can provide powerful explanations for social networks. A recent volume (Lomi & Larsen, 2001) amply demonstrates the quantity and quality of renewed interest (March, 2001) in computational modeling as a strategy to uncover the dynamics of organizations. It is particularly encouraging that several of these studies specifically adopt a network approach to computational modeling (Carley & Hill, 2001; Krackhardt, 2001; Lomi & Larsen, 2001; Prietula, 2001).

Additionally, a particularly promising approach to the study of longitudinal network data is a statistical analytic technique developed by Snijders (2001). The analysis is done on the basis of computer simulations of a probabilistic model for the evolution of the social network. The technique is implemented in a computer software program called SIENA (Simulation Investigation for Empirical Network Analysis).

In summary, the three-tiered MTML model decomposes networks into their multilevel component parts, examines the attributes of nodes, and explores their relations with other multiplex and/or autoregressive networks; *p** techniques provide the basis for statistical analysis of network data, providing an inferential basis similar to more traditional analyses of social attribute data. Computer simulations using multiagent computational modeling environments, such as *Blanche*, provide powerful theory-building and theory-testing tools that can significantly advance the state-of-the-art in research on organizational and communication networks.

Theoretical Network Mechanisms in Social Theories: A Reprise

Chapters 5 through 9 explored a wide variety of social theories to identify theoretical mechanisms relevant to network realizations. Here we briefly review these theories and highlight some of the most important theoretical mechanisms for network research.

Theories of Self- and Mutual Interest

Theories of self interest and theories of mutual interest examine the factors that lead people to act in their own best interest rather than the interest of others, or to act in ways that are for the benefit of the entire collective. Three theories of self-interest examined in chapter 5 were Coleman's theory of social capital, Burt's theory of structural holes, and Williamson's theory of transaction cost economics. The first two theories explore opportunities for investment and profit provided by unconnected regions of networks called structural holes. Here, perceptive entrepreneurs can invest their social or structural capital by linking these unconnected nodes through themselves with the expectation that doing so will generate rewards or benefits in terms of social profit. Structural autonomy is the theoretical mechanism in structural holes theory that generates specific network configurations.

Transaction cost economics explores the various coordination costs involved in organizational production, including information and communication. The fundamental principal driving this theory is that firms seek to minimize these costs when making decisions about how to organize. The tradeoff they must assess is whether it is less costly to search for best market buys than it is to organize hierarchically where the cost to administer hierarchies can often be quite high. Theoretical generative mechanisms that account for markets are exchange and reciprocity. Hierarchy is a generative mechanism that could be used in an MTML p^* analysis to account for vertical organizational structure. From a communication perspective the rule that an agent-based model would follow in generating emergent structure states: "I try to keep the costs of my communication to a minimum."

Chapter 5 also explored the logic of collective action theories with an emphasis on the communication networks that comprise the collective. An alternative form of organization, the network organization, operates on a different principle, joint value maximization, which can reduce both information search costs in markets and administrative costs of hierarchies. Here the agent-based principle that generates structure is, "I try to maximize the collective value of my communication to all others." Public goods theory demonstrated that network connectedness affects who contributes to the creation and/or maintenance of public goods, including the communication public goods of connectivity and communality. The ideal targets for communication campaigns by people who wish to mobilize collective goods are those who are resource rich, who have significant interests in seeing the good realized, and who have extensive ties to others who have similar interests and resources. An important tie between self-interest and mutual-interest theories arises in the case of communication dilemmas. These occur when contributing to the collective good is at odds with self-interest, as may occur in contributing to a discretionary database. The resolution to communication dilemmas is a public goods transformation that aligns individual interests with collective ones.

Contagion, Semantic, and Cognitive Theories

Contagion, semantic, and cognitive theories explain the emergence of communication networks based on individuals' contacts with others as well as their cognitions about others and their relations. *Contagion* theories seek to explain networks as conduits for contagious attitudes and behavior. Here, the primary explanatory metaphor is that merely exposing people to new or different ideas, attitudes, or behavior, is likely to change their existing ideas, attitudes, or behavior. Contagion processes are presumed to operate in similar fashion to the way in which people catch infectious diseases by coming in contact with someone who already has the disease or as neophytes become knowledgeable just by being exposed to new ideas. The network implications of this theory are that network members who are in regular contact with each other should have similar attitudes, opinions, and beliefs. The counterpart to contagion theory, inoculation theory, suggests that giving people small amounts of exposure to attitudes, values, and beliefs will help them develop their own defense mechanisms which will enable them to resist exposure to persuasive messages. From a network perspective this suggests that either small amount of inoculating content should flow through the networks or people should have weak rather than strong ties with infected others, thereby minimizing the likelihood of infection.

The contagion mechanism is also known to operate in interorganizational networks through mimetic processes. Here, organizations copy the best practices of other organizations they come in contact with or imitate those institutions with successful reputations. Isomorphic pressures for legitimation make those organizations that comprise a network in a population more likely to be similar to each other than those population members who are outside the network.

Semantic theories attempt to explain on the basis of networks similarities among individual interpretations of organizational events, public documents, personal experiences, collective histories, organizational symbols, and organizational cultures. The generative mechanisms proposed by a semantic networks perspective that can be incorporated into an MTML model is the extent to which the semantic relations among a network of people can be explained at the individual, dyadic, and the global levels of analysis.

Organizations can also be conceptualized as knowledge networks both within and among organizations in the same or other populations. Knowledge networks are distributed repositories of knowledge elements from a larger knowledge domain that are tied together by knowledge linkages within and among organizations. Theories of *cognitive social structures* examine the cognitions people have of "who knows who" and "who knows who knows who." This set of cognitions comprises the perceived social network among organizational members, and are equally valid within and among organizations. Similarly, theories of *cognitive knowledge structures* examine cognitions that people have of "who knows what" and "who knows who knows what." The former provides the first-order knowledge network that would enable people to directly contact those who have specific knowledge. The second-order network enables people to find others who can help them find those who have the requisite knowledge.

The theory of transactive memory systems explains how interdependent people within a knowledge network, each with their own set of skills and expertise, develop cognitive knowledge networks, which help them identify the skills and expertise of others in the network. These transactive memory systems facilitate the flows of knowledge among people within the network thereby reducing the need for each person to possess skills or expertise available elsewhere in the network.

The theory identifies four interrelated processes by which people develop transactive memory systems: expertise recognition, retrieval coordination, directory updating, and information allocation. *Expertise recognition* is the process by which people identify others in the network who have expertise in various topics. *Retrieval coordination* is the process they use when they face a task for which they do not possess all the necessary knowledge. They do this by coordinating the retrieval of information from among the experts they have identified in the expertise recognition process. *Directory updating* is the process that people use to update their directories of "who knows what?" Finally, *information allocation* is the process by which people who receive information outside their areas of expertise determine which other people in the network would find that information relevant to their respective areas of expertise, thus redistributing the knowledge. The MTML model built to represent these processes uses only the attributes of individuals and relations at the dyadic level. However, the theory posits that these generative mechanisms can lead to a well-developed transactive memory system that has emergent properties, such as knowledge differentiation, which can be measured at the global level.

Finally, from an organizational communication networks perspective *cognitive consistency* theories seek to explain the extent to which a drive for consistency is manifest in people's networks and attitudes. Members' attitudes are viewed as a function of the balance in their networks rather than alternative mechanisms such as contagion. The generative mechanism for cognitive consistency theory is triadic transitivity, which represents the extent to which a person who has a direct relation to another person also has indirect relations to this person via several intermediary others.

Chapter 6 provided several representative MTML models that incorporate the theoretical mechanisms inherent in these contagion, semantic, and cognitive theories. These models decomposed the focal network into its relevant parts (dyadic, triadic, etc.), examined attributes of nodes that can influence the formation of the focal network, and suggested other networks that might be relevant to the emergent process. This family of theories can be used individually or in conjunction with other theories to build and test MTML models for the emergence, maintenance, dissolution, and re-creation of organizational communication networks.

Exchange and Dependency Theories

The logic of exchange and dependency theories suggests that individuals and organizations forge network ties based on their need to obtain informational or material resources from others and their ability to provide their own valuable information or material in return. By seeking exchange ties, actors minimize their dependence on others. Being dependent for resources from others and not being able to offer anything in exchange creates power imbalances in favor of the others. Clearly, actors' goals would be to minimize these power differentials. An additional strategy to reduce power differentials would be to structure resource dependence ties with actors who are not already connected to one another. This may require extending the dependence network to incorporate additional actors. Doing so would increase the ability of focal actors to autonomously broker the dependency relationships without running the risk of others creating coalitions or cartels in their transactions with them. However, by the same logic, individuals and organizations should also seek to structure ties so that they can maximize power differentials with those that depend on them. They can create network ties by offering needed resources to other actors from whom they do not need any resources in exchange. Additionally, they can attempt to create coalitions with other actors who offer similar resources to the target actor. This effort at network consolidation would in effect reduce the number of dependence alternatives and power of the target actor.

Empirical evidence reviewed in chapter 7 indicated that individuals and organizations that structured their ties based on the logic of exchange were indeed more capable of exerting autonomy, enhancing their reputation, and their effectiveness. The accruing power, in turn, gave these actors even greater flexibility in structuring their networks to reinforce the desired dependencies. Since trust can be viewed as a surrogate for committing to an exchange before there is evidence that the other party will reciprocate, it serves as an important precursor to the creation of social exchange relations. As was the case with other theories, the mechanisms and the empirical findings reported in chapter 7 applied to diverse relations such as advice, communication, buyer-seller, or interlocking boards of directorates. Also, as in other chapters, the creation of ties based on social exchange mechanisms were at multiple levels—actor-level properties of the network (e.g., their betweenness centrality), dyadic-level properties of the network (e.g., mutual exchange of different resources), exogenous attributes of the actor (e.g., the resources they possessed), and exogenous relations (e.g., trust).

Homophily, Physical Proximity, Electronic Proximity, and Social Support Theories

In chapter 8 we reviewed four other sets of theoretical mechanisms that also seek to explain why we create, maintain, dissolve, and reconstitute our network ties. The first of these mechanisms, homophily, invokes the adage "birds of a feather flock together." Through processes associated with social identity theory as well as self-categorization theory, individuals and organizations tend to characterize themselves on a handful of key dimensions. Often these dimensions include gender, age, race, religion, product, or service sector, or other organizational demographic characteristics (such as tenure, professional affiliations, age of the industry) or membership in voluntary associations. We noted that the network could influence which of these dimensions emerge as salient in the development of identity and self-categorization. Further, the network also constrains the reference group that individuals and organizations may use for purposes of social comparison and thereby for identity formation of in-groups versus out-groups. While theories of homophily typically rely on individual characteristics, the empirical research reviewed in chapter 8 suggests that organizations also forge ties based on perceived homophily among their employees and other organizations in their industry. Unlike most of the theoretical mechanisms reviewed in this book, the homophily mechanism for creating a network tie, taken by itself, relies primarily on the exogenous attributes of the nodes in the network.

The second mechanism reviewed in chapter 8 was physical proximity. This mechanism proposes a nonlinear influence of physical proximity on the probability of creating a communication tie. The argument is that proximity increases the opportunities for individuals or organizations to observe and learn more about one another, thereby creating conditions conducive to the development of communication ties. These probabilities of communication diminish precipitously as distance among the parties increases. The empirical research on proximity also provided some interesting insights about how relocation and dislocation could influence the maintenance and dissolution of communication ties. Employees who were permanently relocated from their prior place of work experienced much higher stress levels, presumably due to sudden changes in their communication networks, as compared to those who were only temporarily relocated. As was the case in our discussion of other theoretical mechanisms, proximity served to explain the development of communication ties at the individual, departmental, and interorganizational level. At the interorganizational level, the empirical research based on the proximity mechanism gave us one of the few studies that explicitly examined the reconstitution of dissolved ties. Interlock ties were more likely to be reconstituted if departing members represented organizations whose headquarters were physically proximate to that of focal organizations. The generative mechanism to explain the development of communication ties based on proximity relied on one exogenous relation—the proximity relation.

The third mechanism examined in chapter 8 was electronic proximity. The various affordances offered by new media—their richness, bandwidth, portability, embeddedness, and ubiquity—facilitated communication. Broadly speaking, we noted that the theoretical rationale surrounding the influence of new media on communication ties are based on three motivations. Substitution suggests that the creation of communication ties using the new medium would replace the communication tie between the same two actors using older media. Enlargement proposes that the creation of communication ties via one medium would augment and further the communication ties between the same individuals or organizations via other media. Finally, reconfiguration argues that the creation of new communication ties via one medium would reconfigure the relations among actors within the communication network.

The empirical evidence regarding the influence of new media on individuals' and organizational communication networks is decidedly mixed. We argue that this reiterates prior research on the influence of new media on our communication patterns. Rather than exerting a univalent influence, technologies tend to have dual effects, acting in opposite directions at the same time and in spite of each another. We conclude that a more fruitful strategy to examine the influences of technology on communication networks would be to consider the ways in which these reinforce or undermine other theoretical mechanisms influencing the development of communication networks. Specifically, we suggested that the affordances offered by new media might serve to moderate the theoretical mechanisms proposed by contagion theories, theories of collective action, and coordination theories.

We also noted the potential for several additional theories that examine the interrelationships between the genres and use of new media on the one hand and organizing structures and norms on the other to benefit from a more explicit network formulation. While much of the research reported in this section was among individuals, we also reviewed research that demonstrated how investment in electronic data interchange (EDI) protocols reified existing business practices and prevented organizations from considering a reconfiguration of their business relationships. The generative mechanisms for communication via a specific media included the endogenous dyadic relation, as well as exogenous attributes of the actors and exogenous relations such as communication.

Finally, the chapter reviewed ways in which a desire for social support served as the theoretical mechanism for the development of communication ties. There were two primary motivations that explain how the need for social support might structure actors' communication networks. First, being embedded in dense networks enables actors to access material resources and social support that might help them cope with stress and anxiety. Second, it may help to include in the network those who have an understanding of the work circumstances surrounding the focal individual or organization. These others will be better qualified to offer empathy and understanding. Third, in order to maximize their social support, actors may choose to structure their communication networks to include others who are able to provide material and informational resources. Finally, individuals and organizations may seek to forge links with others who will not only be able to provide material and informational resources but are also able to mobilize additional material and informational resources from their respective networks.

We noted that very little of the empirical network research based on this mechanism is conducted in organizational contexts. The limited research reviewed offers some evidence that actors who structured their networks on the basis of a social support mechanism were more likely to generate radical (i.e., frame-breaking) innovation and reported greater job satisfaction. However, another study showed that actors with well-developed social support networks were more likely to report early onset of daily living disability, perhaps because their greater reliance on others eroded over time their confidence in their own ability to do things independently. Another study noted that in blue-collar settings or low security jobs, strong kinship ties could actually exacerbate negative job conditions. In terms of the social support providers in the network, one study reported that actors who engaged in offering social support toward others in their network reported higher levels of emotional exhaustion. Most of the studies reported in this section were at the individual level of analysis, though three studies reported how social support institutions can structure their ties with government, hospitals, and other agencies to facilitate the care of those who come to them in need of help. The generative mechanisms describing how social support can influence the structure of communication ties include actor-level endogenous network properties such as degree centrality, and exogenous actor attributes, that is, their ability to provide material or informational resources.

Coevolutionary Theory

Community coevolution examines how networks of organizational populations and other entities interact with each other in environmental niches to acquire scarce resources. Some environments are munificent; others are sparse. But all have a limited amount of resources, called the carrying capacity, which can support a maximum population or community size. Evolution occurs through processes that generate random and systematic variation in population traits, which are selected on the basis of their fitness for the population and are retained through institutional procedures or transmitted across generations by inheritance or other copying mechanisms. Here, the rule that an agent-based model might employ to generate emergent structure in the population or community is: "I communicate with people in order to improve my fitness in the population network, the fitness of the population's network, or the overall fitness of the community networks."

The primary relations that control coevolutionary development within organizational ecosystems are commensalist and symbiotic. Commensalism varies across a continuum anchored at one end by mutualism and at the other end by competition. Mutualism is a cooperative relationship in which similar members of populations coordinate their actions, thus achieving collectively and to their mutual benefit what no individual could accomplish on its own. Competition occurs when different members of populations seek to obtain the same or similar resources. Often what one gains, the other loses. The center of the continuum is neutrality, where the presence of one population does not affect other populations. Symbiotic relations are dependencies that are based on functional differences. Thus, for example, a member of one population, a banker, provides financial resources to a member of another population, an entrepreneur, who needs the money to implement creative ideas. It is not uncommon for members of populations to enter into both commensalist and symbiotic relations, both within their own populations and with other populations with which they interact.

Though the population ecology perspective has tended to look at isolated populations and to ignore networks of relations, recent work in community ecology has focused on the entire ecosystem where the networks of relations play a central role. Barnett and Carroll (1987) point out that this multilevel property can be seen in that "organizational interdependence can exist at several levels: between individual organizations, between populations of organizations, and between communities of organizations" (p. 100). Thus, as we show in chapter 9, it is possible to build MTML models of community ecologies based in part on commensalist and symbiotic relations within and among population and community networks.

As communities develop, populations tend to increasingly interact with one another. Thus, the density of network ties increases, both within and between populations. This produces two effects. First, populations increasingly acquire resources from each other, thus depending less on the environment. In effect, community coevolution creates a buffering effect or shield against environmental changes. Unfortunately, it also creates an overly dense network, which begins to close on itself, setting up the eventual conditions for its own collapse. When this happens, the resources of the community's populations are released back into the environment, thus providing the basis for the development of a new community.

Small World Networks

Starting in the late 1990s, there has been a resurgence of interest in the "small world" phenomenon (see Buchanan, 2002). The motivations for this interest, spanning several disciplines, were inspired by the design and use of the Web. But this research also provides a potentially powerful framework for understanding the creation, maintenance, dissolution, and reconstitution of networks from an MTML framework. Before we discuss these specific applications and extensions, we begin by reviewing recent developments in small world research.

In his book, *Small Worlds: The Dynamics of Networks Between Order and Randomness*, Duncan Watts (1999) offers one of the most substantial advancement in our understanding of "small worlds" in more than three decades. Paul Erdos, perhaps best known for his foundational contributions to probabilistic graph theory, introduced the concept of *small worlds*. Until recently, most work on the small world phenomena focused on networks among individuals. The phrase acknowledges the considerable surprise ("What a small world!") between two strangers who discover that they are indirectly connected to one another through mutual acquaintances. In the 1950s, two researchers at MIT, Ithiel de Sola Pool and Manfred Kochen, mathematically estimated the number of links that would be required to connect any two strangers in the United States. Based on the assumption that each individual had between a hundred and a thousand acquaintances, many of who might know one another, they conjectured that on the average each person was linked to any other random person in the United States by two or three intermediaries, and almost certainly by no more than four. Their conjecture suggested that perhaps we should not be so surprised by this small world phenomenon.

In 1967 Harvard sociologist Stanley Milgram and his colleagues attempted to empirically test this conjecture. They asked people in Kansas and Nebraska to direct letters to strangers in Boston by forwarding the letters to friends who they thought might have a chance of knowing the strangers in Boston. Milgram discovered that half those letters were delivered to the strangers through no more than five intermediaries. Subsequent studies by Milgram and others replicated these findings between strangers in different towns and even on a single university campus. There appeared to be a universal "six degrees of separation" between any two individuals on the planet. The interest in this finding spread beyond the social science community with John Guare's play (and subsequently a film) titled *Six Degrees of Separation*, and David Lodge's novel *Small World*, a farcical look at academics who were all directly or indirectly connected to each other. In a nod to the pioneering contributions of Paul Erdos, mathematicians around the world marked their prestige by their "Erdos numbers," a measure of how closely they were connected via coauthoring relationships with Paul Erdos. Four hundred and seventy two scholars who had coauthored with the prolific Paul Erdos had an Erdos number of 1! More recently, Brett Tjaden and Glenn Wasson of the University of Virginia created the "Kevin Bacon game" on the Web site (http://www.cs.virginia.edu/oracle/). On this Web site, one can query the Internet Movie Database to identify how many degrees of separation (the "Bacon number") existed between any actor in the world and Kevin Bacon. Of the total number of 452,192 actors in the database, 1,463 had a Bacon number of 1 by having appeared in a movie with Kevin Bacon; 111,714 actors had a Bacon number of 2, signifying their appearance in a movie with someone who had been in a movie with Kevin Bacon; and 273,133 had a Bacon number of 3. In fact, on the average, all actors in the database were just under three degrees of separation from Kevin Bacon. For instance, Raj Kapoor, a famous actor from India's 1950s movie industry is three degrees of separation from Kevin Bacon: Raj Kapoor was in *Awara* (1951) with Shashi Kapoor, Shashi Kapoor was in *Side Streets* (1997) with Peter Appel, Peter Appel was in *Sleepers* (1996) with Kevin Bacon. While these findings might suggest that Kevin Bacon is an extremely central actor in the movie network, qualitatively similar small world findings would have emerged between any two actors.

This is the central conundrum examined by Watts: How is it that many large, sparse (in which each node has only a few connections compared to the total number of nodes), physical, biological, social, and human-designed networks tend to exhibit seemingly universal small world characteristics? Watts defines a small world network as one where the nodes have a high degree of local clustering with a small fraction of the nodes (that is, these nodes are interconnected with one another), while at the same time being no more than a few degrees of separation from all of the remaining nodes. To probe the emergence of small world networks, Watts considers two extreme types of networks that exhibit one, but not the other, of these two characteristics. The first, *regular or lattice* networks, are those where each node is only connected directly to a few neighboring nodes, many of which are also connected to one another. These *regular* networks, like small world networks, demonstrate a high degree of clustering. But, unlike small world networks, they have a high degree of separation from the remaining nodes in the network. Watts refers to this type of network as the "Caveman world" where individuals were closely connected in a cluster to others in their cave but had very high degrees of separation with others outside their cave. The second extreme network considered by Watts is the *random network* where each node is randomly connected to a few other nodes. Since these randomly connected nodes are not likely to be connected to one another, random networks, unlike small world networks, have a low degree of clustering among the nodes. However, like small world networks, these random networks have a low degree of separation between any two nodes in the network. This is because the random connections are more likely to bring far-flung parts of the network closer to one another. Watts refers to this as the "Solaria world," named after the planet in Isaac Asimov's novel where individuals lived in isolation and were just as likely to have connections via robots and computers with others across the planet as they did with their spouses in their local homes.

Clearly, small world networks lie on a continuum between these two extreme regular and random networks such that they have high clustering (like regular networks) and shorter degrees of separation (like random networks). In order to study the transition from regular networks to small world networks, Watts used *construction algorithms* to rewire the nodes. For instance, in the regular network, some of the links from a node to neighboring nodes were removed and redirected to connect to randomly selected nodes in the network. A central finding of this rewiring process, and perhaps the most significant contribution of this book, was the discovery that it took very few of these random rewirings to transition from a regular network to a small world network. In essence, a few of these random connections served as *shortcuts* that abruptly enabled far-flung parts of the network to be indirectly connected by just a few degrees of separation.

A central implication of this finding is that relatively minor changes in the wiring of the network can have dramatic changes in the global structure of the network—that is, in the clustering of the network as well as in the average degrees of separation between the nodes in the network. The ramifications of this tenuous link between microlevel changes and macrolevel properties situate the findings reported in Watts's book at the center stage of contemporary intellectual discourse on complex systems. Not surprisingly, some of the work reported in this book was completed while Watts was in residence at the Santa Fe Institute, which has been a hotbed of theorizing and research on the sciences of complexity. Consistent with the work of other complexity theorists, Watts demonstrates that several small world networks found in nature, society, as well as those designed by humans, represent a delicate balance between order (the regular network) and randomness (via minimal rewiring). Hence, the subtitle of Watts's book: The dynamics of networks between order and randomness.

Having described how small world networks can emerge from a minimal random rewiring of a regular network, Watts next turns his attention to real world networks. Using as examples the collaboration among actors in the Internet Movie Database discussed earlier, the western U.S. power grid, and the neural network of the nematode worm *Caenorhabditis elegans* (the only creature whose neural network has been completely mapped so far), Watts demonstrates that these each meet the criteria of small world networks. He empirically demonstrates that such small world networks are more prevalent in the real world than one would expect by chance.

Intrigued by the widespread prevalence of the small world phenomena in natural, social, and human-designed networks, Watts then focuses on the implications for network dynamics that arise from small world network structure. Specifically, he examines the spread of infectious disease through a structured population, the computational capacity of cellular automata, the evolution of cooperation in game theory, and the synchronization of coupled phase-oscillators. In each of these cases, Watts examines how the dynamics—for instance, the spread of infectious diseases, the spread and sustenance of cooperative strategies among competitive agents, or the ability of crickets to synchronize their chirping—are extremely sensitive to the underlying structure of the networks. In general, he argues that the dynamics exhibited by networks with a small world structure differ qualitatively from regular or random networks. For instance, the spread of a disease may be significantly accelerated in a small world network as compared to a purely regular or a purely random network. These findings suggest the "dark side" of small worlds—the same mechanism that enables two strangers to be amazed when they discover common acquaintances may, in a less welcome surprise, explain how one contracted an infection from the other. In another example, Watts examines, albeit with inconclusive results, how the structure of the small world network impacts the spread of cooperative strategies among competitive agents. The influence of small world network structure on network dynamics have important implications for prior research in these areas that have either ignored the structure of the network or assumed the structure to be approximately regular or random networks. Since, as Watts argues, most real world networks have a small world structure rather than a regular or random structure, the dynamics of a network based on those assumptions are not adequate representations of what may be empirically observed.

Watts acknowledges the preliminary nature of his attempts to characterize small world structures and even more rudimentary exploratory attempts to investigate the impact of small world structures on the dynamics of networks. But his initial forays have helped immeasurably to stimulate a new transdisciplinary stream of research that examines the prevalence of small world networks in a broad spectrum of the physical, life, and social sciences. Even since the publication of Watts and Strogatz's 1998 article in *Nature*, and subsequently Watts's book, *Small Worlds*, researchers have found evidence of small world networks in a wide variety of contexts. For instance, Adamic (1999); Albert, Jeong, and Barabasi (1999); and Kleinberg and Lawrence (2001) have shown that the networks of pages comprising the World Wide Web demonstrate a small world structure where any 2 of the 800 million pages on the Web are on the average separated by approximately 19 degrees of separation (or in this case, hot links). Two Italian scientists, Marchiori and Latora (2000), have shown that the network representing the Boston subway system (the oldest in the United States) exhibits a small world topology. The subway network has a high degree of clustering but also a minimal number of shortcuts that minimizes the degrees of separation between any two randomly selected locations in the Boston area. Others have shown that the network connecting every part of the brain also exhibits similar small world properties.

While Watts's work, and some of the research it has inspired, has focused on *identifying* networks that exhibit small world structures, his ideas are also useful to those who are interested in *designing* small world networks. In general, small world networks with their relatively small degrees of separation between any two nodes, facilitate the efficient transmission of information or other resources across the network without having to overload the network with too many redundant connections. For instance, recent efforts have applied these small world principles to the design of more effective organizations and smarter search agents on the Web. Further, in a recent article in *Nature*, a Cornell University computer scientist, Jon Kleinberg (2000), points to a limitation of, and offers an extension to, the Watts-Strogatz model in describing personal networking. Kleinberg notes that in the model Watts described the rewiring of the regular network is done purely at random. That is, the connection from one node to another node in the regular network is redirected to any other node in the network selected at random. Instead, he argues, in a model that more accurately represents personal networking, the redirected node is not selected purely at random but with a probability of being chosen that is inversely proportional to the square of its geographical distance from the originating node. Kleinberg's argument represents an early attempt at extending Watts's model by introducing one of several mechanisms proposed by social scientific theories about social networks. Specifically, as we described earlier in chapter 8, Kleinberg recognizes the role of physical proximity in determining the likelihood of creating, maintaining, or dissolving social network linkages.

More recently Watts, Dodds, and Newman (2002) extend this further by taking into account two of the mechanisms identified in our book: geographical proximity and homophily on one or more dimensions. Watts et al. (2002) justify this extension on the premise that the small world phenomenon "reveals not only that short paths exist between individuals in a large social network but that ordinary people can find these short paths. This is not a trivial statement, since people rarely have more than local knowledge about the network" (p. 1303). By incorporating these two social mechanisms, the nodes in Watts's simulation now have some agency in their search for other nodes that can relay their message to the intended target. The results of their simulations offer an improved match to the empirical results reported in the Milgram studies. More significantly, their simulations suggest that the best overall performance in searchability seems to be when individuals are homophilous in two or three dimensions. These findings are consistent with independent empirical evidence by Bernard, Killworth, Evans, McCarty, and Shelly (1988) that "individuals across different cultures in small-world experiments typically utilize two or three dimensions when forwarding a message" (Watts et al., 2002, p. 1304).

As we have demonstrated in our presentation of the MTML model throughout this book, social theory has developed an impressive body of literature on the theoretical mechanisms that contribute to the structuring of networks among individuals, organizations, industries, nations, primates, and other animals. It is therefore encouraging to see that some of this work is being incorporated into the small world research on searchable networks. In addition to physical proximity and homophily, MTML mechanisms described in this book that could augment the random rewiring model include, contagion, social exchange, self-interest, mutual interests, and resource dependency, to name a few. Researchers interested in furthering our understanding of the emergence and dynamics of small world networks will find in this literature and the MTML model considerable theoretical and empirical evidence to guide the not-so-random rewiring of Watts's regular networks.

In addition to helping us better understand how we can search social networks to reach other people, research on small worlds has also helped us advance our understanding of how we can search the network of knowledge repositories on the Web. As mentioned earlier, the network of links connecting Web sites demonstrate small world characteristics with around nineteen degrees of separation. This means that starting at any random Web site, we could in approximately nineteen steps reach any other target Web site. But here again we are faced with the conundrum that Watts et al. (2002) confronted. It is one thing to say that any two Web sites are nineteen steps apart. It is quite another to identify how we will select exactly the right steps to get to the target Web site in the smallest number of steps.

This challenge is one we face in all of our searches on the Web. We start with a Web site that is typically a search engine. We then submit our topic of interest to the search engine and hope the results can help us get to the desired Web site with the shortest degrees of separation. In the absence of any additional manipulation, a primitive search engine would simply list— in no particular order all of the Web sites that had the "exact" match to the terms entered. These lists could be inordinately long and hence not very helpful. Increasingly, and fortunately for the user, the developers of search engines are deploying network techniques to help refine the search based on the network structure linking Web sites to one another. For instance, the Google search engine prioritizes the results of a search on the basis of the network prestige score associated with each Web site (Brin & Page, 1998). That is, a Web page that has many links pointing to it could be considered to be more prestigious and hence is more likely to provide the needed information. This would be a measure of prestige based on in-degrees (see chapter 2). However, the search algorithms used by Google goes one step further. They determine the prestige of a Web page not only by the number of other Web pages that point to it, but also the "prestige" of the Web pages that point to it. Of course the prestige scores of these latter Web pages are recursively defined by the number of Web sites that point to it, and their prestige.

Kleinberg and Lawrence (2001) offer an alternative strategy for refining searches and thereby reducing the degrees of separation between a search engine and the intended target of the search. They begin by recognizing the empirically demonstrated fact that the number of links to and from Web pages is distributed according to a *power law* (Barabasi, 2002). In the case of the Web, this means that the proportion of pages with n links to it is approximately n^2. That is, about a quarter of all Web pages in the world have exactly 2 links pointing it, about a ninth of all Web pages have exactly 3 links pointing to it, and so on. This nonrandom "wiring" of the network of Web sites allows them to classify Web pages as hubs and authorities. *Hubs* are pages that point to many authorities, while *authorities* are pages that are pointed to by many hubs. In essence, hubs could be portals (guides, resource lists) that direct traffic on specific topics. Authorities are the pages to which this traffic is directed. In some cases the hubs may be linked to one another (a cohesive sub group) or at least linked to the same authorities (structurally equivalent). Kleinberg and Lawrence (2001) observe, "Knowing the characteristic link structures that identify Web communities, one can examine a large snapshot of the Web for all occasions of the link-based signature of a community" (p. 1850). Hence, unlike Google's use of network analysis techniques to steer the search toward the most prestigious Web pages, Kleinberg and Lawrence (2001) are advocating the use of network analysis techniques to steer the search toward Web pages that indicate the strongest shared community of interest.

Future Network Forms of Organizing

In his classic book, *Images of Organization*, Morgan (1997) recounts how metaphors shape the ways in which we conceptualize and understand the organizations we investigate. They shape the research questions we ask and the methods we use to answer those questions. They privilege certain issues while concealing others. In the industrial era, the machine served as a dominant metaphor shaping our conceptualization of organizations. Reflecting changes in contemporary societal values, the dominance of organization-as-machine metaphor was replaced in succession by organization-as-living systems in the 1970s, organization-as-cultures in the 1980s, and organization-as-computers in the 1990s. With the explosion of the Internet and the Web, there is little argument that the dominant metaphor today is organization-as-networks, as reflected in the title of a section of a recent trade book: "It's the network, stupid!" (Hartman, Sifonis, & Kador, 2000). Embracing the metaphor of organization-as-network has led to an unprecedented focus on the ways in which characteristics of the network influence, and are in turn influenced by, the process of organizing (Contractor & Monge, 2002). Considering organization-as-networks invites a reconceptualization of perennial organizational issues such as information, resources, trust, and cultural values in terms of relations and flows. As such the metaphor prompts researchers to focus on the central issues explored in this book—why we as individuals, groups, and organizations create, maintain, and dissolve our various network relations.

The digital revolution has given us the opportunity to explore novel network forms of organizing. The Japanese visionary and inventor, Kenji Kawakami, is famous for championing *chindogu*—the art of "the unuseless idea." A *chindogu*, an invention that seeks to solve a nagging social need, is fabricated to the highest technological standards and tested by users. But in retrospect it is found to be quite useless. A prototypical *chindogu* is the automated noodle cooler—"a compact fan that fits tidily towards the holding end of one of a pair of chopsticks" allowing one to cool the noodles right before ingesting them (Kawakami & Papia, 1995, p. 42). Alas, history will probably consider many of the novel technologically enabled forms of organizing that we are exploring today to be *chindogus*. The reason for this is that while the technologies are often necessary conditions for us to conceive these new organizational forms, we must rely on our understanding of social mechanisms to assess and possibly enhance their viability. The MTML framework outlined in chapters 1 through 4 and the network mechanisms described in chapters 5 through 9 provide a principled approach to conduct the *"chindogu"* test on many of our organizational innovations.

While it is possible to recount several short-lived attempts at organizing that turned out to be *chindogus*, there are also many early examples of these novel network forms of organizing that have begun to challenge our traditional conceptions of how we organize. We use the term *organize* advisedly because these examples may not fit our notions of conventional organizations. Yet they accomplish many of the same functions and as a result invite us to rethink our more narrow definitions of organizations. One might correctly surmise that many of these examples are in the high-technology arena. Several of these examples are sometimes collectively referred to as peer-to-peer (P2P) forms of organizing (Contractor, 2003).

Consider the following scenario: You are interested in getting a recipe for strawberry rhubarb pie. You have a couple of strategies you can pursue. First, you could go to a library (or log on to the Web) and search a central repository of documents for a recipe. Second, you may ask one or more of your friends if they had a recipe; if they did not, they could ask one or more of their friends for the recipe. If you followed the first strategy, you were a *client* and you obtained that information from a *server* that stored all of the information at one location—the library or a Web site. If you followed the second strategy, you were engaging in peer-to-peer interaction because you bypassed any intermediary central collection of recipes. You may decide that for your purpose it is a lot more effective to pursue one or the other strategy.

In terms of the MTML framework, our goal is to explain the conditions under which you may be more (or less) inclined to initiate a communication link with a central database as opposed to communication links with your peers. Theories of mutual interest (or collective action, see chapter 5) posit that the likelihood of you creating a link to a knowledge repository about recipes is a function of your perceptions of the contributions others make to the quantity and quality of recipes available in the knowledge repository and the costs incurred in retrieving the recipes. On the other hand, theories of transactive memory (see chapter 6) assert that the likelihood of seeking the recipe from a peer would be a function of whom in your network is knowledgeable about recipes or who in your network knows people who are knowledgeable about recipes.

In an earlier age, creating a link to a knowledge repository might mean going to your bookshelf or making a trip to the library. Likewise, creating a link to a peer would have been asking someone in person, writing a letter or calling on the phone. Clearly, the introduction of new technologies has expanded these options. The advent of the Web made it possible for the creation of Web sites to serve information to millions of clients using Web browsers. In some cases you may have contributed recipes to these Web sites or evaluated others' contributions. But your use of the Web sites to retrieve a recipe is not necessarily contingent on your contribution. Of course, one could also use the Internet to e-mail your request for a recipe to a person, listserv, or newsgroup. In both of these examples, the mechanisms associated with electronic proximity (see chapter 7) would augment the theoretical mechanisms posited by theories of mutual interest and transactive memory respectively. Specifically, the new technologies would increase the scope and size of your network and possibly reduce your transaction costs.

More recently, there are novel applications that make it possible to pursue qualitatively superior peer-to-peer strategies. As discussed above, it is possible to e-mail a request for the recipe to a person, a listserv, or a newsgroup. Clearly this is not a very efficient strategy. You may still not be able to get the recipe. Or, you may be inundated with too many of them. Also, many who are not knowledgeable or interested in the recipe may consider reading your request a waste of their time. There is a new generation of peer-to-peer (P2P) applications that addresses these problems. More generally, they make it possible to mobilize resources and organize action in ways that are qualitatively different from what has been possible so far. In the example above, the technology was being used to substitute and enlarge current modes of organizing (see chapter 8). The new generation of P2P applications reconfigures the modes of organizing (Oram, 2001). They fall broadly into three categories: file sharing, computer resource sharing, and communication and collaboration. After we survey these applications we will consider how the MTML framework can help us explain and assess the network forms of organizing that it affords.

First, there are applications that allow peers to *share information* (audio, text, video, and graphics files) directly with one another without going to a Web site. Perhaps the most popular such application was Napster, which allowed individuals to share music files on their computer with millions of their peers anywhere in the world. Some have argued that Napster is not a true peer-to-peer application, because it had an intermediary server that provided a directory of which peers had what songs on their computers. There are other applications, such as Gnutella, FreeNet, and Morpheus, that dispense with the intermediary directory server and are therefore un-arguably peer-to-peer. So, to continue with the previous example, you would fan out your request for a recipe (or a song or any other digital docu-ment) by typing the phrase "strawberry rhubarb pie" on your computer and sending it to a small subset of peers who were connected to the P2P appli-cation network. Their computers would check to see if they had the recipe, in which case they would let you know about its availability; if they did not possess the recipe, they in turn would relay the request to a further subset of their peers. Soon, you would have a list of peers from around the world that had the information you requested. And, all of this search was being conducted in the background without any of the peers being inter-rupted or even being aware of the fact that they might have either shared their recipe with you or forwarded your request for the recipe to other peers on the network.

Second, there are P2P applications aimed at *sharing computing resources* rather than sharing files among peers' computers. Shirky (2001), a leading expert on Internet applications, observes, "At a conservative estimate . . . the world's Net-connected PCs presently host an aggregate of 10 billion megahertz of processing power and 10 thousand terabytes of storage" (p. 23). In many cases, these net-connected PCs have spare storage space on their hard drives. Further, for much of the time, these PCs are not being used—consider the amount of time a screensaver is active on your computer. In 1995, scientists at Berkeley proposed using the computing power of these PCs to help in the search for extraterrestrial civilizations. The SETI (Search for Extraterrestrial Intelligence) Project was collecting a massive amount of radio signals from the skies using radio telescopes. Unfortunately, they did not have the vast computing resources required to analyze these signals to detect extraterrestrial life. To solve their problem, they designed a program called SETI@home. This program worked as a screensaver that a user could download. Whenever the user's computer was idle, this screen saver would be launched and it would connect with the SETI@home data distribution server. It would download a small portion of the data, analyze it on the user's computer and then ship back the results to the SETI@home. As of October 2000, the project had received more than 200 million results from users, making it the largest computation ever performed in the world! Inspired by its success, others are launching similar gridlike applications to help with computational challenges in genetic research, fighting AIDS, and financial data mining. While users volunteered their computing resources for the SETI@Home project, companies such as Popular Power and Distributed Net offered to compensate users for their idle computing resources. On a grander scale, the U.S. National Science Foundation is supporting the development of a *national grid* (Smarr, 1997; Stevens, Woodward, De Fanti, & Catlett, 1997). The goal is to develop a set of software and hardware tools that makes it possible to tap computer processing power off the Internet just as easily as electrical power can be drawn from the electrical distribution grid. In the event of some emergency, say a chemical spill, the different organizations that need to be involved in the crisis management effort can create a virtual network organization and the data available at each of these organizations (soil composition, air quality, water quality, demographics, etc.) can be rapidly collated and analyzed by tapping into computing resources elsewhere on the grid.

Third, some P2P applications help peers *communicate and collaborate* directly with one another. In 1996, a young Israeli firm, Mirabilis, launched the first such application called ICQ ("I seek you"). It allowed users to instantly send messages between PCs connected to the Internet without going through any central server (such as an e-mail server). America Online's Instant Messenger (AIM) program is a similar peer-to-peer application (AOL acquired ICQ in 1998) for users to communicate on a peer-to-peer basis with their "buddies." More recently, Ray Ozzie, who created Lotus Notes, has developed Groove, a peer-to-peer collaboration environment that allows groups of individuals to create a shared space without the presence of a central network server. These environments allow not only for sharing of files but more intensive collaboration such as simultaneous editing of files as well as automatic updating of files even when users are not all connected at the same time.

Finally, some applications combine the peer-to-peer (P2P) applications described above. For instance, programs such as Aimster allow an AOL instant messenger (AIM) user to share files only with others on their "buddy" list. Mojo Nation allows users to pay for downloading files using a digital "currency" (called Mojo), which they can earn by sharing their computer's resources.

Minar and Hedlund (2001) remind us that P2P is not a recent innovation. "The Internet as originally conceived in the late 1960s was a peer-to-peer system. . . . Usenet news implements a decentralized model of control that in some ways is the grandfather of today's new peer-to-per applications such as Gnutella and Freenet" (pp. 4–5). After being eclipsed by the development of the Web and the client-server architecture in the 1990s, the use of peer-to-peer applications has risen dramatically since the turn of the century, and is expected to continue to grow with the advent of millions of Internet-enabled information appliances such as mobile phones and personal digital assistants.

Our reason for identifying these possibilities here is to invite consideration of how these technologies might reconfigure current modes of organizing and how the MTML framework might help us better prepare to design and evaluate those reconfigurations. In terms of the technical network infrastructure, the overwhelming majority of our experiences with the Web today are what we previously called server-client interaction. The server is the central hub and we as clients go to these hubs to retrieve or publish information. As such it mirrors a hierarchical mode of organizing.

On the other hand, P2P applications do not make a distinction between a client and a server. Each user is a server *and* a client (or a *servent*) sharing and retrieving information and computing power, and collaborating directly in shared spaces with other peers bypassing any central servers. As such it mirrors a heterarchical mode of organizing. As Stark (1999) notes, "Whereas hierarchies involve relations of dependence [on the server] . . . heterarchies involve relations of interdependence [among the servents]" (p. 159). These heterarchies have the flexibility of being created on the fly, without the need for any administrative or technical authorization, maintained only as long as they are needed, then dissolved just as easily, and perhaps reconstituted at a later time in a new configuration.

One could consider eBay and Epinions as two companies that are pioneers in the *Napsterization* of the retail experience. The better known, eBay, enables the creation of links that connect demand and supply at the individual level while Epinions considers itself an "eBay of content" (Tolia & Fryer, 2001, p. 21), providing a platform for consumers to share reviews of products and services they have used. Buoyed by the success of these two services, Tolia and Fryer (2001) aver that there is a potential demand for services in a variety of other contexts including time-shares on jet planes and hiring nannies. David Pogue, a columnist for the *New York Times*, shares their enthusiasm. In a column titled "Wish List: 9 Innovations in Search of Inventors," Pogue (2002) seeks the invention of an innovation called Blind Data that would use the Bluetooth technology enabling wireless links within a thirty-foot radius. "Like the Japanese Lovegety toy for teenagers, the Blind Data would be a tiny transmitter, worn on a key ring or pendant. But instead of beeping when just anyone of the opposite sex came nearby, the Blind Data would be a far more discerning gizmo. You would program it with the vital statistics of both you and the kind of soul mate you're seeking. When your transmitter vibrates, it means that somebody else's is vibrating, too. Somebody less than 30 feet away is looking for someone just like you" (p. 61). Clearly this book does not pretend to have delved in any substantive manner into the theoretical mechanisms that facilitate the creation, maintenance, dissolution, or reconstitution of romantic linkages. But we believe that the potential for such P2P applications is just as promising, if not more so, for forging network linkages at the individual, organizational, and interorganizational levels. Indeed, two Web companies that offer such services are elance.com and guru.com. While the examples discussed here only enable the creation of dyadic links among romantic partners or bidders-sellers, the principle illustrated can scale to larger congregations.

The network flexibility and fluidity offered by P2P applications is conducive to the work style of a rapidly growing segment of the workforce that Malone and Laubacher (1998) refer to as the *e-lance economy* and Pink (2001) call the *free agent nation*. Their motivations to create, maintain, dissolve, and reconstitute network links may be unfettered by traditional hierarchical structures, but they will still be shaped by many of the theoretical network mechanisms discussed in this book. Indeed, the absence of hierarchy will privilege many of these multiple mechanisms to influence the emergence of these networks. In order to be viable modes of organizing, workers will still need to contend with issues such as trust, accountability, security, intellectual property, and privacy raised by peer-to-peer environments that bypass the central, reliable, and well-established Web servers we have embraced over the past decade. Let us hasten to add that we are not envisioning a world bereft of hierarchical organizations, or in terms of their technical counterparts, a network sans client-server architecture. In fact, we fully expect both hierarchical and heterarchical forms of organizing to coexist and coevolve—which then raises additional research questions about their relative efficacy for various goals of organizing.

Related to, but distinct from, the P2P trend is the *open source movement* (see Raymond, 2000, for an overview). The history of the open source movement, even though it was not called by that name, can be traced back to the 1960s. During the early development of operating systems and what later came to be known as the Internet, programmers working in universities and at autonomous private labs like AT&T's Bell labs would freely share with another the *source code* for the programs they wrote. Others could take this code, read it, modify it, and extend it. The invention of Usenet (described above as the first major P2P application on the Internet) accelerated the ability of a larger number of programmers around the world to collaboratively develop software.

However, starting in the early 1980s commercial organizations like AT&T began to exercise their intellectual ownership of software including, in the case of AT&T, its version of the Unix operating systems. In order to protect their commercial interests, they only began to distribute the "object" or binary code. The object code was not something programmers could review, modify, or extend. Roughly, one could consider source code as equivalent to providing someone with the recipe for an entrée. The person receiving the source code could cook (or in programmers' parlance, compile) the code. Of course, the person could modify (or in programmers' lingo, tweak) the recipe if they chose. On the other hand, when a person is handed the *object* or *binary code*, they receive the already prepared entrée—without the recipe. This provides recipients very limited opportunity to modify what they get. The open source movement, therefore, reflects the commitment of a very large and growing community of programmers to freely share the recipe of all their programs, allowing others to modify and extend the software on the condition that they in turn distribute it free of charge to all others. The licensing arrangements were initially called the general public license or *copyleft* (as opposed to copyright) and have evolved into a more proprietary-friendly arrangement called the open source definition. The details of the exact licensing conditions are beyond the scope of our discussion here.

While there are thousands of open source projects, there are three that are particularly noteworthy: *Apache*, an open source web server software launched in 1994, got its name from the fact that it was built by programmers who wrote "patches" to the original Web server software developed by the National Center for Supercomputing Applications at the University of Illinois at Urbana-Champaign. It is currently used by more than half of all the Web servers that are publicly observable in the face of stiff competition from Microsoft's and Netscape's suites of Web-server software (Lerner & Tirole, 2000). *Sendmail,* begun in 1979, controls more than 80 percent of the Internet mail transfer traffic, with its closest rival being Microsoft Exchange (Lerner & Tirole, 2000). *Linux* is an operating system that was launched in 1991 by Linus Torvald, a computer science student at the University of Helsinki. A decade later Linux was the operating system on 27 percent (as compared to Microsoft's 41 percent) of all network servers and had 3.9 million users who had installed it on their desktops.

The focus of our discussion of the open source movement is to understand why a movement that writes, distributes, shares, debugs, and extends computer programs for "free" has managed to grow so successfully that it poses a formidable market challenge to established software companies, like Microsoft, which sell proprietary software. The answers do not lie in altruism or the collective religious fervor of a group of like-minded individuals. Instead, taking Linux as an example, Weber (2000, p. 19) argues that

> Beyond these overly simplistic and naïve tales lies a more subtle story of social and political economy, that has important implications for arguments about the logic of production in the "new" economy. A good explanatory story must be social because Linux is a collective good: it is a body of code built, maintained, developed, and extended in a non-proprietary setting where many developers work in a highly parallel way. It must be political because there exist both formal and informal structures and organizations, that function to allocate scarce resources and manage conflicts as well as promote certain practices and values. And self-evidently, it must be economic, because at the core of the Linux process are individuals who engage in some kind of cost-benefit analysis and are maximizing or at least satisficing along some kind of utility function. No single piece of this story—even if "correct"—would by itself explain the outcome. Another way to put this point is simply to argue that Linux rests on a set of microfoundations—the motivations of individual humans that choose freely to contribute—as well as macrofoundations— social and political structures that channel these contributions to a collective end.

This pithy appraisal captures the essence of why the multitheoretical and multilevel framework discussed in this book has such great potential to explain the networks that undergird the development of open source software. The logic of production in the open source movement is fundamentally different from those found in traditional software companies. Yet, this new logic reflects a recombinant ensemble of the same underlying MTML mechanisms that help us understand why we create, maintain, dissolve, and reconstitute our network ties. Raymond (1999), in a contested claim, suggests that traditional software companies operate like a "cathedral" with a grand master plan decided at the top of the hierarchy and implemented in every detail by those lower down in the hierarchy. He likens the open source movement to a "bazaar," where individuals decide autonomously what, if any, will be their specific contributions and who, if any, will be their collaborators. He notes that the incentive to create links with others in the movement and make contributions is guided less by an "exchange" culture (see chapter 7) and more by self-interest (chapter 5). In the short-term, this self-interest is to use the free software to fix the immediate problem they are encountering at work, but also importantly, in the long term, to enhance one's reputation in the movement.

Ironically, given what Raymond (1999) calls the "gift culture" of the movement, the way to build one's reputation is in part based on the value of the gifts a person can offer, which include, in descending levels of value, writing new code, debugging existing code, pointing out bugs in code, and simply using the software thereby enhancing its visibility. Lerner and Tirole (2000, p. 14) note that reputation is a key incentive not only because it offers ego-gratification but also because it serves to signal career concern incentives such as "future job offers, shares in commercial open-source based companies, or future access to the venture capital market."

Clearly the open source movement has demonstrated the viability of a new logic of production. Yet, much remains to be learned about the specific conditions that explain why some of these open source projects (such as the three discussed here) are successful while myriads fail to galvanize a vibrant network. Further, only time—and, hopefully, timely research—will help us understand the long-term sustainability of such movements.

Finally, one must explore the possibility that the real import of the open source movement is its ability to generalize into other arenas. Could the MTML mechanisms that potentially explain the logic of organizing in the software industry also lead us to assess the viability of open source modes of organizing in other diverse areas? Would these findings generalize to processes such as annotating the human genome (Weber, 2000), the structure of biological molecules (Kiernan, 1999), an open directory classification of Web sites (see dmoz.org), or even an open source design of an automobile?

While we ponder those questions, there are some noteworthy examples that are challenging our modes of organizing in areas far removed from the arena of software development. Arquilla and Ronfeldt (2001) identify several recent social movements and ideological campaigns that they identify as *netwars* in which "numerous dispersed small groups using the latest communications technologies could act conjointly across great distances" (p. 2). The groups they consider include terrorists, criminals, separatists, drug cartels, radical activists, nongovernment organizations (NGOs), and civil society advocates. They noted similar network patterns when they examined the organizational forms of seemingly disparate activities such as the al-Qaeda network's terrorist operations (see also Krebs, 2002), the Chechen effort to secede from Russia, the Direct Action Network's operations during the 1999 World Trade Organization summit in Seattle, Greenpeace, the International Campaign to Ban Landmines (ICBL), and the Zapatista National Liberation Army.

Ronfeldt and Arquilla (2001) propose that "the design and performance of such networks depend on what happens across five levels of analysis (which are also levels of practice): (i) organizational level—its organizational design (ii) narrative level—the story being told (iii) doctrinal level—the collaborative strategies and methods (iv) technological level—the information systems in use and (v) social level—the personal ties that assure loyalty and trust." Their use of the term levels is not entirely analogous to our use of that term in the MTML framework. Additionally, it also suggests multiple theoretical mechanisms that must be considered conjointly to help explain the effectiveness of these network forms of organizing.

Further, Arquilla and Ronfeldt's (2001) note that these network forms of organizing enabled these campaigns to engage in *swarming*, which they describe as

> a seemingly amorphous, but deliberately structured, coordinated, strategic way, to strike from all directions at a particular point or points, by means of a sustainable pulsing of force and/or file, close-in as well as from stand-off positions. This notion of "force and/or file" may be literal in the case of military or police operations, but metaphorical in the case of NGO activities, who may, for example, be blocking city intersections or emitting volleys of email and faxes. Swarming will work best—perhaps it will only work—if it is designed mainly around the deployment of myriad, small, dispersed, networked maneuver units. Swarming occurs when the dispersed

units of a network of small (and perhaps some large) forces converge on a target from multiple directions. The overall aim is *sustainable pulsing*—swarm networks must be able to coalesce rapidly and stealthily on a target, then dissever and redisperse, immediately ready to recombine for a new pulse. (p. 12, italics in original)

Arquilla and Ronfeldt's (2001) explanation of swarming is an important illustration of the utility of developing multilevel network models that we advocate in this book. Swarming is an emergent property occurring at the global level of a network. Arquilla and Ronfeldt's description suggests that the likelihood of carrying out a successful swarming activity can only be explained by a careful analysis of the configuration of the network at the actor, dyadic, triadic, and subgroup levels.

Williams (2001) focuses his attention on criminal networks and describes how "organized crime is increasingly operating through fluid network structures rather than more-formal hierarchies" (p. 62). He describes the network structure of the Spence money-laundering network in New York; the Cunterra-Caruana clan that operated primarily in Venezuela and Montreal; outlaw motorcycle gangs in the United States, Canada, Britain, and Scandinavia; immigrant smuggling networks in the United States; and organized crime networks in Russia. Unlike organized crime syndicates of an earlier era, they eschew hierarchies in favor of a more loosely coupled network form of organizing. The structures of these criminal networks are motivated by mechanisms for (1) concealing themselves from law enforcement, (2) cooperating with other criminal entities, (3) boundary spanning across nation-states, (4) exploiting structural holes among corrupt authorities, and (5) enabling them to be robust and resilient when their network is infiltrated.

The rise of network forms of organizing in the examples discussed above is not occurring in isolation. Indeed, in order to effectively compete and cooperate with network forms of organizing in these arguably peripheral sectors of society, other sectors of society are increasingly feeling the need to network their own organizational and interorganizational structures. Bryant, Shumate, and Monge (2002) analyze this coevolutionary process among transnational criminal organizations, multinational corporations, and law enforcement agencies from around the globe. Fountain (2001) addresses how environmental and technological forces are prompting government institutions around the world to redefine the *virtual state*. She argues that the development of government-to-citizen services (G2C), government-to-business (G2B) digital procurement processes, and government-to-government (G2G) connectivity must take into account the institutional arrangements in which these interactions are embedded.

The examples in this section covering the P2P applications, the open source movement, netwars, and the virtual state all underscore the fact that we are entering an era in which individuals, groups, and organizations, enabled by continuing advances in digital technologies, will gauge their success by their *net-literacy*—their ability to link, search, navigate, "recognize," and interact in flexible, adaptive, and adaptable networks (Bach & Stark, 2002). On the darker side, the rise in net-literacy also entails being better prepared to understand and respond to the disruption and destabilization of networks (Carley, 2002). More than ever before, we have a stronger appreciation and critical need for the importance of structuring networks that are robust, fault tolerant, and *self-healing* in the wake of random or targeted attack. Hong (2001) shows how the search and file-sharing strategies used by two P2P applications—Gnutella and Freenet—vary systematically in their efficiency, speed, scalability (ability to cope with large size networks), and fault tolerance (ability to recover from random and targeted attacks to specific nodes). Unfortunately we have very few social scientific theories to understand these capabilities in our social networks.

The Future of Network Theory and Research

The future of network theory and research is nothing if not highly promising. We have come to realize at the beginning of the twenty-first century that we live in a highly connected world and society where the structural interconnections in large part determine what we can and cannot do (Castells, 1996). As we indicated at the beginning of the book, the amount of network theorizing and research has begun to grow geometrically in the past fifteen years. Further, this explosion of work has crossed many disciplines. Watts's small world work reviewed in the previous section is one example. Another, by Faust and Skvoretz (2002), compared forty-two networks from diverse settings, including four different animal species (humans, nonhuman primates, nonprimate mammals, and birds), diverse relational contents, and sizes of the communities. They attempted to determine whether these incredibly diverse networks were "similarly structured despite their surface differences" (p. 268). For instance, they asked, "Is the network of cosponsorship [of bills] among senators structurally more similar to the network of social licking among cows, the network of grooming among monkeys, or the network of advice among managers?" (p. 270). p^* analysis (Wasserman & Pattison, 1996) and correspondence analysis showed that "similarities among the networks are due more to the kind of relation than to the kind of animal" (p. 268). One of their findings was that "the model of social licking among cows best predicts, as a target, cosponsorship among U.S. senators in the 93rd congress" (Faust & Skvoretz, 2002, pp. 283–284). These are incredible findings given that they operate across space and time and in completely different types of social relations and networks. It suggests that there may be deep and significant common social structures across all forms of social behavior. Certainly this is a holy grail worth seeking, even if it doesn't exist, for what we learn in the quest will reveal other equally important insights about communication, organizations, and other social structures.

Appendix:
Data Sets Used in Chapter 2

Crada.atr	Crada.neg
(2i2)	(2i3,i2)
1 1	1 2 1
2 1	1 3 1
3 1	1 4 1
4 1	1 7 1
5 1	1 8 1
6 1	1 9 1
7 1	1 11 1
8 1	1 12 1
9 1	2 1 1
10 2	2 3 1
11 2	3 1 1
12 2	3 2 1
13 2	3 5 1
14 2	3 7 1
15 2	3 8 1
16 2	3 11 1
17 2	3 14 1
	3 16 1
	3 17 1

Crada.neg (*continued*)

4 1 1	11 5 1	17 7 1
4 5 1	11 6 1	17 16 1
4 7 1	11 7 1	
4 9 1	11 8 1	
4 11 1	11 9 1	
4 12 1	11 10 1	
5 1 1	11 12 1	
5 4 1	11 13 1	
5 7 1	11 14 1	
5 8 1	11 15 1	
5 11 1	11 16 1	
5 12 1	11 17 1	
6 7 1	12 1 1	
7 1 1	12 4 1	
7 3 1	12 7 1	
7 4 1	12 11 1	
7 5 1	12 13 1	
7 9 1	12 14 1	
7 11 1	12 15 1	
7 12 1	13 11 1	
7 14 1	13 12 1	
8 9 1	13 14 1	
8 11 1	14 4 1	
8 12 1	14 7 1	
8 14 1	14 8 1	
9 4 1	14 10 1	
9 5 1	14 11 1	
9 7 1	14 12 1	
9 8 1	14 15 1	
9 11 1	15 11 1	
9 12 1	15 14 1	
9 14 1	16 2 1	
10 11 1	16 3 1	
10 14 1	16 7 1	
11 1 1	16 11 1	
11 2 1	16 14 1	
11 3 1	16 15 1	
11 4 1	16 17 1	

References

Abrahamson, E., & Rosenkopf, L. (1997). Social network effects on the extent of innovation diffusion: A computer simulation. *Organization Science, 8,* 289–309.

Adamic, L. A. (1999, September). The small World Web. In S. Abiteboul & A. M. Vercoustre (Eds.), *Lecture notes in computer science; 1696* (pp. 443–452). New York: Springer Verlag. Available online at http://www.hpl.hp.com/shl/papers/smallworld/smallworldpaper.html

Adams, J. S. (1965). Inequity in social exchange. In L. Berkowitz (Ed.), *Advances in experimental social psychology* (pp. 267–300). New York: Academic.

Ahouse, J. J., Bruderer, E., Gelover-Santiago, A., Konno, N., Lazer, D., & Veretnik, S. (1992). Reality kisses the neck of speculation: A report from the NKC workgroup. In L. Nadel & D. Stein (Eds.), *1991 Lectures in Complex Systems, SFI Studies in the Science of Complexity* (Vol. 4, pp. 331–353). Reading, MA: Addison-Wesley.

Ahuja, M. K., & Carley, K. M. (1999). Network structure in virtual organizations. *Organization Science, 10,* 741–757.

Albert, A., Jeong, H., & Barabasi, A. (1999). Diameter of the World Wide Web. *Nature, 401,* 130–131.

Albrecht, T. L., & Hall, B. (1991). Relational and content differences between elites and outsiders in innovation networks. *Human Communication Research, 17,* 535–561.

Albrecht, T., & Ropp, V. A. (1982). The study of network structuring in organizations through the use of method triangulation. *Western Journal of Speech Communication, 46,* 162–178.

Albrecht, T. L., & Ropp, V. A. (1984). Communicating about innovation in networks of three U.S. organizations. *Journal of Communication, 34*, 78–91.

Aldrich, H. (1972). Organizational boundaries and inter-organizational conflict. *Human Relations, 24*, 279–293.

Aldrich, H. (1976). Resource dependence and interorganizational relations: Relations between local employment service offices and social service sector organizations. *Administration and Society, 7*, 419–454.

Aldrich, H. (1979). *Organizations and environments.* Englewood Cliffs, NJ: Prentice Hall.

Aldrich, H. (1982). The origins and persistence of social networks. In P. V. Marsden & N. Lin (Eds.), *Social structure and network analysis* (pp. 281–293). Beverly Hills, CA: Sage.

Aldrich, H. (1999). *Organizations evolving.* Thousand Oaks, CA: Sage.

Aldrich, H., & Kenworthy, A. I. (1999). The accidental entrepreneur: Campbellian antinomies and organizational foundings. In J. A. C. Baum & B. McKelvey (Eds.), *Variations in organization science: In honor of Donald T. Campbell* (pp. 19–34). Thousand Oaks, CA: Sage.

Allen, T. (1970). Communication networks in R&D laboratories. *R&D Management, 1*, 14–21.

Alter, C. (1990). An exploratory study of conflict and coordination in interorganizational service delivery systems. *Academy of Management Journal, 33*, 478–502.

Anderson, C., Wasserman, S., & Crouch, B. (1999). A p^* primer: Logit models for social networks. *Social Networks, 21*, 37–66.

Anderson, P. (1988). The population dynamics of creative destruction. In F. Hoy (Ed.), *Academy of Management Best Papers Proceedings* (pp. 150–154). Anaheim, CA: Academy of Management.

Anderson, P. (1999). Complexity theory and organization science. *Organization Science, 10*, 216–232.

Appadurai, A. (1990). Disjuncture and difference is the global cultural economy. In M. Featherstone (Ed.), *Global culture: Nationalism, globalization, and modernity* (pp. 295–310). London: Sage.

Arquilla, J., & Ronfeldt, D. (2001). The advent of netwar (revisited). In J. Arquilla & D. Ronfeldt (Eds.), *Networks and netwars: The future of terror, crime, and militancy* (pp. 1–25). Santa Monica, CA: Rand.

Arrow, H., McGrath, J. E., & Berdahl, J. L. (2000). *Small groups as complex systems: Formation, coordination, development, and adaptation.* Thousand Oaks, CA: Sage.

Ashby, W. R. (1964). *An introduction to cybernetics.* London, England: Methuen.

Astley, W. G. (1985). The two ecologies: Population and community perspectives on organizational evolution. *Administrative Science Quarterly, 30*, 224–241.

Axelrod, R. (1984). *The evolution of complexity.* New York: Basic.

Axelrod, R. (1997). *The complexity of cooperation.* Princeton, NJ: Princeton University Press.

Axelrod, R., & Cohen, M. D. (1999). *Harnessing complexity: Organizational implications of a scientific frontier.* New York: Free Press.

Bach, J., & Stark, D. (2002). *Link, search, interaction: The Co-Evolution of NGOs and interactive technology.* Unpublished manuscript. Center on Organizational Innovation, Institute for Social and Economic Research and Policy, Columbia University, New York.

Bacharach, S. B., & Lawler, E. J. (1980). *Power and politics in organizations.* San Francisco: Jossey-Bass.

Badaracco, J. L., Jr. (1991). *The knowledge link: How firms compete through strategic alliances.* Boston, MA: Harvard Business School Press.

Baker, W. E. (1987). *Do corporations do business with the bankers on their boards? The consequences of investment bankers as directors.* Paper presented at the Nags Head Conference on Corporate Interlocks, Kill Devil Hills, NC.

Bandura, A. (1986). *Social foundations of thought and action.* Englewood Cliffs, NJ: Prentice Hall.

Banks, D. L., & Carley, K. M. (1996). Models for network evolution. *Journal of Mathematical Sociology, 21,* 173–196.

Bar, F., & Simard, C. (2002). New media implementation and industrial organization. In L. Lievrouw & S. Livingstone (Eds.), *Handbook of New Media* (pp. 254–263). London: Sage.

Barabasi, A. (2002). *Linked: The new science of networks.* Cambridge, MA: Perseus.

Barley, S. R. (1990). The alignment of technology and structure through roles and networks. *Administrative Science Quarterly, 35,* 61–103.

Barley, S. R., & Kunda, G. (1992). Design and devotion: Surges of rational and normative ideologies of control in managerial discourse. *Administrative Science Quarterly, 37,* 363–399.

Barnard, C. I. (1938). *The functions of the executive.* Cambridge, MA: Harvard University Press.

Barnett, G. A., & Jang, H. (1994). *The relationship between network position and attitudes toward the job and organization in a police organization.* Paper presented to the Organizational Communication Division of the International Communication Association, Sydney, Australia.

Barnett, G. A., & Salisbury, J. G. T. (1996). Communication and globalization: A longitudinal analysis of the international telecommunication network. *Journal of World-Systems Research, 2.*

Barnett, W. P. (1990). The organizational ecology of a technological system. *Administrative Science Quarterly, 35,* 31–60.

Barnett, W. P. (1994). The liability of collective action: Growth and change among early American telephone companies. In J. A. C. Baum & J. V. Singh (Eds.), *Evolutionary dynamics of organizations* (pp. 337–354). New York: Oxford University Press.

Barnett, W. P., & Carroll, G. R. (1987). Competition and mutualism among early telephone companies. *Administrative Science Quarterly, 32,* 400–421.

Barnett, W. P., & Carroll, G. R. (1993). How institutional constraints affected the organization of early American telephony. *Journal of Law, Economics, and Organization, 9,* 98–126.

Barnett, W. P., Greve, H. R., & Park, D. Y. (1994). An evolutionary model of organizational performance. *Strategic Management Journal, 15*, 11–28.

Barnett, W. P., Mischke, G. A., & Ocasio, W. (2000). The evolution of collective strategies among organizations. *Organization Studies, 21*, 325–354.

Barney, J. B. (1985). Dimensions of informal social network structure: Toward a contingency theory of informal relations. *Social Networks, 7*, 1–46.

Barrera, M., Jr., & Ainlay, S. L. (1983). The structure of social support: A conceptual and empirical analysis. *Journal of Community Psychology, 11*, 133–143.

Barron, D. N., West, E., & Hannan, M. T. (1994). A time to grow and a time to die: Growth and mortality of credit unions in New York City, 1914–1990. *American Journal of Sociology, 100*, 381–421.

Bass, L. A., & Stein, C. H. (1997). Comparing the structure and stability of network ties using the social support questionnaire and the social network list. *Journal of Social and Personal Relationships, 14*, 123–132.

Batagelj, V., & Mrvar, A. (2002). Pajek 0.85 for Windows. [Computer Software]. University of Ljubljana, Slovenia.

Bateson, G. (1972). Double bind, 1969. In G. Bateson (Ed.), *Steps to an ecology of mind* (pp. 271–278). New York: Ballantine.

Baum, J. A. C. (1996). Organizational ecology. In S. Clegg, C. Hardy, & W. Nord (Eds.), *Handbook of organization studies* (pp. 77–114). Thousand Oaks, CA: Sage.

Baum, J. A. C. (1999). Whole-part coevolutionary competition in organizations. In J. A. C. Baum & B. McKelvey (Eds.), *Variations in organization science: In honor of Donald T. Campbell* (pp. 113–135). Thousand Oaks, CA: Sage.

Baum, J. A. C., & Oliver, C. (1991). Institutional linkages and organizational mortality. *Administrative Science Quarterly, 36*, 187–218.

Baum, J. A. C., & Oliver, C. (1992). Institutional embeddedness and the dynamics of organizational populations. *American Sociological Review, 57*, 540–559.

Baum, J. A. C., & Singh, J. V. (1994). Organizational hierarchies and evolutionary processes: Some reflections on a theory of organizational evolution. In J. A. C. Baum & J. V. Singh (Eds.), *Evolutionary dynamics of organizations* (pp. 3–20). New York: Oxford University Press.

Bavelas, A. (1948). A mathematical model for group structure. *Applied Anthropology, 7*, 16–30.

Bearman, P. (1997). Generalized exchange. *American Journal of Sociology, 102*, 1383–1415.

Becker, G. (1976). *The economic approach to human behavior.* Chicago: University of Chicago Press.

Belliveau, M. A., O'Reilly, C. A., & Wade, J. B. (1996). Social capital at the top: Effects of social similarity and status on CEO compensation. *Academy of Management Journal, 39*, 1568–1593.

Benassi, M., & Gargiulo, M. (June 1993). *Informal hierarchy and managerial flexibility in network organization.* Paper presented to the Third European Conference on Social Network Analysis, Munich, Germany.

Beniger, J. (1986). *The control revolution: Technological and economic origins of the information society*. Cambridge, MA: Harvard University Press.

Benson, J. K. (1975). The interorganizational network as a political economy. *Administrative Science Quarterly, 20*, 229–249.

Berger, C. R. (1987). Communicating under uncertainty. In M. E. Roloff & G. R. Miller (Eds.), *Interpersonal processes: New directions in communication research* (pp. 39–62). Newbury Park, CA: Sage.

Berger, C. R., & Bradac, J. J. (1982). *Language and social knowledge: Uncertainty in interpersonal relations*. London: Edward Arnold.

Berger, J., Cohen, B., & Zelditch, M., Jr. (1966). Status characteristics and expectation states. In J. Berger, M. Zelditch, Jr., & B. Anderson (Eds.), *Sociological theories in progress* (Vol. 1, pp. 29–46). Boston: Houghton-Mifflin.

Berger, P., & Luckmann, T. (1967). *The social construction of reality*. Garden City, NY: Doubleday.

Berkman, L. (1985). The relationship of social networks and social support to morbidity and mortality. In S. Cohen & S. L. Syme (Eds.), *Social support and health* (pp. 241–262). Orlando, FL: Academic Press.

Berkman, L., & Syme, S. L. (1979). Social networks, host resistance, and mortality. *American Journal of Epidemiology, 109*, 186–204.

Bernard, H. R., Killworth, P., & Cronenfeld, D. (1984). The problem of informant accuracy: The validity of retrospective data. *Annual Review of Anthropology, 13*, 495–517.

Bernard, H. R., Killworth, P. D., Evans, M. J., McCarty, C., & Shelly, G. A. (1988). Studying social relations cross-culturally. *Ethnology, 27*, 155–179.

Bernard, H., Killworth, P., & Sailer, L. (1980). Informant accuracy in social network data IV. *Social Networks, 2*, 191–218.

Bernard, H., Killworth, P., & Sailer, L. (1982). Informant accuracy in social network data V. *Social Science Research, 11*, 30–66.

Bienenstock, E. J., & Bonacich, P. (1992). The core as solution to exclusionary networks. *Social Networks, 14*, 231–244.

Bienenstock, E. J., & Bonacich, P. (1997). Network exchange as a cooperative game. *Rationality and Society, 9*, 37–65.

Biggart, N. W., & Hamilton, G. G. (1992). On the limits of a firm-based theory to explain business networks: The western bias of neoclassical economics. In N. Nohria & R. G. Eccles (Eds.), *Networks and organizations: Structure, form, and action* (pp. 471–490). Boston, MA: Harvard Business School Press.

Bizot, E., Smith, N., & Hill, T. (1991). Use of electronic mail in a research and development organization. In J. Morell & M. Fleischer (Eds.), *Advances in the implementation and impact of computer systems* (Vol. 1, pp. 65–92). Greenwich, CT: JAI.

Blalock, H. M., Jr. (1964). *Causal inferences in non-experimental research*. Chapel Hill: University of North Carolina Press.

Blalock, H. M., Jr. (1969). *Theory construction*. Englewood Cliffs, NJ: Prentice Hall.

Blalock, H. M., Jr. (1989). The real and unrealized contributions of quantitative sociology. *American Sociological Review, 54*, 447–460.

Bland, S. H., O'Leary, E. S., Farinaro, E., Jossa, F., Krogh, V., Violanti, J. M., & Trevisan, M. (1997). Social network disturbances and psychological distress following earthquake evacuation. *Journal of Nervous and Mental Disease, 185,* 55–78.

Blau, P. M. (1964). *Exchange and power in social life.* New York: Wiley.

Blau, P. M., & Duncan, O. D. (1967). *The American occupational structure.* New York: Wiley.

Blumer, H. (1969). *Symbolic interactionism: Perspective and method.* Englewood Cliffs, NJ: Prentice Hall.

Bollen, K. A. (1989). *Structural equations with latent variables.* New York: Wiley.

Bonacich, P., & Schneider, S. (1992). Communication networks and collective action. In W. B. G. Liebrand, D. M. Messick, & H. A. M. Wilke (Eds.), *Social dilemmas: Theoretical issues and research findings* (pp. 225–245). New York: Pergamon.

Bond, A. H., & Gasser, L. (1988). *Readings in distributed artificial intelligence.* San Mateo, CA: Kaufmann.

Borgatti, S., Everett, M., & Freeman, L. (2002). UCINET 6. [Computer Software]. Harvard, MA: Analytic Technologies.

Bourdieu, P., & Wacquant, L. J. D. (1992). *An invitation to reflexive sociology.* Chicago: University of Chicago Press.

Bovasso, G. (1992). A structural analysis of the formation of a network organization. *Group and Organization Management, 17,* 86–106.

Boyd, B. (1990). Corporate linkages and organizational environment: A test of the resource dependence model. *Strategic Management Journal, 11,* 419–430.

Brass. D. J. (1981). Structural relationships, job characteristics, and worker satisfaction and performance. *Administrative Science Quarterly, 26,* 331–348.

Brass, D. J. (1984). Being in the right place: A structural analysis of individual influence in an organization. *Administrative Science Quarterly, 29,* 519–539.

Brass, D. J. (1985a). Technology and the structuring of jobs: Employee satisfaction, performance, and influence. *Organizational Behavior and Human Decision Processes, 35,* 216–240.

Brass, D. J. (1985b). Men's and women's networks: A study of interaction patterns and influence in organizations. *Academy of Management Journal, 28,* 327–343.

Brass, D. J. (1995a). A social network perspective on human resources management. *Research in Personnel and Human Resources Management, 13,* 39–79.

Brass, D. J. (1995b). Creativity: It's all in your social network. In C. M. Ford & D. A. Gioia (Eds.), *Creative action in organizations* (pp. 94–99). London: Sage.

Brass, D. J., & Burkhardt, M. E. (1992). Centrality and power in organizations. In N. Nohria & R. G. Eccles (Eds.), *Networks and organizations: Structure, form, and action* (pp. 191–215). Boston, MA: Harvard Business School Press.

Brass, D. J., Butterfield, K. D., & Skaggs, B. C. (1995, June). *The social network structure of unethical behavior.* Paper presented at the International Association of Business and Society, Vienna, Austria.

Brewer, D. D. (1995). The social structural basis of the organization of persons in memory. *Human Nature, 6,* 379–403.

Brin, S. and Page, L. (1998). The anatomy of a large-scale hypertextual web search engine. *Computer Networks, 30,* 107–117. Available online at: http://www–db.stanford.edu/pub/papers/google.pdf

Brittain, J. (1994). Density-independent selection and community evolution. In J. A. C. Baum & J. V. Singh (Eds.), *Evolutionary dynamics of organizations* (pp. 355–378). New York: Oxford University Press.

Brittain, J., & Freeman, J. H. (1980). Organization proliferation and density dependent selection. In J. Kimberly & R. H. Miles (Eds.), *The organizational life cycle* (pp. 291–338). San Francisco: Jossey-Bass.

Brown, J. S., & Duguid, P. (1991). Organizational learning and communities-of-practice: Toward a unified view of working, learning, and innovation. *Organization Science, 2,* 40–57.

Browning, L. D., Beyer, J. M., & Shetler, J. C. (1995). Building cooperation in a competitive industry: SEMATECH and the semiconductor industry. *Academy of Management Journal, 38,* 113–151.

Bryant, J. A. (2002). *From the networks to Nickelodeon to Noggin: A community ecology perspective on the coevolution of children's television organizations in the United States.* Unpublished manuscript, Annenberg School for Communication, University of Southern California.

Bryant, J. A., Shumate, M., & Monge, P. R. (2002). *Globalization and coevolving organizations: Understanding legitimate, illegitimate, and legal organizations as coevolving systems.* Unpublished manuscript, Annenberg School for Communication, University of Southern California.

Buchanan, M. (2002). *Nexus: Small worlds and the ground-breaking science of networks.* New York: Norton.

Buck, S. J. (1998). *The global commons: An introduction.* Washington, DC: Island.

Buckley, W. (1967). *Sociology and modern systems theory.* Englewood Cliffs, NJ: Prentice Hall.

Burgelman, R. A., & Mittman, B. S. (1994). An intraorganizational ecological perspective on managerial risk behavior, performance, and survival: Individual, organizational, and environmental effects. In J. A. C. Baum & J. V. Singh (Eds.), *Evolutionary dynamics of organizations* (pp. 53–75). New York: Oxford University Press.

Burke, P. J. (1997). An identity model for network exchange. *American Sociological Review, 62,* 134–150.

Burkhardt, M. E. (1994). Social interaction effects following a technological change: A longitudinal investigation. *Academy of Management Journal, 37,* 869–896.

Burkhardt, M. E., & Brass, D. J. (1990). Changing patterns or patterns of change: The effects of a change in technology on social network structure and power. *Administrative Science Quarterly, 35,* 104–127.

Burns, L., & Wholey, D. R. (1993). Adoption and abandonment of matrix management programs: Effects of organizational characteristics and interorganizational networks. *Academy of Management Review, 36,* 106–138.

Burns, T., & Stalker, G. M. (1961). *The management of innovation.* London: Tavistock.

Burt, R. S. (1980). Models of network structure. *Annual Review of Sociology, 6,* 79–141.

Burt, R. S. (1982). *Toward a structural theory of action: Network models of stratification, perception, and action.* New York: Academic.

Burt, R. S. (1987). Social contagion and innovation: Cohesion versus structural equivalence. *American Journal of Sociology, 92,* 1287–1335.

Burt, R. S. (1991). Contagion. In R. S. Burt (Ed.), *STRUCTURE Version 4.2: A computer program* (pp. 24–27). New York: Columbia University.

Burt, R. S. (1992). *Structural holes: The social structure of competition.* Cambridge, MA: Harvard University Press.

Burt, R. S. (1997). The contingent value of social capital. *Administrative Science Quarterly, 42,* 339–365.

Burt, R. S. (1998). The gender of social capital. *Rationality and Society, 10,* 5–46.

Burt, R. S. (2001). Structural holes versus network closure as social capital. In N. Lin, K. Cook, & R. S. Burt (Eds.), *Social capital: Theory and research* (pp. 31–56). New York: de Gruyter.

Burt, R. S., & Knez, M. (1996). Trust and third-party gossip. In R. M. Kramer & T. R. Tyler (Eds.), *Trust in organizations: Frontiers of theory and research* (pp. 68–89). Thousand Oaks, CA: Sage.

Byrne, D. E. (1971). *The attraction paradigm.* New York: Academic Press.

Campbell, D. T. (1965). Variation and selective retention in socio-cultural evolution. In H. R. Barringer, G. I. Blanksten, & R. Mack (Eds.), *Social change in developing areas: A reinterpretation of evolutionary theory* (pp. 19–49). Cambridge, MA: Schenkman.

Campbell, D. T. (1974). Evolutionary epistemology. In P. A. Schilpp (Ed.), *The philosophy of Karl L. Popper* (pp. 413–463). LaSalle, IL: Open Court.

Campbell, D. T. (1986). An organizational interpretation of evolution. In D. D. Depew & B. H. Weber (Eds.), *Evolution at a crossroads: The new biology and the new philosophy of science* (pp. 133–167). Cambridge, MA: MIT Press.

Campbell, D. T. (1994). How individual and face-to-face-group selection undermine firm selection in organizational evolution. In J. A. C. Baum & J. V. Singh (Eds.), *Evolutionary dynamics of organizations* (pp. 23–38). New York: Oxford University Press.

Campbell, D. T., & Fiske, D. W. (1959). Convergent and discriminant validation by the multitrait multimethod matrix. *Psychological Bulletin, 56,* 81–105.

Campbell, D. T., & Stanley, J. C. (1966). *Experimental and quasi-experimental designs for research.* Chicago, IL: Rand McNally.

Campbell, K. E., & Lee, B. A. (1990). Gender differences in urban neighboring. *Sociological Quarterly, 31,* 495–512.

Canon, W. (1932). *The wisdom of the body.* Cambridge, MA: Harvard University Press.

Carley, K. M. (1986a). An approach for relating social structure to cognitive structure. *Journal of Mathematical Sociology, 12,* 137–189.

Carley, K. M. (1986b). Knowledge acquisition as a social phenomenon. *Instructional Science, 14,* 381–438.

Carley, K. (1990). Group stability: A socio-cognitive approach. In L. E., B. Markovsky, C. Ridgeway, & H. Walker (Eds.), *Advances in group processes: Theory and research* (Vol. 7, pp. 1 – 44). Greenwich, CT: JAI.

Carley, K. (1991). A theory of group stability. *American Sociological Review, 56,* 331–354.

Carley, K. (1995). Computational and mathematical organizational theory: Perspectives and directions. *Computational Mathematical Organizational Theory, 1,* 39–56.

Carley, K. (1997). Network text analysis: The network position of concepts. In C. Roberts (Ed.), *Text analysis for the social sciences: Methods for drawing statistical inferences from texts and transcripts* (pp. 79–100). Hillsdale, NJ: Erlbaum.

Carley, K. (2002). Smart agents and organizations of the future. In L. Lievrouw & S. Livingstone (Eds.), *Handbook of new media* (pp. 206–220). London: Sage.

Carley, K., & Hill, V. (2001). Structural change and learning within organizations. In A. Lomi & E. R. Larsen (Eds.), *Dynamics of organizations: Computational modeling and organizational theories* (pp. 63–92). Menlo Park, CA: AAAI Press/MIT Press.

Carley, K. M., & Kaufer, D. S. (1993). Semantic connectivity: An approach for analyzing symbols in semantic networks. *Communication Theory, 3,* 183–213.

Carley, K. M., & Krackhardt, D. (1996). Cognitive inconsistencies and non-symmetric friendship. *Social Networks, 18,* 1–27.

Carley, K., Lee, J., & Krackhardt, D. (2001). Destabilizing networks. *Connections, 24,* 79–92.

Carley, K. M., & Newell, A. (1994). The nature of the social agent. *Journal of Mathematical Sociology, 19*(4), 221–262.

Carley, K. & Prietula, M. (Eds.) (1994). *Computational organization theory.* Hillsdale, NJ: Erlbaum.

Carrington, P. J., Scott, J., and Wasserman, S. (Eds.) (2003). *Models and methods in social network analysis.* New York: Cambridge University Press.

Carroll, G. R. (1985). Concentration and specialization: Dynamics of niche width in populations of organizations. *American Journal of Sociology, 90,* 1262–1283.

Carroll, G. R., & Hannan, M. T. (2000). *The demography of corporations and industries.* Princeton, NJ: Princeton University Press.

Carroll, G. R., & Hao, Y. P. (1986). Organizational task and institutional environments in ecological perspective: Findings from the local newspaper industry. *American Journal of Sociology, 91,* 838–973.

Carroll, G. R., & Swaninathan, A. (1992). The organizational ecology of strategic groups in the American brewing industry from 1975–1990. *Corporate and Industrial Change, 1,* 65–97.

Carroll, G. R., & Teo, A. C. (1996). On the social networks of managers. *Academy of Management Journal, 39*, 421–440.

Carroll, T., & Burton, R. (1999). *Exploring 'complex' organizational designs.* Unpublished manuscript, Fuqua School of Business, Duke University.

Castells, M. (1996). *The rise of the network society (Vol. 1. The information age: Economy, society and culture).* Oxford, UK: Blackwell Publishers.

Castells, M. (2001). *The Internet galaxy: Reflections on the Internet, business, and society.* New York: Oxford University Press.

Chamberlain, J. (1974). Provision of collective goods as a function of group size. *Political Science Review, 68*, 707–713.

Chandler, A. D. (1977). *The visible hand: The managerial revolution in American business.* Cambridge, MA: Harvard University Press.

Chang, M., & Harrington, J. E., Jr. (2000). Centralization vs. decentralization in a multi-unit organization: A computational model of a retail chain as a multi-agent adaptive system. *Management Science, 46*, 1427–1440.

Chang, M., & Harrington, J. E., Jr. (in press). Organization of innovation in a multi-unit firm: Coordinating adaptive search on multiple rugged landscapes. In W. Barnett, C. Deissenberg, & G. Feichtinger (Eds.), *Economic Complexity.* New York: Cambridge University Press.

Ching, C., Holsapple, C. W., & Whinston, A. B. (1996). Toward IT support for coordination in network organizations. *Information & Management, 30*, 179–199.

Cicourel, A. (1990). The integration of distributed knowledge in collaborative medical diagnosis. In J. Galegher, R. E. Kraut, and C. Egido (Eds.), *Intellectual teamwork: Social and technological foundations of cooperative work* (pp. 221–242). Hillsdale, NJ: Erlbaum.

Cilliers, P. (1998). *Complexity and postmodernism: Understanding complex systems.* New York: Routledge.

Coase, R. H. (1937). The nature of the firm. *Economica, 4*, 386–405.

Cochran, P. L., Wood, R. A., & Jones, T. B. (1985). The composition of boards of directors and incidence of golden parachutes. *Academy of Management Journal, 28*, 664–671.

Coleman, J. S. (1957). *Community conflict.* New York: Free Press.

Coleman, J. S. (1961). *The adolescent society: The social life of the teenager and its impact on education.* New York: Free Press.

Coleman, J. S. (1973). *The mathematics of collective action.* Chicago, IL: Aldine.

Coleman, J. S. (1986). *Individual interests and collective action: Selected essays.* New York: Cambridge University Press.

Coleman, J. S. (1988). Social capital in the creation of human capital. *American Journal of Sociology, 94*, 95–120.

Coleman, J. S. (1990). *Foundations of social theory.* Cambridge, MA: Harvard University Press.

Conrad, C., & Poole, M. S. (1997). Introduction: Communication and the disposable worker. *Communication Research, 24*, 581–592.

Conrath, D. (1973). Communication environment and its relationship to organizational structure. *Management Science, 4*, 586–603.

Contractor, N. S. (1994). Self-organizing systems perspective in the study of organizational communication. In B. Kovacic (Ed.), *New approaches to organizational communication* (pp. 39–66). Albany: State University of New York Press.

Contractor, N. S. (1997). *Inquiring Knowledge Networks on the Web. Conceptual overview.* http://www.tec.spcomm.uiuc.edu/nosh/IKNOW/sld001.htm

Contractor, N. S. (1999). Self-organizing systems research in the social sciences: Reconciling the metaphors and the models. *Management Communication Quarterly, 13*, 154–166.

Contractor, N. S. (2002). Introduction: New media and organizing. In L. Lievrouw & S. Livingstone (Eds.), *Handbook of new media* (pp. 201–205). London: Sage.

Contractor, N. (2003). Peer to peer. In S. Jones (Ed.), *Encyclopedia of new media* (pp. 359–361). Thousand Oaks, CA: Sage.

Contractor, N., & Bishop, A. P. (2000). Reconfiguring community networks: The case of PrairieKNOW. In T. Ishida (Ed.), *Digital cities: Technologies, experiences, and future perspectives. Lecture Notes in Computer Science* (pp. 151–164). Berlin: Springer-Verlag.

Contractor, N. S., Carley, K., Levitt, R., Monge, P., Wasserman, S., Bar, F., Fulk, J., Hollingshead, A., & Kunz, J. (1998). *Co-Evolution of Knowledge Networks and Twenty-First Century Forms: Computational Modeling and Empirical Testing.* Research proposal funded by the National Science Foundation (Grant # IIS-9980109).

Contractor, N. S., & Eisenberg, E. M. (1990). Communication networks and new media in organizations. In J. Fulk & C. W. Steinfield (Eds.), *Organizations and communication Technology* (pp. 143–172). Newbury Park, CA: Sage.

Contractor, N. S., Eisenberg, E. M., & Monge, P. R. (1996). *Antecedents and outcomes of interpretative diversity.* Unpublished manuscript, Department of Speech Communication, University of Illinois at Urbana-Champaign.

Contractor, N. S., & Grant, S. (1996). The emergence of shared interpretations in organizations: A Self-organizing systems perspective. In J. Watt & A. VanLear (Eds.), *Cycles and dynamic processes in communication processes* (pp. 216–230). Newbury Park, CA: Sage.

Contractor, N. S., & Monge, P. R. (2002). Managing knowledge networks. *Management Communication Quarterly, 16*, 249–258.

Contractor, N. S., O'Keefe, B. J., & Jones, P. M. (1997). *IKNOW: Inquiring Knowledge Networks On the Web.* [Computer software. University of Illinois]. Available at http://iknow.spcomm.uiuc.edu.

Contractor, N. S., & Seibold, D. R. (1993). Theoretical frameworks for the study of structuring processes in group decision support systems: Adaptive structuration theory and self-organizing systems theory. *Human Communication Research, 19*, 528–563.

Contractor, N. S., Seibold, D. R., & Heller, M. A. (1996). Interactional influence in the structuring of media use in groups: Influence of members' perceptions of group decision support system use. *Human Communication Research, 22*, 451–481.

Contractor, N. S, Wasserman, S., & Faust, K. (2000). *Testing multi-level, multi-theoretical hypotheses about networks in 21st century organizational forms: An analytic framework and empirical example.* Paper presented at the annual convention of the International Communication Association, Acapulco, Mexico.

Contractor, N. S., Whitbred, R., Fonti, F., Hyatt, A., O'Keefe, B. J., & Jones, P. M. (2002). Complexity theory and the evolution of networks. Manuscript submitted for publication.

Contractor N., Zink, D., & Chan, M. (1998). IKNOW: A tool to assist and study the creation, maintenance, and dissolution of knowledge networks. In T. Ishida (Ed.), *Community computing and support systems: Lecture notes in computer science 1519* (pp. 201–217). Berlin: Springer-Verlag.

Cook, K. S. (1977). Exchange and power in networks of interorganizational relations. *Sociological Quarterly, 18,* 62–82.

Cook, K. S. (1982). Network structures from an exchange perspective. In P. V. Marsden & N. Lin (Eds.), *Social structure and network analysis* (pp. 177–218). Beverly Hills, CA: Sage.

Cook, K. S., & Emerson, R. M. (1978). Power, equity, and commitment in exchange networks. *American Sociological Review, 43,* 721–739.

Cook, K. S., Emerson, R. M., Gillmore, M. R., & Yamagishi, T. (1983). The distribution of power in exchange networks: Theory and experimental results. *American Journal of Sociology, 89,* 275–305.

Cook, K. S., & Whitmeyer, J. M. (1992). Two approaches to social structure: Exchange theory and network analysis. *Annual Review of Sociology, 18,* 109–127.

Cook, K. S., & Yamagishi, T. (1992). Power in exchange networks: A power-dependence formulation. *Social Networks, 14,* 245.

Cook, T. D., & Campbell, D. T. (1979). *Quasi-experimentation: Design and analysis for field settings.* Chicago, IL: Rand McNally.

Corman, S. R. (1990). A mode of perceived communication in collective networks. *Human Communication Research, 16,* 582–602.

Corman, S. R. (1996). Cellular automata as models of unintended consequences of organizational communication. In J. H. Watt & C. A. Van Lear (Eds.), *Dynamic patterns in communication processes* (pp. 191–212). Thousand Oaks, CA: Sage.

Corman, S. R. (1997). The reticulation of quasi-agents in systems of organizational communication. In G. A. Barnett & L. Thayer (Eds.), *Organization communication emerging perspectives (Vol. 5) The renaissance in systems thinking,* pp. 65–81. Greenwich, CT: Ablex.

Corman, S. R, Kuhn, T., McPhee, R., & K. Dooley (2002). Studying complex discursive systems: Centering resonance analysis of communication. *Human Communication Research, 28,* 157–206.

Corman, S. R., & Scott, C. R. (1994). Perceived networks, activity, foci, and observable communication in social collectives. *Communication Theory, 4,* 171–190.

Cramer, F. (1993). *Chaos and order: The complex structure of living systems.* New York: Wiley.

Crombie, S., & Birley, S. (1992). Networking by female business owners in Northern Ireland. *Journal of Business Venturing, 7,* 237–251.

Cross, R., & Baird, L. (2000). Technology is not enough: Improving performance by building organizational memory. *Sloan Management Review, 41*(3), 41–54.

Cross, R., Nohria, N., & Parker, A. (2002). Six myths about informal networks—And how to overcome them. *Sloan Management Review, 43*(3), 67–76.

Cross, R., Parker, A., Prusak, L., & Borgatti, S. (2001). Knowing what we know: Supporting knowledge creation and sharing in social networks. *Organizational Dynamics, 3*(2), 100–120.

Cross, R., Yan, A., & Louis, M. (2000). Boundary activity in "boundaryless" organizations: A case study of a transformation to a team-based structure. *Human Relations, 53*(6), 841–868.

Crouch, B., & Wasserman, S. (1998). A practical guide to fitting social network models via logistic regression. *Connections, 21,* 87–101.

Crowston, K. (1997). A coordination theory approach to organizational process design. *Organization Science, 8,* 157–175.

Cummings, A. (1997). *The radicalness of employee ideas: An interactive model of co-worker networks and problem-solving styles.* Unpublished doctoral dissertation, College of Business Administration, University of Illinois.

Cutrona, C. E., & Russell, D. W. (1990). Type of social support and specific stress: Toward a theory of optimal matching. In B. R. Sarason, I. G. Sarason, & G. R. Pierce (Eds.), *Social support: An interactional view* (pp. 319–366). New York: Wiley.

Daft, R. L., & Lengel, R. H. (1986). Organizational information requirements, media richness and structural design. *Management Science, 32,* 554–571.

Daft, R. L., & Weick, K. E. (1984). Toward a model of organizations as interpretation systems. *Academy of Management Review, 9,* 284–295.

Danowski, J. A. (1982). Computer-mediated communication: A network-based content analysis using a CBBS conference. In M. Burgoon (Ed.), *Communication yearbook* (Vol. 6, pp. 905–924). Beverly Hills, CA: Sage.

Davies, G. (1996). The employment support network—An intervention to assist displaced workers. *Journal of Employment Counseling, 33,* 146–154.

Davis, G. F. (1991). Agents without principles? The spread of the poison pill through the intercorporate network. *Administrative Science Quarterly, 36,* 583–613.

Davis, J., & Leinhardt, S. (1972). The structure of positive interpersonal relations in small groups. In J. Berger (Ed.), *Sociological theories in progress* (Vol. 2, pp. 218–251). Boston, MA: Houghton-Mifflin.

Davis, K. (1953). A method of studying communication patterns in organizations. *Personnel Psychology, 6,* 301–312.

Dawes, R. M. (1980). Social dilemmas. *Annual Review of Psychology, 31,* 169–193.

Deal, T. E., & Kennedy, A. (1982). *Corporate cultures: The rites and rituals of corporate life.* Reading, MA: Addison-Wesley.

DeFleur, M. L., & Cronin, M. M. (1991). Completeness and accuracy of recall in the diffusion of the news from a newspaper versus a television source. *Sociological Inquiry, 61,* 148–166.

Delacroix, J., & Carroll, G. R. (1983). Organizational foundings: An ecological study of the newspaper industries of Argentina and Ireland. *Administrative Science Quarterly, 28,* 274–291.

Delacroix, J., & Rao, H. (1994). Externalities and ecological theory: Unbundling density dependence. In J. A. C. Baum & J. V. Singh (Eds.), *Evolutionary dynamics of organizations* (pp. 255–268). New York: Oxford University Press.

Delacroix, J., Swaminathan, A., & Solt, M. E. (1989). Density dependence versus population dynamics: An ecological study of failings in the California wine industry. *American Sociological Review, 54,* 245–262.

DeSanctis, G., & Monge, P. R. (1999). Introduction to the special issue: Communication processes for virtual organizations. *Organization Science, 10,* 693–703.

de Saussure, F. (1916/1966). *Course in general linguistics.* New York: McGraw-Hill.

De Soto, C. B. (1960). Learning a social structure. *Journal of Abnormal and Social Psychology, 60,* 417–421.

Deutsch, K. (1963). *The nerves of government: Models of political communication and control.* Glencoe, IL: Free Press.

DiMaggio, P. (1994). The challenge of community evolution. In J. A. C. Baum, & J. V. Singh (Eds.), *Evolutionary dynamics of organizations* (pp. 444–450). New York: Oxford University Press.

DiMaggio, P., Hargittai, E., Neuman, W. R., & Robinson, J. P. (2001). Social implications of the Internet. *Annual Review of Sociology, 27,* 307–336.

DiMaggio, P. J., & Powell, W. W. (1983). The iron cage revisited: Institutional isomorphism and collective rationality in organizational fields. *American Sociological Review, 48,* 147–160.

Domhoff, G. W. (1983). *Who rules America now? A view of the '80s.* Englewood Cliffs, NJ: Prentice Hall.

Doty, D. H., Glick, W. H., & Huber, G. P. (1993). Fit, equifinality, and organizational effectiveness: A test of two configurational theories. *Academy of Management Journal, 36,* 1196–1250.

Drogoul, A., & Ferber, J. (1994). Multi-agent simulation as a tool for studying emergent processes in societies. In J. E. Doran & N. Gilbert (Eds.), *Simulating societies: The computer simulation of social phenomena* (pp. 127–142). London: UCL.

Dunn, W. N., & Ginsberg, A. (1986). A sociocognitive network approach to organizational analysis. *Human Relations, 40,* 955–976.

Durkheim, E. (1895/1964). *The rules of sociological method.* London: Free Press.

Durkheim, E. (1897/1977). *Suicide: A study in sociology* (J. A. Spaulding & G. Simpson, Trans.). New York: Free Press.

Dutton, W. H. (1999). *Society on the Line: Information Politics in the Digital Age.* New York: Oxford University Press.

Dyson, G. B. (1997). *Darwin among the machines: The evolution of global intelligence*. Reading, MA: Perseus Books

Eisenberg, E. M., Farace, R. V., Monge, P. R., Bettinghaus, E. P., Kurchner-Hawkins, R., Miller, K., & Rothman, L. (1985). Communication linkages in interorganizational systems. In B. Dervin & M. Voight (Eds.), *Progress in communication sciences* (Vol. 6, pp. 210–266). Norwood, NJ: Ablex.

Eisenberg, E. M., Monge, P. R., & Miller, K. I. (1984). Involvement in communication networks as a predictor of organizational commitment. *Human Communication Research, 10,* 179–201.

Eisenberg, E. M., Monge, P. R., Poole, M. S., et al. (2000). *Rhizome 2000.* Unpublished manuscript. Department of Communication, University of South Florida.

Eisenberg, M., & Swanson, N. (1996). Organizational network analysis as a tool for program evaluation. *Evaluation & the Health Professions, 19,* 488–507.

Emerson, R. M. (1962). Power-dependence relations. *American Sociological Review, 27,* 31–41.

Emerson, R. M. (1972a). Exchange theory, part 1: A psychological basis for social exchange. In J. Berger, M. Zelditch, & B. Anderson (Eds.), *Sociological theories in progress* (Vol. 2, pp. 38–57). Boston, MA: Houghton Mifflin.

Emerson, R. M. (1972b). Exchange theory, part II: Exchange relations and networks. In J. Berger, M. Zelditch, & B. Anderson (Eds.), *Sociological theories in progress* (Vol. 2, pp. 58–87). Boston, MA: Houghton Mifflin.

Emery, F. E., & Trist, E. L. (1960). Sociotechnical systems. In C. W. Churchman & M. Verhulst (Eds.), *Management science, models and techniques* (pp. 83–97). New York: Pergamon.

Emery, F. E., & Trist, E. L. (1965). The causal texture of organizational environment. *Human Relations, 18,* 21–32.

Epstein, J. M., & Axtell, R. (1996). *Growing artificial societies: Social sciences from the bottom up.* Cambridge, MA: MIT Press.

Erickson, B. (1988). The relational basis of attitudes. In S. D. Berkowitz & B. Wellman (Eds.), *Social structures: A network approach* (pp. 99–121). Cambridge, UK: Cambridge University Press.

Ethington, C. T., Johnson, J. D., Marshall, A., Meyer, M., & Chang, H.-J. (1996). *Gender ratios in organizations: A comparative study of two organizations.* Paper presented at the annual convention of the International Communication Association, Chicago, IL.

Eve, R. A., Horsfall, S., & Lee, M. E. (Eds.) (1997). *Chaos, complexity and sociology: Myths, models, and theories.* London: Sage.

Eveland, J. D., & Bikson, T. K. (1987). Evolving electronic communication networks: An empirical assessment. *Office: Technology and People, 3,* 103–128.

Farace, R. V., Monge, P. R., & Russell, H. M. (1977). *Communicating and organizing.* Reading, MA: Addison-Wesley.

Fararo, T. J. (1973). *Mathematical sociology: An introduction to fundamentals.* New York: Wiley.

Faust, K., & Skvoretz, J. (2002). Comparing networks across space and time, size and species. In R. M. Stolzenberg (Ed.), *Sociological methodology 2002* (Vol. 32, pp. 267–299). Cambridge, MA: Blackwell.

Feeley, T. H., & Barnett, G. A. (1996). Predicting employee turnover from communication networks. *Human Communication Research, 23*, 370–387.

Feld, S. (1981). The focused organization of social ties. *American Journal of Sociology, 86*, 1015–1035.

Fernandez, R. M. (1991). Structural bases of leadership in intraorganizational networks. *Social Psychology Quarterly, 54*, 36–53.

Festinger, L. (1954). A theory of social comparison processes. *Human Relations, 7*, 114–140.

Festinger, L., Schachter, S., & Back, K. (1950). *Social pressures in informal groups: A study of human factors in housing.* Palo Alto, CA: Stanford University Press.

Fine, G. A., & Kleinman, S. (1983). Network and meaning: An interactionist approach to structure. *Symbolic Interaction, 6*, 97–110.

Fiol, C. M. (1989). A semantic analysis of corporate language: Organizational boundaries and joint venturing. *Administrative Science Quarterly, 34*, 277–303.

Fischer, C. (1992). *America calling: A social history of the telephone to 1940.* Berkeley: University of California Press

Flache, A., & Macy, M. W. (1996). The weakness of strong ties: Collective action failure in a highly cohesive group. *Journal of Mathematical Sociology, 21*, 3–28.

Follett, M. P. (1924). *Creative experience.* New York: Longmans, Green.

Fombrun, C. J. (1986). Structural dynamics within and between organizations. *Administrative Science Quarterly, 31*, 403–421.

Forrester, J. W. (1961). *Industrial dynamics.* Cambridge, MA: MIT Press.

Forrester, J. W. (1973). *World dynamics.* Cambridge, MA: MIT Press.

Fountain, J. (2001). *Building the virtual state: Information technology and institutional change.* Washington, DC: Brookings Institution.

Frank, O., & Strauss, D. (1986). Markov graphs. *Journal of the American Statistical Association, 81*, 832–842.

Freeman, L. (1977). A set of measures of centrality based on betweenness. *Sociometry, 40*, 35–41.

Freeman, L. (1979). Centrality in social networks, part 1: Conceptual clarification. *Social Networks, 1*, 215–239.

Freeman, L. C., Romney, A. K., & Freeman, S. C. (1987). Cognitive structure and informant accuracy. *American Anthropologist, 89*, 310–325.

Freeman, L. C. (1992). Filling in the blanks: A theory of cognitive categories and the structure of social affiliation. *Social Psychology Quarterly, 55*, 118–127.

Friedkin, N. E. (1984). Structural cohesion and equivalence explanations of social homogeneity. *Sociological Methods and Research, 12*, 235–261.

Friedkin, N. E. (1998). *A structural theory of social influence.* New York: Cambridge University Press.

Frost, P., Moore, L., Louis, M. R., Lundberg, C., & Martin, J. (1985). *Organizational culture.* Newbury Park, CA: Sage.

Fukuyama, F. (1999). *The great disruption: Human nature and the reconstitution of social order.* New York: Free Press.

Fulk, J. (1993). Social construction of communication technology. *Academy of Management Journal, 36,* 921–950.

Fulk, J., & Boyd, B. (1991). Emerging theories of communication in organizations. *Yearly Review of the Journal of Management, 17,* 407–446.

Fulk, J., & DeSanctis, G. (1999). Articulation of communication technology and organizational form. In G. DeSanctus and J. Fulk (Eds.), *Shaping organizational form: Communication, connection, and community* (pp. 5–32). Thousand Oaks, CA: Sage.

Fulk, J., Flanagin, A. J., Kalman, M. E., Monge, P. R., & Ryan, T. (1996). Connective and communal public goods in interactive communication systems. *Communication Theory, 6,* 60–87.

Fulk, J., Lu, S., Monge, P., & Contractor, N. (1998). *Interactive communication & computing for virtual work communities.* Final Report Submitted to the Annenberg Center for Communication, University of Southern California.

Fulk, J., Schmitz, J., & Ryu, D. (1995). Cognitive elements in the social construction of communication technology. *Management Communication Quarterly, 8,* 259–288.

Fulk, J., Schmitz, J., & Steinfield, C. W. (1990). A social influence model of technology use. In J. Fulk & C. W. Steinfield (Eds.), *Organizations and communication technology* (pp. 117–140). Newbury Park, CA: Sage.

Fulk, J., & Steinfield, C. W. (Eds.) (1990). *Organizations and communication technology.* Newbury Park, CA: Sage.

Fulk, J., Steinfield, C. W., Schmitz, J., & Power, J. G. (1987). A social information processing model of media use in organizations. *Communication Research, 14,* 529–552.

Galaskiewicz, J. (1979). *Exchange networks and community politics.* Newbury Park, CA.: Sage.

Galaskiewicz, J. (1985). Interorganizational relations. *Annual Review of Sociology, 11,* 281–304.

Galaskiewicz, J., & Burt, R. S. (1991). Interorganizational contagion in corporate philanthropy. *Administrative Science Quarterly, 36,* 88–105.

Galaskiewicz, J., & Wasserman, S. (1989). Mimetic and normative processes within an interorganizational field: An empirical test. *Administrative Science Quarterly, 34,* 454–479.

Galbraith, J. R. (1977). *Organization design.* Reading, MA: Addison-Wesley.

Galbraith, J. R. (1995). *Designing organizations: An executive briefing on strategy, structure, and process.* San Francisco: Jossey-Bass.

Gaver, W. (1996). Affordances for interaction: The social is material for design. *Ecological Psychology, 8,* 111–29.

Gell-Mann, M. (1994). *The quark and the jaguar: Adventures in the simple and complex.* New York: Freeman.

Gerlach, M. (1992). *Alliance capitalism.* Berkeley: University of California Press.

Ghoshal, S., & Bartlett, C. A. (1990). The multinational corporation as an interorganizational network. *Academy of Management Review, 15,* 603–625.

Giddens, A. (1976). *New rules of sociological method*. London: Hutchinson.

Giddens, A. (1979). *Central problems in social theory*. Cambridge, MA: Cambridge University Press.

Giddens, A. (1984). *The constitution of society: Outline of the theory of structuration*. Cambridge: Polity.

Giddens, A. (1991). *Modernity and self-identity: Self and society in the late modern age*. Stanford, CA: Stanford University Press.

Giddens, A. (2000). *Runaway world: How globalization is reshaping our lives*. New York: Routledge.

Gilbert, N., & Troitzch, K. G. (1999). *Simulation for the social scientist*. Buckingham: Open University Press.

Glansdorff, P., & Prigogine, I. (1971). *Thermodynamic study of structure, stability and fluctuations*. New York: Wiley.

Goes, J. B., & Park, S. H. (1997). Interorganizational links and innovation: The case of hospital services. *Academy of Management Journal, 40*, 673–696.

Gollob, H. F. (1968). Impression formation and word combination in sentences. *Journal of Personality and Social Psychology, 10*, 341–353.

Goodell, A., Brown, J., & Poole, M. S. (1989). *Organizational networks and climate perceptions: A longitudinal analysis*. Unpublished manuscript. University of Minnesota.

Gore, A., Jr. (1996). The metaphor of distributed intelligence. *Science, 272*, 177.

Gould, R. V. (1991). Multiple networks and mobilization in the Paris Commune, 1871. *American Sociological Review, 56*, 716–729.

Grabher, G. (1993). Rediscovering the social in the economics of interfirm relations. In G. Grabher (Ed.), *The embedded firm: On the socioeconomics of industrial networks* (pp. 1–31). New York: Routledge.

Graen, G. (1976). Role making processes within complex organizations. In M. D. Dunnette (Ed.), *Handbook of industrial and organizational psychology*. Chicago: Rand McNally.

Grandori, A., & Soda, G. (1995). Inter-firm networks: Antecedents, mechanisms, and forms. *Organization Studies, 16*, 183–214.

Granovetter, M. (1973). The strength of weak ties. *American Journal of Sociology, 81*, 1287–1303.

Granovetter, M. (1974). *Getting a job: A study of contacts and careers*. Cambridge, MA: Harvard University Press.

Granovetter, M. (1978). Threshold models of diffusion and collective behavior. *Journal of Mathematical Sociology, 9*, 165–179.

Granovetter, M. (1982). The strength of weak ties: A network theory revisited. In R. Collins (Ed.), *Sociological theory 1983* (pp. 105–130). San Francisco, CA: Jossey-Bass.

Granovetter, M. (1992). Problems of explanations in economic sociology. In N. Nohria & R. G. Eccles (Eds.), *Networks as organizations: Structure, form, and action* (pp. 25–56). Boston, MA: Harvard Business School Press.

Granovetter, M. S. (1985). Economic action and social structure: The problem of embeddedness. *American Journal of Sociology, 91*, 481–510.

Grossberg, L., Wartella, E., & Whitney, C. (1998). *MediaMaking*. Thousand Oaks, CA: Sage.

Gulati, R. (1995). Social structure and alliance formation patterns: A longitudinal analysis. *Administrative Science Quarterly, 40,* 619–652.

Gupta, A. K., & Govindarajan, V. (1991). Knowledge flows and the structure of control within multinational corporations. *Academy of Management Review, 16,* 768–792.

Gurbaxani, V. (1990). Diffusion in computing networks: The case of BITNET. *Communications of the ACM, 33,* 65–75.

Hackman, J. R., & Oldham, G. (1976). Motivation through the design of work: Test of a theory. *Organizational Behavior and Human Performance, 16,* 250–279.

Haines, V. A. (1988). Social network analysis, structuration theory and the holism-individualism debate. *Social Networks, 10,* 157–182.

Hall, A., & Wellman, B. (1985). Social networks and social support. In S. Cohen & S. L. Syme (Eds.), *Social support and health* (pp. 23–41). Orlando, FL: Academic Press.

Hall, S. (1990). Globalization and ethnicity. In A. D. King (Ed.), *Culture, globalization and the world-system* (pp. 25–40). New York: Macmillan.

Hannan, M. T., & Carroll, G. R. (1992). *Dynamics of organizational populations: Density, competition, and legitimation.* New York: Oxford University Press.

Hannan, M. T., & Carroll, G. R. (1995). An introduction to organizational ecology. In G. R. Carroll & M. T. Hannan (Eds.), *Organizations in industry: Strategy, structure, and selection* (pp. 17–31). New York: Oxford University Press.

Hannan, M. T., & Freeman, J. (1977). The population ecology of organizations. *American Journal of Sociology, 82,* 929–984.

Hannan, M. T., & Freeman, J. (1984). Structural inertia and organizational change. *American Sociological Review, 49,* 149–164.

Hanneman, R. A. (1988). *Computer-assisted theory building: Modeling dynamic social systems.* Newbury Park, CA: Sage.

Harary, F., Norman, R. Z., & Cartwright, D. (1965). *Structural models: An introduction to the theory of directed graphs.* New York: Wiley.

Hardin, G. (1968). The tragedy of the commons. *Science, 162,* 1243–1248.

Hardin, R. (1982). *Collective action.* Baltimore, MD: John Hopkins University Press.

Hartman, R. L., & Johnson, J. D. (1989). Social contagion and multiplexity: Communication networks as predictors of commitment and role ambiguity. *Human Communication Research, 15,* 523–548.

Hartman, R. L., & Johnson, J. D. (1990). Formal and informal group structures: An examination of their relationship to role ambiguity. *Social Networks, 12,* 127–151.

Hartman, A., Sifonis, J., & Kador, J. (2000). *Net ready: Strategies for success in the E-conomy.* New York: McGraw Hill.

Harvey, D. (1989). *The condition of postmodernity.* Oxford, UK: Blackwell.

Haunschild, P. R. (1993). Interorganizational imitation: The impact of interlocks on corporate acquisition activity. *Administrative Science Quarterly, 38,* 564–592.

Haunschild, P. R. (1994). How much is that company worth? Interorganizational relationships, uncertainty, and acquisition premiums. *Administrative Science Quarterly, 39,* 391–411.

Haveman, H. A. (1992). Between a rock and a hard place: Organizational change and performance under conditions of fundamental environmental transformation. *Administrative Science Quarterly, 37,* 48–75.

Hawley, A. (1950). *Human ecology: A theory of community structure.* New York: Ronald.

Hawley, A. (1968). Human ecology. In D. L. Sills (Ed.), *The international encyclopedia of the social sciences* (Vol. 4, pp. 328–337). New York: Crowell-Collier & Macmillan.

Hawley, A. (1986). *Human ecology: A theoretical essay.* Chicago, IL: University of Chicago Press.

Haythornthwaite, C. (1996). Social network analysis: An approach and technique for the study of information exchange. *Library & Information Science Research, 18,* 323–342.

Haythornthwaite, C., & Wellman, B. (Eds.) (2001). *The Internet in everyday life.* [Special issue]. *American Behavioral Scientist, 45.*

Head, J. G. (1972). Public goods: The polar case. In R. M. Bird & J. G. Head (Eds.), *Modern fiscal issues: Essays in honour of Carl S. Shoup* (pp. 7–16). Toronto, Ontario, Canada: University of Toronto Press.

Heald, M. R., Contractor, N. S., Koehly, L., & Wasserman, S. (1998). Formal and emergent predictors of coworkers' perceptual congruence on an organization's social structure. *Human Communication Research, 24,* 536–563.

Heckscher, C. (1994). Defining the post-bureaucratic type. In C. Heckscher & A. Donnellon (Eds.), *The post-bureaucratic organization: New perspectives on organizational change* (pp. 14–62). Thousand Oaks, CA: Sage.

Heider, F. (1958). *The psychology of interpersonal relations.* New York: Wiley.

Heise, D. (1969). Affectual dynamics in simple sentences. *Journal of Personality and Social Psychology, 11,* 204–213.

Heise, D. (1970). Potency dynamics in simple sentences. *Journal of Personality and Social Psychology, 16,* 48–54.

Held, D., McGrew, A., Goldblatt, D., & Perraton, J. (1999). *Global transformations: Politics, economics, and culture.* Stanford, CA: Stanford University Press.

Helper, S. (1993). An exit-voice analysis of supplier relations: The case of the U.S. automobile industry. In G. Grabher (Ed.), *The embedded firm: On the socioeconomics of industrial networks* (pp. 141–160). New York: Routledge.

Hinds, P., & Kiesler, S. (1995). Communication across boundaries: Work, structure, and use of communication technologies in a large organization. *Organization Science, 6,* 373–393.

Hoffman, A. N., Stearns, T. M., & Shrader, C. B. (1990). Structure, context, and centrality in interorganizational networks. *Journal of Business Research, 20,* 333–347.

Hofstadter, D. R. (1979). *Godel, Escher, Bach: An eternal golden braid.* New York: Basic.

Hofstede, G. (1984). *Culture's consequences.* London: Sage.

Holland, J. H. (1995). *Hidden order: How adaptation builds complexity.* Reading, MA: Addison-Wesley.

Holland, J. H. (1998). *Emergence: From chaos to order*. Reading, MA: Perseus Books.

Holland, P. W., & Leinhardt, S. (1975). The statistical analysis of local structure in social networks. In D. R. Heise (Ed.), *Sociological methodology, 1976* (pp. 1–45). San Francisco: Jossey Bass.

Holland, P. W., & Leinhardt, S. (1979). *Perspectives on social network research*. New York: Academic.

Hollingshead, A. B. (1998a). Communication, learning, and retrieval in transactive memory systems. *Journal of Experimental Social Psychology, 34*, 423–442.

Hollingshead, A. B. (1998b). Retrieval processes in transactive memory systems. *Journal of Personality and Social Psychology, 74*, 659–671.

Hollingshead, A. B. (1998c). Group and individual training: The impact of practice on performance. *Small Group Research, 29*, 254–280.

Hollingshead, A. B. (2000). Perceptions of expertise and transactive memory in work relationships. *Group Processes and Intergroup Relations, 3*, 257–267.

Hollingshead, A. B., & Contractor, N. S. (2002). New media and organizing at the group level. In L. Lievrouw & S. Livingstone (Eds.), *Handbook of new media* (pp. 221–235). London: Sage.

Hollingshead, A. B., Fulk, J., & Monge, P. (2002). Fostering intranet knowledge-sharing: An integration of transactive memory and public goods approaches. In S. Keisler & P. Hines (Eds.), *Distributed Work: New Research on Working Across Distance Using Technology* (pp. 335–355). Cambridge, MA: MIT Press.

Homans, G. C. (1950). *The human group*. New York: Harcourt Brace.

Homans, G. C. (1958). Social behavior as exchange. *American Journal of Sociology, 19*, 22–24.

Homans, G. C. (1974). *Social behavior: Its elementary forms* (Rev. Ed.). New York: Harcourt Brace.

Hong, T. (2001). Performance. In A. Oram (Ed.). *Peer-to-Peer: Harnessing the power of disruptive technologies* (pp. 203–241). Sebastopol, CA: O'Reilly & Associates, Inc.

Horrigan, K., & Rainie, L. (2002). *Getting serious online*. (Pew Internet & American Life Project, Washington, DC). Available online at: http:// www. pewinternet.org/reports/pdfs/PIP_Getting_Serious_Online3ng .pdf

Huber, G. P., & Daft, R. L. (1987). The information environments of organizations. In L. L. Putnam, F. M. Jablin, K. H. Roberts, & L. W. Porter (Eds.), *Handbook of organizational communication: An interdisciplinary perspective* (pp. 130–164). Newbury Park, CA: Sage.

Huber, G. P., Miller, C. C., & Glick, W. H. (1990). Developing more encompassing theories about organizations: The centralization-effectiveness relationship as an example. *Organization Science, 1*, 11–40.

Hubert, L. J., & Schultz, J. V. (1976). Quadratic assignment as a general data analysis strategy. *British Journal of Mathematical and Statistical Psychology, 29*, 190–241.

Hurlbert, J. S. (1991). Social networks, social circles, and job satisfaction. *Work and Occupations, 18,* 415–430.

Hyatt, A., Contractor, N., & Jones, P. M. (1997). Computational organizational network modeling: Strategies and an example. *Computational and Mathematical Organizational Theory, 4,* 285–300.

Ibarra, H. (1992). Homophily and differential returns: Sex differences in network structure and access in an advertising firm. *Administrative Science Quarterly, 37,* 422–447.

Ibarra, H. (1993a). Network centrality, power, and innovation involvement: Determinants of technical and administrative roles. *Academy of Management Journal, 36,* 471–501.

Ibarra, H. (1993b). Personal networks of women and minorities in management: A conceptual framework. *Academy of Management Review, 18,* 56–87.

Ibarra, H. (1995). Race, opportunity, and diversity of social circles in managerial networks. *Academy of Management Journal, 38,* 673–703.

Ibarra, H., & Andrews, S. B. (1993). Power, social influence, and sense making: Effects of network centrality and proximity on employee perceptions. *Administrative Science Quarterly, 38,* 277–303.

Jablin, F. M. (1980). Organizational communication theory and research: An overview of communication climate and network research. In D. Nimmo (Ed.), *Communication yearbook 4* (pp. 327–347). New Brunswick, NJ: Transaction Books.

Jablin, F., & Krone, K. J. (1987). *Organizational assimilation.* Newbury Park, CA: Sage.

Jackson, M., Poole, M. S., & Kuhn, T. (2002). The social construction of technologies in studies of the workplace. In L. Lievrouw & S. Livingstone (Eds.), *Handbook of new media* (pp. 236–253). London: Sage.

Jang, H., & Barnett, G. A. (1994). Cultural differences in organizational communication: A semantic network analysis. *Bulletin de Methodologie Sociologique, 44,* 31–59.

Johnson, J. D. (1992). Approaches to organizational communication structure. *Journal of Business Research, 25,* 99–113.

Johnson, J. D. (1993). *Organizational communication structure.* Norwood, NJ: Ablex.

Johnson-Laird, P. N. (1983). *Mental models: Toward a cognitive science of language, inference, and consciousness.* Cambridge, MA: Harvard University Press.

Jones, C., Hesterly, W. S., & Borgatti, S. P. (1997). A general theory of network governance: Exchange conditions and social mechanisms. *Academy of Management Review, 22,* 911–945.

Kadushin, C. (1983). Mental health and the interpersonal environment: A reexamination of some effects of social structure on mental health. *American Sociological Review, 48,* 188–198.

Kadushin, C., & Brimm, M. (1990). *Why networking fails: Double binds and the limitations of shadow networks.* Paper presented at the tenth annual International Sunbelt Social Networks Conference, San Diego, California.

Kahneman, D., Slovic, P., & Tversky, A. (1982). *Judgment under uncertainty: Heuristics and biases*. Cambridge, UK: Cambridge University Press.

Kahneman, D., & Tversky, A. (1979). Prospect theory: An analysis of decision under risk. *Econometrica, 47*, 263–291.

Kalman, M. E., Fulk, J., & Monge, P. R. (2001). *Resolving communication dilemmas: A motivational model for information contribution to discretionary databases*. Unpublished manuscript currently under publication review, Annenberg School for Communication, University of Southern California.

Kalman, M. E., Monge, P. R., Fulk, J., & Heino, R. (2002). Resolving communication dilemmas in database-mediate collaboration. *Communication Research, 29*, 125–154.

Kaufer, D. S., & Carley, K. M. (1993). *Communication at a distance: The effect of print on socio-cultural organization and change*. Hillsdale, NJ: Erlbaum.

Kauffman, S. A. (1993). *The origins of order: Self-organizing and selection in evolution*. New York: Oxford University Press.

Kauffman, S. A. (1995). *At home in the universe: The search for the laws of self-organization and complexity*. New York: Oxford University Press.

Kautz, H., Selman, B., & Shah, M. (1997). Combining social networks and collaborative filtering. *Communications of the ACM, 40*, 63–65.

Kawakami, K., & Papia, D. (1995). *101 unuseless Japanese inventions: The art of Chindogu*. New York: Norton.

Kerr, N. L. (1992). Efficacy as a causal and moderating variable in social dilemmas. In W. B. G. Liebrand, D. M. Messick, & H. A. M. Wilke (Eds.), *Social dilemmas: Theoretical issues and research findings* (pp. 59–80). New York: Pergamon.

Khurana, R. (1997). *Director interlocks and outsider CEO selection: A field and statistical examination of the Fortune 500 between 1990–1995*. Unpublished doctoral dissertation, Harvard Business School, Harvard University.

Kiernan, V. (November 5, 1999). The "Open-Source Movement" turns its eye to science. *Chronicle of Higher Education*, A51. Available online at: http://chronicle.com/free/v46/i11/11a05101.htm

Kilduff, M. (1992). The friendship network as a decision-making resource: Disposition moderators of social influences on organizational choice. *Journal of Personality and Social Psychology, 62*, 168–180.

Kilduff, M., & Krackhardt, D. (1993). *Schemas at work: Making sense of organizational relationships*. Unpublished manuscript, Department of Sociology, Pennsylvania State University.

Kilduff, M., & Krackhardt, D. (1994). Bringing the individual back in: A structural analysis of the internal market for reputation in organizations. *Academy of Management Journal, 37*, 87–108.

Kleinberg, J. (2000). Navigation in a small world. *Nature, 406*, 845.

Kleinberg, J., & Lawrence, S. (2001). The structure of the web. *Science, 294*, 1849–1850.

Knoke, D. (1990). *Political networks: The structural perspective*. Cambridge, UK: Cambridge University Press.

Knoke, D. (1993). Networks of elite structure and decision making. *Sociological Methods & Research*, *22*, 23–45.

Knoke, D., and Kuklinski, J. (1982). *Network analysis*. Newbury Park, CA: Sage.

Knorr-Cetina, K. (1981). *The manufacture of knowledge*. Oxford: Pergamon.

Kochen, M. (1989). *The small world*. Norwood, NJ: Ablex.

Kogut, B., Shan, W., & Walker, G. (1993). Knowledge in the network and the network as knowledge: Structuring of new industries. In G. Grabher (Ed.), *The embedded firm: On the socioeconomics of industrial networks* (pp. 67–94). New York: Routledge.

Kontopoulos, K. M. (1993). *The logics of social structure*. New York: Cambridge University Press.

Korzenny, F., & Bauer, C. (1981). Testing the theory of electronic propinquity: Organizational teleconferencing. *Communication Research*, *8*, 479–498.

Kosnik, R. D. (1987). Greenmail: A study of board performance in corporate governance. *Administrative Science Quarterly*, *32*, 163–185.

Krackhardt, D. (1987a). Cognitive social structures. *Social Networks*, *9*, 109–134.

Krackhardt, D. (1987b). QAP—Partialing as a test of spuriousness. *Social Networks*, *9*, 171–186.

Krackhardt, D. (1990). Assessing the political landscape: Structure, cognition, and power in organizations. *Administrative Science Quarterly*, *35*, 342–369.

Krackhardt, D. (1992). The strength of strong ties: The importance of Philos. In N. Nohria & R. Eccles (Eds.), *Networks and organizations: Structure, form and action* (pp. 216–239). Boston: Harvard Business School Press.

Krackhardt, D. (1994). Constraints on the interactive organization as an ideal type. In C. Heckscher & A. Donnellon (Eds.), *The post-bureaucratic organization: New perspectives on organizational change* (pp. 211–222). Thousand Oaks, CA: Sage.

Krackhardt, D. (2001). Viscosity models and the diffusion of controversial innovations. In A. Lomi & E. R. Larsen (Eds.), *Dynamics of organizations: Computational modeling and organizational theories* (pp. 243–268). Menlo Park, CA: AAAI Press/MIT Press.

Krackhardt, D., & Brass, D. J. (1994). Intra-organizational networks: The micro side. In S. Wasserman & J. Galaskiewicz (Eds.), *Advances in social network analysis: Research in the social and behavioral sciences* (pp. 207–229). Thousand Oaks, CA: Sage.

Krackhardt, D., & Hanson, J. R. (1993). Informal networks: The company behind the chart. *Harvard Business Review*, *71*, 104.

Krackhardt, D., & Kilduff, M. (1990). Friendship patterns and culture: The control of organizational diversity. *American Anthropologist*, *92*, 142–154.

Krackhardt, D., & Porter, L. (1986). The snowball effect: Turnover embedded in social networks. *Journal of Applied Psychology*, *71*, 50–55.

Krackhardt, D., & Porter, L. W. (1985). When friends leave: A structural analysis of the relationship between turnover and stayers' attitudes. *Administrative Science Quarterly*, *30*, 242–261.

Krackhardt, D., & Stern, R. N. (1988). Informal networks and organizational crises: An experimental situation. *Social Psychology Quarterly, 51*, 123–140.

Kramer, M. W. (1996). A longitudinal study of peer communication during job transfers: The impact of frequency, quality, and network multiplexity on adjustment. *Human Communication Research, 23*, 59–86.

Krassa, M. A. (1988). Social groups, selective perception, and behavioral contagion in public opinion. *Social Networks, 10*, 109–136.

Kraut, R. E., Egido, C., & Galegher, J. (1990). Patterns of contact and communication in scientific research collaboration. In J. Galegher, R. E. Kraut, & C. Egido (Eds.), *Intellectual teamwork: Social and technological foundations of cooperative work* (pp. 149–172). Hillsdale, NJ: Erlbaum.

Kraut, R., Patterson, M., Lundmark, V., Kiesler, S., Mukopadhyay, T., & Scherlis, W. (1998). Internet paradox: A social technology that reduces social involvement and psychological well-being. *American Psychologist, 53*, 1017–1031.

Krebs, V. (2002). Mapping networks of terrorist cells. *Connections, 24*, 43–52.

Krikorian, D. D., Seibold, D. R., & Goode, P. L. (1997). Reengineering at LAC: A case study of emergent network processes. In B. D. Sypher (Ed.), *Case studies in organizational communication 2: Perspectives on contemporary work life* (pp. 129–144). New York: Guilford.

Labianca, G., Brass, D., & Gray, B. (1998). Social networks and the perceptions of intergroup conflict: The role of negative relationships and third parties. *Academy of Management Journal, 41*, 55–67.

Land, K. C. (1969). Principles of path analysis. In E. F. Borgatta & G. W. Bohrnstedt (Eds.), *Sociological methodology, 1969* (pp. 23–37). San Francisco: Jossey-Bass.

Langford, C. P. H., Bowsher, J., Maloney, J. P., & Lillis, P. P. (1997). Social support: A conceptual analysis. *Journal of Advanced Nursing, 25*, 95–100.

Langton, C., Burkhart, R., Lee, I., Daniels, M., & Lancaster, A. (1998). *The Swarm Simulation System*. Available at: http://www.santafe.edu/projects/swarm

Larson, A. (1992). Network dyads in entrepreneurial settings: A study of the governance of exchange relations. *Administrative Science Quarterly, 37*, 76–14.

Larson, A., & Starr, J. A. (1993). A network model of organization formation. *Entrepreneurship: Theory and Practice, 17*, 5–15.

Lash, S., & Urry, J. (1994). *Economies of signs and space*. Thousand Oaks, CA: Sage.

Lasswell, H. (1948). The structure and function of communication in society. In L. Bryson (Ed.), *The communication of ideas: A series of addresses*. New York: Harper.

Latane, B. (2000). Pressures to uniformity and the evolution of cultural norms: Modeling dynamic social impacts. In D. R. Ilgen & C. L. Hulin (Eds.), *Computational modeling of behavior in organizations: The third scientific discipline*. Washington, DC: American Psychological Association.

Laumann, E. O. (1966). *Prestige and association in an urban community.* Indianapolis, IN: Bobbs–Merrill.

Laumann, E. O., Knoke, D., & Kim, Y. (1985). An organizational approach to state policymaking: A comparative study of energy and health domains. *American Sociological Review, 50,* 1–19.

Laumann, E. O., & Pappi, F. U. (1976). *Networks of collective action.* New York: Academic Press.

Lawrence, R. R., & Lorsch, J. W. (1967). *Organization and environment: Managing differentiation and integration.* Cambridge, MA: Harvard University Press.

Lazarsfeld, P. F. (1941). Remarks on administrative and critical communications research. *Studies in Philosophy and Social Sciences* 9(1).

Lazerson, M. (1993). Factory or putting out? Knitting networks in Modena. In G. Grabher (Ed.), *The embedded firm: On the socioeconomics of industrial networks* (pp. 203–226). New York: Routledge.

Leavitt, H. J. (1951). Some effects of certain communication patterns on group performance. *Journal of Abnormal and Social Psychology, 46,* 38–50.

Leblebici, H., & Salancik, G. R. (1981). Effects of environmental uncertainty on information and decision processes in banks. *Administrative Science Quarterly, 26,* 578–596.

Leenders, R. T. A. J. (1996). Evolution of friendship and best friendship choices. *Journal of Mathematical Sociology, 21,* 133–148.

Lerner, J., & Tirole, J. (2000). *The simple economics of Open Source.* Cambridge, MA: National Bureau of Economic Research, Inc., Working Paper 7600.

Lesperance, Y. (1991). A formal theory of indexical knowledge and action. Technical report. University of Toronto. Computer Systems Research Institute; CSRI-248 Toronto, Ontario, Canada: University of Toronto, Computer Systems Research Institute.

Lessig L. (2001). *The future of ideas: The fate of the commons in a connected world.* New York: Random House.

Levine, J. H., & White, P. (1961). Exchange as a conceptual framework for the study of interorganizational relationships. *Administrative Science Quarterly, 5,* 583–601.

Levinthal, D. A. (1994). Surviving Schumpeterian environments: An evolutionary perspective. In J. A. C. Baum & J. V. Singh (Eds.), *Evolutionary dynamics of organizations* (pp. 167–178). New York: Oxford University Press.

Levinthal, D. A. (2001). Modeling adaptation on rugged landscapes. In A. Lomi & E. R. Larsen (Eds.), *Dynamics of organizations: Computational modeling and organization theories* (pp. 329–348). Cambridge, MA: MIT Press.

Levinthal, D. A., & Warglien, M. (1999). Landscape design: Designing for local action in complex worlds. *Organization Science, 10,* 342–357.

Levitt, R. E., Cohen, G. P., Kunz, J. C., Nass, C. I., Christiansen, T. R. & Jin, Y. (1994). The virtual design team: Simulating how organization structure and information processing tools affect team performance. In K. Carley & M. Prietula (Eds.), *Computational Organization Theory* (pp. 1–18). Hinsdale, NJ: Erlbaum.

Lewin, A. Y., & Volberda, H. W. (1999). Prolegomena on coevolution: A framework for research on strategy and new organizational forms. *Organization Science, 10,* 519–534.

Lewin, A. Y., Long, C. P., & Carroll, T. N. (1999). The coevolution of new organizational forms. *Organization Science, 10,* 535–550.

Lewin, K. (1936). *Principles of topological psychology* (F. Heider and G. Heider, Trans.). New York: McGraw Hill.

Liang, D. W., Moreland, R. L., & Argote, L. (1995). Group versus individual training and group performance: The mediating role of transactive memory. *Personality and Social Psychology Bulletin, 21,* 384–393.

Liebeskind, J. P., Oliver, A. L., Zucker, L, & Brewer, M. (1996). Social networks, learning, and flexibility: Sourcing scientific knowledge in new biotechnology firms. *Organization Science, 7,* 428–443.

Liedka, R. V. (1991). Who do you know in the group? Location of organizations in interpersonal networks. *Social Forces, 70,* 455–474.

Lievrouw, L. A., & Carley, K. (1991). Changing patterns of communication among scientists in an era of "Telescience." *Technology in Society, 12,* 457–477.

Lievrouw, L. A., Rogers, E. M., Lowe, C. U., & Nadel, E. (1987). Triangulation as a research strategy for identifying invisible colleges among biomedical students. *Social Networks, 9,* 217–248.

Lin, N. (2001). Building a network theory of social capital. In N. Lin, K. Cook, & R. S. Burt (Eds.), *Social capital: Theory and research* (pp. 3–30). New York: de Gruyter.

Lin, N., & Ensel, W. M. (1989). Life stress and health: Stressors and resources. *American Sociological Review, 54,* 382–399.

Lin, N., Ensel, W. M., & Vaughn, J. C. (1981). Social resources and strength of ties: Structural factors in occupational status attainment. *American Sociological Review, 46,* 393–405.

Lin, Z., & Carley, K. M. (1995). DYCORP: A computational framework for examining organizational performance under dynamic conditions. *Journal of Mathematical Sociology, 20,* 193–218.

Lincoln, J. R., Gerlach, M. L., & Takahashi, P. (1992). *Keiretsu* networks in the Japanese economy: A dyad analysis of intercorporate ties. *American Sociological Review, 57,* 561–585.

Lincoln, J., & Miller, J. (1979). Work and friendship ties in organizations: A comparative analysis of relational networks. *Administrative Science Quarterly, 24,* 181–199.

Lipnack, J., & Stamps, J. (1997). *Virtual teams: Reaching across space, time and organizations with technology.* New York: Wiley.

Littlepage, G., Robison, W., & Reddington, K. (1997). Effects of task experience and group experience on group performance, member ability, and recognition of expertise. *Organizational Behavior and Human Decision Processes, 69,* 133–147.

Litwak, E., & Hylton, L. F. (1962). Interorganizational analysis: A hypothesis on coordinating agencies. *Administrative Science Quarterly, 6,* 392–420.

Lomi, A., & Larsen, E. R. (2001). Failure as a structural concept: A computational perspective on age dependence in organizational mortality rates. In A. Lomi & E. R. Larsen (Eds.), *Dynamics of organizations: Computational modeling and organizational theories* (pp. 269–303). Menlo Park, CA: AAAI Press/MIT Press.

Lomi, A., & Larsen, E. R. (Eds.) (2001). *Dynamics of organizations: Computational modeling and organizational theories.* Menlo Park, CA: AAAI Press/MIT Press.

Lorrain, F., & White, H. (1971). Structural equivalence of individuals in social networks. *Journal of Mathematical Sociology, 1,* 49–80.

Lott, B. E., & Lott, A. J. (1960). The formation of positive attitudes toward group members. *Journal of Abnormal Social Psychology, 61,* 297–300.

Luhmann, N. (1990). *Essays on self-reference.* New York: Columbia University Press.

Luhmann, N. (1992). Autopoiesis. What is communication? *Communication Theory, 2,* 251–259.

Malone, T. W., & Crowston, K. (1992). What is coordination theory and how can it help design cooperative work systems. In D. Marca & G. Bock (Eds.), *Groupware: Software for computer-supported cooperative work* (pp. 100–115). Washington: IEEE Press.

Malone, T. W., & Laubacher, R. J. (1998, September–October). The dawn of the e-lance economy. *Harvard Business Review, 76,* 145–152.

Malone, T. W., & Rockart, J. F. (1991). Computers, networks, and the corporation. *Scientific American, 265,* 128–136.

March, J. G. (1991). Exploration and exploitation in organizational learning. *Organization Science, 2,* 71–87.

March, J. G. (1994). The evolution of evolution. In J. A. C. Baum & J. V. Singh (Eds.), *Evolutionary dynamics of organizations* (pp. 39–49). New York: Oxford University Press.

March, J. (2001). Foreword. In A. Lomi & E. R. Larsen (Eds.), *Dynamics of organizations: Computational modeling and organizational theories* (pp. ix–xvii). Menlo Park, CA: AAAI Press/MIT Press.

March, J. G., & Weissinger-Baylon, R. (1986). *Ambiguity and command: Organizational perspectives on military decision making.* Marshfield, MA: Pitman.

Marchiori, M, & Latora, V. (2000). Harmony in the small world. *Physica A 285,* 539, http://xxx.lanl.gov/abs/cond-mat/0008357

Markovsky, B. (1997). Network games. *Rationality and Society, 9,* 67–90.

Markovsky, B., Willer, D., & Patton, T. (1988). Power relations in exchange networks. *American Sociological Review, 53,* 220–236.

Markus, M. L. (1990). Toward a "critical mass" theory of interactive media. In J. Fulk & C. Steinfield (Eds.), *Organizations and communication technology* (pp. 194–218). Newbury Park, CA: Sage.

Markus, M. L., & Robey, D. (1988). Information technology and organizational change: Causal structure in theory and research. *Management Science, 34,* 583–598.

Marsden, P. V. (1988). Homogeneity in confiding relations. *Social Networks, 10,* 57–76.

Marsden, P. V. (1990). Network data and measurement. *Annual Review of Sociology, 16,* 435–463.

Marsden, P. V., & Friedkin, N. E. (1994). Network studies of social influence. In S. Wasserman & J. Galaskiewicz (Eds.), *Advances in social network analysis: Research in the social and behavioral sciences* (pp. 3–25). Thousand Oaks, CA: Sage.

Maruyama, M. (1982). Four different causal metatypes in biological and social sciences. In W. C. Schieve & P. M. Allen (Eds.), *Self-organization and dissipative structures: Applications in the physical and social sciences* (pp. 354–361). Austin: University of Texas Press.

Marwell, G., & Oliver, P. (1993). *The critical mass in collective action: A micro-social theory.* Cambridge, UK: Cambridge University Press.

Marwell, G., Oliver, P. E., & Prahl, R. (1988). Social networks and collective action: A theory of the critical mass, III. *American Journal of Sociology, 94,* 502–534.

Mattelart, A. (2000). *Networking the world: 1794–2000* (L. Carey-Libbrecht & J. A. Cohen, Trans.). Minneapolis: University of Minnesota Press. (Original work published 1996)

Mattelart, A., & Mattelart, M. (1998). *Theories of communication: A short introduction* (S. G. Taponier & J. A. Cohen, Trans.). Thousand Oaks, CA: Sage.

Maturana, H. R., & Varela, F. J. (1980). Autopoiesis and cognition: The realization of the living. In R. S. Cohen & M. W. Wartofsky (Eds.), Boston studies in the philosophy of science (Vol. 42). Dordrecht, Holland: Reidel.

McCulloch, W. S. (1945). A heterarchy of values determined by the typology of nervous nets. *Bulletin of Mathematical Biophysics, 7,* 89–93.

McCulloch, W. S. (1965). *Embodiments of mind.* Cambridge, MA: MIT Press.

McElroy, J. C., & Shrader, C. B. (1986). Attribution theories of leadership and network analysis. *Journal of Management, 12,* 351–362.

McGuire, W. J. (1966). Attitudes and opinions. *Annual Review of Psychology, 17,* 475–514.

McKelvey, B. (1982). *Organizational systematics: Taxonomy, evolution, and classification.* Berkeley: University of California Press.

McKelvey, B. (1997). Quasi-natural organization science. *Organization Science, 8,* 352–380.

McKelvey, B. (1999a). Avoiding complexity catastrophe in coevolutionary pockets; Strategies for rugged landscapes. *Organization Science, 10,* 294–321.

McKelvey, B. (1999b). Self-organization, complexity catastrophe, and microstate models at the edge of chaos. In J. A. C. Baum & B. McKelvey (Eds.), *Variations in organization science: In honor of Donald T. Campbell* (pp. 279–307). Thousand Oaks, CA: Sage.

McKelvey, B., & Baum, J. A. C. (1999). Donald T. Campbell's evolving influence on organization science. In J. A. C. Baum & B. McKelvey (Eds.), *Variations in organization science: In honor of Donald T. Campbell* (pp. 1–15). Thousand Oaks, CA: Sage.

McKendrick, D. G., & Carroll, G. R. (2001). On the genesis of organizational forms: Evidence from the market for disk arrays. *Organization Science, 12,* 661–682.

McPhee, R. D., & Corman, S. R. (1995). An activity-based theory of communication networks in organizations, applied to the case of a local church. *Communication Monographs, 62,* 1–20.

McPhee, R. D., & Poole, M. S. (2001). Organizational structures and configurations. In F. M. Jablin & L. L. Putnam (Eds.), *The new handbook of organizational communication: Advances in theory, research, and methods* (pp. 503–543). Thousand Oaks, CA: Sage.

McPherson, J. M., Popielarz, P. A., & Drobnic, S. (1992). Social networks and organizational dynamics. *American Sociological Review, 57,* 153–170.

McPherson, J. M., & Smith-Lovin, L. (1987). Homophily in voluntary organizations: Status distance and the composition of face to face groups. *American Sociological Review, 52,* 370–379.

Merry, U. (1995). *Coping with uncertainty: Insights from the new science of chaos, self-organization, and complexity.* Westport, CT: Praeger.

Merton, R. K. (1949). *Social theory and social structure.* Glencoe, IL: Free Press.

Messick, D. M., & Brewer, M. B. (1983). Solving social dilemmas: A review. In L. Wheeler & P. Shaver (Eds.), *Review of personality and social psychology* (Vol. 4, pp. 11–44). Beverly Hills, CA: Sage.

Meyer, J. W., & Rowan, B. (1977). Institutionalized organizations: Formal structure as myth and ceremony. *American Journal of Sociology, 83,* 340–363.

Mezias, S. J., & Lant, T. K. (1994). Mimetic learning and the evolution of organizational populations. In J. A. C. Baum & J. V. Singh (Eds.), *Evolutionary dynamics of organizations* (pp. 179–198). New York: Oxford University Press.

Michaelson, A., & Contractor, N. (1992). Comparison of relational and positional predictors of group member's perceptions. *Social Psychology Quarterly, 55,* 300–310.

Micro Analysis and Design Simulation Software. (1990). *Getting started with MicroSaint.* [Computer program manual]. Boulder, CO: Micro Analysis and Design Simulation Software Inc.

Miles, R. E. (1980). *Macro organizational behavior.* Santa Monica, CA: Goodyear.

Miles, R. E., & Snow, C. C. (1986). Organizations: New concepts for new forms. *California Management Review, 28,* 62–73.

Miles, R. E., & Snow, C. C. (1992, Summer). Causes of failure in network organizations. *California Management Review, 34,* 53–72.

Miles, R. E., & Snow, C. C. (1995). The new network firm: A spherical structure built on a human investment philosophy. *Organizational Dynamics, 23,* 5–18.

Milgram, S. (1967). The small world problem. *Psychology Today, 2,* 60–67.

Miller, C. C., Glick, W. H., Wang, Y. D., & Huber, G. P. (1991). Understanding technology-structure relationships: Theory development and meta-analytic theory testing. *Academy of Management Journal, 34,* 370–399.

Miller, J. G. (1978). *Living systems.* New York: McGraw-Hill.

Miller, K. I., & Monge, P. R. (1985). Social information and employee anxiety about organizational change. *Human Communication Research, 11,* 365–386.

Minar, M., & Hedland, M. (2001). A network of peers: Peer-to-peer models through the history of the Internet. In A. Oram (Ed.), *Peer-to-peer: Harnessing the power of disruptive technologies* (pp. 3–20). Sebastopol, CA: O'Reilly & Associates.

Miner, A. S. (1994). Seeking adaptive advantage: Evolutionary theory and managerial action. In J. A. C. Baum & J. V. Singh (Eds.), *Evolutionary dynamics of organizations* (pp. 76–89). New York: Oxford University Press.

Miner, A. S., Amburgey, T. L., & Stearns, T. M. (1990). Interorganizational linkages and population dynamics: Buffering and transformational shields. *Administrative Science Quarterly, 35,* 689–713.

Miner, A. S., & Raghavan, S. V. (1999). Interorganizational imitation: A hidden engine of selection. In J. A. C. Baum & B. McKelvey (Eds.), *Variations in organization science: In honor of Donald T. Campbell* (pp. 35–62). Thousand Oaks, CA: Sage.

Minsky, M. A. (1975). A framework for representing knowledge. In P. Winston (Ed.), *The psychology of computer vision.* New York: McGraw-Hill.

Mintz, B., & Schwartz, M. (1985). *The power structure of American business.* Chicago, IL: University of Chicago Press.

Mitchell, J. C. (1973). Networks, norms and institutions. In J. Boissevain & J. C. Mitchell (Eds.), *Network analysis* (pp. 15–35). The Hague, Netherlands: Mouton.

Mizruchi, M. S. (1989). Similarity of political behavior among large American corporations. *American Journal of Sociology, 95,* 401–424.

Mizruchi, M. S. (1992). *The structure of corporate political action.* Cambridge, MA: Harvard University Press.

Mizruchi, M. S. (1996). What do interlocks do? An analysis, critique, and assessment of research on interlocking directorates. *Annual Review of Sociology, 22,* 271–298.

Mizruchi, M. S., & Galaskiewicz, J. (1994). Networks of interorganizational relations. In S. Wasserman and J. Galaskiewicz (Eds.), *Advances in social network analysis: Research in the social and behavioral sciences* (pp. 230–253). Thousand Oaks, CA: Sage.

Mizruchi, M. S., & Stearns, L. B. (1988). A longitudinal study of the formation of interlocking directorates. *Administrative Science Quarterly, 33,* 194–210.

Monge, P. R. (1977). Alternative theoretical bases for the study of human communication. *Communication Quarterly, 25,* 19–29.

Monge, P. R. (1987). The network level of analysis. In C. R. Berger & S. H. Chaffee (Eds.), *Handbook of communication science* (pp. 239–270). Newbury Park, CA: Sage.

Monge, P. R. (1995). Global network organizations. In R. Cesaria & P. Shockley-Zalabak (Eds.), *Organization means communication* (pp. 135–151). Rome, Italy: SIPI.

Monge, P. R. (1998). Communication structures and processes in globalization. *Journal of Communication, 48,* 142–153.

Monge, P. R., & Contractor, N. (1988). Communication networks: Measurement techniques. In C. H. Tardy (Ed.), *A handbook for the study of human communication* (pp. 107–138). Norwood, NJ: Ablex.

Monge, P. R., & Contractor, N. S. (2001). Emergence of communication networks. In F. Jablin & L. L. Putnam (Eds.), *The new handbook of organizational communication* (pp. 440–502). Thousand Oaks, CA: Sage.

Monge, P. R., Cozzens, M. D., & Contractor, N. S. (1992). Communication and motivational predictors of the dynamics of organizational innovation. *Organization Science, 3,* 250–274.

Monge, P. R., & Eisenberg, E. M. (1987). Emergent communication networks. In F. M. Jablin, L. L. Putnam, K. H. Roberts, and L. W. Porter (Eds.), *Handbook of organizational communication* (pp. 304–342). Newbury Park, CA: Sage.

Monge, P. R. & Fulk, J. (1999). Communication technology for global network organizations. In G. DeSanctis & J. Fulk (Eds.), *Shaping organizational form: Communication, connection, community* (pp. 71–100). Thousand Oaks, CA: Sage.

Monge, P. R., Fulk, J., Kalman, M., Flanagin, A. J., Parnassa, C., & Rumsey, S. (1998). Production of collective action in alliance-based interorganizational communication and information systems. *Organization Science, 9,* 411–433.

Monge, P. R., & Kalman, M. (1996). Sequentiality, simultaneity, and synchronicity in human communication. In J. Watt & A. Van Lear (Eds.), *Cycles and dynamic patterns in communication processes* (pp. 71–92). New York: Ablex.

Monge, P. R., Rothman, L. W., Eisenberg, E. M., Miller, K. I., & Kirste, K. K. (1985). The dynamics of organizational proximity. *Management Science, 31,* 1129–1141.

Moore, G. (1992). Gender and informal networks in state government. *Social Science Quarterly, 73,* 46–61.

Moreland, R. L. (1999). Transactive memory: Learning who knows what in work groups and organizations. In L. Thompson, D. Messick, & J. Levine (Eds.), *Sharing knowledge in organizations* (pp. 3–31). Mahwah, NJ: Erlbaum.

Moreland, R. L., & Argote, L. (in press). Transactive memory in dynamic organizations. In R. Peterson & E. Mannix (Eds.), *Understanding the dynamic organization.* Mahwah, NJ: Erlbaum.

Moreland, R. L., Argote, L., & Krishnan, T. (1996). Social shared cognition at work: Transactive memory and group performance. In J. L. Nye and A. M. Brower (Eds.), *What's social about social cognition? Research on socially shared cognition in small groups* (pp. 57–84). Thousand Oaks, CA: Sage.

Morgan, G. (1997). *Images of organization* (2nd ed.). Newbury Park, CA: Sage.

Moscovici, S. (1976). *Social influence and social change.* London: Academic Press.

Nadel, S. F. (1957). *The theory of social structure*. New York: Free Press.

Nardi, B., Whittaker, S., Isaacs, E., Creech, M., Johnson, J., & Hainsworth, J. (2002). Integrating communication and information through ContactMap. *Communications of the ACM, 45*, 89–95.

Nelson, R. E. (1989). The strength of strong ties: Social networks and intergroup conflict in organizations. *Academy of Management Journal, 32*, 377–401.

Nelson, R. R., & Winter, S. G. (1982). *An evolutionary theory of economic change*. Cambridge, MA: Belknap Press of Harvard University Press.

Newell, S., & Clark, P. (1990). The importance of extra-organizational networks in the diffusion and appropriation of new technologies. *Knowledge: Creation, Diffusion, Utilization, 12*, 199–212.

Nishida, T., Takeda, H., Iwazume, M., Maeda, H., & Takaai, M. (1998). The knowledge community: Facilitating human knowledge sharing. In T. Ishida (Ed.), *Community computing: Collaboration over global information networks* (pp. 127–164). Chichester, UK: Wiley.

Nohria, N., & Berkley, J. D. (1994). The virtual organization: Bureaucracy, technology, and the implosion of control. In C. Hekscher & A. Donnellon (Eds.), *The post-bureaucratic organization: New perspectives on organizational change* (pp. 108–128). Thousand Oaks, CA: Sage.

Norling, P. M. (1996). Network or not work: Harnessing technology networks in DuPont. *Research Technology Management, 39*, 42–48.

Norman, D. (1999, May–June). Affordance, conventions, and design. *Interactions*, 38–44.

Norman, R., & Ramirez, R. (1993, July–August). From value chain to value constellation: Designing interactive strategy. *Harvard Business Review, 71*, 65–77.

Numata, J., & Taura, T. (1996). A case study: A network system for knowledge amplification in the product development process. *IEEE Transactions on Engineering Management, 43*, 356–367.

Ogliastri, E., & Davila, C. (1987). The articulation of power and business structures: A study of Colombia. In M. Mizruchi & M. Schwartz (Eds.), *Intercorporate relations* (pp. 233–263). New York: Cambridge University Press.

O'Hara-Devereaux, M., & Johansen, R. (1994). *Globalwork*. San Francisco: Jossey-Bass

Oliver, A. L., & Montgomery, K. (1996). A network approach to outpatient service delivery systems: Resources flow and system influence. *Health Services Research, 30*, 771–789.

Oliver, C. (1990). Determinants of interorganizational relationships: Integration and future directions. *Academy of Management Review, 15*, 241–265.

Oliver, C. (1991). Network relations and loss of organizational autonomy. *Human Relations, 44*, 943–961.

Oliver, P. E. (1980). Rewards and punishments as selective incentives for collective action: Theoretical investigations. *American Journal of Sociology, 8*, 1356–1375.

Oliver, P. E. (1993). Formal models of collective action. *Annual Review of Sociology, 19*, 271–300.

Olson, M., Jr. (1965). *The logic of collective action.* Cambridge, MA: Harvard University Press.

O'Mahony, S., & Barley, S. R. (1999). Do digital telecommunications affect work and organization? The state of our knowledge. *Research in organizational behavior* (Vol. 21, pp. 125–61). Greenwich, CT: JAI.

Oram, A. (Ed.) (2001). *Peer-to-peer: Harnessing the power of disruptive technologies.* Sebastopol, CA: O'Reilly & Associates.

O'Reilly, P. (1988). Methodological issues in social support and social network research. *Social Science and Medicine, 26*, 863–873.

Orlikowski, W. (1992). The duality of technology: Rethinking the concept of technology in organizations. *Organization Science, 3*, 398–427.

Orlikowski, W. (2000). Using technology and constituting structures: A practice lens for studying technology in organizations. *Organization Science, 11*, 404–428.

Padgett, J. F., & Ansell, C. K. (1993). Robust action and the rise of the Medici, 1400–1434. *American Journal of Sociology, 98*, 1259–1319.

Page, S. E. (1997). On incentives and updating in agent-based models. *Computational Economics, 10*, 67–87.

Palazzolo, E. T., Serb, D., She, Y., Su, C., & Contractor, N. (2002). *Co-evolution of communication and knowledge networks as transactive memory systems: Using computational models for theoretical integration and extensions.* Manuscript submitted for publication. University of Illinois at Urbana-Champaign.

Palmer, D., Friedland, R., & Singh, J. V. (1986). The ties that bind: Organizational and class bases of stability in a corporate interlock network. *American Sociological Review, 51*, 781–796.

Palmer, D., Jennings, P. D., & Zhou, X. (1993). Late adoption of the multidivisional form by large U.S. corporations: Institutional, political and economic accounts. *Administrative Science Quarterly, 38*, 100–131.

Papa, M. J. (1990). Communication network patterns and employee performance with new technology. *Communication Research, 17*, 344–368.

Parsons, T. (1937). *The structure of social action.* New York: McGraw-Hill.

Parsons, T. (1951). *The social system.* New York: Free Press.

Paterniti, R., Chellini, F., Sacchetti, & Tognelli, M. (1996). Psychiatric rehabilitation and its relation to the social network. *International Journal of Mental Health, 25*, 83–87.

Pattison, P. (1993). *Algebraic models for social networks.* New York: Cambridge University Press.

Pattison, P. (1994). Social cognition in context: Some applications of social network analysis. In S. Wasserman & J. Galaskiewicz (Eds.), *Advances in social network analysis: Research in the social and behavioral sciences* (pp. 79–109). Thousand Oaks, CA: Sage.

Pattison, P., & Wasserman, S. (1999). Logit models and logistic regressions for social networks, II: Multivariate relations. *British Journal of Mathematical and Statistical Psychology, 52*, 169–193.

Pfeffer, J., & Salancik, G. (1978). *The external control of organizations*. New York: Harper & Row.

Picot, A. (1993). Structures of industrial organization—Implications for information and communication technology. In W. Kaiser (Ed.), *Vision 2000: The evolution of information and communication technology for the information society* (pp. 278–293). Munich, Germany: Munchner Kreis.

Pink, D. H. (2001). *Free agent nation: How America's new independent workers are transforming the way we live*. New York: Warner Brothers.

Piore, M. J. (1975). Notes for a theory of labor market stratification. In R. Edwards, M. Reich, & D. Gordon (Eds.), *Labor market segmentation* (pp. 125–150). Lexington, MA: Heath.

Piore, M. J., & Sabel, C. F. (1984). *The second industrial divide: Possibilities for prosperity*. New York: Basic.

Podolny, J. M., Stuart, T. E., & Hannan, M. T. (1996). Networks, knowledge, and niches: Competition in the worldwide semiconductor industry, 1984–1991. *American Journal of Sociology, 102*, 659–689.

Pogue, D. (2002, March 28). Wish list: 9 innovations in search of inventors. *New York Times*, Circuits, G1.

Polanyi, K. (1957). *The great transformation*. Boston, MA: Beacon.

Pollock, T., Whitbred, R. A., & Contractor, N. (2000). Social information processing and job characteristics: A simultaneous test of two theories with implications for job satisfaction. *Human Communication Research, 26*, 292–330.

Pool, I. de S., Decker, C., Dizard, S., Israel, K., Rubin, P., & Weinstein, B. (1977). Foresight and hindsight: The case of the telephone. In I. de S. Pool (Ed.), *The social impact of the telephone* (pp. 127–157). Cambridge, MA: MIT Press.

Poole, M. S. (1997). A turn of the wheel: The case for renewal of systems inquiry in organizational communication research. In G. Barnett & L. Thayer (Eds.), *Organization communication: Emerging perspectives (Vol. 5. The renaissance in systems thinking*, pp. 47–63). Greenwich, CT: Ablex.

Poole, M. S. (1999). Organizational challenges for the new forms. In G. DeSanctis & J. Fulk (Eds.), *Shaping organizational form: Communication, connection, and community* (pp. 453–471). Thousand Oaks, CA: Sage.

Poole, M. S., & DeSanctis, G. (1990). Understanding the use of group decision support systems: The theory of adaptive structuration. In J. Fulk & C. Steinfield (Eds.), *Organizations and communication technology* (pp. 173–193). Newbury Park: Sage.

Poole, M. S., & McPhee, R. (1983). A structurational example of organizational climate. In L. Putnam & M. Pacanowsky (Eds.), *Organizational communication* (pp. 195–220). Beverly Hills, CA: Sage.

Porter, M. E. (1980). *Competitive strategy: Techniques for analyzing industries and competitors*. New York: Free Press.

Powell, W. W. (1990). Neither market nor hierarchy: Network forms of organization. In L. L. Cummings & B. Staw (Eds.), *Research in organizational behavior* (pp. 295–336). Greenwich, CT: JAI.

Powell, W. W., Koput, K. W., & Smith-Doerr, L. (1996). Interorganizational collaboration and the locus of innovation: Networks of learning in biotechnology. *Administrative Science Quarterly, 41,* 116–145.

Prietula, M. (2001). Advice, trust and gossip among artificial agents. In A. Lomi & E. R. Larsen (Eds.), *Dynamics of organizations: Computational modeling and organizational theories* (pp. 141–177). Menlo Park, CA: AAAI Press/MIT Press.

Prietula, M. J., Carley, K. M., & Gasser, L. (1998). *Simulating organizations: Computational models of institutions and groups.* Menlo Park, CA: AAAI Press; Cambridge, MA: MIT Press.

Prigogine, I., & Stengers, I. (1984). *Order out of chaos: Man's new dialogue with nature.* New York: Bantam.

Provan, K. G. (1983). The federation as an interorganizational linkage network. *Academy of Management Review, 8,* 79–89.

Provan, K. G., & Milward, H. B. (1995). A preliminary theory of interorganizational network effectiveness: A comparative study of four community mental health systems. *Administrative Science Quarterly, 40,* 1–33.

Putnam, R. D. (2000). *Bowling Alone.* New York: Simon & Schuster.

Radcliff-Brown, A. R. (1952; reprint 1959). *Structure and function in primitive society.* New York: Free Press.

Rafaeli, S., & LaRose, R. J. (1993). Electronic bulletin boards and "Public Goods" explanations of collaborative mass media. *Communication Research, 20,* 277–297.

Rao, H., & Singh, J. V. (1999). Types of variation in organizational populations: The speciation of new organizational forms. In J. A. C. Baum & B. McKelvey (Eds.), *Variations in organization science: In honor of Donald T. Campbell* (pp. 63–77). Thousand Oaks, CA: Sage.

Rapoport, A., & Chammah, A. M. (1965). *Prisoner's dilemma: A study in conflict and cooperation.* Ann Arbor: University of Michigan Press.

Ratcliffe, R. E., Gallagher, M. E., & Ratcliff, K. S. (1979). The civic involvement of bankers: An analysis of the influence of economic power and social prominence in the command of civic policy positions. *Social Problems, 26,* 298–313.

Ray, E. B. (1991). The relationship among communication network roles, job stress, and burnout in educational organizations. *Communication Quarterly, 39,* 91–102.

Raymond, E. (1999). The cathedral and the bazaar: Musings on Linux and Open Source by an accidental revolutionary. Sebastopol, CA: O'Reilly.

Rentsch, J. R. (1990). Climate and culture: Interaction and qualitative differences in organizational meanings. *Journal of Applied Psychology, 75,* 668–681.

Rice, R. E. (1993a). Using network concepts to clarify sources and mechanisms of social influence. In G. Barnett & W. Richards, Jr. (Eds.), *Advances in communication network analysis* (pp. 1–21). Norwood, NJ: Ablex.

Rice, R. E. (1993b). Media appropriateness: Using social presence theory to compare traditional and new organizational media. *Human Communication Research, 19,* 451–484.

Rice, R. E. (1994a). Relating electronic mail use and network structure to R & D work networks and performance. *Journal of Management Information Systems, 11,* 9–20.

Rice, R. E. (1994b). Network analysis and computer-mediated communication systems. In S. Wasserman and J. Galaskiewicz (Eds.), *Advances in social network analysis: Research in the social and behavioral sciences* (pp. 167–206). Thousand Oaks, CA: Sage.

Rice, R. E., & Aydin, C. (1991). Attitudes toward new organizational technology: Network proximity as a mechanism for social information processing. *Administrative Science Quarterly, 9,* 219–244.

Rice, R. E., & Danowski, J. (1993). Is it really just like a fancy answering machine? Comparing semantic networks of different types of voice mail users. *Journal of Business Communication, 30,* 369–397.

Rice, R. E., Grant, A., Schmitz, J., & Torobin, J. (1990). Individual and network influences on the adoption of perceived outcomes of electronic messaging. *Social Networks, 12,* 27–55.

Richards, W. D. (1985). Data, models, and assumptions in network analysis. In R. D. McPhee & P. K. Tompkins (Eds.), *Organizational communication: Themes and new directions* (pp. 109–147). Newbury Park, CA: Sage.

Richards, W. D., & Seary, A. (2000). *MultiNet 3.0 for Windows.* [Computer Program]. Vancouver, British Columbia, Canada: Simon Fraser University.

Richmond, B. (2001). *An introduction to systems thinking: STELLA.* Hanover, NH: High Performance Systems.

Richmond, B., & Peterson, S. (1993). STELLA II: An Introduction to systems thinking. Hanover, NH: High Performance Systems.

Ring, P. S., & Van de Ven, A. H. (1992). Structuring cooperative relationships between organizations. *Strategic Management Journal, 13,* 48–498.

Ring, P. S., & Van de Ven, A. H. (1994). Developmental processes of cooperative interorganizational relationships. *Academy of Management Review, 19,* 90–118.

Roberts, K. H., & O'Reilly, C. A. (1978). Organizations as communication structures: An empirical approach. *Human Communication Research, 4,* 283–293.

Roberts, K. H., & O'Reilly, C. A. (1979). Some correlates of communication roles in organizations. *Academy of Management Journal, 22,* 42–57.

Robertson, R. (1992). *Globalization: Social theory and global culture.* Thousand Oaks, CA: Sage.

Robins, G., Elliott, P., & Pattison, P. (2001). Network models for social selection processes. *Social Networks, 23,* 1–30.

Robins, G., Pattison, P., & Elliott, P. (2001). Network models for social influence processes. *Psychometrika, 66,* 161–190.

Robins, G., Pattison, P., & Wasserman, S. (1999). Logit models and logistic regressions for social networks, III: Valued relations. *Psychometrika, 64,* 371–394.

Robinson, D. T. (1996). Identity and friendship: Affective dynamics and network formation. *Advances in Group Processes, 13,* 91–111.

Rock-Evans, R. (1989). *An introduction to data and activity analysis*. Wellesley, MA: QED Information Sciences.

Roethlisberger, F., & Dickson, W. (1939). *Management and the worker*. New York: Wiley.

Rogers, D. O., & Whetten, D. A. (1982). *Interorganizational coordination*. Ames, IA: Iowa State University Press.

Rogers, E. M. (1971). *Communication of innovations*. New York: Free Press.

Rogers, E. M. (1987). Progress, problems, & prospects for network research. *Social Networks, 9,* 285–310.

Rogers, E. M., & Kincaid, D. L. (1981). *Communication networks: Toward a new paradigm for research*. New York: Free Press.

Romanelli, E. (1999). Blind (but not unconditioned) variation: Problems in copying in sociocultural evolution. In J. A. C. Baum & B. McKelvey (Eds.), *Variations in organization science: In honor of Donald T. Campbell* (pp. 79–91). Thousand Oaks, CA: Sage.

Romo, F. P., & Anheier, H. K. (1996). Success and failure in institutional development: A network approach. *American Behavioral Scientist, 39,* 1057–1079.

Ronfeldt, D., & Arquilla, J. (2001). Networks, netwars, and the fight for the future. *First Monday, 6.* Only available online at: http://www.firstmonday.dk/issues/issue6_10/ronfeldt/index.html

Rosenkopf, L., & Nerkar, A. (1999). On the complexity of technological evolution: Exploring coevolution within and across hierarchical levels in optical disc technology. In J. A. C. Baum & B. McKelvey (Eds.), *Variations in organization science: In honor of Donald T. Campbell* (pp. 169–154). Thousand Oaks, CA: Sage.

Rosenkopf, L., & Tushman, M. L. (1994). The coevolution of technology and organization. In J. A. C. Baum & J. V. Singh (Eds.), *Evolutionary dynamics of organizations* (pp. 403–424). New York: Oxford University Press.

Ruef, M. (2000). The emergence of organizational forms: A community ecology approach. *American Journal of Sociology, 106,* 658–714.

Rumelhart, D. E. (1984). Schemata and the cognitive system. In R. S. Wyer, Jr., & T. K. Srull (Eds.), *Handbook of social cognition* (Vol. 1, pp. 161–188). Hillsdale, NJ: Erlbaum.

Rutte, C. G., & Wilke, H. A. M. (1992). Goals, expectations and behavior in a social dilemma situation. In W. B. G. Liebrand, D. M. Messick, & H. A. M. Wilke (Eds.), *Social dilemmas: Theoretical issues and research findings* (pp. 289–305). New York: Pergamon.

Sabidussi, G. (1966). The centrality index of a graph. *Psychometrika, 31,* 581–603.

Salancik, G. R. (1995). Wanted: A good network theory of organization. *Administrative Science Quarterly, 40,* 345–349.

Salancik, G. R., & Pfeffer, J. (1978). A social information processing approach to job attitudes and task design. *Administrative Science Quarterly, 23,* 224–253.

Samuelson, P. (1954). The pure theory of public expenditure. *Review of Economics and Statistics, 36,* 387–389.

Schachter, S. (1959). *The psychology of affiliation*. Stanford, CA: Stanford University Press.

Schachter, S., & Burdick, H. (1955). A field experiment on rumor transmission and distortion. *Journal of Abnormal and Social Psychology, 50,* 363–371.

Schank, R. C., & Abelson, R. P. (1977). *Scripts plans and goals and understanding.* New York: Wiley.

Schelling, T. C. (1978). *Micromotives and macrobehavior.* New York: Norton.

Schermerhorn, J. R. (1977). Information sharing as an interorganizational activity. *Academy of Management Journal, 20,* 148–153

Schmitz, J., & Fulk, J. (1991). Organizational colleagues, information richness, and electronic mail: A test of the social influence model of technology use. *Communication Research, 18,* 487–523.

Scholte, J. A. (2000). *Globalization: A critical introduction.* New York: St. Martin's Press.

Schumpeter, J. A. (1950). *Capitalism, socialism, and democracy.* New York: Harper Collins.

Scott, J. (1988). Trend report: Social network analysis. *Sociology, 22,* 109–127.

Scott, J. (2000). *Social network analysis: A handbook* (2d ed.). Thousand Oaks, CA: Sage.

Scott, W. R. (1987). *Organizations: Rational, natural and open systems.* Englewood Cliffs, NJ: Prentice Hall.

Seabright, M. A., Levinthal, D. A., & Fichman, M. (1992). Role of individual attachments in the dissolution of interorganizational relationships. *Academy of Management Journal, 35,* 122–160.

Seary, A. J. (1999). PSPAR: Sparse matrix version of PSTAR. [Computer Software]. Available at http://www.sfu.ca/~richards/Pages/pspar.html

Seary, A. J., & Richards, W. D. (2000). Fitting to p* models in MultiNet. *Connections, 23,* 84–101. Also at: http://www.sfu.ca/~insna/Connections-Web/Volume23/23–1Seary/Seary-web.html

Seeman, T. E., Bruce, M. L., & McAvay, G. J. (1996). Social network characteristics and onset of ADL disability: MacArthur studies of successful aging. *Journal of Gerontology, 51B,* S191–S200.

Shaw, M. (1964). Communication networks. In L. Berkowitz (Ed.), *Advances in experimental psychology* (Vol. 1., pp. 111–147). New York: Academic Press.

Sherif, M. (1958). Superordinate goals in the reduction of intergroup conflicts. *American Journal of Sociology, 63,* 349–356.

Sherman, J. D., Smith, H., & Mansfield, E. R. (1986). The impact of emergent network structure on organizational socialization. *Journal of Applied Behavioral Science, 22,* 53–63.

Shirky, C. (2001). Listening to Napster. In A. Oram (Ed.), *Peer-to-peer: Harnessing the benefits of a disruptive technology* (pp. 21–37). Sebastopol, CA: O'Reilly.

Short, J. A., Williams, E., & Christie, B. (1976). *The social psychology of telecommunications.* London: Wiley.

Shrader, C. B., Lincoln, J. R., & Hoffman, A. N. (1989). The network structures of organizations: Effects of task contingencies and distributional form. *Human Relations, 42,* 43–66.

Shumate, M. (2002). *The coevolution of social protest groups.* Unpublished manuscript, Annenberg School for Communication, University of Southern California.

Simmel, G. (1922; reprint 1955). *Conflict and the web of group affiliations.* (K. H. Wolff & R. Bendix, Trans.) New York: Free Press.

Simon, A. R., & Marion, W. (1996). *Workgroup computing: Workflow, groupware, and messaging.* New York: McGraw-Hill.

Simon, H. A. (1976). *Administrative behavior.* New York: Macmillan.

Simon, H. A. (1996). *The sciences of the artificial* (3d ed.). Cambridge, MA: MIT Press.

Singh, H., & Harianto, F. (1989). Management-board relationships, takeover risk, and the adoption of golden parachutes. *Academy of Management Journal, 32,* 7–24.

Skvoretz, J., & Fararo, T. J. (1996). Status and participation in task groups: A dynamic network model. *American Journal of Sociology, 101,* 1366–1414.

Skvoretz, J., & Faust, K. (1996). Social structure, networks, and e-state structuralism models. *Journal of Mathematical Sociology, 21,* 57–76.

Skvoretz, J., & Willer, D. (1993). Exclusion and power: A test of four theories of power in exchange networks. *American Sociological Review, 58,* 801–818.

Smarr, L. (1997). Towards the 21st century. *Communications of the ACM, 40,* 11, 29–32.

Smith, A. (1776/1930). *An inquiry into the nature and causes of the wealth of nations.* London: Methuen.

Smith, K. G., Carroll, S. J., & Ashford, S. J. (1995). Intra- and interorganizational cooperation: Toward a research agenda. *Academy of Management Journal, 38,* 7–23.

Snijders, T. A. B. (2001). The statistical evaluation of social network dynamics. In M. E. Sobel & M. P. Becker (Eds.), *Sociological methodology 2001* (pp. 361–395). Boston, MA: Blackwell.

Spencer, H. (1982). *Principles of sociology* (Vol. 2, part 2). New York: Appleton-Century-Crofts.

Spinardi, G., Graham, I., & Williams, R. (1996). EDI and business network redesign: Why the two don't go together. *New Technology, Work and Employment, 11,* 16–27.

Staber, U. H. (1989). Age dependence and historical effects of the failure rates of worker cooperatives. *Economic and Industrial Democracy, 10,* 59–80.

Stark, D. (1999). Heterarchy: Distributing authority and organizing diversity. In J. H. Clippinger III (Ed.), *The biology of business: Decoding the natural laws of enterprise* (pp. 153–179). San Francisco: Jossey Bass.

Stasser, G., Stewart, D. D., & Wittenbaum, G. M. (1995). Expert roles and information exchange during discussion: The importance of knowing who knows what. *Journal of Experimental Social Psychology, 31,* 244–265.

Staw, B., & Ross, J. (1985). Stability in the midst of change. *Journal of Applied Psychology, 70,* 469–480.

Stearns, L. B., & Mizruchi, M. S. (1993). Board composition and corporate financing: The impact of financial institution representation on borrowing. *Academy of Management Journal, 36,* 603–618.

Steinfield, C. W., & Fulk, J. (1990). The theory imperative. In J. Fulk & C. W.

Steinfield (Eds.), *Organizations and communication technology* (pp. 13–25). Newbury Park, CA: Sage.

Sterman, J. (2000). *Business dynamics: Systems thinking and modeling for a complex world.* Boston, MA: Irwin/McGraw-Hill.

Stevens, R., Woodward, P., De Fanti, T., & Catlett, C. (1997). From the I-way to the National Grid. *Communications of the ACM, 40,* 51–60.

Stevenson, W. B. (1990). Formal structure and networks of interaction within organizations. *Social Science Research, 19,* 113–131.

Stevenson, W. B., & Gilly, M. C. (1991). Information processing and problem solving: The migration of problems through formal positions and networks of ties. *Academy of Management Journal, 34,* 918–928.

Stohl, C. (1993). European managers' interpretations of participation: A semantic network analysis. *Human Communication Research, 20,* 97–117.

Stohl, C. (1995). *Organizational communication: Connectedness in action.* Thousand Oaks, CA: Sage.

Stohl, C. (2001). Globalizing organizational communication. In F. M. Jablin, & L. L. Putnam (Eds.), *The new handbook of organizational communication: Advances in theory, research, and methods* (pp. 323–375). Thousand Oaks, CA: Sage.

Stokman, F. N., & Doreian, P. (1996). Concluding remarks. *Journal of Mathematical Sociology, 21,* 197–199.

Stokman, F. N., & Zeggelink, E. P. H. (1996). Is politics power or policy oriented? A comparative analysis of dynamic access models in policy networks. *Journal of Mathematical Sociology, 21,* 77–111.

Strauss, D., & Ikeda, M. (1990). Pseudolikelihood estimation for social networks. *Journal of the American Statistical Association, 85,* 204–212.

Tehranian, M. (1990). *Technologies of power: Information machines and democratic prospects.* Norwood, NJ: Ablex.

Thompson, J. D. (1967). *Organizations in action.* New York: McGraw-Hill.

Tichy, N. M., & Fombrun, C. (1979). Network analysis in organizational settings. *Human Relations, 32,* 923–965.

Tolia, N., & Fryer, B. (2001, January). Power to the people. *Harvard Business Review, 79,* 20–21.

Topper, C. M., & Carley, K. M. (1997, January). *A structural perspective on the emergence of network organizations.* Paper presented at the International Sunbelt Social Networks Conference, San Diego, CA.

Tosi, H. L. (1992). *The environment/organization/person contingency model: A Meso approach to the study of organizations.* Greenwich, CT: JAI.

Trevino, L., Lengel, R., & Daft, R. (1987). Media symbolism, media richness and media choice in organizations: A symbolic interactionist perspective. *Communication Research, 14,* 553–575.

Tsai, W. (2001). Knowledge transfer in intraorganizational networks: Effects of network position and absorptive capacity on business unit innovation and performance. *Academy of Management Journal, 44,* 996–1004.

Tsgarousianou, R., Tambini, D., & Bryan, C. (Eds). (1998). *Cyberdemocracy: Technology, cities and civic networks.* New York: Routledge.

Tsui, A. E., & O'Reilly, C. A. III (1989). Beyond simple demographic effects: The importance of relational demography in superior-subordinate dyads. *Academy of Management Journal, 32,* 402–423.

Tsui, A. S., Egan, T. D., & O'Reilly, C. A. III. (1992). Being different: Relational demography and organizational attachment. *Administrative Science Quarterly, 37,* 549–579.

Turk, H. (1977). Interorganizational networks in urban society: Initial perspectives and comparative research. *American Sociological Review, 35,* 1–20.

Turner, J. C. (1987). *Rediscovering the social group: A self-categorization theory.* Oxford: Blackwell.

Turner, J. C., & Oakes, P. J. (1986). The significance of the social identity concept for social psychology with reference to individualism, interactionism, and social influence. *British Journal of Social Psychology, 25,* 237–252.

Turner, J. C., & Oakes, P. J. (1989). Self-categorization theory and social influence. In P. B. Paulus (Ed.), *Psychology of group influence* (pp. 233–275). Hillsdale, NJ: Erlbaum.

Tushman, M. L., & Anderson, P. (1986). Technological discontinuities and organizational environments. *Administrative Science Quarterly, 31,* 439–465.

Tushman, M. L., & Romanelli, E. (1985). Organizational evolution: A metamorphosis model of convergence and reorientation. In B. Staw & L. Cummings (Eds.), *Research in organizational behavior* (Vol. 7, pp. 171–222). Greenwich, CT: JAI.

Useem, M. (1980). Corporations and the corporate elite. *Annual Review of Sociology, 6,* 41–77.

Useem, M. (1983). *The inner circle: Large corporations and business politics in the U.S. and UK.* New York: Oxford University Press.

Uzzi, B. (1996). The sources and consequences of embeddedness for the economic performance of organizations: The network effect. *American Sociological Review, 61,* 674–698.

Uzzi, B. (1997). Social structure and competition in interfirm networks: The paradox of embeddedness. *Administrative Science Quarterly, 42,* 35–67.

Valente, T. W. (1995). *Network models of the diffusion of innovations.* Cresskill, NJ: Hampton.

Valente, T. W. (1996). Social network thresholds in the diffusion of innovations. *Social Networks, 18,* 69–89.

Van den Bulte, C., & Moenaert, R. K. (1998). The effects of R&D team co-location on communication patterns among R&D marketing and manufacturing. *Management Science, 44,* S1–S18.

Van de Ven, A. H., & Grazman, D. N. (1999). Evolution in a nested hierarchy: A genealogy of Twin Cities health care organizations, 1853–1995. In J. A. C. Baum & B. McKelvey (Eds.), *Variations in organization science: In honor of Donald T. Campbell* (pp. 185–212). Thousand Oaks, CA: Sage.

Van Lange, P. A. M., Liebrand, W. B. G., Messick, D. M., & Wilke, H. A. M. (1992). Introduction and literature review. In W. B. G. Liebrand, D. M. Messick, & H. A. M. Wilke (Eds.), *Social dilemmas: Theoretical issues and research findings* (pp. 3–28). New York: Pergammon.

Vega, W. A., Kolody, B., Valle, R., & Weir, J. (1991). Social networks, social support and their relationship to depression among immigrant Mexican women. *Human Organization, 50,* 154–162.

Von Bertalanffy, L. (1968). *General systems theory: Foundations, development, applications.* New York: Braziller.

Wade, J., O'Reilly, C. A. III, & Chandratat, I. (1990). Golden parachutes: CEOs and the exercise of social influence. *Administrative Science Quarterly, 35,* 587–603.

Wagner, W. G., Pfeffer, J., & O'Reilly, C. A. III (1984). Organizational demography and turnover in top management groups. *Administrative Science Quarterly, 29,* 74–92.

Walker, G. (1985). Network position and cognition in a computer software firm. *Administrative Science Quarterly, 30,* 103–130.

Walker, G., Kogut, B., & Shan, W. (1997). Social capital, structural holes and the formation of an industry network. *Organization Science, 8,* 109–125.

Walker, M. E., Wasserman, S., & Wellman, B. (1994). Statistical models for social support networks. In S. Wasserman and J. Galaskiewicz (Eds.), *Advances in social network analysis: Research in the social and behavioral sciences* (pp. 53–78). Thousand Oaks, CA: Sage.

Wallace, M., Griffin, L., & Rubin, B. (1989). The positional power of American labor, 1963–1977. *American Sociological Review, 54,* 197–214.

Warren, R. (1967). The interorganizational field as a focus for investigation. *Administrative Science Quarterly, 12,* 396–419.

Wasserman, S., & Faust, K. (1994). *Social network analysis: Methods and applications.* New York: Cambridge University Press.

Wasserman, S., & Pattison, P. (1996). Logit models and logistic regressions for social networks: I. An introduction to Markov graphs and p^*. *Psychometrika, 61,* 401–425.

Waters, M. (1995). *Globalization.* New York: Routledge.

Watts, D. J. (1999). *Small worlds: The dynamics of networks between order and randomness.* Princeton, NJ: Princeton University Press.

Watts, D. J. (in press). *Six degrees: The science of a connected age.* New York: Norton.

Watts, D., Dodds, P. S., & Newman, M. E. J. (2002). Identity and search in social networks. *Science, 296,* 1302–1305

Watts, D. J., & Strogatz, S. H. (1998). Collective dynamics of 'small-world' networks. *Nature, 393,* 440–442.

Watzlavick, P., Beavin, J., & Jackson, D. (1966). *Pragmatics of human communication.* New York: Norton.

Weber, M. (1947). *The theory of social and economic organization* (A. H. Henderson & T. Parsons, Eds. & Trans.). Glencoe, IL: Free Press.

Weber, S. (2000). The political economy of Open Source software. (BRIE Working Paper 140). University of California, Berkeley.

Wegner, D. M. (1987). Transactive memory: A contemporary analysis of the group mind. In B. Mullen & G. R. Goethals (Eds.), *Theories of group behavior* (pp. 185–208). New York: Springer-Verlag.

Wegner, D. M. (1995). A computer network model of human transactive memory. *Social Cognition, 13*(3), 319–339.

Wegner, D. M., Erber, R., & Raymond, P. (1991). Transactive memory in close relationships. *Journal of Personality and Social Psychology, 61*, 923–929.

Weick, K. E. (1979). *The social psychology of organizing* (2d ed.). Reading, MA: Addison-Wesley.

Weick, K. E., & Bougon, M. G. (1986). Organizations as cognitive maps: Charting ways to success and failure. In H. P. Sims, Jr., & D. A. Gioia (Eds.), *Social cognition in organizations* (pp. 102–135). San Francisco: Jossey-Bass.

Weiner, N. (1956). *The human use of human beings: Cybernetics and society* (2d. ed.). Garden City, NY: Doubleday.

Wellman, B. (1988). Structural analysis: From method and metaphor to theory and substance. In B. Wellman & S. D. Berkowitz (Eds.), *Social structures: A network approach* (pp. 19–61). Cambridge: Cambridge University Press.

Wellman, B. (1992). Which types of ties and networks provide what kinds of social support? In E. J. Lawler (Ed.), *Advances in group processes* (Vol. 9, pp. 207–235). Greenwich, CT: JAI.

Wellman, B. (2000). Changing connectivity: A future history of Y2.03K. *Sociological Research Online, 4.* Available online at: http://www.socresonline.org.uk/4/4/wellman.html

Wellman, B. (2001). Computer networks as social networks. *Science, 293,* 2031–2034.

Wellman, B., Quan Haase, A., Witte, J., & Hampton, K. (2001). Does the Internet increase, decrease, or supplement social capital? Social networks, participation, and community commitment. *American Behavioral Scientist, 45,* 437–456.

Wellman, B., Salaff, J., Dimitrova, D., Garton, L., Gulia, M., & Haythornthwaite, C. (1996). Computer networks as social networks: Collaborative work, telework, and virtual community. *Annual Review of Sociology, 22,* 213–238.

Wellman, B., & Wortley, S. (1989). Brothers' keepers: Situating kinship relations in broader networks of social support. *Sociological Perspectives, 32,* 273–306.

Wellman, B., & Wortley, S. (1990). Different strokes from different folks: Community ties and social support. *American Journal of Sociology, 96,* 558–588.

Westphal, J. D., Gulati, R., & Shortell, S. M. (1997). Customization or conformity? An institutional and network perspective on the content and consequences of TQM adoption. *Administrative Science Quarterly, 42,* 366–394.

White, D. R., & Reitz, K. P. (1989). Rethinking the role concept: Homomorphisms on social networks. In L. C. Freeman, D. R. White, & A. K. Romney (Eds.), *Research methods in social network analysis* (pp. 429–488). Fairfax, VA: George Mason University Press.

White, H. C., Boorman, S. A., & Breiger, R. L. (1976). Social structure from multiple networks, I: Block-models of roles and positions. *American Journal of Sociology, 81,* 730–780.

Wiener, N. (1948). *Cybernetics or control and communication in the animal and machine.* Cambridge, MA: MIT Press.

Wiener, N. (1956). *The human use of human beings: Cybernetics and society.* New York: De Capo.

Wigand, R. T. (1988). Communication network analysis: History and overview. In G. Goldhaber & G. Barnett (Eds.), *Handbook of organizational communication* (pp. 319–359). New York: Ablex.

Willer, D., & Skvoretz, J. (1997). Network connection and exchange ratios: Theory, predictions, and experimental tests. *Advances in Group Processes, 14,* 199–234.

Williams, P. (2001). Transnational criminal networks. In J. Arquilla & D. Ronfeldt (Eds.), *Networks and Netwars: The future of terror, crime, and militancy* (pp. 61–97). Santa Monica, CA: RAND.

Williamson, O. E. (1975). *Markets and hierarchies: Analysis and antitrust implications, a study of the economics of internal organization.* New York: Free Press.

Williamson, O. E. (1985). *The economic institutions of capitalism: Firms, markets, relational contracting.* New York: Free Press.

Williamson, O. E. (1991). Comparative economic organization: The analysis of discrete structural alternatives. *Administrative Science Quarterly, 36,* 269–296.

Wilson, E. O. (1971). *The insect societies.* Cambridge, MA: Harvard University Press.

Woelfel, J. (1993). Artificial neural networks in policy research: A current assessment. *Journal of Communication, 43,* 62–80.

Woelfel, J., & Fink, E. L. (1980). *The Galileo system: A theory of social measurement and its application.* New York: Academic Press.

Woelfel, J., & Stoyanoff, N. J. (1993). *CATPAC: A neural network for qualitative analysis of text.* Amherst, MA: RAH. Available online at: http://www.galileoco.com/pdf/catpac.pdf

Wright, S. (1931). Evolution in Mendelian populations. *Genetics, 16,* 97.

Wright, S. (1932). The roles of mutation, inbreeding, crossbreeding, and selection in evolution. *Proceedings of the Sixth International Congress on Genetics, 1,* 356.

Yamagishi, T., Gillmore, M. R., & Cook, K. S. (1988). Network connections and the distribution of power in exchange networks. *American Journal of Sociology, 93,* 833–51.

Yates, J. (1989). *Control through communication: The rise of system in American management.* Baltimore, MA: Johns Hopkins University Press.

Yoshino, M. Y., & Rangan, U. A. (1995). *Strategic alliances: An entrepreneurial approach to globalization.* Boston, MA: Harvard Business School Press.

Zack, M. H., & McKenney, J. L. (1995). Social context and interaction in ongoing computer-supported management groups. *Organization Science, 6,* 394–422.

Zahn, G. L. (1991). Face-to-face communication in an office setting: The effects of position, proximity, and exposure. *Communication Research, 18,* 737–754.

Zajac, E. J., & Olsen, C. P. (1993). From transaction cost to transactional value analysis: Implications for the study of interorganizational strategies. *Journal of Management Studies, 30,* 131–145.

Zeggelink, E. P. H. (1993). *Strangers into friends: The evolution of friendship networks using an individual oriented modeling approach.* Amsterdam: Thesis Publishers.

Zeggelink, E. P. H., Stokman, F. N., & van de Bunt, G. G. (1996). The emergence of groups in the evolution of friendship networks. *Journal of Mathematical Sociology, 21,* 29–55.

Zenger, T. R., & Lawrence, B. S. (1989). Organizational demography: The differential effects of age and tenure distributions on technical communication. *Academy of Management Journal, 32,* 353–376.

Zey-Ferrell, M., & Ferrell, O. C. (1982). Role set configuration and opportunity as predictors of unethical behavior in organizations. *Human Relations, 35,* 587–604.

Zinger, J. T., Blanco, H., Zanibbi, L., & Mount, J. (1996). An empirical study of the small business support network—The entrepreneur's perspective. *Canadian Journal of Administrative Sciences, 13,* 347–357.

Author Index

Abelson, R. P., 91
Adamic, L. A., 311
Adams, J. S., 227
Ahouse, J. J., 272–73, 275, 285
Ahuja, M. K., 232
Ainlay, S. L., 237
Albert, A., 311
Albrecht, T. L., 8, 237
Aldrich, H., 8, 163, 210, 242, 248, 249, 252, 253, 255, 257, 258, 259, 261
Allen, T., 228
Alter, C., 212
Amburgey, T. L., 216
Anderson, C., 49, 54
Anderson, P., 85, 87, 96, 246
Andrews, S. B., 146
Anheier, H. K., 217
Ansell, C. K., 39
Appadurai, A., 4
Appel, Peter, 308
Argote, L., 199, 202
Arquilla, J., 324–25
Arrow, H., 234
Ashby, W. R., 96
Asimov, Isaac, 309

Astley, W. G., 247, 250, 256, 257, 259, 260, 261, 267
Axelrod, R., 85, 86, 87
Axtell, R., 103
Aydin, C., 179, 229

Bacharach, S. B., 9
Back, K., 227
Bacon, Kevin, 308
Badaracco, J. L., Jr., 34, 92
Baird, L., 199
Baker, W. E., 147
Bandura, A., 174, 179
Bar, F., 203
Barabasi, A., 311, 313
Barley, S. R., 194, 231, 232
Barnard, C. I., 8
Barnett, G. A., 180, 190, 206, 231
Barnett, W. P., 246, 252, 253, 255, 257, 258, 259, 260, 306
Barrera, M., Jr., 237
Barron, D. N., 252
Bass, L. A., 237
Batagelj, V., 31
Bateson, G., 10, 19

Bauer, C., 227
Baum, J. A. C., 182, 218, 242, 243, 246, 247, 255, 262
Bavelas, A., 16, 150
Bearman, P., 60
Beavin, J., 19
Becker, G., 143, 150
Benassi, M., 146
Beniger, J., 5
Benson, J. K., 214–15
Berdahl, J. L., 234
Berger, J., 222
Berkley, J. D., 220
Berkman, L., 235, 237
Bernard, H. R., 193, 312
Bertalanffy, L. von, 83
Beyer, J. M., 161
Bienenstock, E. J., 209
Biggart, N. W., 148
Bikson, T. K., 9
Birley, S., 226
Bishop, A. P., 198, 229
Bizot, E., 9
Blalock, H. M., Jr., 100
Blanco, H., 238
Bland, S. H., 229
Blau, P. M., 58, 102, 143, 209
Blumer, H., 91
Bock, S. J., 160
Bollen, K. A., 100
Bonacich, P., 166, 209
Bond, A. H., 103
Boorman, S. A., 19
Borgatti, S. P., 31, 46, 199
Bougon, M. G., 85
Bourdieu, P., 143
Bovasso, G., 180, 193
Bowsher, J., 237
Boyd, B., 217, 233
Brass, D. J., 3, 31, 149, 183, 205, 206, 212, 213, 214, 226, 227, *tables 2.1–3*
Breiger, R. L., 19
Brewer, D. D., 197
Brewer, M. B., 165, 193
Brimm, M., 10
Brin, S., 313
Brittain, J., 246, 251, 252, 255

Brown, J. S., 178, 247
Browning, L. D., 161
Bruce, M. L., 238
Bryan, C., 6
Bryant, J. A., 252, 325
Buchanan, M., 307
Buckley, W., 19
Burdick, H., 214
Burgelman, R. A., 255
Burke, P. J., 222
Burkhardt, M. E., 179, 213
Burkhart, R., 103
Burns, L., 10, 149, 181
Burt, R. S., 19, 39, 57, 102, 141, 142, 143, 144, 145, 146, 148, 173, 182, 213, 215, 298
Burton, R., 262
Butterfield, K. D., 206, 214
Byrne, D. E., 224

Campbell, D. T., 242, 249, 255, 256
Campbell, K. E., 237
Cannon, W., 81
Carley, K. M., 10, 62, 67, 91, 93, 99, 100, 102, 103, 174, 186, 189, 191, 192, 203, 223, 232, 297, 326
Carroll, G. R., 148, 212, 246, 252, 253, 257, 258, 259, 306
Carroll, S. J., 20
Carroll, T. N., 262, 271
Cartwright, D., 204
Castells, M., 4, 5, 326
Catlett, C., 318
Chamberlain, J., 160
Chammah, A. M., 87
Chan, M., 92, 197
Chandler, A. D., 18
Chandratat, I., 147
Chang, H.-J., 226
Chang, M., 226, 273, 285–88
Chellini, F., 238
Christie, B., 234
Cicourel, A., 202
Cilliers, P., 13
Clark, P., 149
Coase, R. H., 150
Cochran, P. L., 147

Cohen, B., 222
Cohen, M. D., 85, 86, 87
Coleman, J. S., 19, 60, 62, 96, 120, 142, 159, 223, 298
Conrad, C., 7
Conrath, D., 228
Contractor, N. S., 3, 20, 31, 45, 83–84, 89, 92, 93, 94, 96, 97, 100, 102, 104, 118, 120, 141, 173, 178, 179, 183, 184, 189, 190, 191, 196, 197, 198, 199, 203, 206, 229, 233, 234, 314, 315
Cook, K. S., 209, 212
Cook, T. D., 242
Corman, S. R., 102, 186, 193, 197, 227, 233
Cozzens, M. D., 84
Cramer, F., 97
Crombie, S., 226
Cronenfeld, D., 193
Cronin, M. M., 214
Cross, R., 199, 220
Crouch, B., 49, 54
Crowston, K., 235
Cummings, A., 238
Cutrona, C. E., 237

Daft, R. L., 167, 174, 234
Daniels, M., 103
Danowski, J. A., 186, 190
Darwin, Charles, 268
Davies, G., 239
Davila, C., 217
Davis, G. F., 181
Davis, J., 204
Davis, K., 8
Dawes, R. M., 165
Deal, T. E., 189
Decker, C., 232
De Fanti, T., 318
DeFleur, M. L., 214
Delacroix, J., 246, 249, 251, 252
DeSanctis, G., 4, 5, 10, 119, 234
de Saussure, F., 18
De Soto, C. B., 207
Deutsch, K., 83
Dickson, W., 9
DiMaggio, P. J., 174, 182, 231, 246, 249, 251, 254, 258

Dimitrova, D., 231
Dizard, S., 232
Dodds, P. S., 312
Domhoff, G. W., 217
Dooley, K., 187
Doty, D. H., 9
Drogoul, A., 103
Duguid, P., 247
Duncan, O. D., 143
Dunn, W. N., 187
Durkheim, E., 18, 235
Dutton, W. H., 144
Dyson, G. B., 11

Egan, T. D., 225
Egido, C., 233
Eisenberg, E. M., 3, 7, 20, 34, 67, 173, 183, 186, 187, 189, 190, 205, 206, 227, 229, 234, 238
Elliott, P., 296–97
Emerson, R. M., 58, 209, 212
Emery, F. E., 85, 254
Ensel, W. M., 148, 235
Epstein, J. M., 103
Erber, R., 202
Erdos, Paul, 307–8
Erickson, B., 174
Ethington, C. T., 226
Evans, M. J., 312
Eve, R. A., 85
Eveland, J. D., 9
Everett, M., 31

Farace, R. V., 32, 91
Fararo, T. J., 222
Faust, K., 31, 36, 37, 40, 41, 45, 49, 51, 52, 93, 113–14, 117, 222, 326, 327
Feeley, T. H., 180
Feld, S., 227
Ferber, J., 103
Fernandez, R. M., 213
Ferrell, O. C., 180
Festinger, L., 102, 227
Fichman, M., 218
Fink, E. L., 67, 186
Fiol, C. M., 187
Fischer, C., 232

Fiske, D. W., 242
Flache, A., 170
Flanagin, A. J., 60, 159, 162, 166
Follett, M. P., 8
Fonti, F., 104, 118
Forrester, J. W., 99
Frank, O., 49, 115
Freeman, J. H., 242, 247, 250, 251, 253, 254
Freeman, L. C., 31, 193, 207, 213
Freeman, S. C., 193
Friedkin, N. E., 174, 178, 183
Friedland, R., 11, 218
Frost, P., 19
Fryer, B., 320
Fukuyama, F., 8, 89–90
Fulk, J., 4, 10, 60, 92, 94, 102, 154, 159, 161–62, 165, 166, 170, 174, 179, 203, 220, 233, 234

Galaskiewicz, J., 20, 169, 182, 215, 217, 225
Galbraith, J. R., 10, 18, 102
Galegher, J., 233
Gallagher, M. E., 217
Gargiulo, M., 146
Garton, L., 231
Gasser, L., 103
Gaver, W., 229
Gell-Mann, M., 11, 85
Gerlach, M. L., 215, 216
Giddens, A., 5–6, 19, 102, 197
Gilbert, N., 103
Gillmore, M. R., 209, 212
Gilly, M. C., 8, 68
Ginsberg, A., 187
Glansdorff, P., 89
Glick, W. H., 9
Goes, J. B., 181, 182, 216
Goldblatt, D., 3, 6
Gollob, H. F., 91
Goode, P. L., 9
Goodell, A., 178
Gore, A., Jr., 91
Gould, R. V., 168
Govindarajan, V., 152
Grabher, G., 153

Graen, G., 213
Graham I., 233
Grandori, A., 20
Granovetter, M. S., 5, 46, 68, 147, 148, 152, 153, 169, 183
Grant, A., 169, 179
Grant, S., 102, 191
Gray, B., 214
Grazman, D. N., 255, 256
Greve, H. R., 253
Griffin, L., 215
Grossberg, L., 4
Guare, John, 308
Gulati, R., 34, 68, 181, 218
Gulia, M., 231
Gupta, A. K., 152
Gurbaxani, V., 169

Hackman, J. R., 178
Hall, A., 235
Hall, S., 4
Hamilton, G. G., 148
Hampton, K., 230, 231
Hannan, M. T., 242, 246, 247, 250, 251, 252, 253, 254, 258
Hanneman, R. A., 100, 103
Hanson, J. R., 9
Harary, F., 204
Hardin, G., 165
Hardin, R., 160
Hargittai, E., 231
Harianto, F., 147
Harrington, J. E., Jr., 273, 285–88
Hartman, A., 314
Hartman, R. L., 178
Harvey, D., 4
Haunschild, P. R., 181
Haveman, H. A., 257
Hawley, A., 242, 251, 254, 255, 257, 258, 260
Haythornthwaite, C., 30–31, 229, 231
Head, J. G., 160
Heald, M. R., 196, 199
Heckscher, C., 18
Heider, F., 59, 102, 204, 224
Heino, R., 165, 166
Heise, D., 91

Held, D., 3, 6
Heller, M. A., 179, 184
Helper, S., 151–52
Hesterly, W. S., 46
Hill, T., 9
Hill, V., 297
Hinds, P., 9
Hoffman, A. N., 212
Hofstadter, D. R., 11, 15
Hofstede, G., 191
Holland, J. H., 11, 13, 14–15, 85, 86
Holland, P. W., 59, 204
Hollingshead, A. B., 67, 92, 94, 199, 201, 202, 203, 234
Homans, G. C., 19, 58, 142, 170, 209, 228
Hong, T., 326
Horrigan, K., 230
Huber, G. P., 9
Hubert, L. J., 68
Hurlbert, J. S., 238
Hyatt, A., 102, 104, 118, 120
Hylton, L. F., 34

Ibarra, H., 62, 146, 213, 223, 226
Ikeda, M., 49
Israel, K., 232
Iwazume, M., 197

Jablin, F. M., 9, 180
Jackson, D., 19
Jackson, M., 234
Jang, H., 190, 206
Jennings, P. D., 181
Jeong, H., 311
Johansen, R., 5
Johnson, J. D., 9, 178, 226, 227
Johnson-Laird, P. N., 91
Jones, C., 46
Jones, P. M., 104, 118, 120, 197
Jones, T. B., 147

Kador, J., 314
Kadushin, C., 10, 235–36
Kahneman, D., 145
Kalman, M. E., 16, 60, 159, 162, 165, 166, 167

Kapoor, Raj, 308
Kapoor, Shashi, 308
Kaufer, D. S., 174, 186, 189
Kauffman, S. A., 85, 97, 241, 246, 255, 257, 261–72, 280, 288–90
Kautz, H., 197
Kawakami, K., 315
Kennedy, A., 189
Kenworthy, A. L., 255
Kerr, N. L., 166, 167
Kiernan, V., 323
Kiesler, S., 9, 231
Kilduff, M., 180, 190, 196, 206
Killworth, P. D., 193, 312
Kim, Y., 168
Kincaid, D. L., 19, 67, 174
Kirste, K. K., 227
Kleinberg, J., 311–14
Knez, M., 213
Knoke, D., 168, 216–17
Knorr-Cetina, K., 91
Kochen, M., 307
Koehly, L., 196, 199
Kogut, B., 146, 192
Kontopoulos, K. M., 11, 12, 14, 15, *figs. 1.1–2*
Koput, K. W., 34, 192
Korzenny, F., 227
Kosnik, R. D., 147
Krackhardt, D., 3, 9, 11, 67, 68, 180, 183, 190, 192, 193, 194, 196, 206, 213, 214, 221, 227, 297
Krassa, M. A., 183
Kraut, R. E., 231, 233
Krikorian, D. D., 9
Krishnan, T., 202
Krone, K. J., 180
Kuhn, T., 186, 234
Kunz, J. C., 203

Labianca, G., 214
Lambersteschi family, 39
Lancaster, A., 103
Land, K. C., 101
Langford, C. P. H., 237
Langton, C., 103
Lant, T. K., 249, 255

LaRose, R. J., 169
Larsen, E. R., 297
Larson, A., 214, 218
Lash, S., 6
Lasswell, H., 81
Latane, B., 103
Latora, V., 311
Laubacher, R. J., 7
Laumann, E. O., 168, 215, 223
Lawler, E. J., 9
Lawrence, B. S., 225
Lawrence, S., 311, 313–14
Lazarsfeld, P. F., 81
Lazerson, M., 153
Leavitt, H. J., 17
Lee, B. A., 237
Lee, I., 103
Leenders, R. T. A. J., 226
Leinhardt, S., 59, 204
Lengel, R. H., 174, 234
Lerner, J., 322, 323
Lesperance, Y., 91
Lessig, L., 170
Levine, J. H., 34
Levinthal, D. A., 218, 250, 262, 265
Levitt, R. E., 102, 203
Lewin, K., 16, 271
Liang, D. W., 202
Liebeskind, J. P., 193
Liebrand, W. B. G., 165
Liedka, R. V., 225
Lievrouw, L. A., 10, 189
Lillis, P. P., 237
Lin, N., 142, 148, 235
Lin, Z., 102
Lincoln, J. R., 216, 226
Lipnack, J., 119
Littlepage, G., 202
Litwak, E., 34
Lodge, David, 308
Lomi, A., 297
Long, C. P., 271
Lott, A. J., 102
Lott, B. E., 102
Louis, M. R., 19, 220
Lowe, C. U., 189
Luhmann, N., 95

Lundberg, C., 19
Lundmark, V., 231

Macy, M. W., 170
Maeda, H., 197
Malone, T. W., 6–7, 235
Maloney, J. P., 237
Mansfield, E. R., 180
March, J. G., 248
Marchiori, M., 311
Marion, W., 167
Markovsky, B., 85, 209, 222
Markus, M. L., 163, 164, 169, 232, 233, 234
Marsden, P. V., 31, 174, 183, 193, 223
Marshall, A., 226
Martin, J., 19
Maruyama, M., 81–82
Marwell, G., 60, 120, 161, 163, 164, 165, 171
Mattelart, A., 79, 80
Mattelart, M., 79, 80
Maturana, H. R., 95
McAvay, G. J., 238
McCarty, C., 312
McCulloch, W. S., 11
McElroy, J. C., 213
McGrath, J. E., 234
McGrew, A., 3, 6
McGuire, W. J., 185
McKelvey, B., 11, 15, 17, 68, 97, 242, 247, 252, 255, 261, 262, 263, 265, 266
McKendrick, D. G., 252
McPhee, R. D., 9, 178, 187, 227
McPherson, J. M., 223
Merton, R. K., 81
Messick, D. M., 165
Meyer, J. W., 174
Meyer, M., 226
Mezias, S. J., 249, 255
Michaelson, A., 184
Miles, R. E., 10, 18, 219, 221
Milgram, S., 41, 307–8, 312
Miller, C. C., 9
Miller, J. G., 83, 226
Miller, K. I., 205, 227
Milward, H. B., 216

Miner, A. S., 216, 248, 249, 250, 255
Minsky, M. A., 91
Mintz, B., 217
Mischke, G. A., 258
Mitchell, J. C., 34
Mittman, B. S., 255
Mizruchi, M. S., 20, 169, 182, 217, 218
Moenaert, R. K., 228
Monge, P. R., 3, 4, 5, 7, 10, 16, 20, 31,
    32, 45, 60, 67, 81, 82, 83, 84, 91, 92,
    94, 96, 119, 120, 141, 159, 162, 165,
    166, 186, 187, 189, 190, 203, 205, 206,
    220, 227, 233, 314, 325
Montgomery, K., 216
Moore, G., 226
Moore, L., 19
Moreland, R. L., 94, 199, 201, 202
Morgan, G., 95, 96, 314
Moscovici, S., 184
Mount, J., 238
Mrvar, A., 31
Mukopadhyay, T., 231

Nadel, E., 189
Nadel, S. F., 19
Nardi, B., 197
Nelson, R. R., 242, 247, 248, 249
Nerkar, A., 255
Neuman, W. R., 231
Newell, S., 91, 149
Newman, M. E. J., 312
Nishida, T., 197
Nohria, N., 199, 220
Norman, D., 229
Norman, R. Z., 204, 220

Oakes, P. J., 224, 227
Ocasio, W., 258
Ogliastri, E., 217
O'Hara-Devereaux, M., 5
O'Keefe, B. J., 104, 118, 197
Oldham, G., 178
Oliver, A. L., 193
Oliver, C., 182, 215, 218, 246, 255
Oliver, P. E., 60, 120, 161, 163, 164, 165,
    170, 171, 216
Olsen, C. P., 151, 154, 155

Olson, M., Jr., 160, 161, 163
O'Mahony, S., 231, 232
Oram, A., 317
O'Reilly, C. A. III, 9, 147, 205, 225
O'Reilly, P., 237
Orlikowski, W., 234
Ozzie, Ray, 318

Padgett, J. F., 39
Page, L., 313
Page, S. E., 103
Palazzolo, E. T., 94, 120, 137, 199
Palmer, D., 11, 181, 218, 229
Papa, M. J., 146
Papia, D., 315
Pappi, F. U., 215
Park, D. Y., 253
Park, S. H., 181, 182, 216
Parker, A., 199
Parnassa, C., 159, 162
Parsons, T., 19, 81
Paterniti, R., 238
Pattee, Howard, 12, 14
Patterson, M., 231
Pattison, P., 49, 54, 184, 194, 199, 296–
    97, 327
Patton, T., 209
Perraton, J., 3, 6
Peterson, S., 103
Pfeffer, J., 58, 174, 178–79, 215, 225
Piore, M. J., 4, 148
Podolny, J. M., 252
Pogue, D., 320
Polanyi, K., 14, 148
Pollock, T., 178
Pool, I. de S., 232, 307
Poole, M. S., 7, 9, 100, 178, 220, 221,
    234
Porter, L., 180
Porter, M. E., 220
Powell, W. W., 4, 34, 150, 153, 154, 174,
    182, 192, 249, 254
Power, J. G., 174
Prahl, R., 60, 165
Prietula, M. J., 100, 103, 297
Prigogine, I., 89, 96
Provan, K. G., 216

Prusak, L., 199
Putnam, R. D., 232

Quan Haase, A., 230, 231
Quesnay, Francois, 80

Radcliff-Brown, A. R., 18
Rafaeli, S., 169
Raghavan, S. V., 249
Rainie, L., 230
Ramirez, R., 220
Rao, H., 247, 249
Rapoport, A., 87
Ratcliff, K. S., 217
Ray, E. B., 238
Raymond, E., 321, 323
Raymond, P., 202
Reddington, K., 202
Reitz, K. P., 184
Rentsch, J. R., 178
Rice, R. E., 9, 169, 179, 183, 184, 190,
    229, 231, 232
Richards, W. D., 31, 67, 73, 193
Richmond, B., 103, 108
Robert, Y., 264
Roberts, K. H., 9, 205
Robertson, R., 4
Robey, D., 232, 233
Robins, G., 49, 296–97
Robinson, J. P., 202, 231
Rockart, J. F., 235
Rock-Evans, R., 104
Roethlisberger, F., 9
Rogers, D. O., 169
Rogers, E. M., 19, 20, 67, 149, 174, 189
Romanelli, E., 248, 249, 250, 252, 256,
    261, 267
Romney, A. K., 193
Romo, F. P., 217
Ronfeldt, D., 324–25
Ropp, V. A., 8, 237
Rosenkopf, L., 255, 257, 258
Ross, J., 178
Rothman, L. W., 227
Rowan, B., 174
Rubin, P., 215, 232
Ruef, M., 255, 258, 259

Rumelhart, D. E., 87
Rumsey, S., 159, 162
Russell, D. W., 237
Russell, H. M., 32, 91
Rutte, C. G., 165
Ryan, T., 60, 159, 162, 166
Ryu, D., 179

Sabel, C. F., 4
Sabidussi, G., 213
Sacchetti, G., 238
Sailer, L., 193
Saint-Simon, Claude Henri de, 80
Salaff, J., 231
Salancik, G. R., 20, 58, 174, 178–79, 215
Salisbury, J. G. T., 231
Samuelson, P., 60, 160
Schachter, S., 214, 224, 227
Schank, R. C., 91
Schelling, T. C., 165
Scherlis, W., 231
Schermerhorn, J. R., 225
Schmitz, J., 169, 174, 179, 234
Schneider, S., 166
Scholte, J. A., 4, 5
Schultz, J. V., 68
Schumpeter, J. A., 148
Schwartz, M., 217
Scott, C. R., 193, 197
Scott, J., 31
Scott, W. R., 102
Seabright, M. A., 218
Seary, A. J., 31, 67, 73
Seeman, T. E., 238
Seibold, D. R., 9, 89, 179, 184
Selman, B., 197
Serb, D., 94, 199
Shah, M., 197
Shan, W., 146, 192
Shaw, M., 17
She, Y., 94, 199
Shelly, G. A., 312
Sherif, M., 167, 224
Sherman, J. D., 180
Shetler, J. C., 161
Shirky, C., 317
Short, J. A., 234

Shortell, S. M., 181
Shrader, C. B., 212, 213
Shumate, M., 253, 325
Sifonis, J., 314
Simmel, G., 143–44, 235
Simon, A. R., 167
Simon, H. A., 12, 80, 85, 142
Singh, H., 147
Singh, J. V., 11, 218, 247, 255
Skaggs, B. C., 206, 214
Skvoretz, J., 58, 209, 222, 326, 327
Sloan, Alfred P., 18
Slovic, P., 145
Smarr, L., 318
Smith, A., 79, 142
Smith, H., 180
Smith, K. G., 20
Smith, N., 9
Smith-Doerr, L., 34, 192
Smith-Lovin, L., 223
Snijders, T. A. B., 297
Snow, C. C., 10, 18, 219, 221
Soda, G., 20
Solt, M. E., 251, 252
Soulie, F. F., 264
Spencer, H., 18, 80
Spinardi, G., 233
Staber, U. H., 257
Stamps, J., 119
Stanley, J. C., 242
Stasser, G., 202
Staw, B., 178
Stearns, L. B., 182, 217
Stearns, T. M., 212, 216
Stein, C. H., 237
Steinfield, C. W., 102, 174, 233, 234
Stengers, I., 96
Sterman, J., 99, 103
Stern, R. N., 214
Stevens, R., 318
Stevenson, W. B., 8, 68
Stewart, D. D., 202
Stohl, C., 4, 31, 68, 190–91
Stoyanoff, N. J., 186
Strauss, D., 49, 115
Strogatz, S. H., 311
Stuart, T. E., 252

Su, C., 94, 199
Swaminathan, A., 251, 252, 257
Swanson, N., 238
Syme, S. L., 235, 237

Takaai, M., 197
Takahashi, P., 216
Takeda, H., 197
Tambini, D., 6
Tchuente, M., 264
Tehranian, M., 232
Teo, A. C., 148, 212
Thomas, W. I., 193
Thompson, J. D., 85, 102
Tirole, J., 322, 323
Tjaden, Brett, 308
Tognelli, M., 238
Tolia, N., 320
Torobin, J., 169, 179
Torvald, Linus, 322
Tosi, H. L., 227
Trevino, L., 174
Trist, E. L., 85, 254
Troitzch, K. G., 103
Tsai, W., 34
Tsgarousianou, R., 6
Tsui, A. E., 225
Turner, J. C., 224, 227
Tushman, M. L., 246, 249, 256, 257, 258, 267
Tversky, A., 145

Urry, J., 6
Useem, M., 181, 216, 217
Uzzi, B., 148, 153

Valente, T. W., 169
Van den Bulte, C., 228
Van de Ven, A. H., 255, 256
Van Lange, P. A. M., 165
Varela, F. J., 95
Vaughn, J. C., 148
Volberda, H. W., 271

Wacquant, L. J. D., 143
Wade, J. B., 147
Wagner, W. G., 225

Walker, G., 146, 178, 192
Walker, M. E., 237
Wallace, M., 215
Wang, Y. D., 9
Warglien, M., 262, 265
Warren, R., 34
Wartella, E., 4
Wasserman, S., 31, 36, 37, 40, 41, 45, 49, 51, 52, 93, 113–14, 117, 182, 196, 199, 203, 237, 327
Waters, M., 4
Watts, D. J., 307–12, 326
Watzlavick, P., 19
Weber, M., 8, 17, 19
Weber, S., 322, 323
Wegner, D. M., 94, 199, 201, 202, 203
Weick, K. E., 85, 167, 242
Weiner, N., 82, 83
Weinstein, B., 232
Wellman, B., 20, 47, 229, 230, 231, 235, 237
West, E., 252
Westphal, J. D., 181
Whetten, D. A., 169
Whitbred, R. A., 104, 118, 178
White, D. R., 184
White, H. C., 19
White, P., 34
Whitmeyer, J. M., 209
Whitney, C., 4
Wholey, D. R., 10, 149, 181
Wigand, R. T., 31

Wilke, H. A. M., 165
Willer, D., 58, 209
Williams, E., 234
Williams, P., 325
Williams, R., 233
Williamson, O. E., 150–51, 152, 154, 298
Wilson, E. O., 15
Winter, S. G., 242, 247, 248, 249
Witte, J., 230, 231
Wittenbaum, G. M., 202
Woelfel, J., 67, 186
Wood, R. A., 147
Woodward, P., 318
Wortley, S., 237
Wright, S., 264

Yamagishi, T., 209, 212
Yan, A., 220
Yangchung, P., 246
Yates, J., 234

Zahn, G. L., 228
Zajac, E. J., 151, 154, 155
Zanibbi, L., 238
Zeggelink, E. P. H., 102
Zelditch, M., Jr., 222
Zenger, T. R., 225
Zey-Ferrell, M., 180
Zhou, X., 181
Zinger, J. T., 238, 239
Zink, D., 92, 197
Zucker, L., 193

Subject Index

access, 144–45
access of resources, 212
accuracy, 194, 198, 201, 203
acquaintance networks, 196
acquisition premiums, 181
action process, 163–65
activity focus theory, 227
actor level, 57–58, 61–62, *fig. 2.1,5*
adaptability, 87, 263, 266
adaptive walk, 265
adjacency matrix, 36
adoption models, 169
advertising agency, 226
advice networks, 146, 213, 302
advice relationships, 196
affiliation, 47, 57, 225, 303
affiliation networks, 37, 47
affordances, 234, 235, 303–4
age, 57, 62, 223–24, 225, 303
age dependence, 242, *table 9.1*
agent-based models, 20
    Blanche and, 103–4
    coevolutionary theory and, 306
    collective action theories and, 299
    complexity theory and, 85

    emergent structures and, 21, 88–89
    knowledge networks and, 90–91
    transaction cost economics theory
        and, 298
agents, 86, 103
AIDS, 253, 318
Aimster, 319
algorithmic information content, 85
al-Queda terrorist operations, 324
amplification effect, 214
ANOVA, 47
ant colonies, 15
anticontagion, 180
AOL, 318–19
Apache, 321
apparel economy, 153
a priori knowledge, 99
architectural design software, 154
artifact, 51, 76
artificial intelligence, 91
artificial intelligence techniques, 186
artificial networks, 121
association, 68
asymmetry, 40, 53, 117–18, 174
AT&T, 254, 257, 321

attitudes, 86, 105
in cognitive consistency theory, 204, 205–6, 301
in NK(C) model, 273, 280
toward technologies, 178–80
attribute analysis, 295
attributes, 30–31, 47, 55, 86, 104–5
changes in, 106–7
in cognitive social structures, 194–95
MTML analytic framework and, 48, 294, 295–96
in NK(C) model, 273
in semantic networks, 187
attribute variable, 124–25, 131
attribution theories, 213
authorities, 314
autocatalysis, 89, 95, 267
automakers, 152
automorphic equivalence, 184
autonomy, 11, 17, 146–47, 148, 215, 302
autopoietic systems, 95
autoregressive networks, 295, 296
avatars, 30, 93, 103, 105, 198
Awara, 308

Bacon numbers, 308
badness of fit, 76
balance, 49
balance theory, 46, 88
cognitive consistency and, 204, 206–7
in computational modeling of networks, 102, 118–19
at triadic level of analysis, 59–60, 64, *figs. 2.3,7*
banks, 252, 257
beer companies, 252
behavior, 86, 88, 204, 206
ethical, 210, 213–14
through contagion, 9, 180–82
unethical, 180, 206
belief systems, 272–79, 280–85
Bell labs, 321
Bell System, 253
benefits, 163, 166
Bernoulli distributions, 53, 116
betweenness, 38, 45, 57, 196, 213, 302

bimodal networks, 37
binary attributes, 104
binary networks, 49
binary relations, 36–37, 40
binary variables, 110
binomial distributions, 110, 112
biology, 14, 97, 252, 262, 264–65, 270
biomedical scientists, 189
biotechnology industry, 193, 250
BITNET computer network, 169
Blanche, 20, 21, 103–4, 108–9, 115, 297
computational modeling in, 122–37, *figs. 4.2–4*
Blind Data, 320
blind variations, 248
blockmodeling, 296
Bluetooth technology, 320
Boolean networks, 263–64, 269–70, *fig. 9.1*
boundary-less organizations, 220
boundary spanners, 187
bounded rationality, 142
"bowling alone," 232
brain, 311
brewpubs, 252, 257
bridges, 38
brokers, 143
buffering role, 235, 260
bundled routines and competencies, 247
burnout, 221
"buy or make" decision, 151

Caenorhabditis elegans, 310
capital allocation process, 216
career networks, 10
carpool lanes, 89–90
carrying capacity, 251, 305–6
catalysis, 267
catastrophe theory, 84, 266
categorical attributes, 104–5
CATPAC analysis, 186
causal loop properties, 84
causal models, 55
cellular automata models, 102, 233, 310
centering resonance analysis, 187

centrality, 39
of actors, 195, 302
in collective action theories, 168
exchange relations and, 211, 212–13,
215–16
at global level of analysis, 44–45, 60
at individual level of analysis, 57, 62
job satisfaction and, 206
reputations associated with, 196
in social support theories, 236–37,
305
centralization, 65, 113, 165, 231–32,
287–88. *See also* network
centralization
chains, 17, 41
Challenger, 166
change, 95, 105, 254, 256, 277, 278
change mechanisms, 246
chaos theory, 84
chaotic regime, 269–70
chaotic state, 90, 97, 121
Chechen rebellion, 324
children's television program
organizations, 252
chindogu, 315
choice, 72–73
circle, 17
classical conditioning theory, 102
classical economics, 150
client-server architecture, 315, 319–21
cliques, 21, 43–44, 164, 226, 295
closeness, 38–39, 45, 57, 212
"closing the loop," 72
closure, 95, 259
clustering, 308–9, 311
cocitation analysis, 189
coercive isomorphism, 254
coevolutionary processes, 247, 262
coevolutionary theory, 25, 88, 246–47,
305–7
community ecology and, 257–58
NK(C) model and, 270–72, 278, 280–
88
cognitive attribute variable, 124–25
cognitive balance theory, 59, 64
cognitive communication structures,
24

cognitive consistency, 275–79, 281–85
cognitive consistency theories, 24, 173,
186, 204–7, 301
cognitive dissonance, 278–79
cognitive frustration, 273, 275
cognitive knowledge networks, 91, 92,
198–203, 300
cognitive knowledge structures
theory, 173, 300
cognitive relation variable, 124–25
cognitive social relation, 194
cognitive social structures, 144, 186,
193–98
cognitive social structures theory, 173,
194, 300
cognitive theories, 24, 67, 186–207, 301,
fig. 2.9
cohesion, contagion by, 23, 174–76,
178, 179, 184
cohesion-compliance hypothesis, 170
coin tosses, 52–53, 116–17
Cold War, 285
collaboration technologies, 184, 198,
323
collaborative filters, 197
collaborative problem solving, 17
collective action theories, 22, 88, 159–
72, 298–99
communication technology links
and, 235
in computational model, 120–21
at global level of analysis, 60–61, 65–
66, *figs. 2.4,8*
homophily theory vs., 47
MTML analytic framework and, 94
collective good, 60, 160, 247, 299
collective negative outcome, 165
COMCON, 17, 150
commensalism, 257, 258, 260, 306
commercialists, 253–54
common enemy, 167
commons, 160, 165–66, 170
common understandings, 187
communality, 162, 299
communal networks, 170
communication dilemmas, 24, 165–68,
299

communication functions, 81
communication holes network, 144, *fig. 5.1*
communication linkages, 95, 144–45, 147, 212, 228
communication network analysis, 95
communication rules, 88
communication technologies, 5–6, 10, 102, 197, 231–35
communication ties, 67, 105, 303–4
communication void networks, 144
communities, 237, 271, 272, 305–7
communities of practice, 247, 249
community, 246, 258–60
community dynamics, 257
community ecology, 246, 257–61, 306–7
community interdependence, 242, 246, *table 9.1*
community level of analysis, 252, 271
communityware technologies, 197–98
competencies, 247–49
competition, 247, 251, 253, 257–60, 306
complement, 114, 144
complex adaptive behavior, 88
complex adaptive systems, 87
complex communication networks, 262
complex evolutionary systems, 85
complexity, 11, 17, 85, 246, 272, 310
complexity catastrophe, 266–67
complexity theory, 85–89, 97
complex regime, 97, 269–70
complex systems, 85–89
   self-organizing systems as, 89–97, 269–70
complex systems theory, 79, 83, 262, 310
compliance, 170–71
components, 43–44
compositional emergence, 14
compositional models, 15
computational modeling of networks, 20, 99–138
   in *Blanche*, 122–37
   empirical validation of, 118–21
   executing virtual experiments, 121–22

organizational network models, 102–12
p^* computational network model, 115–18
special issues in, 112–15
computational organizational network models, 102–12
computational organizational theory. *See* COT
computer models, 202–3
computer networks, 92, 203, 229
computer notebook manufacturers, 262–63
computer resources sharing, 317
computer simulations
   Blanche and, 20, 21, 297
   of collective action theory, 170
   of complex systems, 85
   of computational network models, 102, 113, 118
   of contagion, 191–92
   of NK(C) model, 272
   of NK model, 266, 279
   of semantic networks, 189
   of social influence models, 183
concentration, 162
concepts, 103
conditional dependency, 113
conditional uniform distribution, 53
conditioning, 51–53, 296
conditioning theory, 102
configurations, 49–50, 53
connected graphs, 43
connectedness, 9, 44, 152
connected networks, 48, 49
connectivity, 162, 262, 266, 271–72, 299, 326
consensual cognitive social structure, 194, 196
consensus, 194
consistency theories, 71–72, 77, 115. *See also* cognitive consistency theories
constrained generating procedures, 14
constraints
   in coevolutionary theory, 271
   in communities, 260

in electronic propinquity, 232
in evolutionary theory, 263, 265–66
in homophily theory, 226
in network organizations, 221
in NK(C) model, 275, 278–79, 283, 286
in social capital theory, 146
construction algorithms, 309
construction emergence, 14
constructivist perspectives, 174
constructural theory, 191–92
contagion mechanisms, 20, 174–77, 301
  cognitive theories and, 195, 205
  communication technology links and, 234
  in empirical research, 177–82
contagion theories, 22–24, 118, 173–86, 299–300
  in computational model, 123–24, 128
  of networks, 182–86
  physical proximity and, 229
contamination, 23
contextual-ecological variables, 15
contingency tables, 53–54
contingency theory, 102
continuous attributes, 105, 106
control of resources, 213
convergence model of communication, 67, 174
cooperation, 87
cooperation-contingent transformation, 166
cooperation processes, 253, 257–58
cooperative strategies, 310
co-ops, 257
coordination costs, 235, 298
coordination theory, 235, 304
copyleft, 321
core competencies, 247
corporate elites, 210, 216–17
correlation structure, 265
cosmopolites, 149
costs, 163
COT (computational organizational theory), 100–101, *fig. 4.1*
coupled landscapes, 270–72, 281, 283, 285

coupled phase-oscillators, 310
coword occurrence, 189, 190
co-worker networks, 238
CRADA (cooperative research and development agreement), 70–71, 154–55
creativity, 17
credit unions, 252
crickets, 310
criminal networks, 325
critical mass, 163–64, 234–35
critical mass theory, 169
cultural tradition, 19–20
cultural variability, 190–91, 226
cybernetics, 79, 80, 82–83
cyclicality, 42, 59–60, 64, 71–72, 295, 296

"dark side," 310
databases, 103, 105, 198, 299
data generation, 123
decentralization, 17, 44, 232, 287–88
decision-making, 215, 216
degree, 37–38, 57
degrees of separation, 41, 308–11, 313
demise of organizations, 253
demographic homophily, 225–26
demographic processes, 242, *table 9.1*
density
  in coevolutionary theory, 306
  in computational model, 113–14
  in evolutionary theories, 251
  at global level of analysis, 44, 60, 65
  in knowledge structures, 193
  MTML analytic framework and, 21, 46
  network research and, 294
  in p^* analysis, 49
  in semantic networks, 189, 191
  in social support networks, 304–5
density dependence, 242, 246, 251–52, 253, *table 9.1*
density-dependence argument, 251
dependence graph, 115–16
dependencies, 104, 112–13, 294, 296, 306
dependency theories, 24–25, 71, 77, 209–22, 301–2

descriptive network metrics, 47
descriptive statistics, 294
designing of small worlds, 311
determinism, 14, 268
deterministic computational models, 109–12, 115, 232
diachronic emergence, 16
diameter, 41
dichotomous relations, 35, 36, 106
differential cyclicality, 64
differential mutuality, 63
differential network centralization, 66
differential reciprocity, 63
differential tendencies, 72–73
differential transitivity, 64
digital revolution, 315
digraphs, 36
dimensionality of space, 263
Direct Action Network, 324
directionality, 35, 43
directional links, 35, 40
directional networks, 36–37
direct links, 40–41, 43
directory of information, 92
directory updating, 95, 199, 200, 203, 301
direct ties, 77
disconnected graphs, 43
discontinuity, 84
discrete time intervals, 105, 269
discretionary databases, 299
disease metaphor, 22
disembedding, 6–7
dissipative structures, 84
distance, 40–42, 303
distributed knowledge, 91–92
Distributed Net, 318
diversity, 156, 225–26, 254
divisibility, 162
divisional form, 18
DNA, 284–85
dominance hierarchy, 102
double bind, 10
double interacts, 85
downward determinism, 14
drugs, 248
dual effects hypothesis, 232

dyadic atomization, 46
dyadic independence models, 117–18
dyadic level of analysis, 21, 37, 40–42, 46, *table 2.4*
    cognitive social structure theory at, 195
    contagion process at, 174, 205
    CRADA network at, 71–72, 77
    endogenous variables at, 58–59, 304, *fig. 2.2*
    exogenous variables at, 63–64, *fig. 2.6*
    physical proximity at, 228
    semantic theories at, 188–89, 300
    social exchange theory at, 302
    transactive memory systems theory at, 201, 301
    valid statistical inference techniques at, 48
dynamics simulation, 99, 297
Dynamo, 103

eBay, 319–20
ECCO (Episodic Communication in Channels of Organizations) analysis, 8
ecological processes, 242, *table 9.1*
economic exchange, 79–80
economic theories, 148
    transaction cost economics theory, 150–55
ecosystem networks, 255–56
ecosystems, 251, 271, 272, 306
education, 62, 86, 223, 225
effectiveness, 146–47, 216, 302
effective network size, 39–40, 57
efficiency, 9, 40, 57, 147–49
egocentric networks, 39–40, 238
elance.com, 320
e-lancers, 6–7, 320
electronic data interchange (EDI), 233, 304
electronic propinquity, 25, 231–33
electronic proximity theories, 229–35, 303–4, 316
elitism, 193, 210, 216
e-mail, 9, 149, 169, 179, 230, 232, 316

embedded knowledge, 32–34, 92
embeddedness, 5–6, 22, 148, 152–53,
    156–57
emergence
    of belief systems, 272–79
    historical perspectives on, 18
    logics of, 101, 104
    of structure from chaos, 11–15
    time and, 16
emergent networks, 8–16
emergent outcomes, 110, 122
emergent perspective, 233
emergent structures, 85, 88–89, 298,
    306
empirical data, 112–13
empirical network research, 47, 305
empirical research, 84, 100–101, 109
    on cognitive knowledge structures,
        201–3
    on cognitive social structures, 196
    on collective action, 169–70
    on electronic propinquity, 231–33,
        304
    on homophily, 303
    MTML analytic framework and, 296
    on physical proximity, 228–29, 303
    on resource dependency theory, 215
    on semantic networks, 189–91
    on social capital, 147
    using contagion mechanisms, 177–
        82
    using exchange mechanisms, 212–14
    using homophily mechanisms, 225–
        26
    using social support mechanisms,
        237–39
empirical validation, 118–21
empty networks, 48, 49
encoding of information, 201–2
endogenous hypotheses, 77
endogenous variables, 30, 55–61, 304,
    305, *figs. 2.1–4, table 2.4*
enlargement mechanism, 229, 230, 304
entertainment, 81
entrepreneurs
    in coevolutionary theory, 259, 306
    in evolutionary theories, 248

in homophily theory, 226
in population ecology theory, 255,
    257
in public goods theory, 163
in social exchange theory, 214
in transaction cost economics
    theory, 298
environmental niches, 25, 247, 248,
    250–52, 305
environmental processes, 242, 246,
    268, *table 9.1*
Epinions, 319–20
Episodic Communication in Channels
    of Organizations analysis. *See*
    ECCO
epistatic constraints, 275, 278
epistatic linkages, 246, 263, 265–66,
    269, 271, 275–76, 279
equilibrium, 84, 215, 272
equity theory, 227
Erdos numbers, 308
E-state models, 222
ethical behavior, 210, 213–14
ethnicity, 225
ethnographic studies, 153
evolutionary model of organizing, 242
evolutionary processes, 96, 262
evolutionary theory, 25, 88
    of economics, 242
    exogenous prior relations and, 68,
        fig. 2.10
    NK(C) model and, 278
    NK model and, 262–70
    population ecology and, 242–57,
        table 9.1
exchange theories, 20, 24–25, 71, 77,
    88, 182, 209–22, 301–2
exclusion, 160, 209
exit strategy, 151–52
"exit-voice" choice, 151–52
exogenous other relations, 67–68,
    fig. 2.9, table 2.4
exogenous prior relations, 68–69,
    fig. 2.10, table 2.4
exogenous variables, 55, 57, 61–66,
    figs. 2.5–8, table 2.4
    in CRADA network, 72, 77

exogenous variables (*continued*)
  in electronic proximity theory, 304
  in exchange theories, 302
  in MTML analytic framework, 30
  in physical proximity theory, 303
  in social support theories, 305
expectation states theory, 222
experimental design, 242
expertise, 86, 93–95, 105, 192, *table 3.1*
expertise recognition, 199–200, 201–2, 203, 300
explanatory variables, 113–14
exploitation, 249
exploration, 248–49
externalities, 13, 57, 62
extraterrestrial life, 317–18

face-to-face interactions, 184, 197, 228, 234, 256
far-from-equilibrium state, 89, 97, 121
feedback, 84, 152
feedback loops, 13
financial data mining, 318
financial institutions, 216
fitness, 253, 274–79, 306
fitness contributions, 275–77, 281–84, 288
fitness landscapes, 264–67
fitness landscape studies, 262
fitter genotypes, 264
flexibility, 146, 193, 302
flows, 4–7
formal networks, 8–16
Fortune 500 companies, 181
frame-shift mutations, 267, 278
free agent nation, 320
freelancers, 6–7
FreeNet, 317, 319, 326
"free riders," 22, 161, 170
frequency, 174, 210
friendship networks, 102, 146, 206, 213, 214, 226, 296
friendship ties, 67–68, 180, 190
frozen component, 269–70
functional analysis, 81
functional form, 18
functionalism, 79, 80, 81–82

functionalist systems theory, 81–82
functional systems, 81–82

Galileo system, 186
game theory, 87, 310
Gaussian random distribution, 110, 112
gender
  as attribute, 47, 57, 86, 105
  in cognitive social structures, 196
  in homophily theory, 62, 63, 224–27, 303
  in semantic networks, 188
  in social support theories, 237
generalist strategy, 246
generalized exchange theory, 60, 64
General Motors, 18
General Social Survey, 148, 225, 238
general systems theory, 79, 80, 83
generative mechanisms, 88
  centrality as, 168
  of cognitive consistency theory, 204, 301
  of cognitive knowledge networks, 199–201
  of cognitive social structures, 194–96
  of collective action theory, 299
  in computational modeling of networks, 101, 102, 104, 109, 121
  of electronic proximity theory, 304
  hierarchy as, 298
  multiplexity as, 168
  mutuality and reciprocity as, 153
  of semantic theories, 300
  of social support theories, 305
  of transaction cost economics, 298
  of transactive memory systems theory, 301
genes, 262, 271, 273, 284
genetic level, 255
genetic networks, 246
genetic research, 318
genetic traits, 264–65
genotype, 262–63, 273, 279, 280, 284
genotype space, 262–64
geodesics, 40–42
gift culture, 323

globalization, 4–7
global level of analysis, 37, 44–45, *table 2.4*
  cognitive social structure theory at, 195
  endogenous variables at, 60–61, *fig. 2.4*
  exogenous variables at, 65–66, *fig. 2.8*
  semantic theories at, 188–89, 300
  transactive memory systems theory at, 201, 301
  valid statistical inference techniques at, 48
global optima, 266, 277
Gnutella, 317, 319, 326
golden parachute policies, 147
Google search engine, 313–14
government, 66, 71–73, 77, 154–55, 305, *fig. 2.8*
government regulations, 246, 248, 249, *table 9.1*
government-to-business (G2B), 326
government-to-citizen services (G2C), 325
government-to-government (G2G), 326
grapevine, 8, 39
graphs, 36–37, 43, 48–54
greenmail, 147
Greenpeace, 324
Groove, 318
group characteristics, 163
guru.com, 7, 320

Health and Human Services, 198
health care systems, 256, 258
Healthy Start program (Conn.), 238
heterarchies, 11–13, 15, 255, 319, 321, *figs. 1.1–2*
heterogeneities, 103, 191, 225, 288
hierarchical constraint, 40, 57
hierarchies, 9
  in communication networks, 232
  in evolutionary theories, 247
  heterarchies and, 11–12, 15, *fig. 1.1*
  MTML analytic framework and, 298
  organizational forms and, 320, 323

in semantic networks, 188
in transaction cost economics, 150–54, 298
high-technology firms, 190
hill-climbing process, 265–66
historical analysis, 189
historicity, 84
holism, 14, 15–16
homeostatic systems, 81
homogeneity, 191–92
homophily theory, 25, 88, 223–27, 302–3
  collective action theories vs., 47
  in computational model, 118, 124, 128
  CRADA network, 72, 77
  exogenous variables and, 62, 64–65, 66, 303, *figs. 2.5,7*
  small world networks and, 312
hospital studies, 190, 216, 237–38, 247, 305
hubs, 314
human agents, 93–95, 103, 104–5, 198, *table 3.1*
human capital theories, 22, 143
human genome, 323
hybrid models, 45, 47
hypertext, 5
hypodermic needle model, 184
hypothesized structural properties, 49–50, 55, 71–73, 76–77, *table 2.5*

ICQ ("I seek you"), 318
identifying of small worlds, 311
identity, 252
identity theory, 222. *See also* social identity theory
IKNOW (Inquiring Knowledge Networks On the Web), 197
Images of Organization (Morgan), 314
impossibility of exclusion, 160
incentives, 166–67
indegree, 37–38
indirect links, 40–42, 57
individual actor level, 37
individual characteristics, 162–63
individual dispositions model, 178
individualism, 191

individual level of analysis, 21, 37–40, *table 2.4*
   cognitive social structure theory at, 195
   CRADA network at, 72, 77
   endogenous variables at, 57–58, *fig. 2.1*
   exogenous variables at, 61–62, *fig. 2.5*
   in NK(C) model, 278
   physical proximity theory at, 303
   semantic theories at, 188–89, 300
   social exchange theory at, 302
   social support theories at, 305
   valid statistical inference techniques at, 48
individuation, 6
industry. *See* private sector
inertia, 105, 177, 191, 247, 254, 256
inertial theory, 242
infectious disease, 310
inferential statistics, 45, 52, 294–95, 296
informal networks, 8–11, 18
information allocation, 199, 200, 203, 301
informational resources, 236, 305
information flows, 22, 58, 152, 156, 182, 183
information processing theory, 102
information richness, 147
information sharing, 96, 317–19
information technologies, 10, 94, 170, 197, 233
initial conditions, 107–8, 191
initializing stage, 154–55
inner circle, 217
innoculation theory, 299
innovations
   collective action and, 169
   contagion theories and, 182
   evolutionary theory and, 248, 250, 257, 287
   social capital and, 149
   social support and, 305
inoculation theory, 23, 185–86
instant messaging, 229, 230–31, 234–35, 318–19

institutional linkages, 34, 246, *table 9.1*
institutional processes, 246, *table 9.1*
institutional theory, 24, 174, 182
intellectual ownership, 321
intentional variations, 248
interaction, principle of, 183
interaction rules, 86–87
interdependencies, 85, 257, 259
interests, 162, 163
interfirm links, 217–18
interlocking boards of directors, 181–82, 210, 211, 216–19, 302
International Campaign to Ban Landmines, 324
Internet, 7, 170, 229, 232, 316, 318–21
Internet Movie Database, 308, 310
interorganizational alliances, 24, 92, 198
interorganizational communication systems, 96, 192–93
interorganizational consortium, 48–49, 62
interorganizational imitation, 249
interorganizational level
   collective action at, 168–69
   contagion mechanisms at, 177, 181–82
   homophily mechanisms at, 225
   physical proximity at, 229, 303
   social exchange mechanisms at, 210, 212
   social support theories at, 238
   structural holes theory at, 146
interorganizational linkages, 34, 47, 210, 215
interorganizational networks, 57, 149, 214–19, 222
interpretive thematic analysis, 189
interventions, 120
intranets, 203
investments, 210, 298
invisible colleges, 189
"Iron Law of Oligarchy," 221
isolates, 187, 195
isomorphism, 83, 254–55, 299
iterations, 105, 107, 297
   in *Blanche*, 132, *figs. 4.2–4*

Japanese corporate networks, 215, 219
job characteristics model, 178
job satisfaction, 206, 238, 305
job searches, 147, 148, 180
job specialization, 17
jointness of supply, 160
joint value maximization principle, 22, 155, 298
journalistic organizations, 247

keiretsu groupings, 215, 219
kin networks, 238, 305
knowledge, 91
knowledge claims, 278, 284
knowledge differentiation, 201, 203, 301
knowledge flows, 24, 91, 199, 300
knowledge level, 91
knowledge links, 34
knowledge networks, 24, 79–97, 106, 189, 300. See also cognitive knowledge networks
knowledge repositories, 24, 30, 93, 166, 198–99, 203, 315
knowledge structures, 83, 186, 192–93, 197–98
k-plex, 43–44

labor force, 215
laissez-faire system, 79
Land of Lincoln Legal Assistance, 198
latent network, 197
lateral communication networks, 10, 17–18
lattice networks, 309
"Law of N-Squared," 221
"Law of Propinquity," 221
law of requisite variety, 96
leader-member-exchange theory, 213
leadership, 210, 213
learning networks, 192
learning theories, 174
least-upper-boundedness, 9
legitimacy, 254–55
less fit genotypes, 265
liaisons, 38, 187
libraries, 190, 315

linear contingencies, 84
linear systems, 84
lines of authority, 12
linguistics, 18
link density, 295
link level, 58–59
links, 40
Linux, 322
Living Systems (Miller), 83
local connectedness, 25
localites, 149
local networks, 6
local optima, 266, 272
location, 210, 212
logics of emergence, 101, 104
logistic regression, 54
logit, 54
log likelihood, 54
log likelihood values, 77
log linear analysis, 54
longitudinal network data, 297
long-jump adaptations, 267, 278
loose coupling, 85
Lotus Notes, 318
loyalty, 257

maintenance relations, 32
male power base, 226
mandated networks, 8
marital networks, 39
markets, 18, 150–54, 247, 250, 298
market transactions, 156, 298
Markov random graph models, 49, 69
material resources, 236, 305
mathematical equations, 100–101
mathematical models, 169
matrices, 36–37
matrix form of organization, 10, 12, 18, 149
maximally rugged landscapes, 265
maximize, 142
media coverage, 187
media richness, 102
media selection, 234, 303–4
mental health studies, 216, 235, 238
message flow, 60
messages, 5, 186–87

metaphors, 314–15
metarules, 87
methodological designs, 9
methods, 104
microbreweries, 252, 257
microdetermination, 12
microdeterminism, 14–15
Microsoft, 322
Microsoft Exchange, 322
Microsoft Visual C++, 108
migratory knowledge, 32–34, 92
mimetic isomorphism, 254–55
mimetic learning, 249
mimetic processes, 174, 182, 255, 299
Mirabilis, 318
mobilization, 168–69
    of resources, 236–37
model analysis, 123
model building, 123
modularity, 12, 16
Mojo Nation, 319
monopolies, 254
Morpheus, 317
morphogenetic systems, 82, 84
morphostatic systems, 81
MTML analytic framework, 45–54,
        294–97, *table 2.4*
    cognitive social structures and, 195–
        96
    community ecology and, 306
    complex systems and, 89, 94
    for emergent communication
        networks, 242
    generative mechanisms for, 168–69
    knowledge networks and, 92–93
    model of, 54–70, *fig. 2.11*
    organizational forms and, 315–17,
        319, 322–24
    overview of, 20–21, 25, 29–30
    p* network analysis example, 70–77,
        table 2.5
    semantic theories and, 300
    small world networks and, 307, 312–
        13
    transactive memory systems theory
        and, 301
multiagent knowledge networks, 92–95

multiagent simulation environments,
        103
multidivisional form, 18
multilevel analyses, 45, 46–47, 294–95
    of evolutionary theories, 255–56, 259
multilevel hypotheses testing, 46
multilevel systems, 11
multimedia text, 5
multimethod triangulation, 242
multimodal networks, 93–94, *table 3.1*
multinational corporations, 152, 220–21
multiple levels of analysis, 294
multiple orders, 15
multiple organizational forms, 271
multiple-step linkages, 41
multiple theories, 45, 118, 295
multiplexity, 30, 168, 174, 294
multiplex networks, 295, 296
multiplex relations, 35–37
multitheoretical, multilevel
        framework. *See* MTML analytic
        framework
multitheoretical analyses, 45–46
mutations, 265–67, 277–78, 286–87, 306
mutual causality, 84, 89, 96
mutual cooperation, 87
mutual fitness, 258–60
mutual-interest theories, 22, 142, 159–
        72, 235, 298–99
mutualism, 306
mutualists, 253
mutuality
    in computational modeling of
        networks, 113–14
    CRADA network and, 71–73
    at dyadic level of analysis, 40, 58, 63,
        302
    MTML analytic framework and, 21,
        46, 294, 295, 296
    structural equivalence of, 42
mutual links, 53
mutually beneficial outcomes, 257
mutual state, 117–18
mutual ties, 77

Napster, 317
Napsterization, 319

nascent entrepreneurs, 257
Nash equilibrium, 272, 283–84
National Center for Supercomputing
    Applications, 321
National Geographic Society, 229–30
national grid, 318
natural selection, 268–69
Nature, 311
n-clique, 43
negative outcomes, 165
Negopy program, 73
nematode worm (*Caenorhabditis
    elegans*), 310
neoclassical economics, 150
neoinstitutional perspective, 254
nested structures, 11, 15, *fig. 1.1*
net-literacy, 326
Netscape, 322
netwars, 324, 326
network analysis, 29–45, *tables 2.1–3.
    See also Blanche*; MTML analytic
    framework
  electronic proximity theories and,
      229, 233
  semantic networks and, 189
  small world networks and, 314
  social capital theory and, 143
network centralization, 44–45, 52, 60–
    61, 65–66, 294
network consolidation, 215
network decomposition, 295–96
network exchange theory, 58, 209, 222
network extension, 215
network forms, 16–18, 22
network holes, 143
network level of analysis, 21, 189, 246
network linkages, 18–20, 31–34, 228,
    tables 2.1–3
network measures, 35–36
network organizations, 154, 192–93,
    219–21, 221, 298
network properties, 37
network representation, 36–37
network research, 20, 293–94, 326–27
neural networks, 13, 186, 310
newspaper industry, 216, 252
New York Times, 320

niches, 250–52, 257–58, 271
niche-width dynamics, 242, 246,
    table 9.1
9–11 terrorist attacks, 187
NK(C) model, 246, 255, 262, 270–74,
    276–77, 279, 280–88
NK model, 246, 262–70, 271, 278–79
noncooperation, 87
nondirectional links, 35, 42
nondirectional networks, 36–37
nonhuman agents, 93–95, 103, 104–5,
    198, *table 3.1*
nonindependence, 295
nonlinear difference equations, 105,
    106–7
nonlinear interrelationships, 103–4
nonlinear logics, 101
nonlinear systems, 84
nonnetworks, 144
normative isomorphism, 255
n-squared, law of, 221
n-step links, 41
null state, 117–18
null ties, 40
nursing, 236

object code, 321
object-oriented programming, 104
observable communication, 197
occupation, 62, 86
oligarchy, iron law of, 221
Olivetti factory (Naples), 229
one-step mutation, 277–78, **286**
open environmental spa**ce**, **259**
open source movement, 321–23, 326
open-system view of organizations, 85
optical disc technology, 255
optimal landscapes, 266
order, 11, 97, 268–69
ordered regime, 269–70
organizational affiliation, 62, 63, 66, 72
organizational boundaries, 242
organizational change, 254–55, 256
organizational communication, 7, 84,
    231, 301
organizational evolutionary theory, 271
organizational fitness, 249

organizational forms, 11, 17–18, 246, 252–54, 257, 271, 314–26
organizational imperative, 232
organizational lineages, 256
organizational mission, 190, 206
organizational networks, 79, 170
organizational populations, 246–47, 251–60, 267
organizational problem solving networks, 69
organizational research, 242–46, *table 9.1*
organizational success, 251
organizational taxonomies, 242
organizational traits, 262–63
organizers, 163, 164–65
origins of life, 262
outdegree, 37–38
overembeddedness, 221
oversocialized view, 148, 152

p^* analytic techniques
  MTML analytic framework and, 45, 46
  realization of graphs and networks in, 48–54
p^* computational network model, 115–18
p^* logit network models, 54
p^* network analysis example, 70–77, 112, *table 2.5*
p^* social influence models, 297
p^* social selection models, 297
p^* stochastic computational modeling approach, 115
P2P. *See* peer-to-peer applications
Pajek, 31
parameter changes, 120
Paris Commune (1871), 168
partners, 192
part-whole competition, 262
peer approval, 170, 180
peer-to-peer applications (P2P), 316–21, 326
perceptions, 193–98, 202
percolation, 269
peripheral competencies, 247

personal linkage, 34
personal networking, 311–12
perspectivism, 83
Pew Internet and American Life Project, 230
phase transitions, 267, 269, *fig. 9.2*
philosophy, 7, 11, 14
phyletic gradualism, 256
physical connectivity, 162
physical proximity theory, 227–29, 233–35, 303, 312
physics, 14, 83, 97
Planned Parenthood, 198
"poison pill" strategy, 181
police organization, 206
political economy, 214–15
political upheaval, 246, *table 9.1*
poor fit, 102
Popular Power, 318
population dynamics, 242, *table 9.1*
population ecology theory, 242–57, 259, 306
  critique of, 255–57
population level of analysis, 252, 259, 278
populations of organizations, 256, 272–73, 284
positional tradition, 19
positions, 44
power, 210, 212–19, 226
power-dependence relationship, 212, 301–2
power distance index, 191
power grid, 310, 318
power law, 313
POWERPLAY, 102
Powersim, 103
Prairie-KNOW, 198
pregnant women, 238
preponderance, 194
prior activity, 263
prior innovations, 250
prisoner's dilemma game, 87
private goods, 160
private sector, 215
  CRADA network, 71–73, 77, 154–55
  exogenous variables, 66, *fig. 2.8*

probabilistic models, 297
probabilities of ties, 113–15
probability distribution, 110, 118
processing stage, 154, 155
process thinking, 84
production processes, 17
production relations, 32
productivity, 17, 146, 265
product links, 34
proemergent bias, 10
professionalism, 255
profitability, 265, 298
project teams, 92
prominence, 193
propinquity, law of, 221
proximity, 195, 226, 303
proximity theories, 25, 88, 118–19. *See also* electronic proximity theories; physical proximity theory
PSPAR computer program, 30, 54
downloading and installing, 73–77
psychological field theory, 16
psychological theories, 193–94
p-type hierarchy, 12, *fig. 1.1*
public "bads," 160–61
public goods theory, 22, 60, 66, 160–65, 299
public-good transformation, 167
public opinion, 285
publishing industry, 233
punctuated equilibrium, 256, 267

QAP (Quadratic Assignment Procedure), 68
Quadratic Assignment Procedure. *See* QAP
qualitative system changes, 84
quasi-experimental design, 242

race, 226, 227, 303
radical variations, 250
random graph models, 49
random mutations, 287, 306
random networks, 309–11
range, 156, 193
rational choice theory, 142, 222
rationality, 142

reach, 164–65
reachability, 41, 42
realization of graphs and networks, 296
CRADA network, 76, 77
endogenous variables, 55, 58, *table 2.4*
exogenous other relations, 67
exogenous prior relations, 68
exogenous variables, 55, 63, 64, 66, *table 2.4*
generative mechanisms of, 153
in *p** analysis, 48–54
recipes, 314–17
reciprocity, 30, 40
as contagion mechanism, 176
at dyadic level of analysis, 58–59, 63
in *p** analysis, 49–53
tit-for-tat strategy, 88
in transaction cost economics theory, 298
valid statistical inference techniques and, 47–48
reconfiguration mechanism, 229, 230–31, 304
reconfiguration stage, 154, 155
re-creation, 253
reductionism, 14, 15, 83
redundancy, 41–42
reembedding, 6–7
reengineering, 15
referrals, 144–45
reflected exclusivity, principle of, 183
reflexivity, 6
regimes, 269
regression analysis, 47
regular equivalence, 42
regular networks, 309–11
rehabilitation center (Italy), 238
relational-interactional variables, 15
relational ties, 115–16
relational tradition, 19
relations, 30–31, 35, 67, 104, 105–6, 295–96
changes in, 106–7
in cognitive social structures, 194, 195

relation variable, 124–25, 131
religion, 225, 303
replacement, 253
representative linkage, 34
reputation, 196, 302, 323
requisite variety, law of, 96
research design, 109, 122, 128–29
research hypotheses, 45, 48
resistance, variations in, 177
resource dependency theory, 58, 63, 88, 182, 210, *fig. 2.6*
  in interorganizational networks, 214–19
resource exchange, 60, 71, 85, 95
resource heterogeneity, 163, 165
resource poor, 24, 271
resource rich, 24, 299
resources, 162–63
  in coevolutionary theory, 258–60, 306
  in evolutionary theories, 247, 250–52
  in social support theories, 235–36, 305
retail chain stores, 272, 280, 285–88
retention, 247, 249–50, 253, 256, 268
retention mechanisms, 249
retrieval coordination, 199, 200, 203, 300–301
retrieval of information, 201–2
richness, 234
role analyses, 44
routines, 247–49
routinized variations, 250
rugged fitness landscapes, 262–70, 277, 278, 279, 282, 284
rule-governed interaction, 85
rules, 121
rules of interaction, 86–87
rumors, 8

sample space, 49, 51–53
Santa Fe Institute, 310
satisfaction, 17, 205–6
satisfice, 142
savings and loan associations, 257
scale-free, 284
"scapes," 4

"schema consistent," 206
schemata, 87
search engines, 313–14
selection, 247, 249, 256, 268
selection engine, 249
selection-retention mechanisms, 250
selective incentives, 166–67
selectivity, 164–65
self-categorization theory, 224, 302–3
self-healing, 326
self-interest theories, 22, 88, 298–99
  computational network models and, 118–19
  organizational forms and, 323
  public goods theory vs., 161
  theoretical mechanisms of, 20, 155–58
  transaction cost economics theory and, 235
self-organization, 267–70, *fig. 9.2*
self-organization theory, 89
self-organizing complex systems, 89–95, 121
  knowledge networks as, 95–97
self-organizing systems theory, 79, 80, 84, 85
self-referencing, 89
self-referential closure, 95
self-reports, 193–94, 196, 207
self-sufficiency, 260
semantic convergence, 191
semantic networks, 20, 24, 67, 186–92
semantic theories, 173, 186–207, 300–301
semantic ties, 188–89
Sematech alliance, 161
semiconductor industry, 252
Sendmail, 322
servers, 315, 319, 322
SETI (Search for Extraterrestrial Intelligence) Project, 317–18
sex, 226
shadow networks, 10
shared interpretations, emergence of, 102
shared understandings, 187
Shelter for Battered Women, 198

shortcuts, 309, 311, 312

Side Streets, 308

SIENA (Simulation Investigation for Empirical Network Analysis), 297

similarity-attraction hypothesis, 223–24

simulation modeling, 99, 103, 107

simulation software, 108

Six Degrees of Separation (Guare), 308

size dependence, 17, 242, 253, *table 9.1*

skills, 86, 93–94, 199, 300

Sleepers, 308

slugging, 89–90

small businesses (Canada), 238

Small World (Lodge), 308

small world networks, 25, 41, 307–14

Small Worlds (Watts), 307, 311

smooth landscapes, 265

sociability, 235

social capital, 22, 143

social capital theory, 142–49, 298
  theoretical mechanisms of, 156–58

social circles, 235–36, 238

social cognitive theory, 174, 179

social comparison theory, 25, 102, 227, 303

social control, 170

social dilemmas, 165–67

social entrepreneurs, 144–45

social exchange mechanisms, 210, 215, 226

social exchange theory, 46, 58–59, 63–64, 102, 210–12, 302, *fig. 2.2*

social forms, 4

social identity, 224

social identity theory, 227, 302–3

social influence, 24

social influence p^* models, 297

social influence theory, 102, 174, 183–84, 234

social information processing theory, 24, 102, 174, 178–79, 183

social interaction networks, 10

social investments, 145

social learning theory, 24

social network measures, 30–31, *tables 2.1–3*

social networks
  cognitive social structures and, 194
  computer simulations and, 297
  dependence graph and, 115–16
  electronic propinquity and, 229, 231, 234
  knowledge networks and, 95–96, 193
  semantic networks and, 189
  small world networks and, 312–13
  social support theories and, 235
  virtual, 197–98

social sciences, 11, 84, 97, 99–100, 252, 294

social selection p^* models, 297

social support theories, 235–39, 304–5

social theories, 20–25, 29–30, 109, 141, 293, *table 1.1. See also names of theories*

sociology, 18

"Solaria world," 309

source code, 321

space-time compression, 4

space-time distanciation, 5

sparsely connected networks, 44

s-partite graphs, 93–94, *table 3.1*

spatial coordinates, 86

specialist strategy, 246

specialization, 17, 18, 201–2, 252

species, 251–52, 262, 271, 272, 280, 284

specific network realization, 113

specific tie, 113

spontaneous order, 89, 269

square data matrices, 36

stability, 16, 81, 95, 247

stability mechanisms, 246

stable equilibrium state, 121

standardized goods and services, 18

standardized variations, 250

starting values, 107

statistical conditioning, 51–53

statistical methods, 52, 109, 294–95

status differential models, 8

status quo, 81, 82, 250

steel mills, 248

STELLA, 108

STELLA/*iThink*, 103

stereotypes, 199

stochastic computational models, 109–12, 115
storage of information, 201–2, 317
strategies, 87
strength, 30, 35, 36, 174
strength of weak ties, 147–48
stress, 235, 238, 303, 305
strong component, 43
strong ties, 147, 148, 206, 235
structural analysis, 18
structural autonomy, 57–58, 146, 298
structural constraints, 40, 146
structural dependencies, 115–17
structural equation models, 55, 100
structural equivalence, 40, 42
  contagion by, 23–24, 174–76, 178, 179, 180, 182, 184
  in semantic networks, 188–89
structural-functionalism, 79, 80, 81–82
structural holes, 39–40, 57, 60, *fig. 2.1*
structural holes theory, 142–49, 157, 298
structural independence, 117
structural tendencies, 51–53, 55, 65–66, 94
  CRADA network, 70–72, 76, 77
structural theory of action, 102, 174
structuration, 19
structuration theory, 102, 197
structure-preserving systems, 81
structures of knowledge, 24
s-type hierarchy, 12, *fig. 1.1*
subgraphs, 43
subgroup level, 37
subgroup networks, 66, *fig. 2.8*
  CRADA network, 72
subnetworks, 296
substitution mechanism, 229, 230, 304
subway system (Boston), 311
success, 265
supervisor-subordinate relationships, 196
survival, 87, 253, 256, 260, 264, 266
  of the mutually fit, 259
swarming, 324–25
symbiosis, 257, 258, 260, 306
symbiotic relations networks, 247

symbolic interactionist perspectives, 174
symmetric ties, 40
symmetry, 30
synchronization, 310
synchronized aggregation, 14
synchronous emergence, 16
system change, 81–82
systems dynamics simulation programs, 103
systems models, 79–84
systems theory, 19
  critique of, 83–84
  historical perspectives on, 79–83

tangled composite structures, 11–12, 15
tasks, 93–95, *table 3.1*
technological imperative, 232, 233–34
technological processes, 246, *table 9.1*
technologies, 178–80, 247, 253, 304
telephone industry, 232, 253–54, 257
telescience, 10
tenure, 62, 223, 224, 225, 303
tertius gaudens, 143–45
text analysis, 186
theoretical mechanisms, 18, 20–25, *table 1.1*
  for agent-based models, 88
  for coevolutionary NK(C) model, 280–88
  for cognitive theories, 301
  of collective action, 171–72, 304
  for computational modeling, 106–7
  of contagion, 174–82, 191, 301, 304
  for coordination theories, 304
  of electronic proximity, 230–31
  for evolutionary NK model, 272–79
  exchange as, 154, 298
  of fitness-motivated rules, 87
  of homophily, 224–25, 302–3
  of joint value maximization, 155
  MTML and, 46, 60, 94, 301
  for mutual-interest theories, 171–72, 298–99
  of network embeddedness, 153
  of physical proximity, 228, 303

reciprocity as, 298
of resource dependency, 210–12
for self-interest theories, 142, 151,
 155–58, 298–99
of self-organizing systems, 97, 241–42
of semantic networks, 187–89, 301
of social exchange, 210–12, 302
of social support, 235–36, 304
for social theories, 298–307
structural autonomy as, 298
of transactive memory systems, 199
threshold, 169
tie level, 58–59
time
 in Boolean networks, 269
 incremented, 105
 multiple points in, 296
 prior points, 68, 104, 295
time irreversibility, 84
timeless time, 5
timing, 144–45
tit-for-tat strategy, 87–88
TQM (total quality management), 181–
 82
traditional research processes, 100–
 101, *fig. 4.1*
tragedy of the commons, 165–66
traits, 25, 86, 249, 262, 271, 286, 288
trait space, 262, 264–66
transaction cost economics theory, 22,
 150–55, 158, 235, 298
transaction costs, 151, 156
transactive memory systems theory,
 24, 67, 94, 198–203, 300, 315
transcendence, 15
transitive ties, 77
transitive triad, 59–60, 64
transitive triadic structural
 dependency, 115, 118
transitivity, 30
 in cognitive consistency theory, 204–
 5, 301
 in computational modeling of
 networks, 113–14
 in CRADA network, 71–73
 in MTML analytic framework, 294,
 295, 296

in p^* analysis, 51, 52, 53
at triadic level of analysis, 42, 59–60,
 64, 301
triadic level of analysis, 37, 42–44, 46,
 table 2.4
cognitive consistency theory at, 204–
 5, 207
CRADA network at, 71–72, 77
endogenous variables at, 59–60,
 fig. 2.3
exogenous variables at, 64–65,
 fig. 2.7
transitive structural dependencies
 at, 115, 118
valid statistical inference techniques
 at, 48
trial and error learning, 248
trust relations, 156, 210, 211, 213–14,
 302
tunable fitness landscapes, 266
turnover, 180, 225

UCINET, 31
uncertainty avoidance index, 191
undersocialized view, 148, 152
understanding, 187, 305
unethical behavior, 180, 206
unified social systems theory, 81
uniform probability distribution, 50, 53
uniplex relations, 35–37
unitary chain of command, 11
United Negro College Fund, 198
unity-of-command, 9
Unix operating system, 321
upward determinism, 14
Urban League, 198
Usenet, 319, 321
U.S. National Science Foundation, 318

validation, 101–2
valid statistical inference techniques,
 45, 47–48
value chain competencies, 262–63
value chain competitive advantage
 strategies, 262
value chains, 220
"value constellations," 220

valued graphs, 36
valued relations, 35, 36–37, 40
variance, 294, 295
variation, 247–50, 253, 256, 268
Vensim, 103
verbal ambiguities, 100–101, 121
vertical organizational structure, 17,
    150–54, 298
vicarious learning, 249
videoconferencing, 230, 234, 250
virtual, 119
virtual design team, 102
virtual experiments, 110, 119–21
   designing, 128–29
   executing, 121–22
   interpreting the results of, 122
virtual organizations, 149, 197
virtual state, 325, 326
voice mail technology, 190
voice strategy, 152
voluntary organizations, 225, 303
vulnerability, 177

weak component, 43
weak ties, 147, 148, 149
Wealth of Nations, The (Smith), 79

Web, 197, 232, 307, 311, 313–20
webbots, 93, 103, 105, 198
Web sites
   Blanche, 108, 123
   dmoz.org, 323
   elance.com, 320
   guru.com, 7, 320
   Kevin Bacon game, 308
   PSPAR computer program, 73

SETIhome, 318
"Western bias," 148
wine industry, 252
wireless links, 320
word network analysis, 186
work groups, 92, 201, 225, 256
workload, 105
workplace attitudes, 178
work stress, 221
World Trade Organization, 324
World Wide Web. *See* Web

X-Net, 222

Zapatista National Liberation Army,
   324